Investing
with the
Insiders
—Legally

AARON B. FEIGEN, CFA

with DON CHRISTENSEN

SIMON AND SCHUSTER
New York   London   Toronto   Sydney   Tokyo

Published by Simon and Schuster
A Division of Simon & Schuster Inc.
Simon & Schuster Building
Rockefeller Center
1230 Avenue of the Americas
New York, NY 10020

SIMON AND SCHUSTER and colophon are
registered trademarks of
Simon & Schuster Inc.

Designed by Irving Perkins Associates
Manufactured in the United States of America

1 2 3 4 5 6 7 8 9 10

Library of Congress Cataloging-in-
Publication Data

Feigen, Aaron B.
Investing with the insiders legally.

Bibliography: p.
1. Investments—United States. 2. Stocks—
United States. 3. Insider trading in securities—
United States. I. Christensen Don
(Donald James)
II. Title.
HG4910.F38   1988   332.63′2   87-28430
ISBN 0-671-62439-3

Contents

6   Contents

Introduction

The stock market crash of October 19,1987, turned Wall Street upside down. But a year earlier, on November 14, 1986, Wall Street experienced an almost equally startling jolt. That was the day when it was announced that one of the most successful stock market traders of all time—Ivan Boesky—had been caught using "inside information" illegally to profit to the tune of tens of millions of dollars in his stock buying and selling. The media attention that followed this announcement made Boesky as well as others involved with Boesky's schemes, such as investment banker Dennis Levine, nearly household names. It also brought the term "insider trading" into common use to describe behavior that is *always* illegal. The problem with this common perception of "insider trading" is that it is not completely accurate. The truth is that there is a form of "insider trading" *that is absolutely legal.* And, not only is it legal, but you—or any other investor—can profit from it.

To understand this, you must first forget everything you've ever read or heard about "insider trading." Forget Ivan Boesky. Forget Dennis Levine. Forget the general impression you've gathered in the last few years from headlines like "Insider Trading Scandal Rocks Wall Street."

Then consider this little-known fact: Corporate insiders—a company's officers, directors and major shareholders—are permitted by law to buy and sell shares in their own companies. They are also permitted by law to profit from their stock trading.

Then consider another little-known fact: You can find out from publicly-available information how these corporate insiders—who are among the richest and most powerful decision-makers in American business—invest their own stock market dollars. You can find out the names of the companies that people on the inside are investing in and you can find out how much of their money they are investing. With this information in hand, you can identify compelling investment choices for your own stock market portfolio. *All legally.*

This book will tell you how to go about it.

First we'll look at the special way that insiders invest and how they routinely profit from their investments—usually by margins that "beat the market." We'll examine the differences between the illegal actions that got Boesky and others in trouble with the government and the laws that permit corporate insiders to trade legally. Then we'll look at the insider investment activities that are particularly significant as a guide for finding your own stock selections. And we'll explain how to use the specific, special tools for gathering information on insider trading and how to invest just as the insiders do to profit from their special knowledge of the inner workings of their companies and the probable future direction of their companies' stock.

The guidelines provided here have been gathered from over ten years of intensive study and practical experience in analyzing and following insider trading activities. You will discover, as a few of us already have who have been following insiders over the years, that investing with the insiders takes you directly to the heartbeat of the corporate offices of publicly-owned American companies to join in on the investments of the stock market's most consistently successful investors.

In the wake of the October 1987 crash, the activities of insiders have taken on ever more important significance for stock market investors—both amateur and professional. Since insiders are "close to the ground," they are in the best position to judge the true value of their companies while other less-informed investors continue to flounder in an unsettled market atmosphere. Those who carefully watch the investments of insiders will have the best clues in hand for finding out which way to go.

PART ONE:

Uncovering the Insiders' Market

Chapter 1

The Insiders' Edge

IN 1958 when the Great Atlantic and Pacific Tea Company (A&P) sold stock to the public for the first time, the company was the largest retailing organization in the United States. The successful supermarket formula A&P had developed over the decades since its first store opened in 1869 seemed unshakable. An added appeal to stock market investors in 1958 was A&P's many bakeries, coffee-roasting plants and other factories and canneries that helped supply A&P stores with low-cost (and profit-making) company-brand products. In short, A&P was a stock market investor's darling: established, reputable name, stable earnings year after year, good annual dividend.

For the next decade A&P maintained its preeminent retailing position. In 1969 its closest competitor, Safeway, had sales of less than half of A&P's $5.4 billion. A&P's consistent performance during the 1960s kept the price tag for its stock high—as high as $70 per share.

But in the early 1970s things started turning sour. A&P poured more money into manufacturing plants and failed to expand its retail outlets into the growing suburbs. Burdened with crumbling inner-city stores and faced with growing competition, A&P lost ground. And lost it fast.

In 1973 the company lost $51 million. In 1975 it lost $157 million. It closed almost seventeen hundred of its thirty-four hundred outlets. Then competitor Safeway took over the number one grocery-retailing position. And in 1978 another supermarket chain, Kroger, pushed A&P into the number three spot.

Stock market investors reacted to this sorry state of affairs by abandoning the company. In 1978 its stock dropped to $6 a share.

Then in 1979, Germany's largest supermarket organization— Tengelmann— bought 44 percent of A&P's outstanding shares after convincing the Hartford Foundation, a medical research charity that was formed by family members of the original founders of A&P, to sell its controlling block of A&P stock for $7 a share. (Ten years earlier the Hartford Foundation had turned down a $40-a-share offer from another suitor.)

Some Wall Street analysts thought that Tengelmann management would be able to breathe new life into A&P. That interpretation helped the price of the company's stock go up a little. But most analysts and investors thought the Germans had made a big mistake and A&P's dismal performance over the next few years seemed to confirm that prediction. In fact, a survey conducted by Fortune magazine in 1983 of top executives and other leading experts in business and finance named A&P as one of the ten worst corporations of the year. Many investors holding A&P stock sold; others simply ignored the once-powerful retailer.

But there was a small group of investors that bought A&P stock despite the nearly unanimous agreement among the investment community that A&P was a company to avoid.

And they bought a lot of A&P stock.

Beginning in early 1984, Erivan Haub and Helga Haub, the controlling shareholders of Tengelmann who were by then on A&P's board of directors, started adding to the 19-million-share stake they acquired in 1979–80. Although they already effectively owned control of A&P, they renewed their buying with enthusiasm. In February of 1984, they bought about 35,000 shares at prices of about $12 a share. In March of that year they bought another 15,000 shares. In May they added another 140,000 or so shares to their holdings. Month after month, they bought more and more. Some months they bought heavily—as many as 300,000 shares. Other months they made only light purchases, once as low as 2,500 shares.

Others connected with A&P also accumulated stock in the company at the same time. For example, J. B. Burmeister, a vice president of the company, bought more than 17,000 shares over a nineteen-month period. In total, the Haubs and others bought about 1 million A&P shares between January 1984 and October 1985. The prices they paid ranged between $11.88 and $15.88 a share, which were substantially higher than the prices paid for their first purchases.

Considering the negative consensus about A&P's future among Wall Street "experts" and average investors, why did these people continue to buy so many shares of the company's stock—and at ever-higher prices? Were the Haubs and the others throwing good money after bad? Were they out of their minds or stupidly stubborn?

Early 1986 told the story.

When the earnings results for 1985 were announced, they showed double-digit returns on double-digit growth in sales. The company displayed solid profitability. It even declared a dividend—the company's first since 1978. Management predicted that A&P would have sales and earnings growth in 1986 that would outpace the industry average.

In short order, other stock market investors started buying. They didn't buy with the same vigor as they had during the 1960s, but they had enough interest in A&P to drive the price of the company's stock to almost $28 a share by mid-1986 and by mid-1987 to more than $40 a share before the October 1987 crash.

A simple calculation shows that the return that the small group of investors had on the stock they bought during A&P's seemingly dark days was over 100 percent if they had sold in mid-1986 and even more if they had sold in 1987.

Not bad. Now, ask yourself: Do you think that the Haubs and the rest of the people at A&P had a better idea of what was down the road for the company when they were buying at $6, $7, $11, $14 and $15 a share than the people who abandoned their A&P stock at those prices? You can bet on it.

It Wasn't Luck

By anyone's standards, the Haubs and others closely connected with A&P made pretty good investment decisions when they bought stock in 1984 and 1985. Even without the extra push the bull market of 1986–87 probably gave A&P's stock price, the stock was on the rise. Why? Because the company was clearly experiencing a turnaround in its fifteen-year history of poor performance. As the evidence of that turnaround became known to a wider group of stock market investors—as more investors started to believe the company's pronouncements that a turnaround was on the horizon—the perceived value of the company's stock increased and its price followed.

Those A&P directors and officers weren't taking too much of a gamble when they bought their stock. They were making sound business decisions. They knew what the employees of A&P were doing every day to make the hope of a turnaround into a reality. They also probably had a good idea of what their competition was doing and how A&P would fare in the future within the grocery-retailing industry. So, they weighed the business information they had and looked at the selling price of their company's stock. They saw that it was a bargain. They bought it and they made a bundle.

The wise business decision that the A&P officers and directors made is somewhat commonplace within a relatively small group of Wall Street investors of which Ms. Haub, Mr. Burmeister and others are privileged members. Other members of this select group include the officers and directors of other publicly owned companies as well as major shareholders in those companies. This group is collectively (and not always affectionately) referred to as "the insiders."

Insiders do many things during the day that separate them from one another. They have different management styles, different attitudes and prejudices, different sexes, different political points of view, different lifestyles, different ages. But when it comes to investment decisions about buying and selling the stock of their own companies, they come together to share a similar track record: they usually do better than just OK.

Often the insiders are, like the insiders we saw at work at A&P, officers and directors of large, well-known companies. But often they're insiders trading in stocks of companies you never heard of—until it's been too late to get in on the bargain. For example, Apogee Enterprises, a glass manufacturer specializing in curved auto glass, was selling at $2½ a share in late 1983 when insiders started loading up on the company's stock. In early 1985 the stock started going up. By mid-1986 the stock was selling for $20 a share.

Often insiders benefit from a spiraling bull market like the example above. But they also do well with their investments in their individual companies when the stock market on the whole is riding the bear downward. For example, insiders started buying stock in Brunswick Corporation in early 1982 and accumulated hundreds of thousands of shares by the middle of 1983. The stock market as a whole was rising sharply throughout 1983, but in 1984 it experienced its most dramatic drop in ten years. But while the market was dropping, Brunswick's stock advanced about 50 percent from mid-1983 to the fall of 1984 because of a major restructuring of the company's operations when the market as a whole reached its low point.

Often the insiders aren't directly involved with the day-to-day operations of the company whose shares they trade. Instead, they are professional investors or wealthy individuals who are able to identify a company's unrecognized or undeveloped potential early and buy a substantial amount of its stock, establishing an insider position within the company. For example, Harold Simmons, a Dallas businessman, first started buying stock in Cyclops Corporation (a producer of steel products and owner of two chains of specialty retail stores called Busy Beaver Building Centers and Silo) in the spring of 1983 at $21 a share. By February of 1984 he had accumulated 312,000 shares (9 percent of the company's stock) at prices between $21 and $30. Then he sold at $36 a share for an overall profit of about 40 percent, as Simmons's presence itself called attention to the potential of this once highly neglected company. (As sometimes happens, he sold out early; Cyclops was selling for $90 a share in early 1987 prior to a takeover.)

Other times, the insider can be a corporation buying large quantities of stock in other companies, sometimes before a takeover bid. IBM quietly started buying stock in early 1983 of Rolm, Inc. at prices as low as $55 a share. By September 1984, after IBM made an official public announcement of its intention to acquire control of Rolm, the stock rose to $80 a share.

These are just a few of thousands of stories that show how insiders routinely profit from their stock-trading decisions.

If you suspect that the insiders possessed some special knowledge of the probable future direction of the price of their companies' stock, you're probably right. If you think that they had special insights that you (if you were investing in the stock market at the time) or your stockbroker or most other stock market investors didn't—and couldn't—have, again you're probably right.

But you have no cause to be upset. The insiders in each of the examples we've mentioned, as well as thousands of other insiders with similar stories of profitable stock-trading success, did nothing that anyone considered illegal. No one took anyone to court crying about misuse of inside information.

Not only did these insiders do nothing to attract the attention of legal watchdogs, but each time they made stock transactions the specifics of the transactions were made public. For all the world to see. For anyone to study who was interested in knowing how this savvy group of people invested their market dollars.

While the rest of us would consider that our stock-trading activity is a private financial matter on the same level as our income tax returns, the stock trading of insiders is made public by courtesy of the federal government. Ever since 1934, when the Securities and Exchange Commission (SEC) was established to keep watch over the type of questionable business and stock-trading practices that helped bring about the crash of 1929, corporate insiders and major shareholders in publicly owned companies have been required to report to the SEC all the details of their stock-trading transactions—how many shares were bought or sold, on what date, at what price and much more.

Every day in a little room in the building that houses the SEC offices in Washington, D.C., copies of the forms the insiders submit to the SEC that report their stock transactions are put on a table for anyone to look at. Then, every month the Government Printing Office takes most of the data from those SEC forms and publishes it in a thick book called the *Official Summary of Security Transactions and Holdings*. (A computer tape version of the *Official Summary* is also produced by the government.)

There are some professional and amateur stock market investors on the "outside" who pore over these government-produced reports to see how the insiders are trading and then invest based on those insider actions. And as you might expect, those investors on the "outside" have profited right along with those on the "inside" in each of the cases you've already read about—and in many, many more.

Profit Patterns

Those of us outsiders who look to corporate insiders for investment clues sometimes disagree on the specifics of how to interpret the actions insiders take in their stock transactions. But we
all agree on three things:

One: Insiders know more about the future potential value of
the stock of their companies than anyone on the outside could
possibly ever know, because, after all, they are on the "inside."

Two: Insiders do not invest in their own companies because
they are interested in collecting the company's dividends or because they do not have other investment alternatives. Instead,
they invest because they expect to make substantial capital
gains, greater than they could elsewhere, and with more certainty.

Three: Over the long term insiders should be able to consistently outperform the market as a whole in the profitable returns
they enjoy with the stock investments they've made in their
own companies.

There is a substantial amount of statistical research into the
stock-trading habits of corporate insiders conducted over the
past twenty-five years that supports the commonsense thinking
that these three points represent. For example, one of the earliest studies was done as part of a Michigan State University
D.B.A. thesis in 1964 by Donald Rogoff. Rogoff used the SEC's
Official Summary and identified forty-five companies where
three or more insiders bought stock in their company within a
single month and no insiders sold stock. He found that the returns to those insiders over the following six months were over
49 percent, a period during which the market as a whole went
up about 30 percent.

Another study, this one done as part of a Ph.D dissertation at
Ohio State University in 1966 by Gary Glass, looked at insider
trading over fourteen different calendar months and found eight
companies with more insiders buying than selling for each
month. The results were that the average return for this group of
insiders was 24.3 percent compared with the Dow Jones Industrial Average's increase of 6.1 percent.

In yet another study conducted as part of an M.B.A. thesis,
Shannon P. Pratt and Charles W. DeVere of Portland State Uni-

versity in Oregon analyzed fifty-two thousand insider transactions of companies traded on the New York Stock Exchange from 1960 through 1966. Similar to Rogoff, the Pratt and DeVere study looked at companies where three or more different insiders bought stock in a single month and where there was no selling by any insiders. The results? An average gain of 21.2 percent compared to the market average which increased 9.5 percent.

Two other, more extensive studies done separately by Joseph Finnerty, a professor of finance at the University of Massachusetts, and Jeffrey J. Jaffe, a professor at the Wharton School of the University of Pennsylvania, reported similar findings. Finnerty looked at *all* insider transactions over a four-year period (1969–72), instead of just those where there was concentrated insider activity. His analysis showed insiders achieving a return in a twelve-month period that was 8.34 percent *above* the performance of the market as a whole. Jaffe's study, published in 1974, found that insiders *bettered* the stock market's overall performance by an average of 4.94 percent.

Since these early general studies of the returns of insiders as a group were done, there have been many other studies that have looked at different segments of insiders. Some have tracked the performance of various types of insiders—directors, chairmen of the board, vice presidents—to compare how subsets within the insider group fare. Others have looked at individual industries, such as banking, to see if the insider trading anomaly exists. Others have concentrated on the insider activities among small, unknown companies and still others have looked at large, well-known companies.

The findings have almost unanimously been the same. Insiders beat the stock market averages, usually by a wide margin.

Not only do they beat the market averages by buying stock that rises higher than the market as a whole, they also tend to avoid excessive losses when they sell their company's stock. Finnerty, for example, found that the stock of the companies that insiders *sold* during the period he watched tended to do worse than the market as a whole during the twelve-month period following the insiders' sale. (Despite this finding, you will see later that insider *buying* is the activity we watch for investment signals. Insider selling usually is not an important indicator for stock selections based on insider actions.)

Another interesting phenomenon that can be seen in the trading patterns of insiders is their uncanny way of anticipating shifts in the overall direction of the stock market. Over the past twenty years, there has been a tendency for insiders as a group to buy heavily just before the market turned to a bullish trend. (For example, during October and November of 1985 insiders were buying in record numbers. The following five months saw the biggest stock-price jump in Wall Street history up to that point.) Also, studies found that they sell heavily just before the market turns bearish.

This phenomenon can probably be explained logically. Insiders find bargains during times when other investors abandon the market thinking that the doomsday that some stock market "experts" have been predicting for years has finally arrived. The insider, however, is closely focused on his own special situation—his own company—and all he sees is a better bargain price because of the depressed nature of the market. In a way, this automatically enables him to benefit from the historical cyclical nature of the stock market by buying low and then selling high, taking even higher profits, when everyone else jumps on the bull market bandwagon as the cycle comes around again.

The Power of Information

Joseph Finnerty, in his study of insider activities, comes to the conclusion that "insiders, probably because of their access to privileged information, can outperform the market in their stock selections."

Some may consider that an understatement.

If you break down the more than forty million people who own stock in publicly owned U.S. companies into different groups, the insiders connected with the forty thousand or so publicly owned companies do better on average over time than any other group of investors. They do better than institutional investors. They do better than the average pension fund or college endowment fund. They do better than the average mutual fund. They certainly do better than most individual investors.

The reason by now should be very obvious. Insiders have an investment power unequaled by any other group of investors: They have the power of special information.

This is not to say that these insiders are withholding information illegally and duping unsuspecting investors. Frequently the information they use to base their investment decisions on is already public, but has gone unrecognized, or has been ignored by other investors. Sometimes they trade on information that would be irresponsible of them to announce. (For example, maybe there is a new product being developed and the insider may be convinced enough that it will be a winner to invest in its future. But would the insider be acting responsibly by announcing the new product before it had been fully developed, sparking a speculative run-up in the company's stock price before there is proof that its value will rise in the future?) Sometimes the insider is assessing a complex set of circumstances that, for the insider at least, could spell future gains for the company without any specific change in the way the company is being run.

When looking at the investment activities of insiders, remember two things. First, the stock market is like a large flea market or auction parlor—there's some junk, some bargains and a lot of items that are merely OK. Second, the insiders, by the nature of their positions, are able to judge the real, intrinsic value of the "item" they are dealing with. When they see the item selling in the marketplace at below what they "know" it is worth, they can buy it for themselves legally. Add the self-interest factor of human nature, and you can count on them not to act unless they see a personal gain. The more they act, the more they expect to profit. It is as simple and logical as that.

Experience in following the activities of all types of insiders, however, points to the fact that they invest successfully before there is public evidence of some significant development within their companies. While the full-term "birth" of the development can vary from a few months to several years, the development vis-à-vis the insider investment usually is evident when the situation is viewed in hindsight after the "development" occurs.

Let's look at some typical corporate developments that increase the value of a company's stock in the minds of investors on the "outside." (By the way, each example of actual insider investing given throughout this book was originally identified by "outsiders" tracking the activities of the insiders *before* the corporate developments occurred that resulted in a boost in the price of the company's stock.)

Earnings or dividend announcements.   A moment's thought should convince you that when a company announces its earnings for the quarter or its dividends for a year this does not come as a surprise to insiders. A company's accountant isn't the only one who knows. Get an insider to talk candidly about such things and in many cases you'll most likely hear: "I can tell almost exactly what our earnings will be at the end of this quarter. And, unless an earthquake hits our plant in California, I have a pretty good idea of what our earnings for the following quarter will be. For the whole year, for that matter."

But if you were to ask insiders to give a *public* prediction of their company's earnings and dividends, you'd probably get a much more vague answer: "We expect to hold our own within the industry as long as the market conditions remain constant, interest rates stay the same and consumers continue to buy our product as they have in the past." Can you blame a corporate official for giving a prediction like that? Who wants to go out on a limb in public? Insiders can, however, benefit by putting their faith in their own predictive powers by buying the stock of their companies. This power would be particularly profitable if the earnings or dividend announcement represented a turnaround for a previously ailing performance. Could this have been the reason for these insider activities at United Merchants & Manufacturers, an apparel and textile company? The company emerged from Chapter XI bankruptcy in mid-1978, but things were still shaky for several years. Beginning in 1981, however, insiders started buying at $4 a share. Ultimately they accumulated nearly 2 million shares at an average price well under $10 a share. In mid-1984 the company started displaying renewed strength. The stock stood at almost $15 in early 1985 and at $20 in mid-1986. The value of the insiders' stake multiplied into the millions.

New discoveries or products.   The development of a new product can take years. A technological breakthrough can take even longer before a marketable application for it can be found. A company wouldn't want to make an announcement prematurely, but insiders could take a calculated gamble based on their unique assessment of the practicality of the new product or discovery within their marketplace and invest in their own companies. Another possibility is that a company could very well announce the development of a terrific new product, but investors and analysts, being the skeptics that they tend to be, would wait until the product proved itself in the marketplace. The insiders, however, could invest long before the proof becomes evident to others and pick up their company's stock at a much lower price.

In the early 1980s, for example, ICN Pharmaceuticals created a new public company—Viratek—from one of its divisions. At the time the new company went public, ICN maintained a large stake in it, but in 1984 it started reaccumulating an even larger interest. The start-up company showed losses for its early years, but ICN continued to buy thousands of shares throughout 1985 at prices as low as about $11¼ and as high as about $20. By early 1986, ICN had a stake of almost 2 million shares in Viratek. Viratek's 1986 first quarter earnings showed profitability for the first time—coming primarily from royalties on a new drug, Virazole, the company had developed. Reaction to the success of the new drug pushed the price of Viratek's stock to almost $100 a share in 1986.

Spin-off of assets.   A company could be considering—or could have even announced—the sale of some assets that could make it cash-rich and allow it to develop further some other profitable aspect of its business. An insider could take the chance that the proposed spin-off of assets could come true. Maybe this was in the mind of those insiders who purchased hundreds of thousands of shares in Datapoint, a minicomputer maker, during 1984 and 1985 at prices between $12 and $18 a share. In late 1985, the service division of the company was made into a new public company, Intelogic Trace Inc. At the time of the spin-off, Datapoint was selling at about $12 a share. Shareholders were given one share of Intelogic—with an initial value of about $7½ a share—and one share of Datapoint— worth about $4½ a share at the time. By mid-1986, however, the price of Intelogic stock rose to over $16 a share and the Datapoint stock rose to over $9 a share. For the insiders at Datapoint and for other lucky shareholders, Datapoint was worth more as two companies than as one.

Mergers and acquisitions.   A few merger and acquisition stories of well-known companies are reported in minute and colorful detail in the general press. But most of the merger and acquisition of smaller companies rarely see the printed page until the details are all ironed out. Then it's usually too late to make a move to achieve much profit. Insiders, however, are often in the thick of the negotiations every day—months before any merger or acquisition could actually be announced.

These insiders might have thought things would work out well. From August 1985 through November 1985, insiders at Republic Health, an owner and operator of health care facilities, bought nearly 2 million shares in the company at prices between $10 and $17 a share. In March of 1986, the company agreed to a buy-out from an investment group headed by the insiders themselves at roughly $20 a share.

Corporate intelligence.   Insiders not only know what is going on in their own companies, but they also have a finger on the pulse of what is happening among their competitors before the news filters out to the public. The relative success (or failure) of a competitor can have a dramatic effect on the future of an insider's company. For instance, in our earlier example of A&P, the continuing bad performance of the company before 1985 and the relative improved performance of other supermarket chains may have been the spark for this insider: A vice president of the supermarket chain, Shopwell, Inc., started a five-month buying spree of the company's AMEX-listed stock in February 1982. The 26,000 shares of stock he bought had gained him a tidy 300 percent profit within a year. (Ironically, A&P, after its 1985 turnaround, took control of Shopwell in mid-1986.)

Buy-back.   Taking a public company private has occurred with some frequency over the past few years. Since insiders are the very people who are usually involved in the buy-back, they are the first to hear the rumblings in the executive suites where such strategies are conceived. They don't always work out, but some insiders might want to take an early risk on what they see as inevitable long before anyone else catches wind of it.

In late 1983, for example, over 40 percent of the stock of Food-a-Rama Supermarkets, owner and operater of more than two dozen Shop-Rite stores in the Northeast, was held by Joseph Saker and other members of his family. Throughout 1984 and 1985, the Saker family and other insiders purchased thousands of shares at prices between $8¼ and $14. The spring of 1986 brought news that the Sakers were making an offer to minority shareholders for the balance of the outstanding shares in order to take the company private with a package offer valued in the low twenties per share. (Eventually that deal was aborted, but the interim capital gain was impressive.)

Making the Vision Come True

Add another element of power to the insiders' unique position: They have the power of actually doing something to make their investment decisions pay off. After all, why bother to invest in a possibility of a future development based on your special information if you don't do your best to make it happen? The rest of Wall Street's investors can just sit around and hope for the best.

Where Do You Get Your Information?

Let's assume that you're making a conscientious effort to identify some good companies to invest in. You know that among the 1,600 companies listed on the New York Stock Exchange (NYSE), the 950 companies listed on the American Stock Exchange (AMEX) and the 5,000 companies being actively traded Over-the-Counter (OTC) there have to be a few that would give you a good return on your investment.

Let's also assume that you take a conventional route for gathering information about what's going on in the stock market. You'll probably read *The Wall Street Journal* every day as well as either *Business Week, Forbes* and *Fortune* magazines—or perhaps all of them. Then you'll possibly tune into "Wall Street Week" on Public Broadcasting every week. If you're really getting into it, you may also pick up copies of *Barron's* or *Financial World* or the *Journal of Commerce* or *Dun's Business Month*. In addition, you might want to supplement all that with a general investment newsletter like *Value Line Investment Survey*.

Reading all this may spark your interest in specific companies, so you might send away for copies of the company's annual report. Then you might ask your stockbroker for copies of research reports the brokerage house may have. Too, if you're really serious, you might start reading the trade magazines that cover the industry of the company you're thinking of investing in. And if you do all this, you could probably come up with some reasoned investment choices.

More realistically, however, many investors make their choices because their neighbor down the street suggested something. Or their stockbroker—if they have one who pays any attention to their account—called them up to suggest something. Or they noticed in the paper that several thousand people bought shares in IBM—or some other big company—the day before and the price went up a dollar and they felt they didn't want to get caught out in the cold on that one again.

But even if we did our homework methodically by reading the types of publications just mentioned, we would still have a few things going against us.

First, although all those publications print thousands of pages of information on many companies, they don't routinely cover *all* companies. They can't. There's no space or time. So they tend to cover the biggest companies or the companies with the most dramatic stories to tell at the moment.

Every year companies spend millions of dollars on public relations efforts just to get the news of their activities in these publications. *The Wall Street Journal*, for example, receives hundreds of press releases *every day* from companies with stories they think are worth telling. Obviously *The Wall Street Journal* thinks otherwise because most of that news is not reported. Some companies—and public relations directors—are elated when they are simply included in a two-line listing when they announce their earnings for the quarter or the year. Thus you're only getting part of the story on a small number of the seven thousand regularly traded companies.

Even the detailed investment newsletter *Value Line Investment Survey* looks at only about 1700 companies. And if you turn to your stockbroker for research advice, you're going to find that most brokerage houses focus their research on only a few hundred of the largest companies. If you're lucky, however, you might find research on an additional 800 or so companies that are covered by the two or three analysts in the country who are paying attention to them. That leaves you with about 5500 com-

panies you will be hard-pressed to find any information about
—until something happens at those companies that makes them
newsworthy.

The second thing you have going against you when you use
conventional sources of information to make investment decisions is that the information has been distilled and digested and
presented to you with someone else's point of view. If the people who digest the information for you interpret it correctly, you
may not be in bad shape. But what happens if the information
leads you to the wrong conclusion? For example, *Fortune* magazine's survey of business leaders that named A&P among the
"Worst Companies of 1983" appeared during the year when
A&P's stock rose 45 percent in price. In that same survey, the ten
"best" companies were also named. They included: Eastman
Kodak, whose stock went down 12 percent that year; Johnson &
Johnson, down 18 percent; SmithKline Beckman, down 18 percent; Digital Equipment, down 28 percent. The average gain of
the ten "best" companies was .9 percent; the average gain of the
ten "worst" companies was 62 percent. That means that if you
had invested $1,000 in each of the ten "best" companies at the
beginning of the year, you would have had $10,090 at the end of
the year. If you had invested $1,000 in each of the ten "worst"
companies, you would have had $16,200 at year's end.

Compounding the problem of letting others interpret information for you is all the conflicting advice you encounter from
"experts." If you are a regular reader of business publications,
you have probably had the experience of reading an interview
with an expert one day who says that a particular industry's
stocks should be avoided. And then the next day you read advice from another expert who says that the same industry has
terrific future prospects. How do you sort out all these differences of opinion? Who is right?

The third thing you have going against you when using conventional sources of information is that once the news of well-
analyzed companies hits the printed page or an obscure
company surfaces with a dramatic story to tell, it's too late to do
anything about it. If the news is good, you'll be following the
herd to buy. If the news is bad, you'll be following the same
herd to sell.

Here's an alternative to consider: Let the insiders help you
choose the direction you take with your stock market investments. Insiders know more about their companies—more com-

pletely and sooner—than you or the best professional analyst in the world.

The insiders are not always right in their own selections, but you'll find more big future winners among them than the companies covered in today's—or worse, yesterday's—headlines. Their selections won't point the way to every stock market success story, but there will be enough to keep you busy. It will take some work and digging to find out what the insiders are doing —and they'll throw you some curves along the way. But you'll be able to pretty much cut out the middleman and get closer to the decision makers who actually shape the future of their companies and the value of their stocks.

The crash of October 1987 has added considerable validity to watching insider investments. Following the crash, the ability of traditional Wall Street "experts" to view the future for the market as a whole and individual companies in particular was seriously jeopardized by the cloudy economic outlook and the destruction of past styles and principles for making stock market forecasts. On the other hand, insiders who invested in their own companies following the crash have not worried about turbulent market swings. Instead, they have focused on the real, intrinsic value of their companies and bought when they knew the stock was selling at a "bargain" price. Insiders invest for profit. Investing with the insiders can be profitable for you, too —in good times or bad.

Chapter 2

Looking Over the Insider's Shoulder (with a Little Help from the SEC)

I F you think that insiders have an advantage over you today, you should have been around before Congress passed the Securities Act of 1933 and the Securities Exchange Act of 1934. Those two acts were the first set of government regulations to put controls on insider trading (as well as on nearly every other aspect of a publicly traded company's activities). The acts were the first to require public disclosure of corporate insider stock-trading transactions. They paved the way for the creation of the SEC as a watchdog to ensure compliance with the laws.

In those pre-SEC days, insiders' management of their own companies was almost a secondary function. Making personal profit in the stock market at the expense of completely uninformed shareholders seemed to be a greater priority. If, for example, you were an insider then and you received a telegram from the manager of your gunpowder factory in Pennsylvania telling you that the whole thing blew up, you'd rush to sell all the stock you had before anyone else found out about it. Or if your mining operation in Nevada hit on the largest vein of gold in North America, you'd keep the news quiet—or even announce that the results of your company's search for gold was disappointing—until you had time to accumulate a large number of shares at a low price. Then, later, you could tell the rest of the world about your gold find, which would leave you with some greatly appreciated stock.

Another alternative in those days was simply to lie. If you

needed some quick cash, you could announce that your mining operation had found gold and sell off stock you had been holding at a high price to investors who quickly would be running to get a piece of your company's newfound riches. Later, you could, with gloomy apologies, tell those investors that the gold strike that had initially looked so promising had not lived up to expectations.

Or if things looked as if they wouldn't be going well for your company, you could have tried your hand at selling short your company's stock. For the uninitiated, selling short is a profit-making technique to use when you think that a stock is going to go down in price. To achieve this, you sell shares you don't own (you borrow them from your broker) at the current market price. Then, when the price goes down you buy them back at the lower price. This means, for example, if a company's stock is currently selling at $70 a share, you could borrow 100 shares from your broker and sell them. Then, if some bad news is announced and the company's stock fell to $50, you could buy the 100 shares back at the low $50 price and make $20 profit per share.

If you were an insider before 1933, you could sell short as much as you wanted to. As an insider, of course, you would have had a good idea if some bad news about your company was going to be announced and could profit handsomely from selling short. (You could have also manipulated the news to ensure that the stock price would go down.) Several major fortunes were made literally overnight using tactics just like these. In those days, few people thought there was anything wrong with these activities. It was just part of the game.

There were, however, some disgruntled shareholders who felt cheated when they sold their shares in a company to insiders at a low price while the insiders were holding back information that had it been known would have increased the value of the stock.

A couple of these shareholders even tried to sue the insiders in court. These people were viewed as spoilsports. In nearly every case, the court took the side of the insiders. A typical court ruling from one such case in 1916 summed up the prevailing attitude at the time: "The officers are not bound to acquaint a stockholder willing to sell his shares with facts which would enhance the price of the stock. The officers are trustees

for the shareholders only as to the management of the corporation and not in their private dealings."

The Great Crash of 1929 changed that attitude.

Lifting the Veil of Secrecy

Although many factors contributed to the Crash, insiders and
Wall Street professionals got blamed for it. And, although a
complex set of circumstances brought about the Depression,
Wall Street was an easy scapegoat to blame for that as well. The
public called for reform, if not punishment. Wall Streeters
themselves, however, saw things differently and didn't take it
upon themselves to impose their own regulations. So, when
Roosevelt and the New Deal people set up headquarters in
Washington, the government took on the task of drafting a set of
guidelines and controls in hope of restoring trust in the public
stock trading system.

The congressional investigation and hearings that led up to
passage of the Securities Act of 1933 and the Securities Exchange Act of 1934 were raucous. Detailed stories of fraud and
stock manipulation were told by critics of Wall Street. People
who had been profiting by the loose standards of old Wall Street
countered by saying that all was permissible under the name of
free enterprise.

When the investigation zeroed in on insiders, there were two
diverse camps. One argued that all insider trading should be
outlawed because it would be impossible to curb an insider's
use of information unavailable to other investors and that insider buying from an uninformed public (or selling to it) was
inherently unfair, if not fraudulent. The other camp claimed
that insider trading should continue without any restrictions
because, for one reason, it helped push the price of a company's
stock—either up or down—to a level that more realistically reflected its true value. Other arguments from this camp were that
insider profits from stock trading were a legitimate form of corporate compensation for insiders and that the outside investors
who sold their stock to an insider at a low price would have
sold their shares anyway no matter who was on the buying side.

The arguments presented by these two camps continue to rage

today. But the upshot back in 1933 and 1934, as well as all the subsequent laws and court decisions affecting corporate insiders passed down since then, falls between the two extreme views. Insider trading remains legal. The only real differences between today and the time before 1934 is that insiders cannot trade under the cloak of secrecy. Also, their trading is contained somewhat by specific regulations.

Following the Rules

Frankly, the question of whether insider trading is right or wrong is irrelevant to those of us who watch insiders for investment signals. We don't make moral or philosophical judgments. We're interested only in how current laws affect the way insiders *can* invest and the information we can gather from the publicly available documents that corporate insiders file with the SEC.

The current congressional definition of illegal insider trading is very broad and very vague. A few years ago when Congress updated and amended the original Securities Act of 1934 with the Insider Trading Sanctions Act of 1984, illegal insider trading was defined to include trading in securities by any person "in possession of material nonpublic information." The act doesn't go on to fully define "material nonpublic information." But the term has generally come to mean, among people who study such things, some *specific* piece of information that could affect the perceived value of the company's stock—and therefore its price—if it becomes known by stock investors at large.

Someone in possession of "material nonpublic information" could be anyone, not just the corporate officers and directors and major shareholders who are required to file forms with the SEC revealing their stock transactions. It could, for example, be a repairman who maintains the machinery that manufactures a company's product. The repairman probably knows better than anyone else, including his boss and his boss's boss and everyone on up the line, whether the company's manufacturing equipment is going to function properly in the months ahead to fill the orders the company needs to stay profitable. If the repairman sees that the manufacturing equipment is in such a shabby state that it is or will be impossible to fill the company's orders, and if he sells stock in the company in anticipation of lower stock prices in the future when it becomes known to other shareholders that the company is unable to meet production, he would probably be considered to be trading on "material non-public information" and be in violation of the law. If the SEC caught wind of it, the repairman could be in trouble.

But we're not really concerned about the repairman. He isn't required to file public disclosure forms that report his trading transactions as corporate officers and directors and major share-holders are. Only if the repairman personally tipped us off about the state of the manufacturing equipment would he be of any interest to us. Then, however, we'd be in the same pickle with the SEC as the repairman and others of his ilk would be, which we'll discuss in the next chapter.

We also are not interested in the corporate insiders who do not file the proper forms with the SEC even though they should. These insiders are either ignoring the law or don't know that they should be filing. There are a few of both these types of insiders out there. But we don't need to consider them. We're interested only in the corporate insiders who follow the rules. As long as they follow the rules, they are, almost without ex-ception, immune to the wrath of the SEC; and this group makes up, by far, the vast majority of insiders.

But if the statistical studies you read about in Chapter 1 were accurate in their conclusions that corporate insiders consis-tently outperform the market in their stock transactions, and if the individual insider stories you've read about are true, isn't that clear evidence that corporate insiders are routinely trading on "material nonpublic information?" That might be a fair read-ing.

But try to prove it in a case-by-case basis in court. Try to find the smoking pistol that points to the *specific* piece of "material nonpublic information" that the insiders—who followed the rules—used in trading their company's stock. Try to find some piece of information that was not in some way, no matter how subtle, available to the public. It would be nearly impossible. If you tried to lay out all the facts, the result—again, assuming the insiders followed the rules—would merely look like a coinci-dence. The SEC is aware of this, and that is why you will rarely, if ever, see a case brought against the insiders who abide by the rules.

As outside investors poring over the public reports that insiders file, we are looking for the patterns of insider buying and selling that will predict those "coincidences." Remember, the law does not prohibit trading by corporate insiders. Instead, it is designed to curtail the *flagrant* use (and abuse) of information that insiders universally hold. It also, however, recognizes that insiders will profit from their trading actions, but the rules control that to a certain degree.

There are three broad rules the insiders must follow if they want to avoid locking horns with the SEC.

One: Corporate insiders—officers of the company elected by the company's board of directors, the directors themselves and major shareholders—must report every stock transaction in their own companies. They cannot anonymously trade in the market as they did before 1934. This helps the SEC and other interested people monitor insider activities. But, keep in mind, it does not include everyone who could have "material nonpublic information."

Two: Insiders are prohibited from making short sales of their company's stock. This effectively does away with the popular 1920s insider game of profiting from anticipated bad news at the expense of unsuspecting investors. It also keeps an insider from running a company into the ground to create bad news just to achieve personal profit.

Three: The SEC regulations require any profits that insiders realize from trades within a six-month period be returned to the corporation and/or other shareholders. Plus, such profit taking within the six-month time frame carries the possibility of stiff fines and a jail sentence.

The Six-Month Rule

The six-month rule that was first passed in 1934 and strengthened in the Insider Trading Sanctions Act of 1984 dramatically altered the way insiders buy and sell their company's stock. In the old days insiders could jump in and out of the market quickly to make personal profit. They could, for example, run directly from a board of directors meeting that had set dividends and buy stock—if the news was good—or sell—if the news was bad—before anyone else caught wind of it. Insiders could achieve short-swing profits almost without any risk.

Today's laws have put insiders out of the quick-profit business. The rule is strict and specific. Not only must insiders repay the profits they realize from trading within six months, but they must pay *three times* the profits back to the corporation or shareholders. Also, they could be made to pay up to $100,000 in fines to the government. (The 1984 act raised the limit of fines to $100,000 from $10,000 as originally set in 1934. After fifty years, Congress wisely decided that inflation had taken the bite out of a $10,000 fine.) Insiders breaking the six-month rule can now also face up to five years in jail.

As a result of this rule, it is nearly impossible for insiders to manipulate stock prices (legally) for their own benefit. It gives at least six months for news affecting the value of a company's stock to filter out to other investors. Plus, it gives us at least six months to assimilate the information we can gather from the insiders' public reports to the SEC. It also, however, gives insiders de facto legal approval to take profits on investments after being held for six months. This is why insiders who follow the rules have little trouble with the SEC.

Today the insider has plenty of motivation to abstain from the type of investment tactics that angered critics of Wall Street before 1934. Insiders have been changed from short-term speculators, with the power to manipulate stock prices almost at whim, into long-term investors, putting them on more equal footing with other investors. At minimum, the six-month rule does not let them have the opportunity to take advantage of moving quickly on the news of a specific event unknown to investors at large.

These limitations, however, have not discouraged insiders from trading. (Even the passage of the strict act of 1984 has not changed the number of insider transactions reported to the SEC.) The only difference is that insiders must take the long view and try to spot the potential future value of their company's stock months and years ahead instead of hours ahead. This makes their investments riskier than they were before 1934, because unforeseen events can drastically alter the future value of a company's stock during the six months that insiders are required by law to hold their purchases before selling them for a profit. But, as you've seen and will continue to see, insiders still can profit handsomely despite the limitations.

Not surprisingly, practical experience and the statistical studies done by academics have shown that the abnormal gains insiders reap do not usually occur until far beyond the six-month period. The study conducted by Gary Glass at Ohio State, for example, showed that it took an average of ten months for stock held by insiders to garner their abnormal gains. The Pratt and DeVere study saw that the most productive holding time for insiders was about fourteen months, with increasing abnormal returns continuing for as long as two and a half years. These and other studies found that there is very little meaningful or lasting upward price movement during the first two months following an insider's stock purchase.

Time after time, you will see this pattern emerge. Insiders will buy their company's stock and the stock will seem to languish for several months. Then it will increase in value. Sometimes you will see repeated incidences of insider buying spread out over several months (or even years), then suddenly it will stop. When this happens, it can signal that the corporate development or other situation that the insiders are basing their investment decisions on is just beyond the six-month holding barrier.

The six-month rule, and the way that insiders have reacted to it, has a couple of significant ramifications for outside investors who follow the insiders' lead.

First, you must be willing to hold on to shares purchased for an extended period of time—just like the insiders must—before you can expect a good return on your investment. This sometimes can take a great deal of fortitude. You may purchase shares and over the following several months not see any upward movement. You may, in fact, find that the stock falls in price. Understandably, this could make you nervous and you might be tempted to sell to minimize your losses. But this is a mistake. As long as the insiders continue to hold on to their purchases, you can be assured that the corporate development that prompted the insiders to buy in the first place has not come full term in its gestation period. This may happen even though other indicators in the economy or within the company's industry point to continued stagnation or even bad news.

For example, throughout the winter and spring of 1984–85, one of the industries most heavily favored with insider buying was the banking industry. During this period the outlook for banking was pessimistic because of high inflation and interest rates. If you had followed the lead of insiders and bought stock in bank and bank holding companies during those months when their stock prices were falling because of shareholders' negative reaction to the expectation of discouraging company profits, your stockbroker and friends probably would have called you crazy. From a shortsighted point of view, they would have appeared to be correct. But were the insiders crazy? Or were they taking a long-term assessment of future circumstances that pointed to bargains among their companies? The results came well within the eight- to fourteen-month average time span seen in statistical studies when the rewards to insiders became apparent in mid-1985 and continued through 1986. Interest rates dropped and, among other developments affecting the improved performance of banks, home buying boomed.

Another example started during the winter of 1985 and continued into 1986 when insiders within the gas and oil industry bought heavily despite the grim news of falling profits because of plummeting gas and oil prices. Were these insiders crazy also? Or did they too see bargains among the companies that other panicky investors were dumping? Only time will tell. But if the statistical pattern repeats itself, the insiders should have some greatly appreciated stock on their hands no later than early to mid-1988.

The moral of the story, and our first Golden Rule for following insider investments, is: *To profit like an insider, you must stick with a stock just as an insider does, even through periods of bad weather.*

The second ramification the insider's six-month rule has for outsiders following insider actions is that there is a long period of time available to analyze those actions before it is necessary to make an investment decision. This is very helpful to us. It keeps us from prematurely using our investment dollars to follow actions that have not been supported by a display of a consistent investment pattern among insiders. This means, for example, that it is not necessary—in fact, it is not wise—to buy (or sell) immediately on discovering that one insider, or even two or three insiders, within a company has bought (or sold) a single parcel of company stock. Single transactions, or even several transactions, within a short time period (such as one month) do not show enough of a pattern to warrant our serious interest. We want to see a consistent pattern over several months before we can be convinced of the significance of the

insider's point of view about the future of his company—
whether it is positive or negative—before we make a similar
investment decision. Because of the six-month rule, we have the
luxury to sit back for at least six months (and more realistically
eight to fourteen months) and watch what the insiders do before
having to make our own final investment decision.

This brings us to our second Golden Rule: *Don't jump with
your investment dollars at the first twitch of an insider's movement.*

These two golden rules are central to understanding the nature of *legal* stock trading by insiders and the investment opportunities you have in following their actions. They will be
repeated here many times.

Those Revealing Disclosure Forms

If you are not an insider and if you are not on intimate terms
with many insiders who are willing to discuss with you their
common stock investments and the reasons behind their investment decisions (which most likely would be illegal anyway),
start thinking of the SEC as your best friend and ally. Two of the
primary goals of the Securities Act of 1934 were, as one of the
SEC's own publications says: "(a) to provide investors with material financial and other information concerning securities offered for public sale; and (b) to prohibit misrepresentation,
deceit and other fraudulent acts and practices in the sale of securities generally (whether or not required to be registered)."

Ever since that act was passed, the SEC has been trying to live
up to those goals. It ferrets out the latest scams designed to take
unsuspecting investors. And it produces many tons of corporate
disclosure material that gives investors—who are willing to pay
attention to it—information on a seemingly endless list of company activities. These include financial statements, proposed
offerings of securities, location and character of the companies'
principal properties, number of employees, salaries of top executives and information on capital resources and results of operations. The original documents that produce this information
are required to be submitted to the SEC by all companies listed
on the New York Stock Exchange and the American Stock Ex-

change as well as companies with stock traded "over-the-counter" in large enough quantities to be of interest to the general public—about five thousand of the more than thirty thousand over-the-counter companies. (The remaining twenty-five thousand or so companies with stock traded over-the-counter are held closely by so few people or are traded so infrequently that they are of little interest to the SEC and the rest of us.)

A relatively small amount of all of the tons of disclosure documents filed with the SEC is of interest to those who want to know how the insiders are investing. Specifically, there are three public disclosure forms that we look to for information:

- Form 3. Officially called "Initial Statement of Beneficial Ownership of Securities," this form is required to be filed by corporate officers, directors and owners of 10 percent or more of a company's stock when they make their first transaction in that company's stock. Officers and directors are required to file this form whenever their first purchase is 500 or more shares.

- Form 4. Called "Statement of Changes in Beneficial Ownership of Securities," Form 4 is submitted every month when the corporate insider or shareholder of 10 percent or more of a company's stock makes additional transactions in the stock, changing the status reported in Form 3. Form 4 is required on transactions of any quantity of stock. Forms 3 and 4 are required of those who have an established, direct connection with the corporation. These people are the *literal* insiders and we refer to them as the "inside/insiders."

- Schedule 13D. This form, called "The Statement of Intention and Transactions," is required of outside investors—such as wealthy individuals, professional investors and corporations that buy the stock of other companies—when they obtain control of 5 percent or more of a company's securities. We refer to this group of investors, who come from the outside to establish an insider position through the mere size of their investments, as "outside/insiders." When these outside/insiders accumulate 10 percent or more of a company's stock, they are required to file *both* a Schedule 13D *and* the Form 4 used by inside/insiders. (As you will see later, there are differences in the ways "inside/insiders" and "outside/insiders" in-

---

| **FORM 3** | U.S. SECURITIES & EXCHANGE COMMISSION | OMB APPROVAL |

U.S. SECURITIES & EXCHANGE COMMISSION
Washington, D.C. 20549

Initial Statement of Beneficial Ownership of Securities

Filed pursuant to Section 16(a) of the Securities Exchange Act of 1934, Section 17(a) of the
Public Utility Holding Company Act of 1935 or Section 30(f) of the Investment Company Act of 1940

(Please print or type.)

OMB APPROVAL
OMB № 3235-0104
Expires November 30, 1987

1. NAME AND ADDRESS OF REPORTING PERSON	2. STATE OF INCORPORATION	3. IF AN AMENDMENT GIVE DATE OF STATEMENT AMENDED	4. NAME OF COMPANY
LAST FIRST MIDDLE		MO. DAY YR.	
	5. IRS OR SS IDENTIFYING NUMBER OF REPORTING PERSON	6. RELATIONSHIP OF REPORTING PERSON TO COMPANY *(Instruction 5)*	7. DATE OF EVENT REQUIRING
ZIP CODE			MO. DAY YR.

TABLE I. Securities Beneficially Owned

Furnish the information required by the following table as to securities of the company
beneficially owned directly or indirectly by the reporting person, including transferable warrants but
excluding puts, calls, options and other rights or obligations required to be reported in Table II.

(See Instruction 6)

1. TITLE OF SECURITIES OWNED *(Instruction 9)*	2. *(FOR SEC USE ONLY)*	3. AMOUNT OWNED DIRECTLY OR INDIRECTLY *(Instruction 10)*	4. NATURE OF BENEFICIAL OWNERSHIP *(Instruction 11)*	

SEC 1473 (2-85)   REMINDER: THREE COPIES ARE REQUIRED. ONE SHOULD BE MANUALLY SIGNED AND SUITABLE FOR REPRODUCTION   *(OVER)*

FORM 3 (Continued)   **TABLE II. Puts, Calls, Options and Other Rights on Obligations**

Furnish the information required by the following table as to all puts, calls, options and other rights or obligations
(all hereinafter referred to as "options") pursuant to which the reporting person may buy or sell, or be required to
buy or sell, or be required to buy or sell, securities of the company. However transferable warrants issued by the
company which give the right to buy other securities of the company are to be reported in Table 1. Options exempt
under Rule 16a-6 need not be reported.   *(See Instruction 6)*

1. TITLE OF SECURITIES SUBJECT TO OPTION *(Instruction 9)*	2. *(FOR SEC USE ONLY)*	3. NATURE OF OPTION HELD *(Instruction 12)*	4. AMOUNT OF SECURITIES SUBJECT TO OPTION *(Instruction 10)*	5. PURCHASE OR SALE PRICE OF SECURITIES SUBJECT TO OPTION *(Instruction 13)*	6. DATE OF EXPIRATION OF OPTION

Explanation of items in tables:

_____   _____
DATE OF STATEMENT   SIGNATURE OF REPORTING PERSON

NOTE: If the space provided in either table is insufficient, use a continuation
sheet which identifies the table and columns to which it relates.

Page 2

FORM 4		U.S. SECURITIES & EXCHANGE COMMISSION Washington, D.C. 20549		OMB Approval OMB 3235-0287 Expires February 28, 1986

Statement of Changes in Beneficial Ownership of Securities

Filed pursuant to Section 16(a) of the Securities Exchange Act of 1934, Section 17(a) of the
Public Utility Holding Company Act of 1935 or Section 30(f) of the Investment Company Act of 1940

(Please print or type.)

1. NAME AND BUSINESS ADDRESS OF REPORTING PERSON	2. STATE OF INCORPORATION	3. IF AN AMENDMENT GIVE DATE OF STATEMENT AMENDED	4. NAME OF COMPANY
LAST FIRST MIDDLE		MO. DAY YR.	
	5. IRS OR SS IDENTIFYING NUMBER OF REPORTING PERSON	6. STATEMENT FOR CALENDAR MONTH OF	7. DATE OF LAST PREVIOUS STATEMENT	8. RELATIONSHIPS OF REPORTING PERSON TO COMPANY *(Instruction 4)*
(ZIP CODE)		MONTH YEAR	MO. DAY YR.	

TABLE I. Securities Bought, Sold or Otherwise Acquired or Disposed of

Furnish the information required by the following table as to securities of the company bought or sold
or otherwise acquired or disposed of by the reporting person during the month for which this statement is
filed *(See Instruction 5)* and as to securities of the company beneficially owned, directly or indirectly, at the
end of the month. However, transaction involving the acquisition or disposition of puts, calls, options or
other rights or obligations to buy or sell securities of the company shall be reported in Table II.

1. TITLE OF SECURITIES *(Instruction 8)*	2. *(FOR SEC USE ONLY)*	3. DATE OF TRANSACTION *(Instruction 9)*	4. AMOUNT OF SECURITIES ACQUIRES *(Instruction 10)*	5. AMOUNT OF SECURITIES DISPOSED OF *(Instruction 10)*	6. CHARACTER OF TRANSACTION REPORTED *(Instruction 12)*	7. PURCHASE OR SALE PRICE PER SHARE OR OTHER UNIT *(Instruction 13)*	8. AMOUNT OWNED AT END OF MONTH *(Instruction 10)*	9. NATURE OF OWNERSHIP OF SECURITIES OWNED AT END OF MONTH *(Instruction 11)*

SEC 1474 (10-84)   **REMINDER: THREE COPIES ARE REQUIRED. ONE SHOULD BE MANUALLY SIGNED AND SUITABLE FOR REPRODUCTION**   *(OVER)*

FORM 4 (Continued)   TABLE II. Puts, Calls, Options and Other Rights or Obligations

If during the month for which this statement is filed the reporting person acquired or disposed of any put, call,
option or other right or obligation (all hereinafter referred to as "options") to buy or sell, or be required to buy or sell,
securities of the company, furnish the information required by the following table. *(See Instruction 5)* However, the
acquisition or disposition of transferrable warrants issued by the company are to be reported in Table I. Options
exempted by Rule 16a–6 need not be reported.

1. TITLE OF SECURITIES SUBJECT TO OPTION *(Instruction 8)*	2. *(FOR SEC USE ONLY)*	3. DATE OF TRANSACTION *(Instruction 9)*	4. NATURE OF OPTION *(Instruction 13)*	5. AMOUNT OF SECURITIES SUBJECT TO OPTION *(Instruction 10)*	6. CHARACTER OF TRANSACTION, IF ANY, REPORTED *(Instruction 12)*	7. PURCHASE OR SALE PRICE OF SECURITIES SUBJECT TO OPTION *(Instruction 13)*	8. DATE OF EXPIRATION OF OPTION

Explanation of items in tables:

_____   _____
DATE OF STATEMENT   SIGNATURE OF REPORTING PERSON

NOTE: *If the space provided in either table is insufficient, use a continuation
sheet which identifies the table and columns to which it relates.*   *Page 2*

OMB APPROVAL
OMB No. 3235-0145
Expires September 30, 1988

SECURITIES AND EXCHANGE COMMISSION
Washington, D.C. 20549

Schedule 13D

Under the Securities Exchange Act of 1934
(Amendment No. _____)*

_____
(Name of Issuer)

_____
(Title of Class of Securities)

_____
(CUSIP Number)

_____
(Name, Address and Telephone Number of Person
Authorized to Receive Notices and Communications)

_____
(Date of Event which Requires Filing
of this Statement)

If the filing person has previously filed a statement on Schedule 13G to report the acquisition which is the subject of this Schedule 13D, and is filing this schedule because of Rule 13d-1 (b)(3) or (4), check the following box ☐.

Check the following box if a fee is being paid with the statement ☐. (A fee is not required only if the reporting person: (1) has a previous statement on file reporting beneficial ownership of more than five percent of the class of securities described in Item 1; and (2) has filed no amendment subsequent thereto reporting beneficial ownership of five percent or less of such class.) (See Rule 13d-7.)

Note: Six copies of this statement, including all exhibits, should be filed with the Commission. See Rule 13d-1(a) for other parties to whom copies are to be sent.

*The remainder of this cover page shall be filed out for a reporting person's initial filing on this form with respect to the subject class of securities, and for any subsequent amendment containing information which would alter disclosures provided in a prior cover page.

The information required on the remainder of this cover page shall not be deemed to be "filed" for the purpose of Section 18 of the Securities Exchange Act of 1934 ("Act") or otherwise subject to the liabilities of that section of the Act but shall be subject to all other provisions of the Act (however, see the Notes).

(Continued on following page(s))

Page 1 of ___ Pages

CUSIP No. _____   13D

NAME OF REPORTING PERSON S.S. OR I.R.S. IDENTIFICATION NO. OF ABOVE PERSON	
CHECK THE APPROPRIATE BOX IF A MEMBER OF A GROUP*	
SEC USE ONLY	
SOURCE OF FUNDS*	
CHECK BOX IF DISCLOSURE OF LEGAL PROCEEDINGS IS REQUIRED PURSUANT TO ITEMS 2(d) or 2(e)	☐
CITIZENSHIP OR PLACE OF ORGANIZATION	

NUMBER OF SHARES BENEFICIALLY OWNED BY EACH REPORTING PERSON WITH	7	SOLE VOTING POWER
	8	SHARED VOTING POWER
	9	SOLE DISPOSITIVE POWER
	10	SHARED DISPOSITIVE POWER

11	AGGREGATE AMOUNT BENEFICIALLY OWNED BY EACH REPORTING PERSON
12	CHECK BOX IF THE AGGREGATE AMOUNT IN ROW (11) EXCLUDES CERTAIN SHARES* ☐
13	PERCENT OF CLASS REPRESENTED BY AMOUNT IN ROW (11)
14	TYPE OF REPORTING PERSON*

★ SEE INSTRUCTIONS BEFORE FILLING OUT!

vest and there are differences in the criteria we use to judge their actions for investment signals.)

Forms 3 and 4 are required to be submitted to the SEC by the tenth of the month following the actual insider transaction. This means, for example, that a transaction completed on February 14 must be reported by March 10. As you can imagine, the greatest number of filings received at the SEC occur during the first ten days of the month as insiders try to beat the deadline. Schedule 13D forms must be filed within ten days of any changes—no matter what time of the month the transaction occurred.

Copies of these forms are what insider-watchers at the Public Reference Room of the SEC offices in Washington wait for. (Copies of the forms are also required to be filed with either the New York Stock Exchange or the American Stock Exchange if the companies are listed on those exchanges.)

Data from Form 3 and Form 4 are ultimately provided in the SEC's monthly *Official Summary of Security Transactions and Holdings.* Information from Schedule 13D filings, however, is not distributed by the government beyond the SEC's Public Reference Room. The Schedule 13D data must be obtained from nongovernment sources that you will be told about in later chapters.

Let's take a quick look at the information insiders are required to reveal to us by examining the items reported in Form 4, which is very similar to information found in Form 3 and Schedule 13D. (In later chapters, you'll be given guidelines for gaining access to the information in insider reports and how more specifically to interpret it for investment opportunities.)

· *Name of company.* The name of the company, of course, is the one whose stock has been traded. Insiders are required to make separate reports for each different company in which they trade during the month. Insiders who are directors of several different companies, for example, must file separately for each company. Also, each transaction must be reported separately. They cannot be grouped together on a single form— even if the different transactions are made on the same day.

· *Name of the person or organization reporting.* When the insider is an individual, the name given on the form is usually straightforward. Other times, however, the trader is a "group" or organization. This is particularly prevalent among filers of Schedule 13D forms—the *outside*/insiders. Remember that an *outside*/insider is *not* directly connected with the company when an initial investment is made. He is not a corporate director or officer; instead, he becomes an "insider" for our purposes by the mere size of his investment, which is ownership of at least 5 percent of a company's stock. As an outside/insider's involvement with a company becomes more firmly entrenched, he may actually assume the status of a literal insider—whom we call an *inside*/insider—by becoming a director or a corporate officer or by accumulating 10 percent or more of the company's outstanding shares. An outside/insider can be another company or an investment partnership syndicate or a wealthy individual investor. Sometimes you will hear some outside/insiders referred to as "corporate raiders" or "sharks." As you will see later, however, these negative-sounding labels do not always accurately describe large investors who come from the "outside" to establish an insider position at a company they had not previously been associated with.

Many of the wealthiest outside/insiders do not use their own names when investing. Instead, they invest through some other name. For example, Warren Buffett, a well-known outside/insider who has invested brilliantly over the past twenty-five years by identifying undervalued stocks before they took off, does almost all his investing through the company he heads—Berkshire Hathaway, Inc. Knowing who is behind the various organization names can be key to following the investment activities of outside/insiders. A "group" is required to report as a "group" and also individual members of the group must report as individuals. This means that a single transaction by a "group" could be reported several times if there are many members of the "group." If, when looking at the data culled from the reports, the individuals are not identified as part of the group, you could come to the wrong conclusion that there was more trading activity than there actually was.

· *Relationship of reporting person to company.* The information concerning relationship is required only on the inside/insider forms—Form 3 and Form 4. Although insiders are asked to define their position within the company, they are given a broad range of choices. For example, a "vice president" may put down the actual title of "vice president, marketing" or might just use "officer." In either of these cases, the *Official Summary* would simply list the insider as an "officer." Some of the other choices insiders have are "chairman of the board," "director," "beneficial owner of more than 10 percent of the company's stock" and "general partner." Often the insider has a combined relationship, such as "officer and director" or "director and beneficial owner." These distinctions can become important; just as there is a hierarchy within corporations, there seems to be a hierarchy of successful investment decisions among insiders. "Chairmen of the board" and "directors," for example, tend to fare better with their investments than do insiders who are just "officers."

· *Type of securities.* The insider could be trading in different types of securities, such as "convertible preferred stock" or "debentures due in 1989." Usually, however, the type of security is "common stock." And this is normally the only type of security transaction we are interested in following.

· *Date of transaction.* Keeping track of when insiders trade is important. Recent activity is noteworthy, but so is activity stretched out over several months, especially if it shows a consistency of behavior.

· *Type of transaction.* Insiders have a variety of different trading alternatives they can use to acquire or dispose of their shares, for example, "acquired by gift" or "disposition of warrants by exercise." There are, however, only five types of transactions that interest us as analysts of insider activity:

Acquisition by exercise of options

Open-market sale

Private sale

Private purchase

Open-market purchase

Of those five, "open-market purchase" and "private purchase" are by far the most important for our assessment of an insider's view of the future *positive* direction of the stock's price. When an insider is making an open-market purchase, that means he bought stock at full market price in the stock market just as you would if you were buying that stock. Similarly, a "private purchase" is usually made at prices that are the same and often *above* the prices found in the stock market itself. The only difference with a private purchase is that the shares traded hands outside of the stock market system— which is legal and is done every day by big investors. Open-market and private purchases are so important because they generally show that the insider has a solid belief that the company's stock is a bargain at its current full market price. Options, however, are usually purchased by the insider as part of a company compensation plan at a deep discount from the current market price and don't normally tell that the open-market price is much of a bargain. Buying through options becomes important only when it shows an additional reinforcement of insiders' open-market and private purchases. Incidents of sales by insiders are significant only when displayed in a massive way by many insiders. Isolated sales normally do not mean that insiders are abandoning their companies in anticipation of bad times. Instead, it could simply mean that they needed some cash to pay taxes, to buy a new house, to send a child to college, to buy low-cost options and so on. Large private sales, however, are uniquely important, not as a negative, but rather as a bell-ringer, putting us on alert to find who the buyer(s) were. It might presage a major change in control of a company, for example.

- *Size of transaction.* The amount bought (or sold) can also be a very telling piece of information. A purchase of 500 shares might not be as interesting to us as a 5,000-share purchase. But open-market purchases of 500 shares a month by three or four insiders within the same company over a five-month period could be more interesting than a single purchase of 10,000 shares by one insider. The size of transactions tells us how aggressively the insiders are trading.

- *Purchase or sale price per share.* The open-market or private-purchase price paid by the insider is particularly important. This is the price the insider considers to be a bargain. If we decide to follow the insider and buy, we will want to buy at about the same price.

- *Amount of shares owned by the end of the month.* We can weigh the significance of an insider's individual transaction against his total holdings by looking at this data. For example, an insider buying 2,000 shares over three months to add to holdings of 10,000 shares can mean more than an insider who adds 2,000 shares over three months to holdings of 600,000 shares. This is another sign of aggressiveness. The greater the accumulation of shares compared to past holdings, the more aggressive—and significant—the trading.

- *Nature of ownership.* Prior to 1966, insiders exercised a loophole in the law that permitted them to trade shares in someone else's name—usually a spouse or children—and not report the transaction. Now, all such transactions must be reported. "Nature of ownership" refers to the transaction being either "direct"—in the actual name of the insider—or "indirect"—held for the insider in someone else's name. We consider direct and indirect ownership equal since the insider made the investment decision about the stock.

- *Investor's objectives.* Information concerning investment objectives is required only of outside/insiders and therefore is only found on Schedule 13D forms. Inside/insiders—those people who file Form 3 or Form 4—do not provide this information. Typically, the outside/insider's statement of objective in buying stock in a company will sound like this: "Mr. Jones acquired 500,000 shares of XYZ Company for investment purposes. Jones does not have any present plans or proposals relating to the acquisition or disposition of securities of XYZ, but he may at some time in the future determine to acquire additional securities or to dispose of securities of XYZ currently held by him." That doesn't say too much. In reality, outside/insiders could have something else in mind besides a simple investment in a company's stock that they think is a bargain. Sometimes they want to get "inside" to affect changes in a company. Sometimes they are betting on the future of a developing company. And, in the case of corporations, sometimes they buy in anticipation of a takeover move. Whenever an outside/insider makes subsequent reports or amendments to his original Schedule 13D filing, the statement of "investor's objectives" can reveal a significant change, such as a new intention to seek representation on the board of directors which can show aggressiveness on the part of an investor who wants to become involved in the decision-making process at the company.

The Insider Reports at Work

Even with this cursory look at the data you can find in the insider reports submitted to the SEC, you should begin to see how this information can be used to track the investment posture of insiders to identify your own potential investments.

For example, if you had been studying the data in the January 1983 edition of the *Official Summary* for the Royal Crown Companies, makers of Royal Crown Cola, you would have found that two inside/insiders, the chairman of the board William Young and a director named D. Jones, made open-market purchases at the end of 1982 of about 80,000 shares at an average price of $20 a share. That brought their combined holdings to 905,000 shares. You would have also found that the Chesapeake Insurance Company bought about 41,000 shares during the same time period at a $20⅝ average cost per share. Chesapeake Insurance, an investment vehicle used by one of the wealthiest of outside/insiders Victor Posner, then held 1,872,000 shares or 22.8 percent of Royal Crown.

All of this open-market buying showed aggressive stock accumulation. But as an outsider looking at this information, you might have wanted to see more evidence of aggressive buying. And the next month you would have found it. The February 1983 *Official Summary* showed that Chesapeake bought another 112,200 shares at prices between $20½ and $22½. No other significant activity was reported that month, but that trading was interesting by itself.

The next few months showed continued buying by Chesapeake as well as by Young and Jones. By June of 1983, the *Official Summary* would have shown you that Chesapeake had accumulated another 119,000 shares since February at prices between $20 and $24½, raising its stake to 2,105,000 or 25.6 percent of the company's outstanding stock. Also, Young and Jones had purchased an additional 135,000 shares at around $24½.

With this type of evidence in hand, you could have come to the conclusion that the insiders had acquired a huge amount of stock in a very aggressive way and that they must have known what they were doing. Your own purchase of a few shares—let's say 100—in July at $23 a share would have been justified.

Over the next few months, your holdings would have seemed to be comatose. You would have seen the stock go up to $25 a share and then back down to $23 or so. But throughout this time, the inside/insiders and Mr. Posner kept on buying. During July and August, Chesapeake bought another 76,000 shares. Young and Jones acquired another 364,000 shares in a private purchase arrangement at $26.45 a share.

As an outsider watching the insider action, you sit tight. By the end of the year, Chesapeake had acquired 370,000 shares during 1983 to bring its year-end holdings to 2,211,000 shares, or 26.9 percent of the company. Young and Jones had acquired about 600,000 shares during 1983, which raised their combined stake to 1,500,000 shares, or 18.1 percent of the company.

Your stock would have still been hovering around $25 a share. But the new year brought rumors of a buy-out by management. The stock went up to over $32 a share as a wider group of investors started paying serious attention to the action at Royal Crown. Then, bingo. In early January a newly formed corporation headed by Young and Jones made an offer of $37 a share to buy all the outstanding shares of Royal Crown in an effort to take the company private. Posner's Chesapeake made a counter offer of $40 a share. After a few weeks of tug-of-war between the two groups, Young and Jones's corporation agreed to the buy-out offer by Chesapeake and encouraged other shareholders to do the same. Young and Jones made millions on the deal. You would have made $1700, minus commissions to your stock-broker, on your $2300 investment.

Actually, if you had been following the developments at Royal Crown via insider reports beginning in January of 1982, you would have done even better. By the beginning of 1982, Chesapeake had already accumulated over 5 percent of Royal Crown's stock, and the other insiders had begun their stepped-up buying. By February of 1982, there was enough evidence of insider activity to warrant an investment—and some outside did so. In early 1982, you could have bought Royal Crown at about $14 a share. If you had held on to it for the two years that the insiders were continuing to accumulate Royal Crown stock up to the time in 1984 when the buy-out by Posner ended the drama, you would have made a 285 percent profit instead of the mere 74 percent profit you would have made if you waited to make your stock purchase in the summer of 1983.

This actual case is typical in its simplicity.

The actions of these insiders clearly showed a bullish attitude about the company. You could not have come away from the data for this case as displayed in the *Official Summary* with any other interpretation. People like Posner, Young and Jones do not make investments of millions of dollars unless they expect to get something out of it—either a large profit or control of a potentially profitable business.

The SEC as Helpmate

The people in the Royal Crown story were playing a power game to fatten their own pockets. It is interesting to note that Young and Jones made their management buy-out announcement at the beginning of a tax year. It probably was no coincidence that the announcement was made then instead of in December. Actually it might have been that Young and Jones did not even have the financial resources to pull off the buy-out. Perhaps the announcement was simply a ploy to call Posner's hand and quickly sew up a profitable deal for themselves.

Whatever the game these people were playing, the important factors to see here are that they were playing with stock of a publicly owned company—stock you could have owned—and they followed the rules by disclosing their stock transactions—activity you could have found out about. And, although these people would have been unaware of your existence, you could have played in their game with the same ball.

The laws that allow you to watch the activities of deep-pocket investors are very rare in the world. In fact, only two countries other than the United States have similar strict insider disclosure laws—Canada and the United Kingdom. For insiders in other countries it is pretty much anything goes.

Every month the SEC processes ten thousand or more reports of insider transactions—of which perhaps 10 percent is of real interest to us as insider-watchers. The clerical drudgery that the SEC does for us has been going on automatically for over fifty years. It gives us a rich information resource. But the SEC's role in collecting and distributing insider trading information is passive. It just administers the clerical work necessary to fulfill the guidelines drawn up by Congress. The SEC doesn't promote or encourage the use of the insider reports for any purpose. (It also doesn't promote the use of any of the other public disclosure documents it processes.) The information is just there and available. It's up to us to take the initiative to pay attention to it. Also, the SEC doesn't provide any guidelines on how to use the information or how to analyze it. It only supplies the raw data. Again, it's up to us to find ways to interpret it.

The SEC's more active role is focused on making sure that insiders comply with the rules and prosecuting those people who think that the rules are too confining for fulfilling their personal financial dreams. It's a happy circumstance that we outsiders can use the information the SEC rules provide to help fulfill *our* personal financial dreams.

Chapter 3

Notorious Insiders

OBVIOUSLY no one can say that everything that happened before the SEC's creation in 1934 was corruption and fraud and that everything that has happened since 1934 has been sweetness and light. Given human nature and the human forces of greed, power and ego, the SEC has had an uphill battle against people who want to return to the good old days of nineteenth- and early twentieth-century insider trading, and against people who come up with new and improved ways of circumventing the letter and intention of the rules.

Take, for example, the 1979 case of a director of a company called Medfield Corporation. This corporate director learned during a company board meeting held on June 9, 1978, that the company had received a purchase offer from another company for about $20 a share. A few days after the meeting, the corporate director bought 11,600 shares of the company's stock at prices between $15⅞ and $17⅜. Within the same week the board met again and voted to approve the purchase. Our newly stock-rich corporate director voted against the purchase plan. (Was he trying not to appear to be too eager? Or did he want the company to hold out for an even better deal—say, $25 a share?) His stock buying, however, had in itself constituted unusually heavy trading volume for the company's stock and had driven the price of the stock up simply because it caused greater demand for it. This raised some eyebrows. A few other directors at the meeting that approved the purchase plan expressed concern about the amount of volume and price rise over the previous few days—without knowing who had actually done the trading. They were worried that perhaps a director had leaked information about the proposed purchase to others on the outside. The guilty director kept his mouth shut. Later, Medfield publicly announced the company sale. The corporate director made a $26,000 profit when he sold his shares.

It took the SEC over a year to investigate the director, bring him to court and get a conviction. But in the end the director— who quickly left his post—had to repay the $26,000 in profits to the former Medfield shareholders he had bought the stock from. Also, he had to promise never to violate federal securities laws on inside information again. (This was before passage of the more strict laws outlined in the Insider Trading Sanctions Act of 1984.)

Clearly, the Medfield director was acting with total disregard —or contempt—of SEC regulations through blind greed, a personal sense of power, an exaggerated ego or a combination of all three. His actions did not fit into the conventional course that other corporate insiders follow to profit without vexing the SEC. If, for example, he had recognized months before the actual purchase offer that Medfield possessed the qualities that make a company an attractive takeover candidate, he could have bought stock in the company in anticipation that one day in the future —whether it was a few months or a couple of years—there would be a purchase offer. But instead of taking this longsighted view and acting like an investor, he followed the route of the speculator's quest for a fast buck. And the SEC's enforcement team caught him.

On the Trail of the Unruly

The SEC has had a somewhat checkered record for enforcing insider trading rules and uncovering wrongdoing. Over its fifty-plus-year history, there have been periods when the SEC has been aggressive in its enforcement and there have been other periods when dishonest insiders and others have been allowed to go on their merry ways.

When the SEC was formed, the first chairman appointed to the commission was millionaire Joseph Kennedy. It was an ironic choice since Kennedy was an extremely active speculator who in the 1920s and early 1930s frequently practiced tactics that became illegal under the Securities Exchange Act. The thought was, however, that Kennedy, knowing firsthand the evil ways of old Wall Street, would be ideal to beat stock market manipulators at their own game. But Kennedy did very little and the SEC staff was never given the go-ahead to attempt to bring reform to Wall Street. (To be fair to Kennedy, those early years of the SEC coincided with a deeply depressed stock market that was so inactive that there was little chance for anyone to engage in too much manipulation of unsuspecting investors.)

Kennedy left in 1935. As Wall Street grew healthier and as other more aggressive chairmen led the SEC—including William O. Douglas, who later became a Supreme Court justice—the agency grew in size and effectiveness. By 1940 there were seventeen hundred SEC employees—about the same number as there are today. During World War II, however, priorities changed. There wasn't much interest in finding fault with America's own behavior that would distract from the united spirit necessary to see the country through the war years. And after the war, people were so relieved that the country didn't go into another depression that Wall Street was pretty much left alone. By 1949 the SEC staff numbered fewer than a thousand employees.

Throughout the first fifteen years of its existence, the SEC did not pay very much attention at all to insiders or insider trading violations. Most of the SEC's attention was directed toward other activities under its jurisdiction. (It was particularly interested in going after crooked stockbrokers.) In fact, it wasn't until 1951 that the first major case was brought against an insider. And when this case was taken to court, it was not done under the rules specifically governing insiders. Instead, it was tried as a fraud violation under Rule 10b-5, a rule passed in 1942 that was added as a subsection to the Securities Exchange Act of 1934. Rule 10b-5 makes it illegal for a person to defraud anyone else through any device or "to make any untrue statement of a material fact or to omit to state a material fact" in order to mislead.

The 1951 case that tested Rule 10b-5 in regard to insiders and inside information involved Transamerica Corporation. The story went like this. Transamerica was the majority shareholder in a smaller company. There was no problem with Transamerica

owning stock in the smaller company or with its method of filing public disclosure forms which reported its holdings. The
problem came when Transamerica made an offer to buy out the
stock held by minority shareholders to take over complete control of the company. The thing that Transamerica failed to do in
its buy-out offer was to tell the minority shareholders that it had
a plan to liquidate the smaller company's huge inventory of undervalued tobacco. If the minority shareholders had known of
the tobacco inventory and Transamerica's plans for it, they
would have seen that the smaller company's stock was more
valuable than they realized—more valuable than the price
Transamerica was offering. The court ruled that Transamerica
had defrauded the minority shareholders by withholding information that it was privy to by virtue of its insider position.

To this day, Rule 10b-5, which outlaws securities fraud and
which collared Transamerica, is the most common legal device
used by the SEC against those it considers have traded illegally
on inside information. The insider laws themselves are rarely
invoked. But, while the Transamerica case put corporate insiders on warning, the SEC went through a period of inactivity
during the Eisenhower years. By 1954 it had only 770 employees and had become a dying remnant of New Deal legislation.

Expanding SEC Powers

The Kennedy administration—headed, of course, by the son of
the man who had been the SEC's first chairman—breathed new
life into the SEC. It was during these years that the SEC started
trying to expand the definition of insider trading. And it was at
this point that many people think that the SEC began to over-
step its original charter. Through a few landmark court decisions, the SEC achieved a goal of grouping together *all* people
who held inside information as "insiders"—not only the corporate insiders (officers, directors and major shareholders) as defined in the acts of 1933 and 1934.

The first major case to expand the definition came in 1961
and involved a director of the Curtiss-Wright Company, who
was also an official at the stock brokerage firm of Cady, Roberts

& Co. Immediately following a board meeting at Curtiss-Wright that voted to cut the company's dividend, the director telephoned the brokerage firm and reported the news. Using this information, the brokerage house sold the Curtiss-Wright stock it had been holding and sold even more "short" in anticipation of a negative stock market reaction to the forthcoming news. Although the corporate insider did not personally benefit from selling the stock before news of the lower dividend was announced publicly, the court agreed with the SEC's contention that he had illegally tipped the brokerage firm and that Cady, Roberts had illegally used the information. This ruling established the precedent that outsiders who had a "special relationship" with corporate insiders—not just the corporate insiders themselves—were required either to disclose the information they receive from insiders or refrain from trading the stock that could be affected by the information.

A case initiated by the SEC in 1966 took the definition of insider even further. In this case, a geologist working for the Texas Gulf Sulphur Company (now called Texasgulf Inc.) suspected that a 1963 mining site he was assigned to in Timmins, Ontario, in Canada was going to yield a rich source of lead, zinc and copper. He bought stock in the company. He also told a friend about the potential large find. The friend told other people. In a few months all these friends and friends of friends had purchased several thousand shares of the company's stock. The rumor of the mineral find spread. By early 1964 even the financial pages of several newspapers were conjecturing about the possibility of a huge mineral strike. But the company down played the find. (It also quietly bought up adjacent properties to the mine in March 1964.) In April of that year, an engineer at the company and the company's corporate secretary bought stock. Then finally on April 16, 1964, the company officially announced the mineral discovery at a press conference. The company's stock quickly reached almost $60 a share—nearly triple the price the geologist paid back in late 1963.

The SEC took a dozen people to court, including the geologist, the engineer and the corporate secretary. It charged even two directors of the company who had purchased stock *after* the public announcement was made, claiming that the directors had not waited long enough for the news to reach the "average investor." When the case came to court, the people who had purchased shares in late 1963 argued that at the time they were not certain that the mineral find was going to be as rich as it turned out to be and therefore had acted on inconclusive evidence. The two directors who purchased stock a few hours after the news was made public claimed that since news services had beamed the announcement to almost every brokerage firm and bank in the country, the existence of the mine was no longer secret.

The court agreed with those arguments. Only the engineer and the corporate secretary who had purchased stock in April were found guilty of trading on inside information. But the SEC wasn't happy with the decision. The case was taken to a federal appeals court and, in 1968, all the defendants—except for one of the directors who had died—were found guilty.

This was a significant decision because it extended the concept of "insider" to include "anyone in possession of material inside information." Not just corporate insiders, but also all other company employees and anyone who might have heard inside information (or rumors) from someone who would be in a position to know such information. The court ruling also confirmed the SEC's claim that the directors had acted too quickly after the news became public. It did not, however, define how much time an insider must wait after a public announcement before trading. The court agreed with the SEC that timing would "vary from case to case."

This decision sent a jolt through Wall Street. The behavior of the directors, the geologist and his friends had been considered, up until this court decision, legal. Wall Streeters wanted a more precise definition of what the SEC considered insider wrongdoing. Since the stock market feeds on information and rumor, professionals claimed that it would be impossible to function without knowing exactly when one would be doing something wrong.

The SEC refused to make firm guidelines.

Some people had hoped that the Insider Trading Sanctions Act of 1984 would provide a precise definition. It did not. The vagueness of the definition—"anyone in possession of material nonpublic information"—continues to give the SEC a free hand to follow any avenue it wants in the pursuit of those people it may currently consider the wrongdoers. The vague definition also provides the SEC a way to deal in the future with unseemly insider behavior that has not yet been invented. (In the fall of 1987, the SEC and Congress were working together to come up with yet another definition—one that was more specific yet broad enough so as not to allow loopholes. As of this writing no decision about a new definition has been made, but the definitions that have been proposed up until this time would not change the SEC's general approach to "inside trading." Instead, they focus on strengthening the legal point of view that the SEC has already displayed in the cases that it has pursued in the previous few years.)

In recent years the SEC enforcement team has been stepping up its number of cases against illegal insider trading. It has brought more cases involving insider trading to court since 1980 than it carried through in all the previous forty years of its existence.

To catch people trading on "material nonpublic information," the SEC relies mostly on a computer-monitoring system that signals unusual stock-trading activity and on good, old-fashioned informants.

The computer-monitoring system is called MOSS—short for Market Oversight and Surveillance System—which tracks over two thousand stocks every trading day to identify those that show sharply increased buying (or selling) activity or those whose prices rise (or fall) outside of a preset limit that the SEC considers "normal." Whenever the MOSS system identifies a company's stock that is experiencing some type of unusual activity, analysts at the SEC try to determine why. Usually the reason is clear: There has been a public announcement of a major corporate development, such as a just-released earnings statement, or an important publication, such as *The Wall Street Journal* or *The New York Times*, has just published a major favorable (or negative) article profiling the company. When the reason is not immediately evident, SEC analysts will contact the company to find out if there has been some incident that could explain the unusual trading activity or price fluctuation. Usually there is a logical explanation that the SEC analysts have missed. Other times, however, the analysts will discover that there is news about the company that has not yet been announced. When this occurs, the SEC will investigate further to find out who was trading the stock prior to the news announcement and why.

Each of the market exchanges has similar computer surveillance systems. In fact, more SEC investigations and court cases have resulted from the initial findings of the exchanges' monitoring of the companies traded on their own exchanges than MOSS has triggered for the SEC. In total, MOSS and the exchanges' computer systems identify over ten thousand different incidents of unusual trading activity every year. But fewer than two hundred a year are ever investigated thoroughly after the obvious reasons for the unusual activity are taken into account.

While MOSS and the surveillance systems of the exchanges have proven to be helpful electronic bloodhounds, a more productive resource for the SEC has been informants. The SEC likes informants. Not only can they accurately identify the people trading on inside information, they can also testify as eye witnesses in court. Building a case based on data collected through MOSS or one of the exchange's surveillance systems alone is much more difficult—in fact, nearly impossible—because it relies on circumstantial evidence.

The SEC finds its informants in different ways. One way is to catch one member of a group of people involved in an illegal inside trading scheme and convince that person to testify against others in return for a lesser legal charge or a softer punishment. Another way is to rely on the moral responsibility of someone who is aware of illegal trading. Most of the convictions or guilty pleas that the SEC gets from transgressing traders are achieved because of informants.

The SEC likes informants so much that in early 1986 it started toying with the idea of offering them cash rewards. Following in the footsteps of the Internal Revenue Service which for years has been giving cash for information about tax evaders, the SEC reasoned that some of the money that is gathered from a successful case against people trading illegally—either through disgorgement or fines—could legitimately go to informants. Through surveillance systems and informants, the SEC claims that nearly all serious insider trading violations are caught. It acknowledges, however, that small illicit trades are not routinely discovered.

SEC Targets

There are all kinds of "inside information" floating around out there and all kinds of people bumping into it—either accidentally or on purpose. But who are the people the SEC is going after? And what type of insider trading is particularly irksome to the SEC enforcement team?

The "who" generally does not include corporate insiders themselves. This is especially true of those corporate insiders who disclose their stock-trading transactions and follow the rest of the rules. It is more likely that the SEC will catch and prosecute "outsiders" who, like the geologist and his friends in the Texas Gulf Sulphur case, came upon their inside information through some sort of direct experience or from a tip from someone else. In fact, you, as an outside investor, are probably more culpable if you trade because you listened to someone who offered you a hot tip than the thousands of corporate insiders who trade in their own companies' stock (profitably) every year. This isn't too surprising. Corporate insiders are familiar with the specific rules that govern them and they are practiced in using the rules to their advantage. You, on the other hand, are governed by insider trading regulations that are vague and are constantly being redefined.

The kicker to all this is that you face the same punishment that applies to transgressing corporate insiders if you are caught trading on inside information. That means disgorgement of any profits you realize (or losses you avoid) up to three times the amount, plus a $100,000 fine and five years in jail.

When it comes to the type of inside information that the SEC is most concerned with, it is particularly partial to cases involving tender offers. A tender offer, which is a public announcement of someone's intention to acquire stock of a company at a fixed price, is usually used in takeover attempts and greatly appreciates the value of the stock of the target company. Over two thirds of the insider trading cases brought to court since 1980 have involved inside information leaked prior to the public announcement of a tender offer. This also isn't too surprising. The early 1980s saw a rash of acquisition activity and takeover attempts. Clearly, this is where the fast action is. And the illegal activities the SEC is trying to stop with its focus on tender offer situations is the type of increased buying that almost always occurs just a few days or hours before a tender offer is made public.

The huge insider trading scandal that captured headlines in 1986 and 1987 is an excellent illustration of the type of behavior that angers the SEC (and the rest of us). It all started when an informant helped nail a managing director of the brokerage firm Drexel, Burnham, Lambert, Inc. The managing director—Dennis Levine—was a merger and acquisition expert at the company who used sensitive information about pending mergers, acquisitions and buy-outs to personally profit by buying stock just prior to public tender offer announcements at fifty-four different companies. He made illegal profits of over $12.6 million before the SEC had him arrested in May of 1986. After Levine was caught, he too turned informant. Since he obviously had to have gotten his information on the fifty-four different companies from someone, the investigation uncovered a complex labyrinth of tipsters that included lawyers, stockbrokers, bankers and analysts. The biggest catch of all was Ivan Boesky, who up until his run-in with the SEC had acquired legendary status as an enormously successful stock market trader and speculator. Boesky's profits from trading in stocks based on tips from Levine and others ran into the hundreds of millions of dollars.

Many of the people involved in this scandal had previously been lionized as financial geniuses and wizards, particularly among the naïve who like to believe that there are superhuman stock market traders. For those of us who have spent our lives on Wall Street, however, seeing these people pick so many winners with such precise timing and profiting with such astronomical results often prompted skepticism. No one can profit as these people did without using supernatural or illegal means. No stock market investment strategy—including the insider investment strategy presented in this book—can achieve those results. And as it has turned out, many people who had been thought of as financial-world heroes simply weren't playing fair.

There was nothing new in the behavior of those involved in the Levine/Boesky story. People have been trying to get information about soon-to-be-announced tender offers for decades and will continue to do so in upcoming decades. The only thing that made the story hit the front page was the amount of money involved.

The important dynamic to see in the Levine/Boesky affair is that as of this writing *not one corporate insider was implicated in the scandal.* It would be very surprising if any actual insider is ever prosecuted. Because of SEC rules, insiders are forced to be legal investors and not get caught up in the illegal activities that Levine and Boesky found so appealing. In fact, if you look at the fifty or so major indictments and convictions handed down since 1980 against people using inside information, you will find only two actual insiders—Darius Keaton, a director of Santa Fe International, and W. Paul Thayer, former chairman of LTV Corporation and former Reagan administration official.

The people to whom the SEC is paying special attention include the professional traders, brokers, lawyers and bankers like those in the Levine/Boesky case. They also include proofreaders and word processors who work at financial printers, which put together the documents required by tender offer law before the announcements are actually made. One widely reported story involved a reporter for *The Wall Street Journal*—R. Foster Winans—who had used information from forthcoming *Journal* articles to trade illegally. All of these people encounter sensitive information during the course of doing their jobs. The SEC's battle has been to keep them honest.

Boesky's Lesson

However diligent the SEC, if you decide that you want to base your stock trading on "material nonpublic information," the odds are that you won't be caught and prosecuted. The SEC concentrates on finding the biggest offenders who capture headlines and whose fines help pay the huge investigation and prosecution expenses.

Like filing income taxes and filling out the forms with complete honesty, abiding by SEC regulations is largely voluntary. But, like income tax evaders, people *do* get caught, as Mr. Boesky found out.

Generally, if you avoid trading on information that you know is not available to the rest of your fellow investors, you can be assured that SEC agents will not knock on your door. Don't trade on information that you pick up from firsthand experience. And beware of people who claim to have an "inside" tip. They could be right and you would be just as guilty as they.

In short, base your investment decisions on information you gather from public sources, such as newspapers, magazines, radio, television and, of course, SEC public disclosure documents like Form 4 and Schedule 13D. If you confine your trading on "inside information" to the information you gather about corporate insider actions as reported to the SEC in its public disclosure documents, you will never get in trouble with the SEC.

Chapter 4

Insider Investing Versus Traditional Stock Market Strategies

FOLLOWING SEC reports of corporate insider actions for stock selection signals, like other stock market analysis "systems" or "strategies," is a technique for handicapping a pretty baffling horse race. With several thousand horses to choose from—all starting at the gate at different times, with different intrinsic abilities, and affected by a host of conditions from interest rates to changing consumer buying patterns to the outcome of presidential elections—the selection process can be overwhelming, particularly for individual investors who feel that only large organizations with expensive research facilities can beat the odds with any regularity.

The myriad stock market strategies developed over the last hundred or so years, however, have attempted to simplify all this—both for large organizations and individuals—and to bring some order to stock market investing. Although no strategy guarantees 100 percent success at all times, several strategies have served their proponents well over the years. Other systems have quickly died after proving to be ineffective.

The investment strategy of following the insiders' lead is not exactly a new kid on the block. Ever since 1933, when Congress started making corporate insiders disclose their trading activities, many investors and analysts have recognized that these insider reports could provide significant investment signals. But it wasn't until the early 1960s that a few stock market analysts started looking at insider reports in any kind of systematic way. This was prompted by the early statistical studies that proved that insider actions displayed excellent predictive power in pointing the way to the future stock price performance of their companies.

If you are just now starting to pay attention to insiders, you will be benefiting from over twenty-five years of research and trial and error in following insider stock-trading patterns. Two significant developments during the mid-1970s gave insider trading analysis a powerful boost. First was the passage of the Freedom of Information Act of 1974, which required for the first time that forms filed with the SEC by *outside* investors holding more than 5 percent of a company's stock—Schedule 13D—be made public. The second major development that helped insider analysts was the advent of the computer. The computer has allowed us to sort and organize the raw data found in the SEC insider reports with sufficient efficiency to make it "talk."

The success that insider analysts have had since the early 1960s has drawn increased interest among adherents to other stock analysis strategies. Today, these analysts often use insider trading information to augment other information used in their own stock analysis approaches. The well-respected advisory service *Value Line Investment Survey* is an example of a research and analysis organization that uses insider reports as one part of its approach to the stock market. Since the mid-1970s, *Value Line* has included an "index of insider decisions" for each of the seventeen hundred companies it covers every week. There are, of course, other investors—both amateur and professional—who use insider trading reports as the *primary* source of information for their investment strategy. That is the approach supported here.

Whether insider reports are used to supplement other strategies or as the primary source of information for an investment strategy, the interest in insider activities has grown sufficiently to support several suppliers of computer data bases that carry insider report information as well as several advisory newsletters that specialize in gathering and interpreting insider activities. We'll look at both of these types of services in later chapters. The point here, however, is that insider data has gained fairly broad acceptance among many investment experts —although the degree to which the information is used varies greatly from strategy to strategy.

Let's take a closer look at the most widely used stock market investment strategies—random-walk, contrarian, econometric, fundamental, technical—and see how insider trading information fits into these analysis philosophies. Then we'll look at how "following the insiders" works as an investment strategy on its own—completely separate from other approaches.

Random-Walk Theory

The random-walk theory of stock market investing is almost a nonstrategy. Random walkers claim that trading profitably in stocks is largely a matter of luck. They say that attempting to find and buy shares of a stock that is currently undervalued to profit later when the stock's true value becomes evident to other investors—and the price of the stock goes up—is an impossible task. Instead of beating your brains out doing stock analysis by trying to find good values, they say, it would be just as effective to make your stock choices randomly. Buy at random. Pick the dates for your purchases at random. Sell your shares at random. An extreme form of this stock selection approach would have a chimpanzee throw darts at a list of publicly traded companies for the proper choices.

Random-walk enthusiasts are most frequently encountered in academic circles. Wall Street practitioners, on the other hand, usually turn purple with rage at the mention of random-walk theory. The rationale on which random walkers base their beliefs is a concept called the Efficient Market Hypothesis which, essentially, states that at any point in time the price of a company's stock already reflects its true value. This is because investors have at hand all the information currently available about the future of the company, and in turn the probable future of its stock price. The hypothesis further says that when some new information about a company is revealed, investors will buy and sell among themselves almost immediately until the stock's price once again (efficiently) reflects its correct value. The key here is that the new information is always a surprise. Since there are as many good surprises (which would raise the price of a stock) as there are bad surprises (which would lower the value of a company's stock and in turn its price), price changes among stocks move randomly.

Therefore, the random walkers' "strategy" is to put together a diversified portfolio of stocks from many different types of companies that mirrors in microcosm the random nature of the stock market as a whole. Then they sit passively, taking their lumps when randomly occurring bad "surprises" make the value of their holdings go down and taking their rewards when those "surprises" turn out to be good, thereby raising the value of their stocks.

The main reasons that Wall Street practitioners get angry with random walkers is that they know from personal involvement that information about a company's future is not equally distributed among investors. In addition, they recognize that, even when information is distributed equally, investors do not always react to it insightfully or rationally.

For large and well-analyzed companies like IBM, Exxon or General Motors, the efficient market hypothesis might have some validity. Every movement of these companies is fully dissected and widely reported. The current prices of these companies' stocks are probably always a fair estimate of value as perceived by a wide range of investors and analysts at a given time—just as the random walkers claim—until some "surprise" changes the outlook. But relatively few companies receive the type of attention necessary to keep their stocks efficiently priced. In fact, only a small percentage of all publicly traded companies fit into this category. The remaining companies (both large and small) are moderately-to-greatly neglected, receiving very little attention by anyone. At one time, most of today's well-analyzed companies were neglected ones. Apple Computer, for one example. Xerox for another. Even IBM.

Neglected companies stay neglected until something happens that makes the stock market investment community pay attention. Random walkers would say that this is the "surprise" element. But often the "surprise" that dramatically affects the price of a stock or brings an underanalyzed company to the forefront is not all that much of a surprise. Despite what the random walkers believe.

There are countless stories that show that "surprises" could have been anticipated before they changed the direction of a company's stock price. Here's one example—although perhaps a little macabre—that occurred during the spring of 1986. The company: Resorts International, a hotel and gambling casino operator. The "surprise": The death of the company's founder and major stockholder, James M. Crosby. The stock market's reaction: Heavy buying the day after Crosby's death pushed the stock up $26 or 50 percent in one trading day from $51 to $77. The reasoning behind the skyrocketing price: Investors interpreted that the death of Crosby, who had run the company autocratically since creating it in 1968, left Resorts International ripe for a takeover.

Random walkers might point to this as a prime example of investors' efficient reaction to an event that could alter the possible course of a company's future. But even though Crosby's death set off stampede buying of Resorts International stock, reports of his terminal illness had been made public months before. Few investors, however, paid any attention to the effect his possible incapacitation or death could have on the company, until he actually died and the news media widely reported the implications.

An adroit analyst could have anticipated the market's reaction. After all, the interpretation of what could happen to Resorts International on the loss of its leader was not made up on the day he died. But most investors don't bother to try to find the clues about a company that could affect its future. Instead, they wait until everything is said and done and then follow the herd. For random walkers, this means efficiency. But clearly there are inefficiencies that can be found, because most investors simply are unable or unwilling to search them out.

In the Resorts International case there were a few investors who did act before Crosby's death. Including—you guessed it— the corporate insiders and those who followed the insiders. From October 1984 through August 1985, Resorts International insiders accumulated nearly 35,000 shares at an average price of about $42 a share. This is not to say that they were betting on Crosby's death or even that they expected Crosby to step down because of his illness. They could have been buying simply because they saw a healthy future for the company. But it is yet another example of the "coincidence" of a significant corporate development that usually follows an unusual pattern of stock-trading behavior among corporate insiders.

Insiders are definitely not random walkers. They know a good bargain when they see it and they act on it. Surveys of corporate insiders who hold stock in their own companies show them to have very little diversification in their stock portfolios. They are usually heavy with stock of their own companies and light in other companies. While this isn't a good example for the rest of us to follow, the insiders do not accumulate stock in their own companies out of pure loyalty. They feel that they've found something that will appreciate greatly in the future. They have specific reasons for their feelings. And usually they are right.

Random-walk theorists begrudgingly admit that insiders make a dent in the Efficient Market Hypothesis. Burton G. Malkiel, probably the best-known random walker and author of a widely distributed book that has convinced many of the merits of the random-walk theory, *A Random Walk Down Wall Street*, writes: "Stocks purchased by insiders often outperform the stocks in a randomly selected group.... The evidence on insider trading does suggest that the very strongest form of the theory [of market efficiency] may not be valid."

Indeed the entire theory may have been critically disabled by the October 1987 crash.

The Contrarian Strategy

Except for the random-walk approach, all stock market strategies attempt in some way to identify undervalued stocks before the herd of less-informed investors jumps on them to raise the price. These strategies are based on the sage advice crystallized by one of history's most successful stock market players, Bernard Baruch: "Young man, if you want to make money in the stock market, buy stocks when they are low, and sell them when they are high."

Easily said. It takes work to achieve.

Throughout most of his investing career, Baruch followed the dictates of a stock market strategy called contrarian analysis or contrary opinion theory. As the name implies, contrarians invest in the opposite direction of the bulk of investors. When bad news, or a perception of bad news, about a company or the stock market in general sets in and causes the herd of investors to panic and sell a stock down to low prices, the contrarian will buy. Then, when the herd is affected by a buying frenzy that raises stock prices, the contrarian sells.

Contrarians try to read the crowd psychology that motivates most investors. They reason that if a stock is popular—whether that popularity is based on a company's realistic intrinsic value or because the company is enjoying some faddish fashion of the moment—there is no place for the stock to grow because it is already fully appreciated. So, contrarians would avoid buying the stock (or if they already owned a stock that became popular, they would sell it). The flip side to that is similar. When crowd psychology makes a stock or the market as a whole unpopular, there are bargains to be found.

It takes discipline to be a contrarian. Going against the crowd isn't a natural instinct. It requires the firm belief that if you do exactly opposite of the majority, you will ultimately profit. For the contrarian, popular moods and other influences on the market move in cycles.

Indeed, the approach has a considerable amount of strength. Just think of how different your net worth would be today if your parents (or grandparents) had bought into the stock market during the lowest point of the 1930s Depression or if you had bought stock during the stock market's bleak periods of the 1970s and then waited until those bearish times turned to bulls.

Contrarians particularly like finding well-known companies that have experienced bad times (and lost their popular support) but have the seeds for a turnaround performance. Corporate insiders often display this form of contrarian stock selection behavior. When things were rough for Chrysler in the early 1980s, a contrarian might have bought the company's stock. Insiders did. Contrarians might also have bought A&P in the early 1980s when the rest of the market was naysaying the company. Insiders were buying. When all was gloom and doom for the oil industry in 1986, a contrarian probably would have bought. Insiders did.

The difference between insiders acting as contrarians and other investors who follow the contrarian approach is that insiders have a clearer vision of the light at the end of the tunnel. They know what is going on within their company that will make their currently unpopular stock achieve popularity in the future. Other investing contrarians can only have faith in the belief that the "crowd" was wrong.

Some contrarians use insider analysis along with their other stock selection techniques. When a stock is identified as losing popular support, a contrarian could look at insider activities for insights into how insiders view the "crowd's" reaction to their company's stock. If there is heavy buying among insiders, it probably means that they are picking up a bargain with the expectation that the unpopularity is temporary. This would confirm the contrarian's overall analysis. If, however, insiders are dumping stock right along with the "crowd," it should give the contrarian pause. (And if there is no insider buying or selling, it would give a neutral signal to contrarians.) There is one contrary opinion that a contrarian—or you—usually wouldn't want to hold: One that is contrary to the insiders.

The Econometric Approach

Econometric analysis takes a global view. It says that big economic forces, such as current government monetary policy, unemployment rates, inflation rates and taxes, are the dominant underpinnings that support everything in the stock market. As those supports change so will the prospects for the stock market as a whole and for specific industries and companies.

The analysts who follow an econometric strategy make their forecasts by looking at the current relationship of a combination of statistical economic indicators and then compare that current status to the way a similar combination of factors affected the stock market in the past. Usually an econometric prediction is based on a mathematical formula using dozens or even hundreds of different economic indicators—from the gross national product to last week's volume of car sales to the amount of help-wanted advertising appearing in last month's newspapers. All this work is almost always done by a computer; it isn't the kind of analysis you can make with your pocket calculator. Then, using an econometric model, the strategist works downward from analyzing the overall economy to its effect on different industries and then to specific companies.

One indicator that some econometric analysts fold into the rest of the data they use is, not surprisingly, the trading actions of insiders. When stock purchases among all insiders number higher than normal—meaning the sum of insider buying by *all* insiders in *all* companies not just within individual companies —it gives the econometric strategist the clue that these knowledgeable investors are expecting, as a group, to find bullish times ahead in the stock market on the whole. When the ratio of insider selling to buying is greater, it may predict a bearish future. Although no econometrician would use this indicator alone as a way of predicting the future direction of the stock market, it has displayed a fairly good track record in the past for anticipating swings in overall market behavior. This could be explained, however, by the fact that in the recent past the market experienced relatively short periods of bullish activity followed closely by short periods of bearish activity and back and forth. Insiders as a group could have been following their contrarian instincts during those periods—buying low when their stock looked like bargains and selling high to make profits.

While some analysts have touted an index of all insider buying and selling as a barometer for predicting the overall direction of the market, the approach in this book does not apply any credence to it. In following the insiders for over ten years, there's no convincing evidence that this index can provide clues for making market predictions. There are too many instances when market swings did not follow the group actions of all insiders. The most dramatic example of this was the fairly heavy insider buying in the months just prior to the 1987 crash. Insider investments are unrelated to the atmosphere that pushes market swings.

Insiders as individuals are not miniature econometric analysts. The big economic picture is not as important to them as the events and developments affecting their specific companies. Although he may unconsciously take into account broad economic considerations while making an investment decision, the insider's view is usually a myopic one, focused almost entirely on the unique set of circumstances found at that one company. When following insiders for investment signals, sometimes you will find that they are bucking the economic trends. This shouldn't be alarming to you. It just means that the insiders see their company unaffected by the trends.

Take, for example, the story of Hadson Petroleum, a gas and oil company based in Oklahoma City. In the second half of 1985 —when oil and gas prices were falling and most investors were selling their shares in energy companies—Hadson insiders bought tens of thousands of shares in their OTC-listed company at an average price of about $2½. By the end of 1986—when the outlook for oil and gas companies continued to look bad and most energy stocks continued to fall—Hadson stock reached $7 per share. (This was a return for the insiders, and others who bought Hadson on the heels of the insiders, of about 275 percent in less than a year.) Why did this little energy company's stock fare so well when others were doing poorly? The answer was revealed in the company's 1985 annual report which was distributed in the spring of 1986. The company's revenues for 1985 showed a 700 percent increase over the previous year, and earnings per share rose to 34¢ in 1985 from 10¢ a share in 1984. The reason for this improved performance that went against the general tide within the industry? Hadson had accumulated pipeline distribution for its product, which meant that instead of being dependent on the *price* of its product (which was declining) for profitability, its sales and profitability were more dependent on the *volume* of its product that was delivered (which was increasing). When this news hit the investment community at large, it drove the value and price of the company's stock up— despite the generally poor performance of other companies in the industry. In all likelihood, Hadson's performance will reach even greater heights when gas and oil prices go up, since it will benefit from *both* the sales price and sales volume of its product.

The Hadson insiders, disregarding the advice given by many econometric analysts that the gas and oil industry was a segment of the stock market to avoid in late 1985, saw the unique circumstances of their particular situation before making their investment decisions.

The Technical Approach

The technician, often called a "chartist," looks almost entirely at price movements and trading volume to try to predict the future direction of a stock's performance. The technician reasons that all information gleaned and analyzed by other investors as well as the psychology of crowd emotion is reflected in a stock's chart. So, rather than attempting to understand the reality behind price movement, the technician is interested only in riding the wave. If the technician interprets that wave to mean that the stock will continue to go up, that's a buy signal. And when it appears that investors are turning away from a stock, that's a sell signal.

There are almost as many different ways to interpret the charts as there are technicians. Underneath all this disagreement, however, is the common belief that past trends in buying or selling will be repeated in the future.

Although some technical analysis is used to try to predict long-term trends, most technicians concentrate on very short-term price movements. When you hear of stock market strategies that emphasize "market timing" or individual investors who "ride the tape," the terms are usually describing some form of technical analysis. By constantly watching the minute variations in up-and-down movement of the market as a whole as well as individual stocks, talented technical analysts can be very successful. But the approach usually requires paying constant attention to the stock market and quick in-and-out trading. The technical approach is not "investing" in the traditional sense, but is instead a *trading* technique that feeds off the current momentum of the stock market. As successful as the approach often can be, it is only for the stronghearted with plenty of time to devote to it. (The crash of October 1987 dealt the technical approach a particularly hard blow. The past patterns that the technicians had used to make their forecasts before the crash were destroyed, and it will take some time before new patterns can be established to enable the technical analysis approach to regain its former validity.)

In a certain sense, the insider investing strategy does share some similarities with technical analysis. Technicians believe that trading and volume patterns observed in the past will give a clue to future direction. An insider analyst believes the same thing. Except, instead of looking at the total trading patterns of the consensus of all traders, we are looking at a small segment of traders—the insiders. The insiders' actions reflect *specific knowledge* about the future of their companies, while the consensus of traders—which the traditional technician watches—reflects a perception of the value of a company's stock by *all* investors at that particular time. Like the technician who follows general trading patterns, we ride the wave of the insiders' investment actions with the assurance that past evidence of insider behavior indicates that similar behavior in the present will point the way to future stock returns in a somewhat predictable fashion.

Furthermore, while the traditional technician has no interest in attempting to find out the reasons behind the stock-trading patterns he follows, we have no way of knowing exactly *why* the group we are following acts in the way it does—only the

insiders themselves know for sure the reasons for their investment actions. We, therefore, must base our conclusions on the
patterns of insider actions and not on the impossible-to-
determine information they are using to make their decisions.
From that point of view, an insider investment approach is similar to the technical approach. But, unlike most technicians, the
insider strategist follows a traditional "buy and hold" investment philosophy rather than one that depends on fast turnaround trading speculation.

The Fundamental Approach

Contrarian and econometric strategies are actually offshoots of
the more widely followed approach called fundamental analysis. Like followers of contrarianism and econometrics, fundamentalists attempt to assess the basic worth of a company and
then look to see if the company's stock is currently being sold at
a price that accurately reflects that worth. If the stock is selling
for more than the company's inherent value, fundamentalists
consider the stock to be overvalued and therefore it should not
be bought. (Or if the overvalued stock is currently being held in
a portfolio, it should be sold.) When a stock is selling for less
than the company's inherent value, the fundamentalist considers that a buy signal. Thus, unlike the contrarian strategy,
which interprets the psychology of the crowd, and econometrics, which looks at a set of outside economic indicators for the
big picture, fundamentalists concentrate on the health of a company in relation to other companies.

Because there are so many people following this philosophy,
there are numerous splinters that go about it in different specific
ways. But usually a fundamentalist will evaluate a company
based on objective factors, such as past earnings and dividend
performance, and subjective factors, such as an assessment of
the company's management capabilities and the future probability of the continued (or changing) success of its products or services.

There are various objective factors that fundamentalists use as
barometers for identifying undervalued or overvalued stocks.

Let's look at two of the most important ones: price/earnings ratios and book value.

A stock's price/earnings ratio, most commonly referred to as "P/E ratio," is the current price of the company's stock divided by the company's annual earnings per share. Therefore, if the stock's price is $10 and the company's earnings per share is $1, the stock has a P/E ratio of 10. In other words, the stock is selling at ten times the company's earnings. At any given moment, the stocks of different companies carry different P/E ratios. Some may be selling at a hundred (or more) times their earnings; others may be selling as low as two times earnings. The fundamentalist will look at the average P/E ratio of all companies combined—or within specific industries or groups of companies—at a given moment to see if there are companies with stock being sold below that average. Those below the average are possible undervalued stocks. For example, in simplified terms, let's say that the average P/E ratio of all companies in an industry group is 10. To a fundamentalist, a company selling at a ratio between 2 and 5 could be considered a good value to buy. The idea here is that when other investors wake up to this good value it will drive the price of the stock up to put it more in line with the average P/E ratio of the rest of the stock market (or those companies within a specific industry group).

When fundamentalists turn their attention to a company's book value, they are looking at the company's total net assets— after all its liabilities, including debt, have been subtracted— divided by the number of shares of stock there are outstanding. So, for example, if a company's total net assets are $50 million and there are 5 million shares of stock being held by stockholders, the book value would be $10 per share. Usually the actual price of a company's stock is above its book value—except during times when the stock market is extremely depressed. But by comparing the average price of the stocks of all companies in relation to their book values, a fundamentalist might find companies that are selling under the average. This would imply that those companies have undervalued stock. In other words, if at a particular time, the average company's stock is selling at 100 percent more than its book value, a company's stock selling at only 25 percent or 50 percent above its book value could be an undervalued stock.

No self-respecting fundamentalist would limit an analysis to

P/E ratios or book values. Other statistical and subjective information would be weighed, such as the amount of a company's
working capital or cash on hand, its debt, its dividend yield, its
return on equity, its new products, its markets and technologic
prospects and a host of other factors. The use of P/E ratios and
book value, however, illustrates both the strength and weakness
of the fundamental stock selection strategy. Its strength lies in
the fundamentalist's attempt to assess the reality that lies behind the price of a stock. Although at times the stock market
seems to have a life of its own without any relation to the reality
of a company's performance—when crowd euphoria for a particular stock, for example, drives the price up out of proportion
or when crowd fear drives it down to an undeserved low—
there is usually some logical explanation to prices. Through
analysis, the fundamentalists are simply trying to spot in advance those stocks selling at levels different from their proper
price.

But the weakness that every fundamentalist must face is that
statistics based on past performance don't necessarily have anything to do with future performance, which is particularly the
case in the aftermath of the cataclysmic October 1987 crash. To
supplement an analysis of past performance, many fundamentalists try to project possible future earnings and other statistics
about a company. As you can imagine, when an analyst gets into
this area of crystal ball predictions of specifics, the ground gets
a little shaky. A thorough fundamentalist, who isn't bound by
statistics alone, will interview company management to detect
its views of a company's future and also will try to analyze the
soundness of the company's business and its growth potential
—compared to competing companies and trends in the economy—to come up with a probable forecast for the company and
its stock. A fundamentalist will also look for seemingly insignificant clues that give a window view of the changing value of a
company.

This type of sleuthing was the reason for the stock price increase experienced by a company called Oppenheimer Industries, a cattle agency and ranch broker, during the winter and
spring of 1986. In January of that year, Oppenheimer was selling
on the American Stock Exchange at about $6½. At the end of
January, the company announced its 1985 earnings—a 29¢ return per share on sales of $6.9 million as compared to its 1984
record of 18¢ earnings per share on sales of $5.7 million. A nice

improvement, but nothing to get too excited about. On publication of this news, the company's stock actually went down a few pennies. But during the second week in February of 1986, the stock went up dramatically to nearly $10 a share. The company issued a news release on February 12 saying that there was no reason for the price rise. Another similar news release was circulated in the middle of March when the company's stock had gone up to $11 a share. Later that spring the company's stock was selling at over $18 a share. Still, the company said it had no idea why.

A mystery? Not really. A tiny tidbit about the company had, in fact, been revealed on February 6, 1986, when it was announced that Oppenheimer had sold four and a half acres of vacant land near downtown Kansas City for $1.7 million. This real estate, which had been included in the company's listing of assets at a much lower valuation, suddenly put a different price tag on the company's other real estate holdings and therefore on its stock. With the new information in hand, an attentive fundamentalist would have figured out quickly that Oppenheimer's previously unrecognized real estate riches added significantly to its book value. One estimate put this at an additional $17 a share. If the fundamentalist bought stock at about $8 a share on the heels of the announcement of the sale in Kansas City, the return in the following few weeks would have been more than a little satisfying.

A similar story happened to Alexander's, Inc., a chain of department stores in the New York City area. Although the sales and earnings performance of this retailer had been spotty over the years, a fundamental analysis that started circulating in 1985 among some investors showed that the company held rapidly appreciating real estate—including a block-size chunk of Manhattan across the street from Bloomingdale's, an extremely successful department store. (The company also owns prime property in suburban areas.) Alexander's announced in the mid-1980s that it had vague plans for tearing down the twenty-year-old store it had on the site in Manhattan and replacing it with a building complex of offices, apartments and smaller stores. In mid-1986 Alexander's stock sold for over $40 a share. Fundamentalists who saw the hidden value of Alexander's real estate could have picked up the stock for as low as $23 in 1985. There still may be a chance as of this writing that Alexander's hasn't gone up as much as possible, since most investors will wait to buy the stock until they hear that the wrecking ball has started work on that piece of property in Manhattan. But by then, of course, the game will be over.

These are just two examples of how an investor digging for fundamental clues to the future of a company can profit. This is why full-service brokerage firms spend millions of dollars every year for fundamental analysis.

Of all the stock selection strategies, investing based on insider actions is most closely related to fundamental analysis. Insiders are themselves the best fundamentalists. They have at their fingertips all the statistical information that outside fundamentalists have, plus a lot of other information that might not be readily available to outsiders, which gives their conjectures about future performance considerably more credibility than the forecasts that outside fundamentalists are capable of.

Actually, the choices that insiders make sometimes coincide with the analysis made by outside fundamentalists. More often, however, insiders make their choices far in advance of even the most alert fundamentalists or make selections that are never caught by fundamentalists until some bombshell development becomes evident. The same two companies, Oppenheimer Industries and Alexander's, Inc., are perfect examples.

Beginning in April of 1985, Harold Oppenheimer, chairman of the board of Oppenheimer Industries, started a concentrated buying spree in the open market of stock in his company. In April he bought 6,700 shares at an average price of $7; in June, 8,000 more shares were purchased at an average $6 price; in July he added 3,300 shares to his cache at about $6 a share; in August he purchased another 2,600 shares at an average cost of $6 a share; and in September of 1985 he made a whopping purchase of over 1 million shares at an average of only $5 a share. This huge September purchase was made almost exactly six months (remember the six-month rule governing corporate insiders!) before the sale of those four and a half acres in Kansas City which triggered interest in the company and quickly brought about a reassessment of Oppenheimer Industries' intrinsic value.

In 1985 Mr. Oppenheimer plunked down over $10 million of his own money for the privilege of owning all that stock. As a fundamentalist, perhaps he had a realization of the value of the company's real estate holdings or perhaps he bought the stock for some other fundamental reason no one has recognized yet.

(A really clever fundamentalist could probably have analyzed the company's real estate and its value based on the current real estate market and come to the same conclusion in 1985 that became clearly evident in February of 1986. But that would have taken a lot of work and there was nothing in Oppenheimer Industries' past that would have called attention to the company for that type of in-depth analysis.)

Mr. Oppenheimer's buying was the type of extraordinarily unusual trading pattern that should spark the interest of investors following insiders. You could have picked up a good bargain at $5 a share if you had been paying attention—as some of us did. Oppenheimer himself turned the value of his $10 million stock purchases in 1985 to almost $30 million worth of stock in less than a year. Subsequently nothing happened at Oppenheimer. No deals were announced and no more real estate was sold. As is common in situations like this, the short-term speculators who bought heavily as the company's stock was on the way up lost interest in it when it stopped rising. Those speculators turned to concerted dumping as the stock's price fell back to below $6 a share in late 1986. At the beginning of 1987 the stock had recovered to about $8 a share, which was still considerably higher than the price paid by the insider and those of us who followed the insider's lead back in 1985. But this higher price could have been considered an even better buy because of the evidence of large real estate asset value plus the fact that the insiders were holding pat. They did not sell when the stock reached its high in 1986 to take big profits. Instead, they continued to hold their shares, and even bought thousands more when the stock's price fell back, which more than implies that they still consider a bright future for Oppenheimer Industries stock.

The insider scenario for Alexander's, Inc. was somewhat different. In this case the major players were outsiders who became so enamored of Alexander's potential that they bought heavily enough to become insiders. There were two major groups of investors. One was the Bass Group, a family-run Texas-based investment company, and the other was Interstate Properties, a New Jersey real estate group. Beginning as early as 1980, Interstate started buying hundreds of thousands of shares at prices as low as $10. It sank over $10 million into Alexander's. The Basses started their buying in early 1984 at prices that averaged about $23 a share for total holdings that cost them over $17 million. Clearly, a fundamental analysis of Alexander's real estate prompted these two groups to invest so heavily. And, once again, investors following these savvy outside/insiders profitably rode their coattails at an early stage before the research departments of large brokerage firms caught on to what was happening. At the end of 1986, the Bass Group sold its holdings for a huge profit to New York real estate magnate Donald Trump. Trump, who has a reputation for getting things done, is expected to actually develop Alexander's real estate potential. Although he paid nearly $50 a share for his holdings, Trump will probably also see the value of the stock increase in the next few years after his work is done.

These stories are not meant to condemn fundamental stock selection strategies. Methodical and investigative fundamental analysis can turn up excellent stock choices, including many that insiders never invest in themselves. In fact, as a close ally to fundamental analysis, insider analysis has already taken its place among the screens used by many fundamentalists. Insider trading information can be used to confirm a selection identified by traditional methods, such as P/E ratios and book value. If a fundamentalist feels that a company is carrying an unusually low P/E ratio, for example, a look at what the insiders have been doing in recent months may show that they too have considered the stock to be undervalued in comparison to other companies. Or if heavy insider selling was going on it may signify that the company's stock wasn't as much of a bargain as its low P/E ratio may indicate.

While insider investing information can help fundamentalists sort out potential winners and losers, investors who follow insiders as the *primary* signals for investments cannot rely on traditional fundamental measurements to confirm the decisions made by the insiders being followed. These traditional measurements could be misleading. In the case of Oppenheimer Industries, for example, the fundamentals—earnings, dividends, book value and so on—were OK, but there was nothing exciting about them that would imply that Oppenheimer was an undervalued or even a particularly wise investment choice. It was a sleeper that had only its insider's solid belief in the company's future going for it—until the Kansas City real estate sale showed the company's hand. The Alexander's, Inc. story didn't even have OK fundamentals going for it. A poor earnings record and seemingly ineffective retailing acumen within its management made the company an unlikely choice based on readily apparent fundamentals. It was only the behavior of some heavy-duty outside/insiders that made this stock interesting. In both of these cases, the unusual pattern of insider behavior would have been enough—and *was* enough—for investors following insiders, despite the other fundamental indicators.

Insider Investing on Its Own

If the stock market is like a horse race, then the various strategies for selecting stocks are similar to the ways people pick horses to bet on at the track. A random walker selects his horses by closing his eyes and letting his finger land on the scratch sheet. A contrarian picks the horse with long odds in hopes of making a big killing. The technician looks at the recent past performance of each horse and watches how other people were betting before making a decision just before the race begins. The fundamentalist assesses the horse's complete past performance, watches it walk up to the gate to try to judge its spirit on that day and, in addition, looks at the jockey's record and personality, the weather conditions, and probably buys a tip sheet—the track's equivalent of a research report—to see how others are interpreting the possible outcome.

Each of these approaches represents a plan of attack that makes some sense. But if you had the opportunity, wouldn't you rather bet the way the horse trainers and owners do? That's the insider investing strategy in a nutshell: betting with the trainers and owners.

Following this approach requires more than a little bit of blind faith. Since you don't know in advance *why* the trainers and owners are betting the way they do, you can only believe that they generally know more and have a better reading on the situation than you do—no matter how carefully you analyze the scratch sheet and assess the track conditions.

Such blind faith is not without logic. It is based on an understanding of and a belief in the basics of human nature. A horse owner's human nature may motivate him to provide his animal with the best food, training, soft hay for its stall and fresh Kentucky air between races. But when he steps up to the betting window, all the concern and hopes he has for his horse goes drifting away in the breeze. Now he is concerned only with himself and the return he can make on his bet. If he is convinced his horse has a good chance of winning, he'll bet on it. Otherwise, he'll choose another horse with better prospects. That's human nature.

It's probably the element of human nature that motivated Harold Oppenheimer to put over $10 million on the nose of Oppenheimer Industries. And it's also most likely the motivating force behind all the other insider actions you've read about so far.

Some may argue that it is also in insiders' human nature to become emotionally involved with the company they work for and helped build, and that purchases of their own company's stock can be emotionally motivated. Up to a certain point this may be true. Seeing an insider buy a thousand shares or even a few thousand shares may make sense from an emotional attachment perspective. But when he starts buying tens of thousands of shares and spends hundreds of thousands or millions of dollars to do it (and does it time and time again), the emotional explanation isn't as valid—unless the insider is insane. As far as insanity goes, we can give the insider who is investing heavily the benefit of the doubt. Few truly insane people are able to achieve the status of an insider or accumulate the money necessary to invest in a way that defines heavy investment. We can therefore safely assume that heavy investments are motivated by financial self-interests and are based on the same type of sound business decisions that got the insider to his or her position in the first place.

Not everyone is cut out for following on faith the actions of strangers for investment signals, even though those strangers have a very good record for picking winners. Test your faith quotient. If you looked back at the insider stories you've read about so far but disregarded the final outcome, would you have been convinced to put a few of your own dollars into these companies—without knowing anything else about the company except the investment activities of the insiders? Would Harold Oppenheimer's purchase of 2 million shares of Oppenheimer Industries or the Haubs' purchase of nearly a million shares of A&P or the Bass Group's investment in Alexander's signaled to you that these people had a good perspective on the future?

If not—if you do not believe that these insiders were continually accumulating stock over a long period of time with the expectation of a big return in the future—then you probably do not have the temperament to follow insiders for investment signals.

There is no practical way to confirm the insiders' investment decisions to give you an idea of the likelihood of success. Traditional criteria for judging the soundness of a company's stock wouldn't be much help. As we've already seen, they can be misleading. Actually, it is often in the insiders' best interest to keep others in the dark until they are finished placing their own bets at good prices.

Studying a company's historical balance sheet won't reveal the forward-looking insights that the insiders are using. Projecting possible future earnings, dividends and company developments based on readily accessible information is a futile exercise, because you won't be able to find all the minute particles of objective and subjective data that the insiders assimilate on their way to making their own investment decisions. And it would be silly, of course, to think that if you telephoned the insiders themselves and asked a few questions about the reasons for their investments you would be given the complete answers you're looking for. Therefore, all you have is faith in their knowledgeable and very human behavior.

For those of you who still are uneasy about investing your money by following the actions of these strangers, consider the faith you may put into the recommendations of traditionally recognized "authorities." Many people listen attentively to stockbrokers, newsletter writers and other investment advisors who provide recommendations—for a price. That's fine. Some of these advisors have excellent track records. But do you always know how these authorities themselves invest or even how they have come to their conclusions? And in the case of stockbrokers, do you always know if they have your best interests at heart? Certainly the crash of October 1987, which came so unexpectedly, does no credit to traditional Wall Street experts.

Insiders, on the other hand, are investors only, investors who have the privileged position of being very close to the action. They do not sell their insights. They would probably prefer that you did not even know how they were investing.

Of all these "authorities," which one holds the greatest credibility? Our vote is for the insiders—those savvy investors who speak to you only through the actions they take with their own money.

The Ghost of Benjamin Graham

In the same year that Congress passed the Securities Exchange Act of 1934, the first edition of one of the most significant and influential books on investments was published. The principal author of the book, entitled *Security Analysis,* and of three subsequent editions was Benjamin Graham. Graham was the first articulate exponent of *value investing*—that is investing based on measuring a company's intrinsic worth and its probable performance in the future. Graham is considered the father of the fundamental analysis approach to stock market investing.

Although some may think that Graham's principles for *long-term* value investing, created nearly sixty years ago, could have little relevance in a stock-market atmosphere that increasingly stresses *short-term* trading speculation, the genius of Graham's concepts is *very* relevant today to the way insiders invest and the way we invest as insider-watchers. Graham identified two basic requirements for securities selection. The first tells us to make a projection of a company's value several years into the future and to make that projection independent of the stock market's current view of the value of the company's stock. This means looking at the company's asset value, its probable income, earnings and so forth to find out what a company is *really* worth today and project what it can be expected to be worth in the future. The second requirement is to compare that assessment of value to the price the company's stock is currently selling for in the stock market. If the stock is selling for a discount from its real worth then the company's stock is *undervalued*— it's a "bargain."

As you have seen earlier in this chapter, these two requirements are the underlying principles that fundamental analysts use for making their stock selections and recommendations. You should also recognize that these two requirements are the principles that the *insiders* use to make their selections. They look to the current and *future* value of their specific companies before making their investment decisions, because the six-month holding rule that governs the way insiders can invest does not allow them to play on the *short-term* price movements of the stock market. The insiders are expert appraisers of value—in fact, they are the most expert appraisers of value because of their unique "insider" access to comprehensive information about their companies. "Outside" appraisers of value—fundamental analysts—actually must go to the insiders for *their* information, which can remove the fundamentalists' appraisal from reality. As insider-watchers, we skip over attempts to make our own evaluation of a company's value—which, considering the complexities of doing such a thing accurately, could make our conclusions foggy—and look only at the actions that the experts take with their own money. And, quite simply, the more actions we see, the more compelling the investment for our own stock portfolio.

Graham further went on to say that after an undervalued stock is identified and bought, there are three ways that the holder of that stock can expect to achieve a proper price in the stock market. The first way is to simply wait for the market to ultimately come to an appreciation of the company's real worth. The second way is to force management of the company to take action to bring about proper valuation. And the third, if you can't get management to work out the proper valuation, is to take over yourself and displace management.

As an individual investor with small or even moderately large holdings in a company, you could realistically expect only one of the three ways to work: the first—waiting. But as a co-investor with insiders you have people with considerable amount of real "inside" power working for you to bring about full valuation following Graham's other two paths. Since inside/insiders *are* management, they can force themselves to take action—all, of course, based on their own financial self-interests. And displacing management is often the route taken by outside/insiders, which has earned them—rightly or wrongly—labels such as "raider" and "shark."

Although Graham died without assessing a stock selection strategy based on following insider actions in terms of his own concepts, we can say with confidence and without upsetting his ghost that the insider investment strategy is pure Benjamin Graham. In fact, by following the lead of insiders—those most expert of expert appraisers of value—we could say that we are practicing the purest form of Benjamin Graham's principles. This is because the accurate assessment of a company's probable future value and ability to achieve its highest value is all wrapped up in one neat package in the form of the insiders' power. When viewed in this way, the insider investment strategy is not unusual or offbeat in any way. It is, instead, a most orthodox and traditional form of security analysis. It's just that we go about it on a somewhat different course.

That Ol' Devil Risk

Uncertainty. That's the bugaboo investors grapple with constantly when choosing among different investment options. For the extremely fainthearted, keeping funds in a bank's government-insured savings account that yields a steady 5½ percent return is all the uncertainty that can be tolerated. For the real gambler, getting involved in the rough-and-tumble world of commodity futures trading can be an exciting game that could bring some hefty profits.

Somewhere in between these two extremes is investing in the stock market.

Of course, common stock investing has its risks. At times investors abandon the stock market when the risks of owning stocks appear to outweigh the possible returns. For example, during periods of high interest rates, many investors would rather keep their money earning a comfortable 10 percent or more in a money market account rather than brave the relatively choppy waters of the stock market. When these periods of high interest rates occur, the stock market usually reacts with a bearish decline; since many investors are pulling their money out in search of a more certain return, there is less demand for all stocks and therefore prices go down. The opposite occurs, of course, during periods of low interest rates. If investors can't get a decent return elsewhere, they are willing to turn to the stock market and experience a little risk in the hope of getting a better return on their investment dollars.

Influences such as interest rates contribute to fluctuations in the stock market as a whole. When rising (or falling) interest rates—or some other occurrence—cause the stock market to decline (or rise), it affects nearly all stocks. This is one type of risk that a stock market investor encounters. It is referred to as *systemic* risk and it is caused by overall market factors. Another type of risk—called *unsystemic* risk—is related to the performance of a specific company—its earnings, dividends and so forth. On this basis, a company's stock will fluctuate depending on these *nonmarket* factors. When they are negative the stock will usually go down in price, when they are positive they will usually go up in price—regardless of what the general market is doing.

When we consider the risks in following insider investments, we first have to look at those investments from the insider's point of view. Because of the laws affecting the way insiders can invest they are forced to take the long view of their investments (the six-month rule, again). And because they are forced to take this long view, it is nearly impossible for them to predict the circumstances that will affect the price of the stock from systemic or market risk factors. Market factors change too quickly to be taken into consideration with an investment that *must* be held for at least six months. Even if you have not been actively involved in stock market investing, you probably have heard news stories in the past few years that report one day the stock market made its biggest overall advance in history and then a few days later had its biggest drop in history. Those big swings cannot be predicted in advance, although they usually affect the prices of most stocks on a daily basis. Because of the unpredictable nature of market risk, the insider must focus on the *nonmarket* factors affecting his specific company that will in the future (at least six months ahead) dramatically influence the perception of other investors about the value of the company's stock. As a result of this focus on nonmarket factors, almost all insider investments fall into the category of what is called a "special situation stock."

In Sylvia Porter's *New Money Book for the 80's*, she defines a special situation stock as "a stock in which you're likely to make a profit as a result of a new or impending specific and unusual development either within the company or in the outside environment affecting the company. What makes this special is that few investors recognize the impending change, and the improvement has not yet been reflected in the price of the stock. In either case, the development is setting the stage for a substantial upsurge in the company's earnings—and usually you'll be able to make your profit no matter what the short-term swings in the general stock market."

This is exactly what the insiders are doing—spotting special situation stocks—regardless of the overall movement of the market. Their unique positions allow them to see the special situation nature of their companies' stock so correctly and consistently.

The insiders' point of view is that stocks they buy have very low *long-term* risk or likelihood of losing money. However, during the time that it takes to work out the "special situation" the company's stock will be vulnerable to market factors. And the stock's price could be very volatile during the holding period. As outsiders investing along with the insiders, we can never know the time in which the insider expects to achieve his profits. Therefore, like attempting to confirm insiders' actions through traditional measurements of a stock's current relative health, applying market risk measurements to insider investments will not provide any meaningful assessment of the future direction or risk probability of the "special situation" stock chosen by insiders.

(It should be pointed out to those of you who are concerned with market risk assessments that several of the statistical studies that have shown abnormal returns on insider investments have also shown that the abnormal returns exist even when market risk is taken into consideration. Essentially, this means the abnormal returns that insiders enjoy are not achieved because they are investing only in high-risk stocks—ones that would naturally outperform the average stock in bull markets. Insider trading is evident in *all* types of companies. From small, emerging companies that traditionally carry high systemic risk to companies with traditionally low systemic risk like utilities and large well-known companies. It's a very democratic phenomenon.)

Does this imply, however, that following insiders for investment signals is completely without risk? Unfortunately, no. Despite their excellent track record, insiders sometimes make mistakes. And they can make whoppers if they go wrong. Also, sometimes insiders invest too early for the taste of impatient outside investors who want to make a fast killing and are unwilling to wait for the development on which the insider is basing an investment decision to come full term.

One insider who miscalculated his company's future prospects was H. E. Chiles. An oil field magnate who has a track record of success dating back to the late 1930s, Chiles accumulated over 500,000 shares in the company he founded and heads, Western Company of North America, from March 1985 through July 1985 at prices between $3.87 and $7 a share for a total cost to him during 1985 of over $2.5 million. (These purchases brought his total holdings in the company to over 3 million shares.) Western Company, an oil field services company, was severely hurt during the oil-glut period of late 1985 and early 1986, and by April of 1986 it had to default on most of its $580 million debt. The company started liquidating its assets and the stock dropped dramatically to below $1 a share. Chiles, who had also owned the Dallas-Fort Worth baseball team, the Texas Rangers, lost a huge amount of money. His stock, which was worth about $350 million at its peak in 1981, dwindled to only about $12 million in mid-1986.

Another case where insider-watchers would have lost right along with the insiders themselves was American Adventure, a campgrounds developer. Insiders at American Adventure bought nearly 125,000 shares during 1984 at a cost of over $1 million at prices between $9.63 and $12.63 per share. In late 1984, the stock had gone up over $14 a share—due in part to successes seen in similar campground businesses—but in late 1985, after the government forced the company to redefine its accounting operations and asset measurement, its stock fell sharply and steadily until mid-1986 when it was selling at about 50¢ a share.

The fact that insiders can be fallible does not negate the investment approach of following insiders for investment signals. We are all "insiders" with regard to our personal lives. But just because we sometimes make a mistake, it does not mean that we give up on using our best judgment in making decisions. The insiders at Western Company and American Adventure invested with full expectation of achieving a good return. The events that followed obviously did not match their expectations.

It is the high incidences of *correct* judgment by insiders that makes the approach valid. However, when we find evidence of heavy insider investments among several different companies, it is impossible to forecast with absolute certainty the probability of a successful outcome with one insider "choice" as compared to others. As you've seen, insiders can *sometimes* be wrong in their assessments of the future of their companies and the price direction of their companies' stock. To guard against the risk of following only insider situations that ultimately turn sour— even though the number of these cases should be very low— you must *diversify*, that is, build a portfolio of not one or two but several insider "picks." The procedures for portfolio diversification are described in Chapter 11. Another element of risk encountered in stock market investing is that of outright management fraud. But this is thankfully a rare happening, particularly in insider situations, where it would be analogous to personal financial suicide.

But If Everyone Did It . . .

Notwithstanding the occasional investment misjudgments on the part of insiders, if the idea of following the lead of insiders holds so much promise for identifying undervalued stocks, how could it possibly work if everyone started paying serious attention to what insiders are doing?

This has been a question posed since the first studies on insider trading during the early 1960s were conducted. Again and again over the years, stock market experts have warned that as the existence of the public nature of insider trading transactions becomes more widely understood it would dilute the effectiveness of the strategy. This is because, they reason, so many people would jump on the coattails of insiders that it would raise the price of the company's stock and would make a seemingly undervalued stock immediately overvalued.

This hasn't happened. And it probably won't happen in the future, for a couple of good reasons. First, "everyone" doesn't follow any one strategy. If everyone did, contrarians wouldn't be as successful as they are because everyone would be a contrarian. If everyone followed the technicians' philosophy, there wouldn't be anyone to create the patterns that the technicians feed off of. If everyone was a traditional fundamentalist, this group of strategists would never be able to find an undervalued security. And if everyone was a random walker, no one would be doing the analysis necessary to make the market as efficient as it is.

Second, adherents of any of these traditional stock market strategies are not likely to be converted by any discussion of the possibilities that following insiders hold. As far as they are concerned, their systems work and will continue to work in the future. In other words, the field is still open for you, just as it has been for decades.

Even if more people *do* start paying attention to insider trading, there is a built-in safeguard against buying into a stock when it has become overvalued. By using common sense and not paying much more for the stock than the insiders' own purchase price, you limit yourself to investing at prices the insiders consider a bargain. If a particular stock's price rises quickly before you are able to identify it as an insider's choice, just move on to another company's stock that *can* be purchased at the insider's price. There are more than enough new stock candidates turning up each month—and week.

There *has* been increased trading based on insider activities in the past few years and it has brought with it a situation that occurs with some regularity. Investors, seeing the bullish actions of insiders, buy. This creates more demand for the stock. In addition, technical strategists—who watch volume of trading and look for blips in increased stock prices—sometimes jump on this activity, creating even more demand for the company's stock. The increased demand, of course, tends to raise the stock's price. But then, traders, either out of fear or impatience, will start selling the stock and the price goes down. Remember, the insiders' buying itself is *not* the event that increases the true value of the company's stock. It is merely a predictive measure that some very knowledgeable people expect that the stock will go up. It is only after the real event becomes evident—a takeover, a performance turnaround, a buy-out and so on—that the "efficient" aspect of the market recognizes the change in the company's value and the stock will go up and stay there. When investors who follow insiders buy heavily and technical strategists also buy heavily, it often causes a *short-term* rise in the company's stock price that is not based on the reality of the market's reevaluation of the company's situation. (Insiders themselves can rarely benefit from this short-term rise because of the six-month holding rule. And, therefore, it is nearly impossible for them to manipulate insider-watchers by buying heavily in order to create an artificial short-term price rise from which they could profit.)

When the demand slows, the price of the stock will go down, which causes fear among some investors, who will dump their holdings (and lose money), causing the stock to fall even more. These people do not have the objectivity or temperament to hold the stock until the situation—on which the insiders first based their investment decision—ultimately comes to pass.

That can cause a sickening feeling among the rest of us, because as other investors dump their holdings and as previous buyers —including the insiders—hold back, it can produce very big percentage drops. Of course, such a drop can also create even greater opportunity for those with good nerves and a solid, long-term investment perspective. This is because the dumping can carry the price of the stock down to levels that are *below* the prices paid by the insiders themselves.

Don't assume, therefore, that, just because you are not able to purchase shares at the insider's price when you first discover interesting insider activity, you will have lost out on an opportunity. In other words, if insider trading draws attention to a stock and raises its price through heavy demand by insider-watchers and others, wait until the dust settles and the price comes down again before purchasing yourself. Then you can hold on to the stock until the *real* situation occurs that raises (and stabilizes) the stock's price.

PART TWO:

Getting to Know the Players

Chapter 5

The "Rules" of the Game

W<small>E</small> know that insiders know more than we do. We know that they consistently profit from investments in their own companies—usually with returns much greater than the stock market as a whole. We know, since we are not insiders ourselves and cannot expect insiders to discuss candidly with us the reasons behind their trading actions, that all we have to tell us about their investments are the publicly available reports they file with the SEC. But how do we know when we look at these SEC reports—or read about insider activities in newspaper or magazine articles or in investment advisory newsletters—which insider investments are significant enough to signal us to invest our own dollars?

A general, and simple, answer to that question is: When they display a consistent pattern of unusual behavior.

The next question, of course, is: What constitutes "consistent" and "unusual" behavior? To begin with, you should understand that *any* type of stock trading by *any* corporate insider is "unusual" behavior. Only a small percentage of insiders actually trade every year. A quick look at the numbers shows how rare insider trading is.

There are more than thirty thousand public companies reporting to the SEC, and we can estimate that there is an average of about ten to twelve insiders at each of these companies. That gives us approximately four hundred thousand people who come within the SEC's definition of corporate insiders and who are required to report their trading in the stock of their companies. (No one has actually tried to count the number of insiders. The figures given here are very rough—and conservative—estimates. There are probably several hundred thousand more inside/insiders as well as outside/insiders.)

Now compare our conservative estimate of four hundred thousand insiders to the number of insider trading transactions reported to the SEC. Every month about ten to twelve thousand reports are filed, and in one year the total number of transactions reported is usually less than a hundred and fifty thousand. These separate reports are not filed by a hundred and fifty thousand individual insiders. Many of them, who are actively trading in the stock of their own companies, submit several reports during the year. Some individuals actually file hundreds of reports in a year. It's hard to determine the precise number of different insiders who file with the SEC in a given year. But, for argument's sake, let's say that each individual files an average of four reports a year. That conservative estimate leaves us with only about forty thousand individual insiders trading in a year.

In other words, it would appear that roughly 90 percent of insiders are not actively trading in the stock of their own companies in any given year. That means that we, as outsiders, are unable to get any clues about the attitudes of the vast majority of insiders concerning the future direction of their companies' stock performance. This is not to say, however, that the companies without insider trading activity are poor investment choices. There are many excellent choices among them. It's just that you can't identify them through the insider investment strategy. You have to use another stock selection strategy to assess their potential.

But you can concentrate on the 10 percent or so of insiders who *are* trading. Their activities provide a "window" on the inner workings of their companies. And that's as close as you can get—*legally*—to inside information that you can use to invest with.

Assessing the Unusual

Since *any* trading by *any* corporate insider is unusual, all insider trading demands our attention. But of that insider trading, some trading behavior is more "unusual" than other behavior.

The more unusual the behavior, the more attention we should pay to it.

When we look at the trading of *inside*/insiders we must keep a few things in mind. For example, many companies provide their key employees with stock option plans. Under most of these plans, insiders are able to buy stock at a discount from the prevailing price paid for it by outside investors buying stock of the same company in the open market. As you can imagine, since almost any option purchase guarantees an insider a big profit, most of the stock that insiders buy is purchased under some type of stock option plan. When, however, an insider buys in the open market at the prevailing full price (or makes a private purchase of stock at the current full market price), it is behavior that is much more unusual.

But not all open-market purchases are as unusual as others. When, for example, an insider makes large purchases in the open market, they are much more unusual than small purchases. Further, when more than one insider at a company is making open-market purchases at the same time, it is an even rarer occurrence.

On top of such "unusual" behavior comes "consistent" behavior. A single large open-market purchase by one insider in one month is unusual. But a series of large (or even small) purchases stretched out over several months provides a pattern of consistency that may override the unusualness of a single large purchase.

When an *outside*/insider comes on the scene—which you will remember requires an investment large enough to control at least 5 percent of a company's outstanding shares—the situation becomes *significantly* unusual. The incidents of *inside*/insider trading are rare when viewed in the context of the total number of people who *could* trade, but the number of *outside*/insider investments is rarer still.

When there is trading by *both* inside/insiders and outside/insiders in the same company, it is by far the most unusual—and most interesting to those of us on the outside—of any type of situation.

As an example, in late 1984 inside/insiders at RB Industries, a New York Stock Exchange-listed furniture retailer, owned about 1.3 million shares of the company's stock. Specifically, the major shareholding insiders were Myron Kaplan, a director of the company, James Nathan, president of RB Industries and a

director, as well as Joseph Sinay, chairman of the board and one
of the principal organizers of the company, and other members
of the Sinay family. Kaplan and Nathan, who were also directors
and officers of another NYSE-listed company called House of
Fabrics, had accumulated most of their holdings jointly in the
open market throughout 1984 at an average cost per share of
approximately $9¾. By the end of 1984, Kaplan and Nathan
held about 600,000 shares or about 14 percent of the company.
This buying was significant because it came at a time when RB
Industries was experiencing a severe earnings downturn, causing the company's stock to drop sharply from a high in 1984 of
$24 a share to a low of about $8. This inside/insider behavior
was interesting for outside investors by early 1985 as a possible
signal that RB's performance was expected—by the insiders at
least—to turn around.

But the real reason for all the buying, it appeared, was that
there was an internal struggle for control of the company. Kaplan and Nathan, as a team, were vying for complete control
against Joseph Sinay and the Sinay family. At the beginning of
1985, Sinay controlled about 500,000 shares or approximately
12 percent of the company's stock.

The struggle continued until June 4, 1985, when Kaplan and
Nathan sold their shares, in a private stock transaction conducted away from the stock exchange, at $10 per share. The $10
sale price was 10 percent *above* the price on the open market.
The purchasers of the stock were the Sinay family and RB Industries itself. Sinay, after shelling out over $2 million of his
family's money for the privilege of paying a premium to Kaplan
and Nathan for their stock, had achieved consolidation of control of the company. Kaplan and Nathan resigned from the board
of directors.

But had Sinay made a bad bargain? Throughout the end of
1985 and into 1986 it appeared that he had. From all outward
indications, the company continued to be plagued by a poor
short-term earnings outlook. The company's stock fell further—
down to almost $5 a share. But open-market buying of several
thousand shares by other inside/insiders—specifically, Stanley
Goff, secretary of the company and a board member, and James
Brightman, an officer of the company—from July of 1985
through early 1986 at prices ranging from $5.38 a share to $8.80
a share, implied that the turnaround that Kaplan and Nathan
were probably buying into in late 1984 and the improved per-

formance that Sinay was most likely certain of when he paid over $2 million dollars for stock at $10 a share were still "cooking."

The behavior by these inside/insiders was "unusual"—large purchases made at open-market prices and at prices *above* the open-market price—and "consistent"—continual buying over an extended period of time by not just one insider who wanted to protect his personal power base (Sinay) but by other insiders as well (Goff and Brightman).

At the beginning of 1987, RB Industries' stock stood at about $7. (In late 1985 it reached a low of $5¼ and then rallied briefly in early 1986 to $10 a share because of better—but not great— news about the company's performance.) This $7 price tag was still far below the average price insiders paid for their shares during 1985 and early 1986. Viewing this price at the beginning of 1987 and taking into consideration the "self-interest" aspect of human nature, it is apparent that Sinay and the other insiders would not only want to do everything they could to protect the investments they made in 1985 and 1986, but would also be expected to push to make sure that they make a nice profit. This means you reasonably could have expected that something would happen to make RB Industries' stock rise significantly above $10 a share. We could not have known when this would happen. It could have been in 1987 or it could take a few years. But there was certainly a high probability that it would happen. At the beginning of 1987, with RB Industries' stock standing at $7, this company's stock was a first-rate candidate for capital gain investment by outsiders who followed the "consistent pattern of unusual behavior" displayed by these inside/insiders.

But there's another element to the RB Industries story that made it even more significant. Throughout the period of the battle for control of the company between Sinay and Kaplan/ Nathan, Jeffrey Neuman, a former "financier" with Drexel, Burnham, Lambert, Inc., had been investing in RB Industries' stock as an "outsider." Through frequent and steady trips to the open market, Neuman had accumulated 301,000 shares, or 8.9 percent of the company's stock, by the beginning of August 1985. His average price per share was about $8. In his Schedule 13D filing, Neuman stated that his reason for acquiring the stock was "for long-term investment purposes only." Reading this statement of his investment objective and knowing something about his past investment activities, we would have had every reason to believe that Neuman meant just that. Neuman is an experienced Wall Streeter who would not have made an investment of over $2 million naïvely or carelessly. Also, Neuman had had no history of takeover activity. We would have come away from this Schedule 13D document with the thought that Neuman probably simply recognized some intrinsic value in the company that had not been fully appreciated by other less astute investors. Any conjecture as to the specific reasons for Neuman's large investment (as well as the investments by the inside/insiders) would have been a useless parlor game. It would have been sufficient to know that these people considered RB Industries to be a good buy at $8 and $10 a share and put up their money in evidence.

This evidence of the "consistent pattern of unusual behavior" by inside/insiders and outside/insider Neuman was clearly apparent by the end of September 1985, the point at which you would have had all the information—from the *Official Summary* and other sources—about these investors' actions during the first half of 1985. It would have been enough to justify an investment into RB Industries.

At the end of September and the beginning of October 1985, the price for RB Industries' stock had fallen some more on the heels of an announcement by the company that it expected "substantial" losses during its fourth quarter. That announcement was tempered with news that the company was eliminating surplus inventory, consolidating operations and redeploying assets, which would mean probable improved performance in the future. But many investors chose to overlook the long-term good news of the announcement and focused only on the short-term bad news of losses in the fourth quarter. They sold in large numbers and the stock fell in price as demand for it lessened.

Ignoring that announcement altogether, however, and following the bullish behavior of the insiders alone, you could have—as some of us did—bought the stock for about $6¼, which was far below the average price paid by insiders. If you had held on to the stock for about six months, you would have found your investment increase in value by about 30 percent when the stock's price rebounded to $8¼. This price was still below the price insiders paid, so you would not have wanted to sell, even though you could have made a tidy 30 percent profit. In fact, you could have been justified in buying *more* RB Industries stock at the higher price with the secure expectation that the insiders themselves would not be happy until the stock's price went well over $10 a share.

As it turns out, the beginning of June 1987 brought a dramatic turn of events at RB Industries. At that time it was revealed that a British company, Yearpledge, had accumulated over 25 percent ownership of the company. Most of those shares were acquired in private transactions (some from Sinay) at a $10 per share price. (The open-market price at the time was hovering at $9 a share.) Yearpledge's stated purpose for acquiring the large stake—nearly 1 million shares—was for "investment purposes." But it was a clear indication that whatever was "cooking" at RB Industries was beginning to come to a boil in June 1987.

The "consistent pattern of unusual behavior" evident throughout 1985 in the RB Industries' story passes the litmus test of three key factors that should be applied to all inside trading:

One: *The large quantity of shares traded or the amount of money involved.* Not only did the insiders buy hundreds of thousands of shares, they spent millions of dollars to do it.

Two: *The high frequency of trades.* The insiders—both inside/insiders and outside/insider Neuman—made numerous trips to the open market over a period of at least eighteen months to accumulate their holdings.

Three: *The aggressiveness of the trading.* The insiders bought heavily during times of negative company news and were even willing to pay a premium—in Sinay's case—for their shares.

Analysis and Intrepretation

When we are faced with the raw data of insider trading we must make decisions about which of them display the qualities of quantity, frequency and aggressiveness that would justify our following the insiders' lead.

In the RB Industries story, the evidence of all three is overwhelming. In hindsight, we would say that the best time to have purchased the stock would have been in late September/early October of 1985 at about $6 a share. This is when we would have known everything about Sinay's $2 million-plus purchase of stock from Kaplan and Nathan. Too, we would have had the evidence on the continuing purchasing pattern of outside/insider Neuman as well as buying by another inside/insider, Stanley Goff. Without this hindsight convenience, however, a strong case could be made for our own investment purchase of RB Industries' stock at the *beginning* of 1985 at about $9 a share. This is when we would have had the evidence of heavy buying by Kaplan and Nathan. We would not have known about Sinay's forthcoming purchase, of course. And we would not have known anything about outsider Neuman's purchases because by then he had not accumulated 5 percent of the company's outstanding shares and therefore had not yet filed a Schedule 13D. But investing based on Kaplan's and Nathan's activities alone would have been justified. It was unusual and consistent. A purchase of RB Industries stock in early 1985 based on these insiders' trading patterns would not have been "wrong."

The point here is that a "consistent pattern of unusual behavior" can take many different forms. The criteria for judging this phenomenon cannot be reduced to a simple formula. You cannot say, for example, that whenever seven insiders over a three-month period buy stock that is worth ten thousand dollars or more, it signals a "buy" for outsiders.

Unfortunately, it isn't that automatic.

Over the years, however, many people have tried to come up with simple formulas based solely on criteria applied objectively to raw data found in the *Official Summary*—with no subjective analysis of the human behavior that lies behind the raw data. These formulas are most evident in the statistical studies of corporate insider trading. One such study considered a "buy" whenever three or more different insiders made open-market purchases in a single month and no insiders sold shares of stock. Another study said that whenever the number of insider buying transactions in the open market over five sequential months was greater than the number of insider selling transactions, it was a "buy" signal. Another grouped the number of insider open-market buying and option-buying transactions together in one month and weighed that against the number of selling transactions; if there were more buying transactions than selling in a given month, it was considered a "buy." (Similar formulas have been concocted for "sell" signals. For example, the number of insiders selling in a month being greater than the number of insiders buying is considered a bearish attitude that signals outside investors to avoid the company's stock or to sell it.)

At first blush, all of these formulas seem to have merit. They seem to achieve successfully the goal of boiling down complex human behavior into simple mathematical calculations. But closer inspection shows how little sense they make. For example, a formula that counts the number of different insiders buying in a month may consider that three insiders who bought 1,000 shares each in one month signaled a "buy." But it would have ignored a case where one insider bought 500,000 shares in one month and there were no other insiders buying. That doesn't make sense.

Nor does it make sense to say that if five insiders sold 2,000 shares each in a month—which might have been purchased at a discount in an option plan in the first place—and two insiders bought 50,000 shares each that a "sell" signal is given because more insiders sold than bought. This approach, of course, doesn't take into account the bullish signals the insiders gave through the size of the buys.

The same potentially misleading conclusions could be drawn if you look only at the number of trading transactions. For example, there could be an insider who sells 300 shares a day for two weeks—ten different transactions totaling 3,000 shares— while one insider could be buying 20,000 shares in three transactions. This doesn't necessarily show a "sell" signal just because there are more sell transactions than buys. Counting the number of insiders trading or counting the number of insider transactions alone does not take into consideration important elements like the quantity of shares involved or the amount of money involved.

When you try to apply criteria of quantity in an objective manner, you can also get into trouble. For example, one study defined important transactions as those involving purchases of twenty thousand dollars or more. But it disregarded buying patterns of insiders who may make daily trips into the stock market to buy small quantities—say, 300 shares one day, 500 the next, 100 the next and so on—until a total accumulation over several months reaches several hundred thousand or even a million or more shares. (Actually, frequent small purchases over an extended period of time is a common display of "unusual" behavior. By following this avenue, the insider keeps the demand low with small frequent purchases and thereby does not alert the market that a large total purchase is going on. A single large purchase or even several moderately large purchases can trigger increased demand, especially in a lightly traded smaller company, which could raise the price of the company's stock. That's something that an insider who is building a large cache of stock would not want to happen.)

Obviously, the criteria used in these different formulas (and there are many others with similar weaknesses) cannot take into account all the possible variations that show a "consistent pattern of unusual behavior." They *could* be successful in identifying some interesting situations, but they would have missed a great deal and would actually have discovered very few *extraordinary* insider stories. In fact, most of the stories of successful insider trading you've read about here would not have been caught by any single one of these formulas.

Counting the number of different insiders trading, for example, would have disregarded the "consistent pattern of unusual behavior" you saw at A&P, Rolm, Viratek, Foodarama, Royal Crown Cola, Resorts International, Oppenheimer Industries, Hadson Petroleum and Alexander's, Inc. In each of these cases, it was large or frequent trades by one or two insiders spread out over several months that was unusual and consistent, not large numbers of different insiders.

Counting the number of "buy" transactions in relation to the number of "sell" transactions also would have been misleading in many of the stories told so far in this book. For instance, in the A&P story there were several months when the number of "sell" transactions was greater than the number of "buy" transactions. On closer inspection, however, you would have found that the "sells" involved quantities of stock that were only a fraction of the size of the quantities of the "buys." Even if you attempted to account for the size of transactions in addition to the number of transactions, you could come up with the wrong conclusion. For example, in the RB Industries' story the directors who were attempting to wrest control of the company (Kaplan and Nathan) sold hundreds of thousands of shares in the company in June of 1985. In that same month, RB Industries' chairman of the board Joseph Sinay, who was consolidating his control, *purchased* hundreds of thousands of shares. Would this have meant that the large "sell" transactions canceled out the large "buy" transactions, thus giving a neutral signal? Of course not. A subjective analysis of the situation—which took into account *who* purchased the Kaplan/Nathan shares and the fact that a 10 percent premium over the then open-market price was paid for those shares—would have told you that the insider attitude about the company was very bullish indeed. It was far from a "neutral" situation.

It should be obvious just from this cursory look at the variables found in the behavior of insiders that a formula—simple or complex—could not realistically take into account all the possibilities inherent in the stock-trading activities of insiders. Indeed, most of the "formulas" that provide strictly objective criteria for assessing insider trading have been created by academics as part of their statistical studies of the returns insiders enjoy with their investments. The academics, of course, needed a set of completely objective criteria as part of the methodology upon which equally objective statistical measurements could be used to assess the eventual returns the insiders achieved after their trading. Considering the unavoidable weaknesses that such objective formulas contain, it is surprising that so many statistical studies found insider trading as profitable as they did.

Fortunately for us, as analysts of insider trading patterns and behavior, we are not bound by the confines of purely statistical methodology. We can bring a subjective interpretation to the raw data we find in the insiders' public disclosure documents.

That is not to say, however, that "reading" the insiders is entirely subjective. There is an objective side to it as well. Insider analysis is like the procedure for sorting and processing eggs. Eggs are sorted by machine into different size categories. But to this day, despite technological advances, each egg must be examined by a human being using the process called "candling," in which the egg is passed in front of a bright light so that its contents can be seen. Only a human being can determine if the egg contains a blood spot or some other flaw. Similarly, analyzing the behavior of insiders can start with a mechanical sorting of actions into those that are of interest—such as open-market purchases and private purchases made at open-market prices— and those that are not of interest—such as stock acquired by gift or other acquisitions obtained at a cost far below the open-market price. But insiders happen to be human beings and tend not to act with enough consistency from one situation to another to enable us to set highly specific boundaries that will encompass the multiple variations possible on the same investment theme. Therefore, a final assessment, beyond the initial sorting by mechanical means, must be made through human insight into the insiders' very human behavior.

Using Common Sense

If you want to analyze insider trading successfully and get really close to the insider action, you must develop a commonsense attitude about the human behavior lying behind the trading actions the insiders display in their public disclosure forms. To some, simplistic formulas may make sense, but do they make *common* sense?

Let's attempt here, then, to bring some commonsense thinking to the process of analyzing and interpreting the actions of insiders. There are, in general, ten commonsense rules of thumb, and the factors they raise will give you an idea of the issues to keep in mind when you judge information about insider trading. That information could be in the form of raw data found in Form 3 and Form 4 (or in the *Official Summary*) or in Schedule 13D. Or you may encounter the information in investment advisory newsletters or in newspaper or magazine articles.

These rules of thumb are not commandments that apply equally in every situation. In some situations, one or two will supersede all the others. In other cases, these ten rules of thumb, which are not in any particular order of importance, and other rules of thumb you will read about throughout the rest of this book will fit neatly together to give you the investment answers you're looking for. There's no need to try to memorize these rules, but you should keep them handy when you get to the point of actually deciding to make an investment based on insider actions.

TEN COMMONSENSE RULES OF THUMB

1. *Watch the activities of both inside/insiders and outside/ insiders.* Trading by inside/insiders is one story. Trading by outside/insiders is another story. But when there is trading by inside/insiders and outside/insiders at the same company, that's the *whole* story. Not all situations, of course, involve both groups of insiders. But when a situation does occur, you don't want to miss it. In the RB Industries scenario, for example, the

heavy buying by chairman of the board Joseph Sinay and his family could have been interpreted—if you had been watching only the trading by inside/insiders—merely as an ego move by Sinay to solidify his control of a company that he helped to develop. The presence of Neuman's outside/insider $2 million-plus investment, however, tells you that someone without highly personal interests at stake viewed the company as a good investment and added considerable credence to Sinay's invest-ment decision to buy hundreds of thousands of shares of the company at a premium above the then open-market price. In this, and other cases you'll read about in later chapters, keeping a bifocal view of insider activities is essential.

2. *Open-market purchases are usually more significant than sales or purchases made through option plans.* Every share of stock that an insider buys in the open market is a solid vote of confidence that the insider considers that price to be a pretty good deal. Since this open-market price is the price we have to pay for the privilege of owning shares in a company, it is very interesting news to hear that an insider thinks it is a good enough bargain for him. Most stock purchases made under a company's stock option plan are acquired at a deep discount from the open-market price. An options purchase is much less of a vote of confidence. It usually does not warrant the same amount of interest as an open-market purchase. When we con-sider the importance of sales by insiders, we should remember that they can occur for many reasons besides a bearish outlook by the insider. He may simply be selling to raise cash to buy a house or a car, to pay taxes or to buy more low-cost options. Selling by insiders does not routinely cancel out the open-market purchase insiders are making. Option purchases and selling usually are interesting only when they are overwhelm-ingly large. (More about options and selling in the next chapter.)

3. *Private purchases can be more significant than open-market purchases—particularly if the cost of the private pur-chase is above open-market prices.* Private purchases are made away from the glare of the open market and they can in-volve some large special deals among insiders. Usually you will learn about these transactions only through SEC public disclo-sure documents. When a private transaction involves a pur-chase at prices above open-market prices, it tells us that the insider doing the purchasing is aggressive and extremely opti-

mistic about the future direction of the stock's price movement. Identifying companies where there are private purchases and open-market purchases—while ignoring all other types of transactions—is a sensible way initially to screen insider reports to find potentially interesting situations. After you identify companies with those types of activities, you can look more closely at other insider actions.

4. *The absence of selling—when there is buying—is more significant than the presence of selling.* While most insider selling—in smallish quantities at least—is done to raise cash for personal reasons, situations that show open-market or private purchases with *no* selling can be reasonably interpreted as meaning that the insiders who are holding shares are not using this source to raise cash. They probably see an imminent increase in value for their shares and are holding on to them, looking to other sources to answer their cash needs. In other words, *no* selling by insiders is a bullish sign, but selling is not necessarily a bearish sign.

5. *Large transactions are important, but so is a "large" series of small transactions.* Single large transactions, involving either a large number of shares or a large amount of money, command the most serious attention. But persistent buying (or selling) in small quantities can build up large holdings (or diminish large holdings) in a significant way. However, we don't need to look closely at every nickel-and-dime transaction. When doing an initial screen of insider reports using open-market and private purchases as our primary identifier of potentially interesting situations, we can add another criterion to our screen: buy transactions involving at least 500 shares or more. This is large enough to discount small, scattered trading, but it is small enough to encompass most serious buying situations. After we've sorted companies by purchases of 500 shares or more, we can look more closely at each of the companies to see what other trading has occurred.

6. *Several different insiders acting in the same way is significant, but don't ignore the lone wolf.* It's reassuring to see different people trading in a similar fashion. The more people "voting" the same way, the more confident we can be about the general attitude insiders have about the future of their company's stock. But lone wolf trading—as we saw with Harold

Oppenheimer and his huge one-year buying spree at Oppenheimer Industries—cannot be summarily dismissed. When
there is lone wolf trading, however, we need to look carefully at
who is trading. In the Oppenheimer case, it was the chairman of
the board, a position we can assume carries with it a greater
overview knowledge of the company than other insider positions have. If the lone wolf had been a low-level officer—who
we can assume has less access to information about the company—the trading would not have held as much importance.
(More about the hierarchy of insiders in the next chapter.)

7. *Repeated behavior stretched over a long period of time is
usually more important than concentrated trading during a
short time span.* A single large transaction or even several
transactions by different insiders within a short time span—say,
one or even two months—could be very interesting. But we
usually want to see consistent behavior over a longer period of
time—say, three, four or even five or more months, depending
on the amount of activity—before making our own investment
move. We may miss some good opportunities by following this
conservative route, but we will also avoid unpleasant experiences by speculating on a limited display of "unusual behavior." Remember the Golden Rule: Do not jump on the first
twitch of an insider's movement.

8. *Recent activity is more important than past activity, but
recent activity should be weighed against historical behavior.* Current information about insider trading tells you the
current attitudes insiders have about their investments. But current trading should not be viewed in isolation against past behavior. Here are a few examples of how important a comparison
of current to past behavior can be: Large purchases by insiders
in a previous month may be interesting. But if that current activity follows several months of smaller purchases, it probably signals a stepped-up acquisition trend that makes the situation
even more interesting. If current buying shows purchases at
ever-increasing prices over past behavior, we can assume that
the insider continues to see the stock's price as a bargain. If,
however, an insider's current trading activity dwindles in comparison to past patterns—or even stops—as the price of the
stock rises, we can assume that the insider sees the stock rising
toward its expected peak. Of course, insider purchases that stop
can also have very positive significance, meaning that the in-

sider has begun his "waiting" period for the corporate development to brew. (Remember the SEC's six-month rule limiting insiders' profit taking within six months of a purchase.)

9. *The actual prices insiders pay for their shares are more important than the average price paid.* We want to invest in a company favored by insiders at prices not much above the same price they paid. It would be great if we could buy at a lower price than the lowest price paid by an insider, but that isn't always possible. Since we take a conservative—as opposed to a speculative—view of insider actions and want to see a "consistent pattern of unusual behavior," it may take several months or even a year of watching monthly trading before all the evidence points to the reasonableness of our own investment. Throughout that watching period, insiders may buy heavily one month, lightly one month, skip a month, then trade heavily again. They might be buying at different price levels. For example, let's say that an insider bought steadily at $10, $11 and $14 a share. Instead of looking at the *average* price paid—say, $12 a share— and binding ourselves to that test for our own purchases, we need to look at the most recent actual price paid. If the insider accumulated shares at ever-increasing prices, we can be justified in paying the higher price—or even slightly higher than the highest price paid. Practical experience in following insiders for more than ten years has shown that insiders usually achieve at least a 25 percent return on the investments they've made beyond their own *highest* purchase price. That means we can pay a premium for shares above the insider's price—but probably not more than 25 percent. A more attractive situation, however, occurs when the "consistent pattern of unusual behavior" finds the insider buying steadily at ever-decreasing prices. Then, of course, we will want to buy at the lower prices and not wait until the price "recovers" to the insider's average price.

10. *The importance of the size of transactions, the number of transactions and the number of insiders involved may differ with different-size companies.* Many large corporations may have one hundred or more corporate insiders who are required to report their transactions to the SEC. In many smaller companies, there may be only a handful of insiders. Large corporations will have hundreds of millions of outstanding shares; many small companies have only a couple of million shares. We can't expect to find the same number of people trading in the same

type of quantities at the smaller company as we do in larger companies. Therefore, insider trading at a larger company usually requires more stringent tests than trading by insiders at smaller companies.

Thinking Like an Insider

The most important thing to remember about these ten rules of thumb, as well as the others you will encounter in the following chapters, is that the rules themselves are not as significant as the commonsense thinking that lies behind them. Once you become more familiar with the various patterns of insider investments and are able to think like the insiders, you'll begin to view their trading from *their* perspective. Then you won't need "rules" to identify the instances of a "consistent pattern of unusual behavior" that will point you in the direction of compelling stock investments.

An added thought to keep in mind is that the stock market crash of October 19, 1987 has become a watershed date in Wall Street history. The investment actions of insiders should be viewed in relation to that date. Generally speaking, actions following the crash will be of particular importance compared to actions taken before the crash. New opportunities were created by the across-the-board lower prices caused by the crash. Other situations that were brewing before the crash may have changed because of its effects. The investments of insiders following the crash have provided important trail markers of where to put your stock market dollars.

Chapter 6

The Inside/Insiders

BOTH groups of insiders—inside/insiders and outside/insiders—are on the lookout for a good investment value, and when it comes to reading their actions for investment signals, the ten commonsense rules of thumb presented in the last chapter can be applied almost equally as tests for either inside/insider actions and outside/insider actions. But there are some special considerations that separate these two different groups of insiders. In this chapter we'll look at some additional commonsense thinking to apply to your reading of inside/insiders, and the following chapter will take a closer look at outside/insiders.

In on the Know

Think of a typical family as a corporation with husband, wife and children as "insiders." Now, assess how much each of the "insiders" in this family knows about its overall financial and emotional health and future outlook. Probably none of its members knows *everything* about all matters that could affect the family's future. But husband and wife, as chairman of the board and chief executive officer, most likely have a better idea of how things will turn out—at least from a financial point of view—than do the children, the vice presidents.

This same hierarchy of information distribution can be applied to the family of insiders at corporations. We can safely presume that the insiders holding the most top-level positions have a better grasp of a wider range of information than insiders on lower levels.

A provocative study conducted by Professors Kenneth Nunn (University of Connecticut), Gerald Madden (Northeastern University) and Michael Gombola (Southern Illinois University) attempted to assesss just that commonsense assumption. The study, the results of which were published in the Spring 1983 edition of *The Journal of Portfolio Management* in an article appropriately entitled "Are Some Insiders More 'Inside' Than Others?" tested the returns that different types of insiders had on their investments. The basic hypothesis presented by the researchers was that chief executive officers and directors of companies had the greatest access to sensitive information. They reasoned that since the chief executive officer had the most direct and indirect responsibility for promoting all major corporate policies, and since directors had the responsibility for advising the chief executive officer on all strategic decisions, these two groups held the primary position in the information hierarchy. Other insiders, they surmised, would have much less access to information: Vice presidents with responsibility limited to specific functions would have little opportunity to receive information outside their sphere of interest; major shareholders of 10 percent or more of a company's stock, usually referred to as *beneficial owners*, who did not have any day-to-day connection with the company's operations would not normally be included in major corporate decisions.

With these basic assumptions, the researchers watched the investments by the separate groups of insiders from February 1974 through August 1978 to see if, indeed, chief executive officers and directors, who presumably had access to more information, would enjoy greater returns than vice presidents and beneficial owners, who had much less information. Like in other statistical studies, the researchers devised a simple "formula" for selecting the insider activities to follow. Unfortunately, like other formulas, it contained serious limitations. For example, the researchers counted only open-market purchases of ten thousand dollars or more to signal their "buys"—leaving out the situations with a series of smaller purchases that could have added up to a large acquisition. Also, they threw out transactions by insiders who held dual positions—for example, by a vice president who was also a director. In reality, insiders holding two or more positions could possibly be the *most* knowledgeable.

Despite the limitations of the criteria used to select the insider activity to follow, the study found that all groups of insiders achieved abnormal profits. But they also discovered, true to their original hypothesis, that chief executive officers and directors achieved a much greater abnormal return than did vice presidents and beneficial owners. The researchers' concluded: "... the results show that CEOs and DIRs are able to time purchases much better than either BOs [beneficial owners] and VPs.... On a comparative basis, the findings indicate that CEOs and DIRs outperform BOs and VPs by a wide margin on stock purchases. This result is also consistent with the hypothesis that access to inside information is directly related to the insider's functional role within the organization. Hence, access to non-public information does not appear to be equal across insider groups."

This study corresponds closely with observations gathered through practical experience in following insiders. But a few other embellishments can be added to the researchers conclusions.

First, "chief executive officers" and "directors" are not the only titles that describe the topmost level of insider who could be, as the researchers say, at "the informational focal point of the organization." Other insiders at this level would include "president," "chief financial officer," "chairman of the board" and "chief operating officer." These titles, of course, are often interchangeable from company to company, but you shouldn't limit yourself to chief executive officers and directors when identifying those insiders with the best informational overview.

Second, whenever an insider carries two or more labels—that is, "officer and director"—you can assume that he has access to information on the same level as the highest level of his titles. Therefore, an insider who is a "vice president and director" should be considered on the same level as a "director," because a "director" holds a higher level within the hierarchy of insiders. A "beneficial owner and president" would be considered a "president." And so forth.

Third, buying transactions by the top-level insiders that show a "consistent pattern of behavior" tend to precede some type of "deal"—a takeover of the insider's company by another company, an acquisition of another company, a merger, a spin-off of assets. Heavy buying by insiders on the vice president level usually precedes general good news, such as increased earnings performance, launching of a successful new product, forthcoming evidence of a turnaround. When there is buying by both top-level and lower-level insiders, you can assume there is a variety of positive factors triggering them to buy.

At the end of their *Journal of Portfolio Management* article, Nunn and his co-researchers offer a piece of advice to those who follow insiders for investment signals: "[Outside] investors could shorten their search process and perhaps improve their results by focusing only on the purchases of CEOs and directors." But this statement is perhaps too sweeping. Buying by insiders on the vice president level *can* be significant. Ignoring behavior that predicts a general sound future for a company could mean ignoring a worthwhile stock investment. But when we see vice-president-level buying—without similar behavior by top-level insiders—we need to be somewhat more cautious and stringent with our tests. The evidence of buying among vice presidents should be consistent among several vice presidents over several months. Also, we wouldn't want to follow the behavior of a lone wolf if the single-person trading was a vice president without any connection—such as a directorship—to top-level information. Leave serious consideration of lone wolf investing to the key insiders. As reinforcers of top insider buying, however, vice presidents can play a reassuring role. For example, if a president of a company is buying lightly and one or more vice presidents are also buying lightly, it is a more interesting situation than the president buying lightly alone or if only two vice presidents are buying lightly.

When Selling Is Important

Inside/insiders have two compelling motivations for buying stock in the open market or in a private purchase arrangement at prices at or above open-market prices. One motivation is much more compelling than the other—profit making or, to be more blunt, greed. The insiders buy because they expect to make a lot of money. The less compelling motivation is political. When an inside/insider first joins a company—particularly as a director or in some other highly visible inside/insider position such as a chief executive officer—he or she usually feels that it's necessary to make at least a token purchase of the company's stock. Otherwise some shareholder may raise an embarrassing observation at a shareholders' meeting that questions the insider's own faith in a company in which he or she owns no shares.

Clearly, our motivation in following insiders for investment clues more closely matches the motivation of greed. We don't care about an insider's political status. Therefore, another commonsense rule of thumb tells us that we can usually ignore the information we find on the inside/insider's Form 3 filing. Form 3, as you may recall, is the "Initial Statement of Beneficial Ownership of Securities" and it is used only once when the insider buys his or her first block of stock in the company. We can assume that this first purchase satisfied the insider's political motivation. It is when we see buying in subsequent Form 4 filings ("Statement of Changes in Beneficial Ownership of Securities") that we can draw conclusions about the profit-making motivation in action.

When it comes to selling, however, inside/insiders, as we have already mentioned, have a multitude of motivations for their actions. They may need the cash for personal reasons. They may want to sell some shares at open-market prices so that they can turn around and buy some low-cost shares through an option plan. They may decide that the stake they have in their own company is too large in relation to the rest of their investment portfolio and sell to raise money to diversify a little. They may even want to sell at a loss to lower their tax liability in a year when they made a little too much money through other avenues.

With all these compelling reasons for selling, it's no wonder that most insider transactions involve selling. Organizations that put together indexes of insider transactions usually consider it normal when about 60 percent of all such trading—that is, trading by all insiders at all companies—are "sell" transactins and 40 percent are "buy" transactions. The "buy" transactions counted in this 40 percent include all types of buying, not just open-market buying and private purchases. It is from this normalcy of 60 percent "sell" compared to 40 percent "buy" that some analysts judge the overall direction of the stock market. They reason that when selling goes higher than 60 percent, it foretells an overall bearish direction for the market. (There have been some months in the past fifty-odd years when the number of sell transactions actually reached almost 90 percent of the total number of transactions reported to the SEC.) When buying goes above the "normal" 40 percent mark, these analysts interpret this to mean that bullish times are ahead.

An index of this type has next to no relevance for our total insider investment strategy. We are not interested in the combined activities of insiders at all companies; we are interested only in the insider activities at *specific* companies and the investment opportunities they reveal regardless of the overall outlook and performance of the market. An insider's index may, however, fit into another stock market strategy, such as in econometric analysis, as a broad economic indicator.

Index measurements of insider transactions do tell us, however, that a preponderance of sell transactions over buy transactions is the normal course of events. When you consider that most of the buy transactions are actually acquisitions through options, you can see that selling in relation to open-market and private purchases makes the high percentage of selling even more "normal." Therefore we can ignore most selling transactions most of the time.

Insider selling becomes significant for us only when it displays another human motivation just as intense as the greed that sends most insiders to the open market. That is the motivation of fear. Fear of loss. Fear of not getting the best price for your holdings before the rest of the market's investors find out that your company is headed for bad times or before they realize that perhaps your company's stock is overpriced.

But, in light of the fact that most transactions are "sells," how can you tell when fear is the motive? Like an assessment of insider buying, insider selling that shows a "consistent pattern of unusual behavior" is the action to watch. The size of the sell transaction is important (both the number of shares and the amount of money involved). So is the amount of shares the insider is unloading in comparison to his or her total holdings. The number of insiders selling is also important. All this, then, must be compared to buying activity. Is there open-market buying going on at the same time as the selling? Or does the only buying going on involve low-cost options? If there is open-market buying—particularly by top-level insiders in significant quantities—you can assume that selling—particularly by lower-level insiders in moderate quantities—is being motivated by reasons other than fear. Therefore, the evidence of selling, before we can presume that it is based on fear, has to be significant.

Here's an example of stock dumping. In 1983 Apple Computer Inc. was riding a wave of faddish popularity. Those were the days, you may recall, that the personal computer was being touted as the next "necessity" for the American household. Every home would have one, the promoters told us, and every member of the family would use it for tasks ranging from Junior's homework to storing Christmas card lists to keeping tax records. Investors thought that Apple Computer was going to be the primary company to provide all those millions of computers. People liked Apple Computer's aggressive and imaginative marketing approach. They even liked the product's cute name. It seemed that everyone wanted to buy shares in Apple Computer. That frenzy of investing by "average" investors—as well as by institutional investors—pushed Apple's stock price from about $26 at the start of 1983 to a high of $63¼ in June 1983.

But was this investment stampede justified by reality? Or was it a fantasy? Insider actions during this period gave some clues that most investors chose to ignore. On April 29, 1983, Steven Jobs, one of the founders of the company and then its chairman of the board, sold 500,000 shares in the open market at a price of $50⅜ a share. He got over twenty-five million dollars on this sale. A sale of this magnitude is unusual, and it's difficult to explain a person's need for twenty-five million dollars on the basis that he wanted cash for personal reasons like buying a new house. A couple of hundred thousand dollars is understandable or maybe a million or two. But twenty-five million? All at one time? It is also hard to imagine that Jobs needed that much money to pay taxes. And, if Jobs agreed with so many other investors that Apple had a limitless future, why would he have sold at that point to diversify his investments? Was the motivation fear of loss or a recognition that Apple's stock price had gone beyond—or was quickly reaching—a level of reality?

Jobs's selling was unusual by itself, but the actions of other insiders at the same time made the sell story consistent. Over a seven-month period from mid-January to mid-August 1983, ten other Apple Computer insiders sold in a similar fashion as Jobs.

In almost weekly selling trips to the open market, they collectively sold nearly one and a half million shares for a total sale price of over sixty million dollars. Consistent and unusual.

By fall of 1983, Apple's bubble had burst. Investors and analysts finally put two and two together and realized that every American family *wouldn't* be buying personal computers. (A couple of thousand dollars is a little too much to pay to keep your Christmas card list in order and to help Junior with his homework.) Also, investors realized, that if Americans *did* ever find personal computers a necessity there was a new and very strong competitor—IBM—which probably would capture much of the market from relatively small Apple. These insightful, but overdue, judgments helped drive Apple's stock down to under $20 a share by November 1983. Many investors lost a lot of money. But the insiders made out very well.

The type of stock dumping seen in the Apple Computer example—and there are others, including heavy selling by IBM insiders from the end of 1985 to the middle of 1986 that preceded bad earnings news that made the company's stock fall sharply beginning in the spring of 1986—isn't of much concern to investors who used the insider investment strategy to pick stocks in the first place. The behavior by Apple's insiders would have told us to avoid the stock. Not because the selling was so heavy, but because there was very little open-market *buying* showing a "consistent pattern of unusual behavior" that would have attracted our attention. Remember it is the evidence of *buying* that interests us. Selling, when there are strong votes of buying, can be ignored, because the presence of selling is normal.

Also, we will rarely, if ever, see dumping by insiders of stocks we are holding that had first been identified through an analysis of insider *buying*. That's because we will have sold our shares before the data on insider profit-taking is available. We don't wait for the data on insider actions to tell us when it is time to sell our shares. Considering the probable two-month waiting time caused by the SEC's reporting process, it may be too late to know when to sell our shares based on insider actions. Instead, we normally sell our shares when the event or development that appears related to heavy insider buying occurs. The event brings the company's stock to the attention of a wider group of investors and thereby raises its price.

For example, in the Resorts International story an insider-watcher probably bought at $46.50 in the fall of 1985 at about the same price as the insiders. In early spring of 1986, when an event occurred that raised the stock's price (the death of the founder of the company that made Resorts International a possible takeover candidate), the stock went up to $77. An insider follower would have been justified in selling at that price—without knowing whether the insiders had sold. The game was over by the time the development became apparent, which, incidentally, could have sparked an overreaction by investors who raised the price of the stock beyond reality. An insider follower could have rightly taken advantage of the situation and made a 66 percent profit.

The same situation occurred with Oppenheimer Industries. In fall of 1985 insider-watchers bought at $5 a share—the same price the insider bought at. In February of 1986 when Oppenheimer Industries sold a portion of its Kansas City real estate, which caused a reassessment of the company's true value and sparked enough interest in the company to raise its stock to $18 a share, inside-watchers had a compelling reason to sell. No waiting around for signals from the insiders. The event that we had been expecting—not knowing, of course, what it was or when it would happen—apparently occurred. Insider-watchers who sold at that time made a nice profit, although they might not have done as well as the insiders ultimately do. But taking a handsome profit and moving on to a new insider favorite is all part of the insider-watcher's game plan. (When to sell shares that were first purchased using the insider investment strategy will be covered in greater detail in a later chapter.)

The message here, in short, is that selling is unimportant as a factor in choosing a stock unless it overwhelms the insiders open-market buying and private purchases.

A Final Word on Options

Normally it's true that an insider's buying of his company's stock at a deep discount under an option plan has very little significance. But not all options are purchased at a deep discount. Some are actually bought at close to market prices. Therefore, when we see option buying at full market price we

can consider that as bullish as open-market and private purchases. The deeper the discount the less significance we can
give it. As another rule of thumb, when options are purchased at
prices that are equal to 50 percent and above of the open-market
price, we can consider that to be a positive reinforcement of any
open-market buying that may be occurring at the same time.

Companies provide option plans as part of their compensation for executives. Another company "gift" comes in the form
of employee share ownership plans—called *ESOPS*. These
plans, usually part of a pension program, often buy shares in the
open market. But when you run across ESOP purchases in SEC
documents, you can ignore them. ESOP buying doesn't necessarily display value buying. There is no personal human motivation behind the purchases. Although insiders are directing
the purchases of an ESOP, they are not doing it for *themselves*
with money out of their *own pockets*.

Chapter 7

The Outside/Insiders

Edgar Bronfman, Sr., currently the head of Canada's wealthiest family dynasty, which controls the world's largest liquor distributor, Seagram, knows his way around money. The Bronfmans have taken Seagram, since its start in 1924, from an active supplier of liquor to U.S. bootleggers during Prohibition and built it into a truly self-sufficient liquor/whiskey/wine empire that controls every step of its manufacturing and distilling process—except the making of bottles and the printing of labels—including grain elevators to store the raw material for its vodka, gin and whiskey and an operation that makes the oak barrels used to age the top-shelf stuff.

But keeping the world stocked up on such well-known beverages as Chivas Regal, 7 Crown, Ronrico rum, and Paul Masson and Christian Brothers wine isn't the only money-making tactic the Bronfmans have. Since the early 1960s, the Bronfmans, using Seagram as their investment vehicle, have made large investments in several different companies in an attempt to get a toehold into other industries. During the 1970s, they concentrated on oil and gas businesses. Their biggest success during that period was an investment into a crude oil producer, Texas Pacific. The company's oil exploration in Europe, Asia and offshore in the Gulf of Mexico in the late 1970s was so successful that in 1980 Sun Oil paid Seagram $2.3 billion for its oil reserves.

Throughout the early and mid-1980s, however, the Bronfmans particularly concentrated their investments in one company—

Du Pont. Seagram first got involved with Du Pont in a somewhat circuitous way. In 1980–81 Seagram attempted a takeover of Conoco, an oil and coal company. But Du Pont wanted it too, and in 1981 it won the battle for Conoco. In return for the holdings it had accumulated in Conoco during its takeover attempt, Du Pont gave Seagram 47 million shares of Du Pont's stock— worth about $2.5 billion at the time—which gave the Bronfmans 20 percent of Du Pont's outstanding shares. This was a larger block of stock than the Du Pont family itself controlled.

Despite the huge size of this stake, most analysts considered the Du Pont shares a consolation prize for Seagram that the Bronfmans would quickly cash in as soon as they found another likely takeover candidate. The analysts believed that since Du Pont was already such a big company it had very few prospects for growth and therefore very little chance for a sharp upturn in its stock's price. The Bronfmans, the analysts concluded, would not want to hold on to such a sluggish performer for very long.

To almost everyone's surprise, Edgar Bronfman took a seat on Du Pont's board of directors and, instead of selling his stake in the company, actually started accumulating more Du Pont shares. In 1982 Bronfman used Seagram's money to buy an additional 3.3 million shares. In late 1983 and early 1984, Seagram purchased another 1.5 million or so shares. By early 1986, following more buying trips to the open market, Seagram held nearly 55 million Du Pont shares or about 22.5 percent of the company. Moreover, most of this stock accumulation occurred during periods of double-digit interest rates when the Bronfmans could have gotten a better short-term return on their dollars if they had simply put their money in a bank rather than expecting Du Pont's then comparatively low 8 percent dividend payments to make them richer.

The Bronfman investment in Du Pont has not gone unnoticed by Wall Street watchers, although both the Bronfmans and Du Pont continually try to downplay the relationship. Many analysts just think that the Bronfmans are foolish. Another widespread—and highly amusing—interpretation of the Bronfmans' motivation for accumulating all that Du Pont stock is that they are using Du Pont to buy themselves respectability within the corporate community by owning a large stake of staid, respectable Du Pont as some type of atonement for their Prohibition-days image as rumrunners. But the Bronfmans are not foolish; they are knowledgeable businesspeople. And their investment of several billion dollars—money that could have gone into expanding or improving Seagram's primary businesses and into investments into other companies—is more sensibly explained by a more compelling human motivation: honest and respectable "greed."

By the beginning of 1987, the Bronfmans had already seen their investment increase in value by over $1 billion, an appreciation of roughly 40 percent over the total cost of their holdings. At that time, Du Pont's stock price went above $100 a share. In comparison, the Bronfmans' highest price paid up to that point was about $56 a share—although much of it was acquired at lower prices, as low as $32 a share.

The Bronfmans seemed happy with the situation. They weren't selling. In fact, they had made an agreement in early 1986 with Du Pont not to purchase more than 25 percent of the company's stock before 1999, which, of course, rules out a Seagram takeover attempt of Du Pont until the turn of the century. They also promised to offer Du Pont the first right to buy its shares if it decided to sell. But the Bronfmans don't seem eager to sell out. Instead, they have pressured Du Pont into giving them more seats on the board of directors (a total of five out of twenty-nine spots) and on Du Pont's finance committee (a total of two out of eleven). Du Pont seemed happy with the situation as well. Du Pont's management has praised Seagram's influence for bringing valuable acumen in financial matters and consumer marketing to Du Pont.

As outside/insiders—who, strictly speaking, are now inside/insiders because they hold more than 10 percent of the company's stock and control several positions of influence within Du Pont—the Bronfmans clearly identified a good thing when they got involved with Du Pont and they are sticking with it to the tune of billions of dollars. And, clearly, anyone following in the footsteps of the Bronfmans by having invested in Du Pont through the middle of 1985, when they stopped their buying at about $56 a share, would have made a good decision.

The Bronfman activities at Du Pont are in one way typical of an outside/insider investment pattern that is interesting for those of us who follow insiders for investment clues. But in another way, the situation is atypical of what most people would normally associate with an outside/insider investment.

The typical aspect in this case is that the outside/insider took a large amount of money that was accumulated in the first place through savvy business dealings and invested it in a company following a "consistent pattern of unusual behavior." This behavior told us that these very smart business people have, in their best judgment, found an investment that they fully expect to pay off in a big way.

The atypical aspect is that the Bronfmans and Du Pont appear to be so friendly. The Bronfmans seem to be happy with their somewhat passive role, and DuPont currently doesn't seem to be too afraid of the Bronfmans' substantial presence as "outsiders"—although things may change in 1999 when the Bronfmans' agreement not to buy more than 25 percent of the company runs out (or sooner, if the agreement is "rewritten" or another work-out plan develops, that is, for example, a sale to a third-party group). Although many outside/insiders maintain a fairly passive role in the inner workings of the companies they invest in, the more common popular image of the outside/insider is not that benign.

"They're All Bums"

Outside/insiders have been called a lot of nasty names. "Corporate raider" and "shark" are a couple of the nicer ones. "Rapist," "racketeer," "opportunist" and "SOB" are a sampling of the not so nice.

A few of the wealthy individuals, professional investors and corporations that invest heavily in other companies and make up our outside/insider group are thought of as nice people—sometimes even as "white knights" who come to the rescue of companies that are victims of hostile takeover attempts by outside/insiders which the companies' management view as undesirable. But most of the time, the outside/insider is characterized as a vampire sucking the blood of innocent, law-abiding companies that are just trying to make an honest buck. These outside/insiders, their critics say, are interested only in depleting corporate treasuries and assets for their own personal profit. One of the schemes they are accused of is to take over a company at a low cost or through highly leveraged debt, then sell off its assets once they have taken control and pocket the profits—making the company a mere shell of its former self and leaving shareholders much poorer for the experience. Another scheme is to threaten a hostile takeover and force the company to reach into its cash reserves (or sell off assets to raise cash) and buy back the outside/insider stock holdings at a premium price—a procedure usually called "greenmail." This too, people say, lessens the value of the company and leaves shareholders grasping an empty bag.

Is this negative image justified? Are the facts consistent with the perception that outside/insiders divert corporate assets to the detriment of other stockholders?

Once again let's turn to statistical research to see if we can find some answers. A study conducted by Clifford Holderness and Dennis Sheehan, professors at the University of Rochester, followed the investments of six famous—or, rather, infamous—outside/insiders from 1977 through 1982. The six men included in the study were Carl Icahn, Irwin Jacobs, Carl Lindner, David Murdock, Victor Posner and Charles Bluhdorn. (Bluhdorn has since died, but at the time of the study he was the head of Gulf & Western and considered one of the most ruthless corporate raiders.) As of the beginning of 1987, all of the others are still very active outside/insider investors, although Victor Posner was indicted for tax evasion in the mid-1980s and may end up directing his huge empire from behind prison walls. Holderness and Sheehan's study, the results of which were published in the December 1985 edition of the Journal of Financial Economics, looked at each of the Schedule 13D filings by these six investors and tracked the target company's stock performance over two years after the initial filings.

Collectively, the six investors filed Schedule 13Ds for a total of ninety-nine different NYSE- and AMEX-listed companies during that time period. After all the data were collected and the results adjusted for systemic market risk, the researchers found that, contrary to the popular belief that these six "raiders" decreased the value of shareholders' stock, on average "stockholders of target firms earned statistically significant positive abnormal returns." The study found that the stockholders benefited whether the end result of the initial investment was a takeover, a merger, a buy-out taking the company private or simply a "toehold" 5 percent investment by the raiders.

The study even found that stockholders enjoyed abnormal returns when the end result was the paying of "greenmail" to the raiders. While it was true that the "greenmail" usually involved the company's paying the raiders a premium over the then-current market price for their stock and for no one else's, the open-market price itself had risen *abnormally* between the time that the outside/insiders came on the scene and the "greenmail" was paid. The other stockholders may have been angry that they couldn't get the premium price for their shares. But if they held shares that had originally been purchased at the price the outside/insiders had paid, they still would have enjoyed an increase in their shares' value.

The findings in this study are consistent with other similar studies and with practical experience in following outside/insider investing for over a decade. But if the evidence shown in this and other studies is true—and it is—why does outside/insider investing spark average abnormal returns for *all* shareholders? And who is spreading the myth that outside/insider investors are "raiders?"

First, let's look at the probable reasons for the average abnormal returns for all stockholders. Holderness and Sheehan offered two hypotheses for the phenomenon. (They acknowledge, however, that the hypotheses are not supported by objective evidence but are instead subjective assessments based on their findings.) The first of their hypotheses is that the six investors helped improve the management of the target firms. The second is that the six consistently identified underpriced stocks in the first place. Actually, the reason for the abnormal returns is most often a combination of these two assumptions about outside/insider investing patterns along with a few other dynamics.

Like any true investor, an outside/insider, whether an individual "raider" or a corporation investing in another company, is looking for a bargain, something that in some way will appreciate in value and make him richer. The difference between the outside/insider and other "average" investors is that they are already rich. Very rich. (They have to be rich—or have access to huge funds—to be able to afford to accumulate 5 percent or more of a company's outstanding stock.) These people have already developed the skills that enable them to identify situations that will make money. It is not surprising, therefore, to expect them to use their skills to find companies with some realizable intrinsic value that has not been fully appreciated in the marketplace.

Besides being rich, outside/insiders have another quality that most other investors do not have. They have clout. As major shareholders, they can accomplish a great deal in achieving the goal of increasing the value of their investment that other people cannot. They can use strong-arm tactics like taking over the company and replacing top management with more aggressive managers who will use a company's resources in a more profitable way. Or they can use less dramatic methods of influencing management to improve the performance of the company or to bring the full value of a previously ignored or neglected company to the attention of more investors.

All this is done to the benefit of *all* stockholders.

Don't think, however, that outside/insiders are champions of shareholders rights. They are interested only in themselves and their own pockets. They don't care much about any other shareholders. If the price of a stock goes up because of an outside/insider's actions and you benefit, it is only a by-product of the outside/insider's selfish goals. But since they are shareholders with a large interest in making their holdings appreciate in value, their motivation matches your self-interest as a fellow shareholder. It's just that they can do something about it and you usually can't.

Since outside/insider investments more often than not accompany an appreciation in the value of a company's stock, who is creating and spreading the negative "raiders" and "sharks" image of outside/insiders? The answer is the people who bear the brunt of the hostilities that outside/insiders sometimes display when they are working to make their investments pay off. Namely, the management of the target companies.

Top executives of target companies have somewhat different self-interests than outside/insider investors and other shareholders, like you, have. You and the outside/insiders generally are interested in seeing the value of your holdings increase. The people who make up a company's top management, even though they also may be shareholders, are more interested in keeping their good-paying jobs and their positions of unquestioned power. Keeping the power base and status that come with a top position in a company is a human motivation that is normal but should never be underestimated.

Top management—those people with the most to lose personally—are the ones who cry "raider" and "shark" the loudest. They also get the most sympathy from financial reporters and others. Outside/insiders, particularly ones who use hostile tactics to get management to do something to make their investments increase in value, are interlopers upsetting the status quo. Nobody likes an interloper, even if the interloper's influence could benefit a larger group of people—the shareholders.

Think of how insulting it is to management to be faced with a hostile outside/insider presence. To begin with, the outside/insider has identified the company in the first place because he or she has found some value that has not been fully cultivated. This, of course, implies that management hasn't done everything it could to realize the company's potential. Then, this interloper has ideas for putting the company on the road to greater riches, ideas that management previously didn't think of itself or wouldn't do. So, to hold off these insulting attacks by "raiders," management will spend bundles of a company's money in legal costs, greenmail or struggles against an outside/insider's shareholder proxy fight, all in the name of protecting shareholders' rights.

Management sometimes will also use emotional appeals to the government and employees of the company that point out how a takeover could possibly change and "upset" their lives. Since most people don't like change, this rallies support for management—whose motivation, if viewed realistically, is just to protect its own hide. But since management is able to pull the right emotional strings, you will often see an outpouring of petitions and other shows of support for management against outside/insiders. This kind of story often is sympathetically reported by the financial and general media, taking matters out of context in highlighting the experiences of individual employees whose lives could be upset by change.

These supporters of the status quo, however, fail to understand or are unwilling to accept a basic principle of our capitalist economic system, namely, that companies—these businesses —do not exist for the convenience of employees. Instead, the ultimate goal for the creation and continuation of a company is to enrich the owners—the shareholders. Those who can accept this fact of life do not have a problem with the outside/insiders or other "owners" of a company who are trying to do all they can to make their invests appreciate, even though their tactics may upset the lives of individuals. Rather, they use it to their own advantage—as the outside/insiders do and as you can do too.

Here's an example of management's desperate struggle against an outside/insider. The company was NL Industries, a NYSE-listed chemical producer and petroleum services company. In early 1986, Coniston Partners, a professional investment team made up of three former Wall Streeters, took a large stake in the company to the tune of nearly $35 million at an average price per share of about $12.70. Following some struggles with management, Coniston Partners convinced NL's board to take steps to enhance the value of its shares—namely, by dividing the company into two separate entities with one concentrating on the petroleum aspect of its business (which wasn't worth much at the time) and one concentrating on the chemical aspect (which was worth plenty). But before NL had a chance to put the Coniston Partners' plan in operation, another outside/insider, Dallas-based "raider" Harold Simmons, had accumulated 20 percent of the company's stock at about $13 a share and announced a takeover move. Simmons offered NL shareholders $15.125 a share for their holdings—a greater value than NL shareholders had seen in years. But management didn't like that, saying that the price was inadequate. To fight this takeover, NL's management first drew up an antitakeover document that required such stringent qualifications for a takeover that it essentially made it impossible for anyone to buy the company successfully. (These antitakeover plans—which have been pressed upon shareholders at an increasing number of companies in the past few years—are often referred to as "poison pills." A common feature of these plans is a very generous provision for the company's management in the event that a takeover is successful and executives lose their jobs—the so-called golden parachutes. The NL Industries plan was later judged illegal in court.)

NL Industries, frightened by the Simmons threat, decided to actually spin off the chemicals part of the company and create a new company, NL Chemicals, in an effort to bring immediate recognition of the company's true value. NL's management also started a public advertising campaign in July 1986 to convince its shareholders not to sell out to Simmons. In a couple of full-page ads in The New York Times and The Wall Street Journal, management tried to make a case for its actions. The ads themselves provide some interesting insights into the thinking of NL's management and board of directors. Included in one ad was a telling admission: "The Board believes that NL's stock has historically been undervalued, in part because analysts and portfolio managers specializing in one of NL's two major business segments may have found the other segment difficult to understand." (NL's low price was someone else's fault, you see.) Then the same ad makes an insightful assessment of the motive behind the Harold Simmons and the Coniston Partners presence: "The Board also believes that the undervaluation of NL has been a major reason for the attempts by the Simmons Group, and earlier by Coniston Partners, to seek controlling positions in NL." (No kidding.) Then management wanted some sympathy: "These attempts, which the Board believes have been detrimental to the best interests of NL shareholders, have forced the management of NL to devote substantial time, energy and cost to takeover and merger issues, and over the long term the diversion of management's attention to those matters would be detrimental to NL's business and profitability." (Here we see that the interloper had upset the status quo.)

The point of the ad was to keep shareholders from selling to Simmons before NL management was able to put together the spin-off of NL Chemicals. In a separate ad, NL quoted industry analysts who said that as two separate companies NL Industries' stock could trade between $4 and $6 a share within twelve months after the spin-off and the new NL Chemicals could be worth from $12 to $16 a share—a combined possible value of between $16 and $22 a share. This was clearly more than Simmons was willing to pay. All management seemed to want was a little time to get things rolling. It pleaded: "We urge you not to tender any of your NL securities to Mr. Simmons. We believe they are worth more than he is offering."

As an NL shareholder, you should have had a few questions for NL's management: If the board knew all along that NL's stock had "historically been undervalued" and since there was a way to achieve a more realistic valuation—by spinning off part of the company—why wasn't it done before? If management really had shareholders' interests at heart, why did it take an interloper to force NL to do something to make the shareholders' investment properly valued? If Coniston Partners and Harold Simmons had not come along, would NL's management have undertaken the steps to bring about full valuation of the shareholders investment or would it have continued on its past course of keeping the stock undervalued?

Clearly, Coniston Partners and Harold Simmons played catalyst roles in bringing about changes in NL Industries that benefited all shareholders. And NL's antitakeover tactics didn't work. Simmons was able to accumulate over 50 percent of the company's common stock by mid-August 1986 and took control of the company. Thereafter, the idea of making NL Industries into two separate companies was abandoned. However, stockholders were given one share of "preferred" stock for each common share held which represented the chemicals aspect of the company. By the middle of 1987, the common stock—which represented the petroleum aspect of the company—stood at about $7½ and the preferred stock—which represented the chemical aspect—was selling at about $15 a share. This was a combined value of over $22 a share, which was much, much higher than the value the shareholders had before the Coniston Partners and Harold Simmons came on the scene.

Were the villains in this story the "raiders" who brought about the change that improved the perceived value of NL's stock? Or were the villains the previously complacent NL management who acted to improve the stock's performance probably only through fear of losing their power positions?

NL shareholders should have sent the Coniston Partners and Harold Simmons thank-you notes.

Leading the Way

Passive or hostile, "raider" or "white knight," an outside/insider investment has several different possible final outcomes:

- Takeover of the target company by the original investor
- Takeover of the target company by a third party—either a "white knight," another unwanted suitor or the company's management in a buy-out deal
- Repurchase of the outside/insider's shares by the company— the dreaded greenmail
- Shares sold in the open market or to another investor in a private transaction

These different outcomes occur with varying degrees of frequency. Statistically, some type of completed takeover is the most common final event seen following an outside/insider's initial Schedule 13D filing—although not necessarily by that particular outside/insider. The next most prevalent ending finds the original investor selling his or her shares in the open market or to another investor. Greenmail payment is the least common final outcome and may disappear entirely if current congressional critics have their way.

Another statistical study of investments by outside/insiders, conducted by Wayne Mikkelson, a professor at the University of Oregon, and Richard Ruback, a professor at the Massachusetts Institute of Technology, gives some interesting insights into the type of activity you can expect when following outside/insiders for investment clues. The study, which was published in the December 1985 edition of the *Journal of Financial Economics*, tracked all initial Schedule 13D filings by corporations from 1978 through 1980. (The study did not include Schedule 13D filings by individuals. But almost all accumulation of 5 percent or more of a company's stock is done under the name of a corporation, even though a single individual may be the leading force behind the acquisition. Edgar Bronfman uses Seagram as his investment vehicle, for example. Harold Simmons, whom you saw at work at NL Industries, uses several different investment vehicles, including Amalgamated Sugar Company, Contran Corporation and LLC Corporation.)

The researchers identified 473 separate initial filings reporting investments in as many different companies. (Mikkelson and Ruback did not track subsequent filings that would have reported additional purchases.) The researchers then followed the activities of each of those 473 investments for three years. They found that 206 of the initial investments—44 percent of the total—preceded some type of completed takeover within three years. Another 52 investors—11 percent—sold their shares in the open market or to another investor in a private purchase. Company repurchases (greenmail) accounted for 40—8 percent—of the final outcomes. They also found that 160, or nearly one third, of the situations they identified had no outcome within three years of the initial filing.

The researchers tracked the stock performance for each target company from the point of the initial Schedule 13D filing through the end of the three-year period the study covered. They found that there were abnormal above-average returns for all shareholders with each type of final outcome—including situations involving greenmail. The stock of the target companies in situations that had no outcome within the three-year period actually decreased in value, on average. It is important to note, however, that the outside/insiders held on to these apparent losers throughout this three-year period. When outside/insiders sold they did so at a profit with average abnormal positive returns.

The study does not tell us how many outside/insiders, who were holding on to the stocks that went down in value, *continued to accumulate more shares* in companies whose stock prices were falling over three years. It does tell us, however, that they tended *not to sell* even though the performance appears— in the short term, at least—to be negative. Clearly the outside/insiders anticipated future gains beyond the three-year period covered in this study. (Most likely they were following a common outside/insider path of buying *more* shares while the price for the stock was low and before the corporate development that was anticipated was fully worked out. You will often see insiders buy over a period of several years before payday occurs.) This brings us back to one of our golden rules: To profit like an insider, you must stick with a stock the way an insider does, even through periods of seemingly bad weather.

Even when you consider that there were average negative returns throughout three years in the situations that had not yet come to a final development, two thirds of the total 473 situations displayed average abnormal *positive* returns within three years. Not bad. There aren't many stock market investors who enjoy average positive abnormal returns on two thirds of their investments within three years. Remember, "average positive abnormal returns" translates into stock performance that "beats the market."

As outside investors looking at this study we learn that most outside/insider investments are overwhelmingly profitable. But clearly it isn't possible for us to invest in *all* of the target companies that big-money outside/insiders identify. There aren't many investors who can invest in 473 different companies over a three-year period. (And since 1980, when this study was completed, there has been a sharp rise in the number of incidences of outside/insider investments.)

Not only is it not possible to invest in all these companies, it is not desirable to follow every outside/insider investment with our own investment. Like all other assessments of insider investment activities, we want to see a "consistent pattern of unusual behavior" before we make our own moves.

Often this means that events will happen so quickly on the heels of a Schedule 13D filing that we won't have the time to analyze the situation and still be able to jump in at the same price the outside/insider bought at—or even at a premium of up to 25 percent over the outside/insider's highest price. This situation most commonly occurs when an initial Schedule 13D filing reveals takeover intentions. When that happens the game is very often over. It receives wide coverage in the financial press and many investors will be attracted to the situation which could raise the price of the stock very quickly. But this doesn't mean that you should ignore these situations. Sometimes you *will* be able to invest at the outside/insider's level and considering the extremely high incidences of a completed takeover—either by the original outside/insider investor or a third party—you will usually come out ahead.

But Schedule 13D filings that do *not* reveal an initial intention of a takeover move will be the ones that hold the greatest opportunities for us. With these we will have more time to assess the "consistent" and "unusual" aspects for investment clues. Like our assessment of any insider activity, we want to see trading patterns that display aggressiveness in quantity of shares purchased and frequency of trips to the open market (or through private purchases at or above open-market prices). And we want to apply commonsense reasoning to outside/insider actions.

This means that an initial Schedule 13D filing that shows a 5 percent ownership is interesting, but subsequent filings that show ever-increasing buying is more interesting. As we have stated earlier, when there is both inside/insider buying *and* outside/insider buying it is more interesting than situations when there is only outside/insider activity. Also, it is more interesting when we see a company investing in another company that is involved in the same or related business. For example, an automotive parts manufacturer's investment into an automotive parts *retailer* is much more interesting than an investment by a mining company into a grocery store chain. We can assume that companies investing within their own or related industry group have greater insights into the future of those targets than companies with completely unrelated backgrounds.

When we come across situations where there is more than one outside/insider investing in the same company, it can be the most interesting opportunity. For example, outside/insiders started investing in Pittsburgh-based Cyclops Corporation back in late 1982 when the company had diversified business activities of producing steel products, constructing nonresidential buildings and ownership of two specialty retail chains, Busy Beaver Building Centers and Silo. The first outside/insider attracted to Cyclops was Harold Simmons. By early 1983 Simmons had purchased 5.3 percent of Cyclops (about 182,000 shares) at prices between $21 and $30. Throughout 1983 he continued to buy until he owned about 312,000 shares—9 percent of the company—before he sold out in February 1984 at $36 a share with about a 40 percent profit in less than two years.

A large amount of Simmons's holdings was purchased by another outside/insider player, Harris Associates, a Chicago-based investment firm. Another chunk of Simmons's stake was purchased by yet another outside/insider, the Steinhart Fund. By the end of 1984 Harris owned about 425,000 shares (11.3 percent of the company)—purchased at an average price of about $38 a share—and the Steinhart Fund owned about 208,000 shares (5.8 percent of the company)—acquired at about $36 a share. Then, in late 1984 another outside/insider came on the scene, the Coniston Partners. Through the middle of 1985 it purchased almost 370,000 shares (9.7 percent of the company) at prices ranging from $35 to $49 a share. Incredibly, yet another outside/insider jumped on board in early 1985. This player was home builder Kaufman & Broad—a company that had itself been the target of outside/insider advances. Kaufman & Broad bought about 292,000 shares (7.7 percent of the company) at an approximate average price of $48 a share.

By the middle of 1985 these four outside/insiders owned almost 35 percent of Cyclops's stock. Few other investors—except those of us who were following SEC reports—paid very much attention to Cyclops. But here were four big investors (five if you count Simmons who dropped out with his 40 percent profit) with track records of success that had all been attracted to this company. Why? There was untapped value inherent in Cyclops's operations, which these outside/insiders discovered, unassisted by any Wall Street analyst recommendations or reports. In 1986 the outside/insider investors started prodding Cyclops's management to take action to achieve greater valuation by spinning off divisions of the company and consolidating the company's strengths, namely, its discount specialty retail store operations. But before those plans were put in operation, a British electrical equipment retailer made a tender offer for the company at $90¼ in February of 1987 followed by a second, winning bidder at $95 a share in April 1987. Not a bad showing for these four "investors," but nothing that made many headlines in the financial news media.

The Cyclops story shows the kind of trading behavior we like to see: large, frequent, aggressive open-market and private purchase buys.

Types of Outside/Insiders

There are three broad categories of outside/insiders you will find making investments:

· Individuals and families

· Partnerships and investment syndicates

· Domestic and foreign corporations

All of these different categories of investors approach their investments in somewhat different ways—with different ultimate goals and different ways of achieving those goals. Your understanding of how they operate can be significant when making your decision about following their investments with your own.

When we look at the people who make up the individuals and families category, we almost always find a strong personality with an equally strong investment vision directing the investment action. It is in this category that you will find the widest spectrum of outside/insider behavior—from the most passive to the most aggressive.

A well-known and highly successful individual who is at the relatively passive end of this investment spectrum is Warren Buffett. Buffett is a fundamental investor in the classic sense. He searches out what he considers to be an undervalued situation and, in most cases in recent years, keeps a complete hands-off position with an investment choice until the value of the stock appreciates—which often takes years. Interestingly, it was not always so: Buffett (via his investment vehicle, Berkshire Hathaway) got started by moving into actual management. His main break came with obtaining control of GEICO Corporation in the early 1980s. His heavy buying at about the $14 per share level was followed by a price slump to nearly $10 a share before the rise began which took the price to over $100 in 1986. (Companies actually welcome stock purchases by Buffett. His investments are usually viewed as a vote of confidence in a company's future.) He has been extremely successful in his thirty-plus years of investing. Buffett's primary investment vehicle, Berkshire Hathaway, is ostensibly an apparel retailing and textile business. But the real business is stock selection and investment. The retailing and textile businesses of Berkshire have been only marginally profitable—and often unprofitable—for years. Despite this, the $7 a share that Buffett paid for control of Berkshire in 1965 was worth an unbelievable $3,100 a share at the beginning of 1987. Shareholders in this OTC-listed company are clearly not interested in the performance of Berkshire's retailing and textile businesses; they are holding Berkshire stock as they would shares in a mutual fund. (Of course, it isn't necessary to buy shares of Berkshire to follow Buffett's investments; many of them are reported in Schedule 13D and Form 4 filings.)

On the opposite end of the spectrum are people like Carl Icahn whose style is to jump into an investment target (or actually take it over) and stir things up dramatically to put the company on the path he thinks is best to achieve increased stock value. People like Icahn—whose most recent well-publicized success came in taking over faltering airline TWA in a bloody battle and then directing the company's turnaround in profitability—are those who are usually labeled "raiders." For Icahn and other "raiders" making something happen to increase a stock's value is one aspect of their investment approach. Another common shared aspect of their personalities is their drive to build an empire with themselves at the helm personally directing all the shots. The success of their enterprises, therefore, is highly dependent on their own energies and managerial brilliance—which can sometimes be uneven.

Most of the individual and family investors, however, fall in between these two extremes of the spectrum, and they receive the least amount of publicity. This group isn't as passive as a Warren Buffett. Like investors such as Icahn, these people also try to use their influence to prod a company in a direction that will ultimately appreciate the value of their holdings, but they normally do it with less flamboyance and fewer strong-arm tactics than does a Carl Icahn. Examples of this type of outside/insider would include the Pritzker brothers of Chicago, who concentrate on building up smallish companies that are in some trouble, Carl Lindner of Cincinnati, who is involved in a wide range of different businesses, and Gene Phillips of Dallas, who seems to concentrate on finding stable companies with bright futures instead of searching out troubled situations and then getting involved only when management welcomes his presence. A specially gifted "operator" is Larry Tisch of Loews Corporation, who does very few deals—such as CNA Financial and, most recently, CBS, Inc.—but does them very well.

Knowing the personalities, investment styles and track records of these different outside/insiders can add significantly to your *subjective* reading of outside/insider investments. Periodically you will run across articles in the general financial press (and even in general newspapers) that detail their careers and provide insights into their investment philosophies. Study these profiles. You might even want to clip them out and keep a file of them that you can refer to when these outside/insiders' big investments spark your interest in a particular company. (One section of the Bibliography at the end of this book gives a list of important articles published in the last few years about most of the major players.)

With this kind of information in hand, you can assess your own investment temperament in relation to the outside/insider you are planning to follow. For example, you may be more comfortable with a Warren Buffett or with someone like Canada's George Mann, whose overall investment philosophy is directed by looking at the "downside" risk of an investment instead of optimistically looking at its "upside" potential. On the other hand, you may like the style of more daredevil investors like an Asher Edelman or a Saul Steinberg who often jump into risky situations that sometimes bring big results relatively rapidly, and other times some big losses. By looking beyond the mere objective evidence of heavy buying by these different people and taking into consideration their track records and styles, you can make a more intelligent decision about your *own* investment. If you do not know anything about these people or if you are not comfortable with them, don't follow their investments with your own. Instead, go with those situations with people you *are* comfortable with or know something about.

When we look at the special characteristics of the second

broad category of outside/insider—"partnerships and investment syndicates"—we usually find people acting in a way similar to those in the middle range of the "individual and family"
category. These investors take large enough positions in companies so that they can exert pressure on the company to make
something happen to appreciate the value of its stock. But they
will rarely take over a company or try to directly manage its
day-to-day operations. Most of these partnerships and investment syndicates are headed by people who have worked professionally as financiers, analysts or in some other big-money
investment capacity at leading brokerage firms or investment
banks such as Merrill Lynch or Goldman Sachs or Drexel Lambert before starting their own investment enterprises. The Coniston Partners that you saw at work in the NL Industries and
Cyclops stories is an example of this type of investing group.
Two of the three men who make up Coniston Partners—Keith
Gollust and Paul Tierney—are former corporate finance experts
at Merrill Lynch. The third partner is Gus Oliver, a lawyer who
cut his investment teeth at the major law firm of Skadden, Arps,
Slate, Meagher & Flom.

Others you will find in this category of outside/insiders are
people like Edward C. "Ned" Johnson, president of FMR Corporation. FMR Corporation directs many of the best-known mutual
funds in the world—the Fidelity family of funds including the
Magellan Fund. Johnson often puts together a consortium of
high-roller investors to invest in situations outside of his company's mutual fund investment activities. When you see investments by this type of group (and there are others such as
investments by Max Heine and Michael Price who head Mutual
Shares Corporation), you are not following the investments of
the mutual funds. Instead, you are following the actions of the
individuals of the mutual funds' management as they invest
their *own* money.

This kind of behavior on the part of individual mutual fund
managers may raise the question in your mind that if their funds
held as much promise as they claim, why are they making outside investments? If the mutual funds provide the kind of diversified stock investment that is good enough for other people's
money, why isn't it good enough for 100 percent of the managers' *own* money? An explanation is that the mutual fund investment is necessarily a passive one, whereas an investment
partnership or syndicate can actively get involved in helping

change the direction and fortunes of a company. By law a mutual fund can hold only a relatively small percentage of a company's total outstanding shares—too small to allow a mutual fund to be influential on the inner workings of a company. Ned Johnson and others who invest heavily in specific companies outside of their mutual fund investments can do things such as demanding representation on a company's board of directors and then work to bring about the change necessary to wake up a sleepy company with potential or shift its assets around to make other investors pay attention to the company. This is something that is impossible to do as a mutual fund manager. So here we see two different kinds of investing—passive and active. It is not an indication that Johnson or others are turning their backs on their own mutual funds.

For our final broad category of outside/insiders—"domestic and foreign corporations"—the investing you will see is normally done with an eye on eventual acquisition of the target company. An official takeover announcement by one company that has been buying shares in another company can happen very quickly after the buying starts. Or the buying can go on over an extended time period—sometimes several years—before a tender offer is made. As we mentioned previously, you usually will not be able to invest in situations when the takeover announcement comes quickly on the heels of the start of a company's stock buying. It's those situations when a company buys continually and steadily over a long period that hold the greatest opportunities for us.

This type of slow and steady buying is particularly evident among foreign companies buying the stock of U.S. companies. When foreign companies invest heavily, they usually mean business. They are serious about their investments and have a clear goal in mind—a takeover. Their final move often coincides with a time when the value of the dollar on the world's monetary market is low. The foreign company buys quietly so as not to alert the market that a large acquisition is occurring and then scoops up the rest of the shares using cheap dollars.

Here's an example of a typical investment pattern seen among foreign corporations: In the early 1980s, a German company named Vorwerk started buying stock in Ranco, Inc., an Ohio manufacturer of heating and air-conditioning equipment devices. Through frequent trips to the open market, Vorwerk amassed nearly 1 million shares or about 24 percent of the com-

pany at prices between about $17 and $24 a share. At the end of
1986, the company's stock stood at about $26. In the middle of
January 1987, when the value of the dollar was very low, Vorwerk offered $40 a share to take over the company.

A Cautionary Note

It's necessary to backpedal a little here and add a caveat to the
overall positive view of following outside/insider investments.
Although it is statistically true that most outside/insider investments precede abnormal positive returns for all shareholders—
even in cases that eventually result in the paying of greenmail to
the outside/insider—there is a "danger zone" when you should
follow outside/insiders with extreme caution. This danger zone
exists because the rule prohibiting insiders from selling shares
for a profit until being held for six months does not apply to
outside/insiders until they have acquired 10 percent or more of
the company's stock. This means that between the time when
outside/insiders acquired 5 percent of the company's stock—
when a Schedule 13D filing is first required—and their accumulation of 10 percent or more, the outside/insiders can jump
out of a situation very quickly.

This ability to sell out quickly can have some dire conse-
quences on investments that had been made based on the out-
side/insiders' actions during the danger zone time. For example,
a well-known outside/insider will accumulate 7 or 8 or 9 percent of a company's stock. Often an accumulation like that, particularly if it is of the stock of a well-known company, can
attract considerable attention by the general financial press. The
press will hype this outside/insider presence—often with the
encouragement of the outside/insider himself—drawing attention to the situation. Other investors, thinking that something
dramatic is going to happen quickly, will jump on this news and
invest in the company. This added demand, of course, can cause
a sharp increase in the stock's price. As we previously mentioned, a sharp short-term price rise often occurs following huge
investments by insiders—especially well-known outside/in-
sider investments in well-known companies. The outside/in-
sider, who does not own 10 percent or more of a company's

stock and is therefore not bound by the six-month holding rule, can take advantage of this short-term rise and sell out at a very handsome profit. This sale will in turn deflate the stock's price. And the people who bought on the news of an outside/insider's original purchase will have lost a lot of money. There are several outside/insider investors who have been accused of playing this stock market manipulation game.

Also during this same period is when a high incidence of greenmail payments occurs. An outside/insider can strike fear in the hearts of a vulnerable company's management by buying less than 10 percent of the company's stock and then very publicly detail the changes he plans to make—including firing current management. Since the outside/insider doesn't hold that much stock, management may think that it would be expeditious to pay the "shark" off quickly. While statistically other shareholders may also enjoy an increase in the value of their holdings, avoiding following an outside/insider who only has greenmail in mind is a good idea. (We should again note that the whole problem of greenmail may soon become moot since there is legislation before Congress that would outlaw the practice.)

So when an outside/insider's holdings are *below* 10 percent of the company's outstanding shares, you should view that investment with skepticism, particularly if the outside/insider is too willing to talk about the investment and actually welcomes publicity about the situation. In these cases the outside/insider is possibly simply trying to manipulate you or the management of the target company. It is much more attractive to see an outside/ insider go over the 10 percent ownership hump and continually acquire more shares toward 15 percent, 20 percent and more ownership while at the same time trying to downplay the investment or even to keep it quiet. By keeping the news of the stock accumulation out of financial press headlines, the outside/insider can continue to buy more shares at bargain prices. Those people who call attention to their stock buying probably have something other than a *real* investment in mind.

Generally, therefore, we want to avoid following an investment by outside/insiders who hold less than 10 percent of a company's stock. It is after the point when the outside/insider has become deeply embroiled in the company and cannot jump out quickly with profits because of an artificial or unrealistic price rise that we can be serious about our *own* investment.

There are cases, however, when an investment below the 10

percent level can be significant. One such situation occurs when the outside/insider investor does not have a history of stock market manipulation or taking greenmail. For an example we can look once again at Warren Buffett, who has never taken a dime of greenmail and doesn't appear to invest just to dupe other investors. But to know the past behavior of outside/insiders on which you can make assumptions about future behavior, you should, as we have mentioned previously, familiarize yourself with their investment careers before making your own investment.

Another situation where an outside/insider purchase of less than 10 percent can be important is when you also see heavy inside/insider purchases. A small outside/insider presence can confirm the bullish attitude of inside/insiders—as we saw in the RB Industries story in Chapter 5. And when we see an outside/insider come on the scene with a small overall holding and there are already other different outside/insiders involved with the company, we can view that as further evidence of a value situation—as we saw in the Cyclops story earlier in this chapter.

All this can be summarized in another general rule of thumb: Do not invest with an outside/insider who holds less than 10 percent of a company's stock, except when (a) you are absolutely certain that the outside/insider does not have a history of taking greenmail or selling out quickly, (b) there is evidence of heavy inside/insider investing or (c) where there are two or more other outside/insiders who hold 5 percent or more of the company's stock.

PART THREE:

Tracking Down the Insider Action

Chapter 8

Sifting for Nuggets

EVERY day in the Public Reference Room at the SEC offices in Washington you'll find about fifty people working, almost all of them some type of professional researcher. Some are stringers from newspapers and news service bureaus who feed their employers news about the latest developments as soon as public disclosure documents—particularly from Schedule 13D filings of prominent outside/insiders—are released. Others work for law firms or the research departments of large brokerage houses. But most of them work for the fifteen or so information service organizations that specialize in collecting timely data from SEC documents—including filings by insiders as well as information from the nearly three hundred different other public disclosure forms required by securities law—and quickly distributing it to people such as investment bankers, brokerage firm analysts and professional and amateur investors.

Because the information service people are so thorough and because we can get the information we need about corporate insider trading through printed and computer-generated sources, we don't ever need to step foot inside the Public Reference Room.

Beyond the Public Reference Room

The people who subscribe to SEC information services for instantaneous reports of the latest filings pay a premium to be the first to know of important developments. Some retain two or even three different service bureaus to ensure that they receive the news fast. It's all done in an effort to get a leg up on other investors. The hottest and most newsworthy of the SEC documents for these people is the Schedule 13D. In fact, a Schedule 13D filing can be so newsworthy that the SEC releases all of them simultaneously in the Public Reference Room and the press room down the hall.

Here's an example of what the people who want immediate knowledge of Schedule 13D filings hope to achieve: Tuesday morning a well-known outside/insider—someone like Carl Icahn or Saul Steinberg—files a Schedule 13D that shows he has accumulated 9 percent of a company's stock and is ready to buy the rest of the company's stock for $75 a share. At the moment on Tuesday morning when the subscriber to an SEC information service gets the news, the stock of the company that is the target of the takeover offer is priced at $64 and he immediately buys it. By Wednesday afternoon or Thursday morning, after the news of the Schedule 13D filings gets broader circulation through newspaper, television and computer data base reports, a wider group of investors will find out that the target company's stock has been reevaluated at a much higher price. More investors will try to buy it in the anticipation that they soon may receive at least $75 per share. And by Friday afternoon the company's stock which sold for $64 on Tuesday morning may very well reach $72 or more in reaction to the increased demand. The investor who bought Tuesday morning on receipt of the news from an information service bureau obviously will have profited very well in a very short period of time.

Most of the people who practice this stock market trading technique are arbitrageurs. For those unfamiliar with this particular breed of stock market investor, arbitrageurs—often simply referred to as "arbs"—practice the art of arbitrage. If you wanted to play one version of the arbitrage game, you would buy the stock of a company targeted for a takeover and at the same time you would sell short the stock of the company *attempting* the takeover. Since takeover targets usually enjoy increased valuation during the period of time prior to the final conclusion of a takeover attempt, you would expect to profit by jumping on the stock at the earliest news of a takeover announcement. At the same time of your purchase of the target company's stock you would also sell short the stock of the company attempting to make the takeover because you would expect the price of the stock of that company to go down. This is because the company would have to use up at least some of its assets to buy the other company. Therefore the company making the acquisition would become less valuable as it got closer to the actual time when the takeover is completed.

For example, if Carl Icahn wanted to buy out XYZ company and used TWA as his source of funds, the price of XYZ Company most likely would go up to at least the amount Icahn was offering as his buy-out price. TWA's stock price, on the other hand, would most likely go down because the company would have to shell out some of its money (or sell off some of its assets) in order to buy XYZ Company—giving it a lower book value and in return a lower stock price reflecting that lower book value. So, an arbitrageur can expect to make money on two fronts: by buying stock in the takeover target company and expecting the price to go up, and by selling short the stock of the acquiring company and expecting the price of that company's stock to go down. Clearly, the sooner arbitrageurs have information about an intended takeover, the sooner they can begin trading at the most advantageous prices. In recent years, however, many of the arbitrageurs operate "naked"; that is, they buy only the target stock and do not cover that purchase by hedging through the sale of the acquiring company's shares.

Many of the people involved in the illegal insider trading that captured headlines in 1986 and 1987 were somehow connected with arbitrage. But they didn't wait until the *public* announcement of a tender offer or takeover attempt to make their arbitrage moves. Instead, they found out about an upcoming announcement through tips from others. This, of course, allowed them to buy shares at even lower prices and without competition from other arbitrageurs who were acting legally. Although the arbitrage game is *very* profitable for some people, it is a fast-paced approach to stock market trading that is best left to professionals. To become an effective arbitrageur, you would need to give full-time attention to it and have ready access to a considerable amount of funds to invest on a moment's notice.

For the average investor looking to SEC disclosure documents for investment signals, the need for fast knowledge of the latest filings is not as intense as it is for arbitrageurs or other professional traders who jump on Schedule 13D filings that announce takeover bids. These professional traders are looking for situations that will provide them with a high probability of quick profits. Their well-oiled investment machinery is usually so efficient that it often effectively locks us out of situations when a takeover announcement accompanies a Schedule 13D filing. Sometimes, however, the takeover process can drag on for so long that arbitrageurs and other professional traders get bored with the situation. They may stop trading or even sell out to grab onto another takeover situation with the promise of quicker returns. The result of this may actually push the price of the takeover target's stock down to a level that makes it attractive for us.

Although arbitrageurs are almost solely interested in outside/insiders who have officially announced a takeover intention, our approach to watching outside/insiders (as well as inside/insiders) shares a couple of similarities with the arbitrageurs'. First, like an arbitrageur, we want to follow the lead of the deep-pocket players, the decision makers whose actions point us to investments that have a high probability of giving us a good return on our investment dollar. Unlike the arbitrageur, however, we have the patience to buy and hold—based on our reading of insider actions—in anticipation of long-term capital gains on our investment. The arbitrageur is generally interested in trading maneuvers that result in a fast turnaround and profit.

This is not to say, however, that all our investments will take years to pay off. Some may come to fruition within a matter of weeks or months from the time that we actually buy. But we can't predict the timetable because we don't know exactly why the insiders are investing the way they are. Also, we don't know what the insiders are doing to make their own investments pay off, or the timetable they have set for themselves to bring about a stock appreciation. Arbitrageurs, on the other hand, have latched onto firmly announced takeover intentions because the price and timetable for these types of situations are much, much more predictable. Statistically, the returns on the final outcome of our investments should be very similar to those of an arbitrageur (if not better). But most of the situations that would interest us would never interest the arbitrageur or even most professional traders. The action is just too slow for their operations.

The other aspect of this investment game that we share with the arbitrageur—and we share it more completely—is that our need for information cannot be satisfied by conventional sources. *The Wall Street Journal, The New York Times, Barron's, Business Week, Fortune, Forbes, Financial World* and so on will not tell us what we need to know. These are all wonderful publications and reading them provides an excellent overview of the current general business climate. But they do not, cannot and will not give us the information about insiders that we need. From time to time general business publications will report on insider activities, but rarely with the detail or consistency necessary for making investment decisions. *The Wall Street Journal,* for example, periodically prints a list of recent insider transactions that its editors consider noteworthy. However, the list is small and incomplete. It concentrates on isolated, large, single transactions, usually "sell" transactions. Because the list is not comprehensive, it is completely worthless for our purposes. You cannot come to any accurate conclusions based on such scanty information.

So, like arbitrageurs, we need to be familiar with the special information sources that deliver comprehensive coverage of the doings at the SEC's Public Reference Room in Washington.

There are three sources of detailed information that you can use to find out about insider investments:

- *SEC documents* or the *printed* official sources of raw data about insider trading activities

- *Advisory newsletters* specializing in reporting on insider activity and recommending stocks favored by insider buying

- *Computer data bases* offering insider trading data that is accessed via a personal computer telephone hookup

Time and Money

Since none of these information sources is conveniently found at newsstands and since no one is going to hand you comprehensive insider trading data on a silver platter, you yourself must gain access to this specialized information (which will cost you a few dollars) and analyze the information (which will take some time). It will be well worth it.

As someone first starting to follow insider investments, your best bet would be to use one of the several advisory newsletters as the source of insider trading information. Generally speaking, these newsletters do an excellent job of sorting through the mountains of raw data found in SEC documents and screening it for evidence of the most important insider situations. The cost of a year's subscription to these various newsletters ranges from a hundred to three hundred and fifty dollars. But if you use them carefully by keeping in mind the advice given in the following chapters, you will come up with investment candidates that hold greater probable profitable returns for you than the selections you could gather by reading general financial publications or from recommendations of friends or even from your stockbroker. These candidates should more than justify the cost and it shouldn't take you more than a couple of hours a month to do the necessary analysis of the investment possibilities that the newsletters identify for you.

As you get more involved with insider investing and become more familiar with the various types of insider trading patterns, you may want to try your hand at insider trading research using original SEC documents or the printed sources of raw data. Following this do-it-yourself route can cost you less money. (A subscription to the *Official Summary of Security Transactions and Holdings* costs only $59 a year as of this writing.) But you can expect to spend *at least* thirty hours a month sorting through those printed sources and screening them for investment candidates. And then you may want to go beyond printed sources and use computer-assisted research and the computer data bases of insider trading transactions that are available.

An alternative to selecting and buying stocks through your own reading of insider activities is to place your investment dollars in a mutual fund. There are over a thousand different mutual funds in operation in this country, and some of them look at insider disclosure information for at least part of the approach they take in selecting the stocks to include in their portfolios. For example, Peter Lynch, who is the manager of Fidelity's Magellan Fund, was asked in 1986 by Louis Rukeyser on the Public Broadcasting Service's weekly television program

"Wall Street Week" if he had any advice for average investors for selecting companies to invest in. His response was to watch what the insiders are doing because they provided a "very good, reliable indicator" of a stock's direction. If Mr. Lynch is giving out that kind of advice, it more than implies that Fidelity's mutual fund managers are paying some attention to insider activity.

The exact criteria that mutual funds use on their way to stock selections are usually considered proprietary and are not generally revealed in detail. It's hard to tell, therefore, which funds are using insider trading information and which are not. However, there are two mutual funds currently in existence that make selections based *primarily* on SEC insider disclosure information. One is the Wealth Monitors Fund, P.O. Box 419003, Kansas City, MO 64141, (816) 221-5545. This fund, which began investing in 1986, watches major outside/insiders and their Schedule 13D filings for investment signals. The other fund is The Insider Reports Fund, 120 Broadway, New York, NY 10271, (212) 349-2372. The author of this book is the investment advisor to this fund, whose focus is on the trading patterns of *both* inside/insiders and outside/insiders as the basis for making investment choices.

If you want to take a more do-it-yourself route, it can be exciting, fun and rewarding—particularly if you have a Sherlock Holmes-type ability for deducing the elementary. But since most people do not have the time to devote to the sort of research necessary to use the raw data found in printed sources of insider information, the next three chapters outline an analysis and investment approach using an advisory newsletter of your choice as your source of information. The final section of this book—"Resources—Using Official Data and On-Line Data Bases"—details the steps you need to take to read and analyze raw data from printed or computer sources. The guidelines provided in this final section can put you on a level of insider analysis that exceeds the work done by many *professional* insider-watchers. This is a comprehensive view of reading insider activities that is not necessary for the average investor to successfully invest with the insiders—even though the techniques outlined there can point the way to compelling investment choices that are never covered in advisory newsletters. Although this final section will be of interest primarily to professional analysts and serious investment hobbyists, you are urged to read this section even if you do not plan to ever get to this level. The information there will give you more insights into your reading of advisory newsletters.

Actually, using computer data bases for research can be the fastest, least expensive and most comprehensive way of finding out what the insiders are up to. But this is true for you only if you fulfill two big "ifs." *If* you already own the computer hardware necessary to access computer data bases and *if* you are already proficient in doing computer data base research. Provided you do fulfill these two ifs, you will be interested in the final section of the book. However, for those of you who do not have the time to read printed sources of raw data or have access to a computer, using advisory newsletters will give you more than enough *superb* investment choices to fill your stock portfolio.

Chapter 9

Advisory Newsletters

W ITH about a thousand different newsletters published, covering a variety of investment angles from stocks to precious metals to commodities, the newsletter industry has attracted over five hundred thousand subscribers. There are several newsletters that pay attention to insider activity. Most of them, such as *Value Line Investment Survey* and *The Zweig Forecast*, use insider trading data as supplementary input into their traditional approaches to stock analysis. (*Value Line* takes a fundamentalist view; *Zweig Forecast* uses a technical approach.) There are a handful, however, that look to insider activity as the primary source for investment signals.

These insider newsletters differ dramatically from one another in the way they "read" insider trading. Some look at inside/insider activity only; others concentrate solely on outside/insider trading. Only a few routinely look at both inside/insider and outside/insider disclosure information.

Some of the newsletters interpret insider activity through a rigid formula—for example, one based solely on the number of different insiders trading in a similar way. Others add fundamental or econometric considerations to insider trading data to come up with their "buy" and "sell" recommendations. Many of them disagree with the point of view and interpretive advice you've read in this book. For example, most of the advisory services categorically disregard insider private-trading transactions as unimportant. As you've seen in these pages, a private transaction—particularly one involving an insider buying stock

at prices above the then open-market price—can be a significant indication of his attitude about the probable *future* direction of the stock's price. Also, you'll find that some newsletters
consider that insider purchases made through an option plan
are equal in importance to those made in the open market. Here,
however, you've read that since option purchases are usually
made at a deep discount from open-market prices, they are a
much less bullish sign. And you'll find that most advisory
newsletters put a considerable emphasis on the incidence of insider selling, whereas the approach in this book generally disre-
gards insider sales. There seem to be as many different ways to
look at insider trading data as there are serious insider-
watchers.

Despite the disparity in points of view, these newsletters
sometimes come to the same conclusions about the best investment choices based on insider trading. In the fall of 1986, for
example, almost every insider newsletter was recommending
OTC-listed Henley Group (at a buy price of about $19 a share)
and NYSE-listed Apache Petroleum (at a buy price of about
$9½). Obviously, the evidence of bullish insider attitudes is
often so overwhelming that there can be no question about the
interpretation. There are times, however, when you will find
that one newsletter is ballyhooing a particular company while
another newsletter is sending out a red alert to sell or to avoid
that same company's stock. But all this does not negate the
value of the work done by these various advisory services or the
investment candidates you can gather from them.

The first thing you need to do, therefore, is find the newsletters that you feel comfortable with both in terms of their philosophical approach to insider investments and their methods for
tracking insider activities. Each of the newsletters profiled in
this chapter is reputable and has a solid publication history.
(Subscription rates and other details are accurate as of 1987.)
Each will send a sample issue in response to a subscription in-
quiry. Take a look at them and decide which is best for you.
(Incidentally, many large public libraries subscribe to one or
more of these newsletters.)

CONSENSUS OF INSIDERS
P.O. Box 24349
Fort Lauderdale, FL 33307

(305) 776-3994

Thirty-six issues annually. One-year subscription: $147.

Consensus of Insiders was founded in 1962 by the granddaddy of systematic insider watching, Perry Wysong. Now editor emeritus of the newsletter, Wysong coined the phrase "You can't know what they know, but you can do what they do."

The newsletter follows inside/insiders only, with no consideration given to the effect of outside/insider trading. Wysong's approach to following insiders, which continues to be the backbone of the newsletter's stock recommendation policy, maintains that it is the *number of different* insiders trading in the same way that is important—regardless of the size of the transaction (either number of shares or amount of money involved) or the position of the insider within the company. The approach considers open-market purchases and purchases made under option plans as equally positive signs. Any open-market sales are considered a negative. (Private transactions are ignored.) The newsletter looks at insider activity over a six-month time frame. It adds together the total number of insiders buying in the open market and those exercising options and subtracts from that figure the total number of insiders selling. Then the company is assigned an "Insider Grade" that runs from "A" (the best) to "F" (the worst). Therefore, if five different insiders bought in the open market and three insiders exercised options, you would have a positive total of "8." And if two insiders sold stock in the same company over the same six months, the "2" would be subtracted from the "8" to give a total positive signal of "6." Since the positives greatly outweigh the negatives the newsletter would probably assign an "Insider Grade" of "A" to the company's stock. On the other end of the spectrum, if the insiders are only selling with no one buying, the company would probably get a "D" or "F." In the center, with a "C" or "D," you may find a situation where three insiders sold and only one insider bought, which would give the company a negative rating of "−2." Of course, the negative rating would be assigned even if the three insiders sold a total of 4,000 shares and the single buying insider had accumulated 500,000 shares over six months.

This grading formula is provided in each issue of the newsletter for about fifteen hundred different companies. Also, once a month a summary of the twenty stocks favored by the most

company officials is given. The newsletter never tells the prices
that insiders actually paid for their holdings. A hint about the
appropriate purchase price that "outside" investors should follow can be found in the newsletter's monthly updated model
portfolio. As each new company appears on the portfolio list,
the price per share at the point it was added to the portfolio is
shown. However, not all companies with an "Insiders Grade" of
"A" or those included on the list of twenty stocks favored by the
most company officials find their way into the model portfolio.
The newsletter uses another rating system—called "Investment
Rank"—to further narrow down its portfolio choices. The exact
weighting system that produces the "Investment Rank," which
assigns a rate from "9" (the best) down to "1" (the worst) for
each of the stocks covered in the newsletter, is a closely guarded
secret. In general terms, however, the "Investment Rank" is
based on an appraisal that includes insider activity plus the
company's "earnings history and predictions, relative strength
analysis, and other fundamental and technical considerations."

THE INSIDER OUTLOOK
120 Broadway
New York, NY 10271
(212) 349-2372
Twelve issues annually. One-year subscription: $195.

The authors of this book are the editors of The Insider Outlook,
which looks at both inside/insider and outside/insider trading.
Four or five companies are featured monthly and each stock
selected for inclusion usually will have had heavy insider
open-market and/or private transaction purchases over an extended period of time. The exact objective and subjective criteria used to choose the featured stocks are detailed in the last
section of this book.

For each featured stock, a summary of the insider transaction
specifics are provided—including name and position of the insider, the amount of shares involved in the trades, the prices
paid for shares and the dates of the trades. Besides the specifics
about the insider trades, recent news about the company that
may explain the reasons for the insiders' investments is given.
Also, as new developments affect previously featured selections, the newsletter details them—whether the "news" is addi-

tional insider buying or developments within the company that may affect the future value of the stock's price.

For an additional cost of fifteen dollars per request, subscribers will be sent a computer printout of all insider transactions in the last twelve months for any publicly traded company. An interpretation or analysis is not provided with this raw data, but by using the guidelines in the last section of this book, the computer printout can be analyzed to determine the insiders' current view of the company.

THE INSIDERS
3471 North Federal Highway
Fort Lauderdale, FL 33306
(800) 327-6720 [In Florida, call (305) 563-9000]
Twenty-four issues annually, published every two weeks. One-year subscription: $100.

Editor/publisher Norman Fosback first got interested in insiders while studying at Portland (Oregon) State University. One of his professors was Shannon Pratt, who, along with Charles DeVere, conducted one of the first statistical studies of the abnormal positive returns that insiders enjoy with their common stock trades. *The Insiders* follows inside/insider activity only. Schedule 13D filers (outside/insiders) do not receive any attention in this newsletter.

Through his study of inside/insider trading, Fosback has developed a weighting system he applies to *all* publicly traded stocks to come up with a rating index that grades each stock from "0" to "10." Those with a rating of "0" are considered the worst and should be sold (or certainly avoided). Those with a "10" are the newsletter's best candidates for investment. To come up with these ratings—of which about twenty-five hundred are printed in each issue, with the remaining unlisted companies carrying a "5" rating that is considered "neutral"— Fosback applies criteria such as evidence of open-market purchase, number of different insiders trading ("lone wolf" investing is not well thought of here), position of the insider within the company, size and the dates of the trades. Insiders trading in companies where there is insider buying industrywide are given extra consideration.

The ratings listing gives the name of the company and the

number of individual insiders who have bought or sold shares
in the past year as well as Fosback's rating. Like *Consensus of
Insiders, The Insiders* ratings list does not tell you the price
paid by insiders for their shares. However, insider transaction
details, including prices paid, from the past three months are
provided for all stocks with "8," "9" or "10" ratings. Also,
whenever a new buy recommendation appears in the newsletter
it is given a short descriptive analysis.

Besides the ratings and buy and sell recommendations, *The
Insiders* maintains a portfolio—which is beneficially owned by
associates of the Institute of Econometric Research—that tells
you what to buy, what to continue to hold and what to sell.

THE INSIDERS' CHRONICLE
P.O. Box 272977
Boca Raton, FL 33427
(305) 394-3404
Fifty issues annually (not published Thanksgiving and Christmas)
and four quarterly summaries. One-year subscription: $350.

Chronicle editor William Mehlman considers himself an investigative reporter and not an investment advisor. Instead of
making buy and sell recommendations, Mehlman identifies
significant insider activity—from both inside/insider Form 3
and Form 4 and from outside/insider Schedule 13D filings—
and then tries to find out the reasons behind it. Each issue of the
newsletter features a lengthy and in-depth analysis of one particularly interesting situation that has been favored by insider
purchases. The analysis looks at the company's fundamentals
and past stock performance record. It also provides the details
on any recent news developments or company announcements
that may affect the future direction of the stock—and could explain the insiders' purchases. Mehlman tries to talk with the
insiders themselves and if they are too tight-lipped, he'll talk
with analysts covering the company to see if they can provide
some insights. Sometimes he finds apparent reasons for the insiders' actions; other times the insider buying remains a mystery despite careful digging for publicly available information.

Besides the main "Insider Alert" article, which features off-
the-beaten-track companies you probably won't hear about in
the general financial news media, there are shorter descriptions
of six or so other insider favorites. A "Short Takes" column fo-

cuses on companies with outside/insider activity. And one page is devoted to quick analyses of four or five of the companies involved in the largest inside/insider purchases during the past few weeks.

Several pages of each issue provide a list of all open-market and private transaction buys and sells submitted to the SEC the week before. All companies listed on both major exchanges and traded over-the-counter are included, except for "penny stock" issues. Purchases made through option plans are excluded as are other transactions, such as gifts, that are of little interest to insider-watchers. This running compilation of the latest important filings can be a helpful initial screening source if you plan to take a more do-it-yourself approach to following insider investments. The newsletter's quarterly summaries provide a comprehensive list of all the transactions reported in each individual issue of the preceding three months.

Also included is a list of the previous week's initial Schedule 13D filings. Schedule 13D amendments, however, are not reported.

SPECIAL SITUATION REPORT
P.O. Box 167
Rochester, NY 14601
(716) 232-1240
Sixteen issues annually, published every three weeks. One-year subscription: $230.

The special situations covered in *Special Situation Report* are possible takeovers. Editor Charles LaLoggia watches Schedule 13D filings—and only Schedule 13D filings, with no interest in inside/insider activity—to find companies with stock that is being quietly and steadily purchased by well-known "raiders" or corporations in related businesses. LaLoggia ignores those initial Schedule 13Ds that have an accompanying notice of takeover intent. Instead, he concentrates on activity that hasn't made the business page headlines—yet.

Each issue contains a list of about two dozen "buy" recommendations. The recommendations stay on the list as buys until the actual takeover becomes official or until some other event occurs that makes a takeover unlikely. Then, the buys become "sells." A buy can be on the list for three or more years as the takeover machinery continues to churn.

As new takeover candidates are added to the list, short descriptive analyses explain LaLoggia's reasoning behind the recommendations. He looks at the past performance of the
outside/insider and the possible fundamental reasons for the interest in the target company. As an analyst interested in takeover action, LaLoggia ignores activity that simply looks like a
passive investment for potential capital gains on the part of the
outside/insider. Therefore, outside/insiders like Warren Buffett
or FMR Corporation, who tend to invest because of their fundamentalist reading of an undervalued stock, would not be
thought of as a "special situation."

Besides the recommendations based on Schedule 13D filings,
the newsletter also offers an editorial assessment of the market
as a whole. This stock market overview is primarily based on
LaLoggia's technical interpretation of past activity displayed in
various types of stock performance charts.

STREET SMART INVESTING
2651 Strang Boulevard
Yorktown Heights, NY 10598
(914) 962-4646
Twenty-four issues annually, published every two weeks. One-year
subscription: $350.

Schedule 13D filers are the focus of this advisory service. Investment signals are taken from well-known outside/insiders
like Carl Lindner, Carl Icahn and the Bass Brothers as well as
less well-known newcomers. Also, editor Kiril Sokoloff likes to
keep an eye on corporation investments into other companies
in related industries. Although outside/insider activity sparks
Sokoloff's initial interest in a company, he also checks on in-
side/insider trading for each of the companies he reports on.

Each issue features three or four lengthy descriptions of new
investment possibilities, which include detailed information on
the outside/insider's trades (dates of transactions, number of
shares purchased, amount of money invested) and background
on his past investment activities. Some fundamental analysis of
the possible reasons for the investment is also given. Sokoloff is
particularly attracted to situations involving investments by
several outside/insiders into the same company. In addition to
the featured companies, the newsletter provides follow-up information on four or five previously recommended companies.

VICKERS WEEKLY INSIDER REPORT
P.O. Box 59
Brookside, NJ 07926
(201) 539-1336
Fifty-one issues annually. One-year subscription: $137.

The *Vickers Weekly Insider Report* concentrates on providing data from Form 3 and Form 4 filings submitted to the SEC the week before, listing all open-market buy and sell trades of 500 or more shares on exchange-listed stocks. Over-the-counter trades are not reported unless they exceed 1,000 shares. Private transactions are listed only when they involve more than 10,000 shares. Pertinent trading information is given for each of the transactions listed: date of transaction, price, size of transaction, current size of holdings and name and position of insider. This raw data, which is sorted out to include most of the types of inside/insider transactions of interest, would be very useful to the do-it-yourselfer who wants to keep an eye on *all* insider investments—not just the ones featured as recommendations by this or other newsletters. (Following the guidelines in the final section of this book makes this possible.)

Besides transaction details, the newsletter also provides a "Weekly Insider Index" which rates about twelve hundred stocks according to the criteria of a weighting system that includes "number of buy or sell transactions; percentage of each transaction to an insider's total holdings; unanimity (all buys or all sales of any company)." The weighting system also takes into account the direction of the market as a whole and the performance of each industry. The ten companies getting the highest ratings in this index are identified separately as are the ten companies with the lowest ratings.

Also included each week is an editorial commentary by editor Ed Buck which usually focuses on the general current trading patterns of all insiders in all companies and the possible clues they may provide for predicting the direction of the market as a whole.

WEALTH MONITORS
Suite 220
1001 East 101st Terrace
Kansas City, MO 64131
(816) 941-7990
Twelve issues annually. One-year subscription: $250.

Like the analysts at *Special Situation Report* and *Street Smart Investing, Wealth Monitors* concentrates on Schedule 13D filers. But for editor/publisher Michael Lamb all Schedule 13D filers are not the same. He focuses on the two dozen or so outside/insider heavy hitters whom he calls the Power Investors. Among his current favorites are the Bass Brothers, Warren Buffett, Irwin Jacobs, Carl Lindner, Saul Steinberg and the Coniston Partners. Following these Power Investors, Lamb believes, offers the best opportunity for profit for average investors—more so than following other less well-known outside/insiders or corporation investments—because these people have the ability to "force the action" to make their own (and in turn your) investment pay off in a big way.

Each issue of the newsletter features about a dozen buy and sell recommendations, but Lamb doesn't recommend *every* company that his Power Investors have taken positions in. He weighs a company's fundamentals and other criteria such as the quality of management of the company before making a recommendation. Lamb rarely grasps onto an outside/insider's coattails upon an initial Schedule 13D filing. He usually waits until his Power Investors have dug their heels deeply into a situation.

The First Step

Clearly, all of these newsletters share the goal of identifying and assessing the "consistent patterns of unusual behavior" of insiders, although they go about it in somewhat different ways. Their value to you as an individual investor with a limited amount of time available to spend following insider investments is that they comb through tens of thousands of insider SEC reports every year to come up with those situations that hold the greatest promise. With this data in hand, you will have fulfilled the essential first step toward finding the investment selections that are best for you.

Chapter 10

Making Your Selections

IF you are new to the insider investment approach, you may be tempted, when you begin receiving insider advisory newsletters, to start investing immediately in the situations that they recommend or feature. Fight this temptation. There is no need to rush into any stock-buying program. Stock investments based on insider actions have been going on for years and will continue in the years ahead. Just because there appear to be some compelling investment choices today doesn't mean that those are the *best* choices you'll ever find or that other compelling choices will not appear tomorrow.

When the insiders invest in a way that shows us an aggressive and bullish attitude about the future of their company's stock, they have made reasoned, unemotional business decisions about their investments. You should be equally reasonable and unemotional about *your* investments, if not more so. If you are not completely confident about a possible investment candidate, don't buy it. You don't want to lose sleep over any investment decision you make. It's not necessary.

The insider investment strategy is not dependent on making split-second decisions and jumping in and out of the market to make the profits you are looking for. Remember the laws regulating how insiders can invest make them take the view of the potential *long-term capital gain* appreciation of their investments. You, when you follow insiders, must also take this long-term perspective. When you buy a stock based on insider actions, you are making a long-term commitment because you will never know in advance how long it will take before the pay off comes. You could be lucky and a stock you buy might pay off in a couple of weeks, but it could take a couple of years. If you are hesitant about making a commitment like this for a particular stock, then just don't buy it. Despite the positive returns others have enjoyed by following the insider strategy over the years, you should never allow yourself to be caught up in any kind of feverish attitude that takes away from an objective investment stance.

When using insider advisory newsletters as your source of information about insider activities and possible investments for your own stock portfolio, there are two ways you can approach the information. The first way is somewhat passive. Here you would find a newsletter that you feel completely comfortable with—both in terms of its philosophical approach to insider investing and the criteria used to assess the "consistent pattern of unusual behavior" that points the way to interesting investment opportunities. Then you would follow the newsletter's buy and sell recommendations exactly as presented. This approach requires the least amount of time on your part—as long as you have the financial flexibility to invest near the time that the newsletter makes its recommendations. And, obviously, if you can afford several such newsletters, there is a clear advantage to focusing on only those stocks favored in common by all.

The second approach to advisory newsletter information is to apply more screening tests to the recommendations, cutting down the list to find the ones that hold the greatest potential for future stock price appreciation. This approach requires more time on your part in "reading" the newsletters and analyzing the information in them. But the time required to do this carefully isn't all that great and it will give you a list of investment candidates that exceeds the basic selection criteria of the newsletter.

Following Newsletter Recommendations

As you saw in the last chapter, there is a wide difference in the criteria used by the various insider advisory newsletters in selecting the insider situations to recommend or feature. Some require more stringent insider investment evidence than others before a recommendation is made. However, you can feel assured that at the very minimum the newsletters match the criteria used by academics in their statistical studies of insider investments. And since those studies almost universally found that insiders as a group reap abnormal positive returns on their investments, you can reasonably expect to find the same type of performance in your own portfolio if you follow just about any of the currently published insider newsletters and their recommendations.

Of course, no newsletter will promise or guarantee any type of returns. It's against the law—both the law of the government and the law of common sense—for anyone to make such promises. But even if you do take this passive approach in following newsletter recommendations with your own investments, there are two rules you should follow:

- Make sure you purchase shares close to the prices paid by the insiders themselves.

- Wait at least two weeks following receipt of the newsletter recommendation before buying.

The single most important factor that will affect your success in following the insiders is buying your shares at prices that match—or nearly match—the prices the insiders paid. This is the price that they consider to be a bargain. A stock's price at the time a newsletter is printed or its price at the time you receive the newsletter could be very different from the insiders' own purchase price. Your newsletter *must* tell you about the prices insiders paid or you do not have the information you need to make a good investment decision. If your newsletter does not give you this data somewhere on its pages, cancel the subscription and get another newsletter.

We recommended earlier that you could consider buying your own shares at a price over an insider's highest purchase price by up to 25 percent and still feel comfortable about the future price appreciation of your holdings. However, if you are passively following an advisory newsletter's recommendation without any further tests of the insiders' aggressive buying patterns, you generally would not want to pay this premium for your shares. Save premium buying for those situations in which insider buying behavior overwhelmingly points to a certain outcome. You cannot be sure of this, however, if you are just following a newsletter's recommendation passively.

The second rule governing this passive approach is not to buy too quickly. A newsletter's recommendation can be a very powerful thing. With some lightly traded stocks, a hundred or even fewer people buying the stock can cause a sharp demand that is unusual and that will quickly raise the price. The newsletter's recommendation alone may very well cause a stock's price to go up quickly—sometimes in a matter of hours after the recommendation is published. Don't be impetuous. Wait. Within a few weeks, a stock that had been neglected prior to a newsletter recommendation will most likely return to being neglected after the newsletter's subscribers have bought. At that point, its price will go down—possibly to levels *lower* than prior to the newsletter recommendation. That's when you can pick up your bargains.

Remember, the insider buying activity as well as the newsletter recommendation are not the real reasons that a stock becomes reevaluated in the stock market. We have to wait until the corporate development on which the insiders based their investment decisions occurs and the "efficient" aspect of the market recognizes the true—and new—value of the stock before we can expect payday on our selections. So, wait at least two weeks after you get your newsletter recommendation. If, after that time, the stock's price is at an acceptable level as defined by the insiders' own purchase price, and if it is not showing increased volume of trading or rising prices, then go ahead and buy. But if you see the price going up, wait some more. It may be three weeks or three months before the price goes down again to an acceptable level. But that's OK, because as we know there is no need to rush. One of our golden rules can be expanded on: Don't jump with your investment dollars at the first twitch of an insider's movement or a newsletter's recommendation.

More Stringent Selection Tests

Although almost every advisory newsletter can be valuable in pointing you in the direction of insider favorites, there aren't many individual investors who can add all of them to their portfolios. Newsletters are constantly coming up with new recommendations—otherwise they wouldn't be called *newsletters*. *The Insiders' Chronicle,* for example, features more than fifty in-depth analyses of different companies in a year, as does our own *Insider Outlook. The Insiders'* model portfolio can typically include forty or so different stocks. If you're like most individual investors you won't be able to invest in that many situations and, in fact, it isn't a very good idea to have a portfolio with so many different stocks. So, you'll need to cut that list down to size.

Some of the recommendations you come across will automatically have to be discarded because you will not be able to buy into them when the stock's price is not near the insiders' own purchase price. But even taking that dynamic into account, you probably will still have too many choices.

To sift out the best candidates from among your newsletter's recommendations, let's apply a little logic. Since a newsletter's initial recommendation of a stock is based on some criteria that in some way measure insider trading actions in terms of quantity of shares involved, frequency of trades and/or aggressiveness, if the same stock gets a repeated recommendation, *based on new evidence of continued insider buying,* then that situation shows even more insider aggressiveness. And those insider investment candidates that show the greatest number of repeated newsletter recommendations over time hold the greatest probable favorable outcome. In other words, if insider behavior fulfills a newsletter's criteria for a stock recommendation once, it's an even better choice for you if it fulfills the same selection criteria twice or even more times.

Here is a six-step game plan for using your newsletter to find the most aggressively traded stocks from among its recommendations or featured selections. The screening work necessary on your part shouldn't take more than a few hours every six months:

Step One: Gather at least six consecutive months of issues of your newsletter. If you are just starting with a newsletter subscription do not act on any of the recommendations for at least six months. You can read the newsletters as they are delivered, but save them. In fact, you may want to consider leaving them unopened for six months until you are ready to review the insider activities they report at the end of this period. Or you could request that your subscription start with the last six months of previously published issues so that you can begin your screening tests when you receive them.

Step Two: Make a list that includes each stock that has been recommended or featured in the issues published during those six months. Put your newsletters in chronological order with the oldest issue on top. Get a few sheets of paper and write down in a column the names of companies's stocks as they are *first* recommended or featured in your newsletter. At this point include the name of a company only once—even though you may see the name mentioned again in subsequent issues. And don't pay any attention to the analysis the newsletter may provide. (You might want to try to put the names in alphabetical order so that you can find them quickly later.) If your newsletter has a "model portfolio" of previously recommended stocks, put *all* of those on your master list as well.

Step Three: Each time the newsletter reports evidence of NEW insider buying at a company on your master list, put a check mark beside the company's name. Start back with the oldest newsletter issue. Disregarding the first time the company is mentioned as a recommendation or as a featured stock, find evidence of additional insider buying at any of the companies on your master list. In some cases this will be in the form of a descriptive discussion of the company in your newsletter; for example, "Once again we see insider buying at..." Or it could be shown in raw data form. For example, *The Insiders' Chronicle* does not provide follow-up discussions of previously featured companies, but it does print a fairly comprehensive list of the insider SEC filings from the week before in each issue. Look to this list for evidence of *new* insider buying on previously featured companies. This same type of data can be found in *Vickers Weekly Insider Report.* Whatever newsletter you have, look in every possible spot for this additional report on continued insider buying. And every time you find a new piece of evidence or a repeated recommendation based on new evidence, put a check mark next to the name of the company on your master list. (You might also want to note the issue date of the newsletter that showed this new evidence or recommendation so that you can refer to that issue later.)

Do not, however, put a check mark next to a company's name if the newsletter recommendation is simply a reiteration of an old recommendation based on the same insider activity that it originally used to make its selection. Instead, you want to focus on the *new and additional* insider buying that goes beyond the newsletter's original recommendation.

Step Four: Isolate the companies with the greatest number of check marks on your master list from those with no or very few additional notations of continued insider buying. Sometimes the companies on your list will see two, three or four additional check marks that indicate more insider buying beyond the newsletter's original recommendation criteria. (If you subscribe to a weekly or biweekly newsletter you may find your highest scoring companies getting ten or more check marks.) Quite simply, the companies on your master list with the greatest number of check marks are your best investment candidates. The companies on the low scoring end with few or no check marks— and most of the names on your list will be in this category—should be put aside, at least for now. Concentrate on the highest-scoring candidates. These are the ones that show the greatest amount of aggressive insider activity.

If you find that none of the names on your master list receives any additional insider signals during the six-month scoring period, which is highly unlikely, then just keep watching your newsletter issues until the names do show up again. Admittedly, this is a very conservative and cautious way of sorting out advisory newsletter recommendations. But it identifies those situations that exceed the original recommendation standards of your newsletter. And with this approach you can be more certain about the probability of a successful outcome with your own investments because your high-scoring candidates will have insiders working for you who have more at stake than the lower-scoring candidates. While this additional screening procedure can help you predict the *probability* of a successful outcome from among possible choices, it cannot predict the *degree* of the successful outcome. Candidates with low "scores" that ultimately enjoy a successful outcome may very well appreciate in value at a higher rate (and faster) than your best-"scoring" candidates. But by following the most conservative and cautious route you minimize risk. And while you may find that it is a little discouraging to see some big fish get away, you should be content that over time you will net enough big fish to make the total catch a good one.

Step Five: Compare the trading activity at your highest-scoring candidates to find the best ones among them. With the names of your best candidates in hand, go back through the

newsletters and take a very close look at the insider trading data
the newsletter tells you about. Look at *all* of the trading data as
far back as possible, not just within the last six months. You're
looking at the complete overall picture now. Then rank your
candidates based on this data, using the general rules of thumb
you have read about in this book. That means, for example,
those companies where there has been buying by both inside/
insiders and outside/insiders, or where there are two or more
outside/insiders investing would go to the top of your investment candidate-ranking list. Or if there is only inside/insider
trading, then look at *who* is buying, *how much* they have bought
and the percentage of the *increase in their holdings* during their
accumulation period. As we've seen, heavy buying concentrated
among top-level insiders is more significant than that by lower-
level insiders. Bigger purchases are more important than
smaller purchases, but not if the smaller purchases add up to a
very large one. And if insiders at one company increase their
holdings by 200 percent or 300 percent, it is much more interesting than buying that increases an insider's holdings only by
10 percent—even when the 10 percent increase involved more
shares or more money than the situations with higher percentage increases.

Try to consider all of the various ways for judging aggressive
insider buying. Your very best candidates should quickly pop
out at you if you have absorbed the concepts described in earlier
chapters. And finally, after you have identified your best investment choice (or choices), you must also look at the current market price compared to the prices paid by the insiders themselves
before making your own buying move.

Step Six: Repeat the screening process. You can wait six
months or so and let your newsletters gather in the corner before sorting through them in the way we have outlined. Or you
can read each newsletter as it arrives and continue the scoring
procedures on a routine basis. Whatever you do, keep your original master list, including the names of the companies that you
discarded previously. Add new recommendations as they come
and score every company as it receives repeated notices of new
buying by insiders. After some experience, you will evolve your
own scoring patterns for selecting the most compelling investment choices from your newsletter. You may notice, for example, whenever a newsletter recommendation receives five
additional mentions of continued insider buying, that is the

level of aggressiveness you need to see before you make your own investment. Or it could be only three additional mentions or maybe up to ten. It all depends on the newsletter you use and your own investment personality. Don't jump to conclusions about any pattern, however, after just six months of scoring the various potential candidates. A year's worth of newsletter reading would be better.

Narrowing the Field Further

Even with this very conservative and stringent approach to selecting the best investment candidates, you may still find that there are too many selections for you to invest in at a particular moment. Yet, there comes a point when all of the various investment candidates you've found are equally excellent. Using advisory newsletter recommendations and applying additional screening criteria for judging the insider's view of the future value of a company's stock could lead you to several dozen or more compelling investment possibilities in a year. (If you follow the guidelines outlined in the final section of this book, you could come up with several hundred or more in a year.) At The Insider Reports Fund we invest in as many of these as possible, but as an individual investor you must continue to pare this list down.

There are a few different commonsense approaches you can use to do this. But, before getting into those, there are a few approaches that you should *not* use to cut your list of investment candidates down to size.

First, don't automatically assume that the situations involving insider investments with the largest amounts of money are the best. Consider these two hypothetical situations. You find out that the Bass Brothers invested $20 million for 11 percent of Jack and Jill Pail Company. At the same time you see that Joe Smith, president of Zippity-Do-Dah Southern Baked Pies, and Billy Jones, chairman of the company's board, have invested a total of $300,000 in the stock of their company. Both situations, you decide, fulfill the criteria of aggressiveness, consistency, and so forth. Which one of these two—based solely on the activities of the insiders—is the better investment choice for you?

The answer is that you can't tell. In fact, both are still equally good investment choices. The Bass Brothers' $20 million investment represents money that is a relative drop in the bucket compared to the total assets they control. The $300,000 investment by Smith and Jones could very well be their total investment worth. Although the Bass Brothers don't like to lose, their money is spread out over many different investments and they can assume more risk with any single one of their investments than Smith and Jones can with their investments. That could lead you to the logical conclusion that Smith and Jones are more certain of the profitable outcome of their investment and therefore the selection of Zippity-Do-Dah is a better choice for you than Jack and Jill Pail. But, on the other hand, we know that the Bass Brothers have a fairly consistent history of picking winners while we know nothing or very little of the past investment experience of Smith and Jones. So, that leads us back to the conclusion that both of these situations are pretty much equal.

The second pitfall that you should avoid when narrowing down investment choices is to pick *only* companies you have heard of or that make products or provide services you are familiar with. Aggressive insider activity at "blue-chip" or "big board" corporations is no better than aggressive insider activity at small, currently obscure over-the-counter companies. And don't think that just because you personally like a company's products or services that that has anything whatsoever to do with an investment decision. Being impressed with a company's name or its products is an emotional reaction. If you focus on companies that impress you, you run the very real risk of having your image of the company color your reading of the insider activity. You may end up talking yourself into seeing aggressive insider trading that is not really there. You will also be missing the valid activity at less well-known companies. You must, therefore, maintain complete objectivity. This is one of the most difficult hurdles for the average investor to conquer.

You may think this piece of advice goes against the old adage that says to "invest in what you know best." But remember that in the context of the insider investment strategy, you are not investing in what *you* know best but rather are investing with those people who are investing in what *they* know best. And they know it better than *anyone* else.

In fact, to invest successfully with the insider investment strategy, you don't even have to know what business the company is in. All you need to do is keep an objective eye on the trading activity of the insiders and leave it to *them* to know what business they are in. In short, when you encounter evidence of a "consistent pattern of unusual behavior" at a well-known company, don't think that it is somehow better or will precede a more certain positive outcome than the aggressive insider behavior at a company you've never heard of. The situations remain equal.

You are particularly susceptible to yet another pitfall if you are an adherent to some other investment strategy. That is, don't think you can use criteria from traditional forms of fundamental or technical analysis to "confirm" the investment decisions of insiders. To think that can be presumptuous. It assumes that you have the ability to look at fundamental data—such as the information found in a company's balance sheet as published in its annual report—or to chart a company's past stock performance and discover something that the insiders are not already aware of. You can be assured that the insiders are very familiar with their companies' fundamentals and their past stock performance patterns. Doesn't it make simple common sense that an insider will assimilate all the fundamental and stock performance data available before buying stock in an aggressive way that displays a "consistent pattern of unusual behavior?" If you were an insider, wouldn't *you* take into account your company's past balance sheet and stock performance before investing? Of course, it makes plain common sense. And, of course, you would use all the information at hand before investing heavily in your own company.

Sometimes insiders appear to be investing *because of* the company's fundamentals or past stock performance. Other times, they apparently invest *despite* the readily available evidence you can find through traditional forms of fundamental or technical analysis. If, for example, you identify an interesting insider buying situation and look at its fundamentals and see that the company's stock is selling below its book value or has a low P/E ratio, you can feel reassured that you have been directed to an undervalued stock in a traditional fundamental sense. When you do see these positive traditional fundamental signs for an undervalued stock—and your advisory newsletter will often point them out—you can consider this an extra "plus" in evaluating your various candidates.

On the other hand, if the stock that the insiders favor is selling *above* book value or has a *high* P/E ratio or even is showing losses, you should not automatically dismiss the situation. These insiders may be investing based on a company's assets that are not fully reflected in the published data that is used to determine its book value. As we've seen in several examples already, a company's true value can be hidden for years until an event takes place that reveals its *real* value. Often this involves real estate that is carried on a company's books as being much less valuable than its actual current market worth. And when we look at a P/E ratio, we must never forget that it is based on *past* performance, while the insider has knowledge (or at least a very good idea) about the company's probable *future* earnings performance. So, a P/E ratio that looks high today because of last year's earnings may suddenly look very low when some future earnings report is made public.

When using technical analysis techniques, you could also be given the wrong impression about the potential future direction of the company's stock. As a technician, you would probably not be interested in a stock that is falling. But an insider-watcher who sees heavy buying by insiders as the price of a stock goes down can read that to mean the insiders see the stock as a bargain that will at some time in the future regain its popularity or even surpass its past performance when the favorable events they anticipate occur. Often, however, you will see insiders buying when the past stock performance would look flat if it were charted. Technical analysts would not be interested in companies with little or no up-and-down activity. But the insiders undoubtedly are investing in those situations because they expect something to happen in the future that will make their stock break away from the past flat performance. Certainly we can assume that no sane insider invests in order to lose money. Mistakes, yes; financial suicide, no.

Therefore, positive signals from traditional forms of fundamental and technical analysis can be emotionally reassuring "confirmations" of aggressive insider buying for an "outside" investor. But they shouldn't be the deciding factors for choosing between a company with seemingly "good" traditional analysis evidence and a company with "bad-looking" data. All of those traditional measurements are irrelevant when you consider that the insider has already taken them into consideration while he looks *forward* to the future event or events involving his company that we cannot legally predict through any type of measurement of past corporate or stock price performance. "Good" traditional measurements or "bad," companies with equal insider evidence of a "consistent pattern of unusual behavior" remain equally compelling investment candidates for you.

Now that you have an idea of how *not* to cut down your list of excellent investment possibilities, here are three different approaches you could use successfully to pick from the list of *already prequalified* candidates:

1. *"Good news clues."* With this approach you attempt to find publicly available news items that apparently explain the reasons behind the insiders' heavy buying and then invest in the companies with the best news about possible future corporate developments.

2. *"No news is good news."* Here you take a contrarian point of view and invest in insider favorites where there is *no* apparent reason for the insider activity—or even when there is bad news being spread about the company at the same time the insiders are investing heavily.

3. *"Bet the jockey."* Since your investment hinges on the accuracy of the insiders' investment decision, you could use this approach and find out everything there is to know about the insiders involved in the trading at the companies you're watching. You can attempt to trace their past history of investment success, their experience in the field they are investing in and their connections with other related companies. Those people you feel most comfortable with may be the "investment advisors" to follow. This is a particularly strong approach in outside/insider screening.

Each of these three approaches makes sense within the insider investment strategy. You can choose the approach you want to take based on your own investment temperament, whether you are conservative or have a more speculative bent. Actually as you become more experienced with following insiders you will probably find that the best way to pick your finalists is to use all three approaches in varying degrees depending on the situation.

These three different approaches, which we'll look at more carefully soon, require information beyond the data of insider trading activity. Often this additional information will be provided by your advisory newsletter in an analysis description of recommended stocks. When the information is not available in your newsletter, you can usually get what you need from your stockbroker—if you use a "full-service" brokerage firm as opposed to a "discount" broker. When you use a full-service broker you are paying a full premium commission on your stock purchases. That commission goes to support research departments and the apparatus that stands behind providing investment information and advice to clients. (A discount broker simply executes the buy and sell orders you place and normally will not provide any additional service.)

Don't be shy about asking your full-service broker the few simple questions that the screening approaches we will discuss require. If your broker balks at giving you this information or if he implies that you're being a pain in the neck, get another broker. On the other hand, don't abuse your broker by being too demanding. If you've narrowed your investment selections down to two or three, asking your broker for some additional information on those companies is justifiable. But don't give him a list of twenty or thirty different companies and expect to be greeted with enthusiasm. And don't pressure the broker to get you the information you request by noon or the next morning. You don't need anything that fast. Your full-service broker can be a very good friend and resource if you both respect the boundaries of the relationship.

If you want to take a more do-it-yourself approach and save money by using a discount brokerage firm to carry out your buy and sell orders, you are going to have to take a short trip to the library to find the additional information not provided in your newsletter. Or, if you have a computer hookup to financial data bases, you will have to spend a few minutes doing data base research for the information.

Let's look now at the three different final screening approaches more closely and at the types of additional information you need to gather.

1. "Good news clues."

While you can never know as much as an insider, there are some situations where you will be able to find a positive piece of news about a company that appears to be connected with the aggressive insider buying that you see. Usually, however, that piece of news is *not* headline material. Instead, it is a seemingly insignificant item that doesn't have an immediate effect on the company's fortunes but could have a dramatic impact on its future.

For example: If you had been following insider activity during the last half of 1986, you might have noticed a flurry of buying at Showboat, Inc. Showboat, Inc., which is listed on the New York Stock Exchange, operates the Showboat Casino/Hotel and Country Club in Las Vegas. During the first seven months of 1986, three directors of the company, two of whom also held top-level officer positions, reported open-market purchases of a total of nearly 8,000 shares at prices between $16⅞ and $20⅛. The total amount the three insiders spent for these shares was about $152,000—an average cost per share of approximately $19. This wasn't a spectacular display of insider buying, but it certainly was positive. At the same time, however, there was a large outside/insider open-market purchase of about 270,000 shares at a total cost of about $5.4 million (approximately $20⅛ per share) by FMR Corporation and Fidelity International, which, of course, are two of the investment vehicles controlled by Ned Johnson of Fidelity mutual fund fame.

Why was all this inside/insider and outside/insider investing going on? While we can't know *exactly* the reasons behind it, if you had researched news announcements from the company during the first half of 1986, you would have found that it had revealed plans to build a large casino/hotel complex in Atlantic City. Barring unforeseen difficulties, the company expected to open the facility in late 1987. This new casino/hotel would about double the company's money-making capacity. And considering the success that Showboat has had with its Las Vegas operations, the company could also about double its profitability by the end of the decade. When (and if) this happens, Showboat as a company will certainly be worth more than it was when it was only operating one gambling facility. And its stock price can be expected to respond to this change.

Knowing the news about the company's plans for Atlantic City, you could say that there was an *apparent* reason that explained the insider investments. They invested in 1986 at about $20 a share in the expectation that in the future other investors will also find the company a valuable investment choice. Most investors, as we know, will wait until the new casino/hotel actually opens or until there is proof that the company does indeed increase its profitability. But it seems that the

inside/insiders and the outside/insiders had enough faith in the
probability of success in Showboat's Atlantic City venture to say
to us through their investment activity that at $20 a share the
company was a bargain.

The important thing to see in this example is that the news
item that apparently explains the reason for the insiders' actions
had something to do with the company's *future* performance.
Not *past* performance. Showboat's past earnings, dividends and
so forth through 1986 were stable, but there was nothing to tell
you that the future would be significantly different. Therefore,
when you go looking for good news items or information about
the company that explains insider activity, watch only for
stories that project the company's fortunes *forward*. For example, an announcement of a new product that has not been mar-
keted or is just new on the market. Or a restructuring of the
company's debt that could put it on a stronger financial footing
in the future. Or a realignment of top management or an infusion of new management. Or an announcement of the company's involvement in a new, yet related, aspect of its primary
business.

Think new. Ignore the past—no matter how glorious or dismal. The past is history—it is dead except for the "past" track
record of the players. They are insiders who are looking only
forward, and "new" developments that are announced are the
things that could explain bullish insider activity.

If you are a conservative investor, sorting your insider investment candidates based on news announcements that seem to
explain *why* the insiders are investing is possibly your best approach. Remember, however, the information you find out may
not be the real reasons behind the insider investments. They are
simply *apparent* reasons. But these apparent reasons can in a
sense "confirm" in your own mind that the insiders are investing based on a concrete expectation of a future development.
Also, the "good news clues" can sometimes give you a timetable
for your investment appreciation.

In the Showboat, Inc. case, for example, you know that the
Atlantic City operation is not likely to open until late 1987 or
early 1988 and it will take at least a year of operations before the
evidence of profitability will prove to most investors what the
insiders already apparently expected back in 1986. This means
that the big return may not occur until 1989 or even 1990. By
that time, of course, the company's stock probably will no

longer be a "bargain." And that most likely is the reason the insiders invested in 1986. These insiders may actually continue their purchases if they see that the stock remains a bargain. But when a great number of other investors jump in and raise the stock's price, it will be too late to buy it and expect a big future return, unless the company announces some other plan in the meantime to expand beyond the Atlantic City operation. But, you, as an insider-watcher, may have seriously considered a 1986 investment into Showboat, because you have the patience to wait—just like the insiders. (Actually, as it turned out, the Atlantic City facility opened in March 1987. And in May 1987, Showboat's stock price hovered at about $30 before the company split its stock two for one in early June—all of which delivered a gain for the insiders and the investors who followed the insiders of about 50 percent in less than a year.)

Information you'll need: When reading the analysis of a company in your newsletter, look for coverage about the announcements the company may have made about *future* developments. Again, ignore the reporting about *past* performance, including traditional fundamental measurements of a company's current health. If your newsletter tells you about an impending development but qualifies the potentially good *future* news by pointing out possible risks, you should focus on the *positive* aspects of the news since that is why the insiders are making their own buying move. For example, in the Showboat, Inc. story there are many possible things that could go wrong before the company's Atlantic City casino/hotel becomes profitable. But the insiders have certainly weighed those potential risks and decided that a profitable return on their investments was more probable than loss.

If there is no indication in your newsletter about publicly announced developments and if you have an established relationship with a full-service broker, ask the broker: "Have there been any announcements or developments coming from XYZ Company in the last few months." (It is advisable to gather news like this from at least the previous six months—the last year is even better.) The broker may come back to you with only a brief answer such as "Showboat announced that it's going to build a casino in Atlantic City next year." Usually that type of response should be enough for you to connect the announcement as the apparent reason for the insiders' investments. Other times the news may sound negative, but is really positive. For example, "It announced that it is restructuring its debt" or "New management has taken over." But here again, you should view such news from the positive angle.

For the do-it-yourself approach involving a trip to the library, there are two steps to researching the companies on your list. First, you look for the company's name in bibliographic indexes of newspapers and periodicals. After identifying articles about the company, you then get your hands on the complete article which you must read through for those "good news clues."

The two primary bibliographic indexes you will use are the *National Newspaper Index* and *Business Periodicals Index*. *National Newspaper Index* provides a detailed indexing of the *Christian Science Monitor, The New York Times* and *The Wall Street Journal*. *Business Periodicals Index* covers a broad range of business publications including *Fortune, Forbes* and *Barron's* as well as specialized business magazines and journals. (If you are not familiar with library research techniques, ask the librarian to help guide you to the proper sources. But don't settle for a company's annual report. You want *news*, not accounting figures and self-serving stories about a company's past performance.)

A more completely comprehensive source, which includes news that you will find in national publications as well as the company announcements which never appeared in general circulation publications, is Standard & Poor's Corporation Records *Daily News* and *Cumulative News*. (These are the sources your broker will most likely use to answer your questions.) Ask your librarian how to use these sources for news items of the companies on your potential investment list. While these Standard & Poor's sources are more comprehensive, the news reported is greatly abbreviated in form and will not usually be as detailed as the news reports you find in national publications. So, don't use the Standard & Poor's sources to the exclusion of the other bibliographic indexes and the original articles found in national publications. And when checking for publicly announced news, you should research from the present back to about a year prior to the date of the initial insider buying transaction which started the "consistent pattern of unusual behavior" that sparked your interest in the company in the first place.

If you have access to computer on-line data bases, the procedures you follow to find "good news clues" are very similar to the ones you use when turning to the printed sources of information found in a library. For example, if you are a subscriber to the Dow Jones News/Retrieval (see Chapter 15 for details), you can use the data base's Text-Search Services. With this data base all you need to do is type in the name of the company you want to research and you will be shown all the news stories that mentioned the company in *The Wall Street Journal* since 1984 as well as in selected stories from *Barron's* and from the Dow Jones News Wire Service since June 1979. Similar services are available on ADP Network Services, Quotron, Dialog and Knowledge Index.

2. *"No news is good news."*

One of the major strengths of the insider investing strategy is that it points the way to companies that are currently neglected or at least underappreciated by most stock market investors. This factor of neglect or underappreciation is the reason that a company's stock is the "bargain" that heavy insider buying indicates it is. Insiders through their buying activities tell us that they consider the company's stock to be undervalued and that at some time in the future they will cash in on the real value either through sale, merger or liquidation—or when other investors come to recognize the true full value of the stock and through *their* buying elevate its price.

It stands to reason, therefore, that the more an insider favorite is neglected or underappreciated, the greater the "bargain." And, it stands to reason, that the more a company's stock is a "bargain" today because of neglect, the greater is the potential for a dramatic price increase when a positive corporate development occurs and the company is "discovered."

One important measurement of neglect is the *absence* of publicly available news about a company. Out of necessity, the less information investors have about a company, the less opportunity they have to react—which keeps a company "neglected." You can take that thought a step further. The more negative the publicly available news about a company is, the more disfavor its stock gathers from the bulk of investors.

When either of these two elements—the absence of news or negative news—occurs concurrently with evidence of heavy insider buying it tells us something important: The insiders have reasons to believe that the company's current status of intensive neglect—caused by no news—or investor disfavor—caused by negative news—is unwarranted in view of future corporate developments. Thus, the "no news is good news" approach to sorting out excellent insider investment candidates completely turns around the "good news clues" approach. Now the *less* you can find out about a company or the *worse* the news coinciding with heavy insider buying the *better*.

There are two other measurements you can use to determine the degree of neglect or the amount of disfavor a company is currently experiencing. The first is to find out how many professional securities analysts are following the company. The fewer their number, the more neglected the company is. The second measurement is to find out the number of institutional investors—such as banks, mutual funds and insurance companies—that hold stock in the company. The smaller the amount of institutional investor holdings, the more disfavored the company is.

Therefore, no news, bad news, few securities analysts and a small amount of institutional investment all can be considered positive signals when there is evidence of heavy insider buying at the company. This is a variation on a contrarian strategist's approach. Because a company is so neglected and disfavored now, when the positive corporate development occurs in the future—as predicted through the evidence of heavy insider buying—it will be a much more startling surprise to the vast majority of investors than are situations where "good news clues" have been publicly available to *any* investor willing to pay attention to them. And that could mean that the neglected or disfavored company's stock will rise with a much more dramatic percentage when the positive corporate development becomes evident.

This approach to sorting out your best investment candidates may seem more speculative than the "good news clues" approach. That's because there's nothing to hold on to as a *reason* for investing in the company—other than the evidence of insider buying. But if you accept the original truisms that insiders know more about the *future* value of their company's stock and consistently profit from their investments, this "no news is good news" approach is really no more speculative. It is clear, however, that it requires strong nerves and self-confidence, particularly when the stock you buy does nothing during its "cooking period" while the market as a whole goes through the roof, as it did in 1986 and early 1987. Actually, many of the examples you've already read about fit into this category of great neglect and/or disfavor, including A&P, Hadson Petroleum, Oppenheimer Industries, United Merchants & Manufacturers and RB Industries.

Information you'll need: You may read in the your newsletter something like this: "Insiders are buying at XYZ Company despite four consecutive quarters of ever-lower earnings." Jump on that bad news if you follow this final screening approach. Or if the newsletter routinely provides news of its recommendations and can't find anything about the company that is newsworthy, you can consider that a positive signal as well.

When working with your full-service broker, the questions to ask are: "Have there been any announcements or news developments at XYZ Company in the last few months? How many different institutional investors hold stock in the company and how many financial analysts are covering the company? Does your firm have any research reports on the company?" Then judge the broker's responses in view of the way they measure neglect and/or disfavor. If there aren't any news items available or if the recent developments at the company are negative, that tells you the company could be experiencing both neglect or disfavor. As a rule of thumb, if fewer than five institutional investors are currently holding stock in the company, it is a sign that the company is in disfavor. If fewer than five financial analysts are covering the company, you can consider it greatly neglected. If there are more than twenty-five analysts covering the company, it probably isn't neglected at all. If your full-service brokerage firm does not have any research reports on the company, that's another sign of neglect.

If you are following the "no news is good news" approach, the more negative the responses to these questions, the better your insider investment candidate should look to you. The difficult part here is the psychological strain you will have to learn to endure. Paradoxically, when the situation looks its worst, it really is at its best for buying—always, of course, with adequate insider "support."

For the do-it-yourselfer using library or computer data base sources, the process for research is the same as for the "good news clues" approach: check the *National Newspaper Index*, *Business Periodicals Index*, Standard & Poor's *Daily News* and

Cumulative News or the on-line data base equivalents. With this approach, of course, the less you find out or the more bad-sounding the news, the better your investment candidate would appear to be.

To find out information about the other two measurements of a company's neglect and/or investor disfavor—the number of securities analysts and the amount of institutional investment —the first source you should check is *Neilson's Directory of Wall Street Research,* which you should be able to find in the business section of most large public libraries. This directory lists all companies that receive research coverage by one or more security analysts. It also lists the names of the institutional investors holding stock in each of the companies and the amount of stock held.

Although the Neilson's directory is comprehensive, this annual publication's information is at least a year old. More up-to-date information on the degree of neglect from analysts can be found in Standard & Poor's weekly *Earnings Forecaster.* If your investment candidate is not listed in this, or if only a few analysts are reporting earnings estimates, you can consider the company to be greatly neglected. Current institutional investing is tracked monthly in Standard & Poor's *Stock Guide.* Again, the smaller the amount of investment by these organizations the better. And watch for a drop in institutional investment from one month to the next. The sharper the drop, the more disfavor the company is attracting and the more interesting the concurrent heavy insider buying becomes.

3. *"Bet the jockey."*

At the racetrack, one popular betting strategy is to review the track records of the jockeys in each race and then bet on the horse being ridden by the jockey who has the best history of bringing home the greatest number of winners with the highest total purses. This same approach can be used to sort out your best insider investment candidates.

You have already done this to a certain degree when you initially screen investment possibilities by giving greater weight to the activities of top-level inside/insiders than to lower-level executives and by paying special attention to outside/insiders with whom you are familiar. At this point, however, you may want to carry this type of judgment even further. To "bet the jockey" you want to know everything you can about the past career and investment performance of the people you are betting with. What is their experience? How long have they been in the industry of the company that they are investing in? How successful have they been? Have their careers and past investments been erratic or consistent? Are they involved with companies other than the one they are investing in? Are those companies in the same or related businesses? Do you feel comfortable with their past career, management and investment decisions?

The "bet the jockey" approach can be used alone or it can be used in combination with either of the two approaches discussed previously. Knowing exactly *whom* you are betting with adds another dimension to those two other methods of narrowing down your investment choices.

When assessing the background of inside/insiders you will want to look at the possible ways they are involved in other companies. For example, if you find out that Billy Jones of the Zippity-Do-Dah pie factory is also on the board of directors of General Mills, you might want to apply greater credence to his investment decision than you would if he weren't involved in any other company or if he were on the board of directors of a river dredging company. Or you may find that your "jockey" is on the board of directors of several different companies. (It's not uncommon to find people serving as a director at five or more companies.) If he is and he is investing heavily into only one of those companies, it probably tells you that from among all the choices that he is very close to he has identified one company's stock that holds particular promise. This could be a very positive sign.

Also, you might want to see if the inside/insider has led a company in the past into innovative areas or directed its turnaround. Both of these pieces of information can be considered positive. On the other hand, has the insider been involved with a company that has gone bankrupt? Or has he had executive experience only as the president of an advertising agency before heading a bank? These past experiences could be considered negative in relation to the past profiles of the insiders at your other investment candidates.

With outside/insiders you also will want to weigh their past successes and failures before betting with them. Plus, as mentioned in Chapter 7, you may want to find the people whose investment personalities you feel most comfortable with. Do you like the slow-and-steady-wins-the-race types like Warren Buffett, Ned Johnson, Carl Lindner or David Murdock? Or do you enjoy getting your adrenaline going with faster, big hit-or-miss types like Asher Edelman, Irwin Jacobs or Saul Steinberg? Among outside/insiders there are people to match nearly any type of investment temperament.

As you get more intimately involved with collecting and analyzing insider trading information, the names of many of the players will become more and more familiar to you—just as you may already be familiar with a great number of people who are sports figures, movie stars and politicians. The insiders are the "stars" of corporate America. And you will find that the business world isn't all that large. The incidences of personal interrelationships among insiders are high.

Any assessment of the credibility of insiders will, to a certain degree, be subjective. When you find information about these people, there will be some you will like and others you will dislike without being able to point to specific objective criteria. But as in the choice of many business relationships, when all is seemingly equal a final decision is often based on how much you like someone. And since the insiders are your "investment advisors," it isn't necessarily a bad thing to go with the people you trust and feel most comfortable with.

Information you'll need: Often your newsletter will provide short capsule profiles of active insiders or point out the relationships they have with other companies and other insiders. Other times, as you have potential investment candidates in mind, you will come across stories in general newspapers or financial publications that tell about an insider's career. For inside/insiders these profiles often appear within articles announcing "personnel changes." Clip them out and keep them just as you should with the profiles that you come across on the outside/insiders.

Information on people is not easily obtainable from your stockbroker. Nor is it as readily accessible as the information required in our first two screening approaches. But if you're willing to take a trip to the library, you'll be surprised how much information you can find out about people with a little digging.

The first printed sources you would use at the library are the same ones that you used in the previously discussed sorting methods—the *Business Periodicals Index* and the *National News Index*. But instead of looking under the name of the company, you look under the name of the person. The same holds for computer on-line data base searches; enter in the name of the person you want to know about instead of the company.

Besides the articles you find in nationally circulated publications, you should also check to see which companies the insiders are involved with. Volume 3 of Standard & Poor's *Register of Corporations* provides an alphabetical listing of people who are directors and executives at every company listed in the directory. For each individual's name, the names of all the companies he or she is associated with is provided. With this very valuable information, you will be able to tell the interrelationships of the insider's major business connections. You may also want to look through *Who's Who in America* and *Who's Who in Finance and Industry* for other clues. Actually, you can start your search by looking in Marquis's *Who's Who Index to Who's Who Books*, which tells you which *Who's Who* the person is listed in.

Two more references you might want to check: the company's annual report and proxy statement. (A proxy statement is a public, SEC-mandated document which, among other important information about what inside/insiders hold in stock, gives notice of the time and place of the annual stockholders' meeting.) While we've steered away from annual reports, these publications often do provide biographical information about officers and directors. Of particular interest is the number of years the insider has been connected with the company. If the insider has been with the company for many years and is just now investing heavily, it may imply that the insider has recognized an opportunity for profit that had not existed in the past.

A Note about Research

Narrowing down your investment selections by any one, or all three, of these approaches, may sound complicated and time-consuming at first. But once you grow accustomed to the process, it will become almost second nature to you. Remember, the insiders you are watching have already done the most valuable work and research for you in making their own investments. You have only to take the time and the necessary steps to identify *which* insider situation seems the most promising to you.

Chapter 11

Mapping Out an Investment Strategy

O NCE you have identified some exciting insider situations, it's time to take the plunge.

If you already have an existing portfolio of stocks and are not ready to expand it, replace your current holdings with insider favorites when you are ready to sell the old ones. This isn't a recommendation to dump your current holdings for insider selections. If you had good reasons for selecting them in the first place, keep them until you would have normally sold them following whatever strategy you originally used. Then start investing in insider situations. If you are a beginning investor, build a portfolio slowly when you are satisfied that you have found the best insider "picks" available. If nothing looks good enough to you this month, wait a month or so until something better comes along. There's no need to rush into investments that you are not completely comfortable with.

Once you make a decision to start investing in insider favorites, you are going to be directing your own stock investment destiny. So let's look at the strategies you'll need to follow to make your investments as profitable as possible.

The Importance of Diversification

The concept of portfolio diversification tells us that it is better to hold a variety of different stocks than to have just one or two. The wisdom here is very simple: Don't put all your eggs in one basket—even if you plan to watch the basket intently.

Entire volumes have been written about this simple (yet essential) investment tactic. But the importance of it should be so obvious to you that it will not be belabored here. Suffice it to say that despite the strength of the insider investment strategy's selection process, there is no guarantee that *all* of your final choices will pay off. Even if 95 percent of your best investment candidates ultimately turn out to be winners, you could have the misfortune of investing in those situations that turn out to be disasters. By diversifying your portfolio with different stocks, you reduce the risk of having only latched onto losers.

But since the incidences of an eventual profitable outcome from stock selections based on aggressive insider buying are high, it is not necessary for an individual investor to hold hundreds of different stocks to guard against those relatively small number of situations that ultimately turn bad. At the minimum, however, you should hold the stocks of five different companies. Optimally, ten or twelve is a good number. But fifteen or more different stocks in a portfolio is not necessary for an individual investor. At the Insider Reports Fund we may have one hundred or more stocks in the fund's portfolio at any one point. But we spend full time tracking the developments at those various companies and managing the portfolio. You, as an individual investor, may not be able or wish to do this time-consuming work effectively. The time you *do* have available would be better spent tracking down insider trading activity to find new investment candidates. Then you will always have a few ready to replace old ones as they come full term in their gestation.

Most of the many pages of theory and advice about portfolio diversification concerns *how* to diversify. One popular thought —particularly among the Efficient Market/Random Walk people —is to build a portfolio with an eye on its overall potential sensitivity to systemic or market-factor risk. This usually is done by looking at each individual stock in the portfolio and assigning a measurement of its potential future sensitivity to market movement based on how that stock fared in the past in relation to market factors. (The measurement used is usually referred to as *beta*.) In other words, if a certain company's stock price was very sensitive to market factors in the past—if the stock's price had a history of swinging widely as the overall market went up and down—it would be considered to have a risky future because of its probable volatility. Other stocks that have not had a history of sensitivity to overall market movements would be considered less risky.

The portfolio diversification philosophy that grows out of this measurement of past performance says that an individual can choose the amount of risk he or she is willing to take by combining a certain number of high-risk stocks and a certain number of low-risk stocks. The reason that someone would want high-risk stocks, the supporters of this philosophy tell us, is because volatile stocks tend to go up higher than the market as a whole during bull times, which means that someone with a high-risk (high beta) portfolio expects to do better than the market when the market is rising. The risky part comes when the market goes down. Then these stocks which had been volatile in the past are expected to go down more than the market as a whole. Low-risk stocks, on the other hand, tend to go up less during bull markets, but they also tend to go down less during bad times. An individual investor using the systemic or beta-risk measurement approach to portfolio diversification would choose those stocks that add up to the risk measurement that represents the amount of risk he or she is willing to carry—the more risk one can assume in the expectation of greater returns, the higher the beta rating of the portfolio.

Another popular diversification idea is to be sure to diversify by industry. This approach says that the various stocks in your portfolio should be of companies chosen from completely different, unrelated industry groups. With this type of portfolio, the theorists say, you are protected against disasters that may befall any particular company because of an industrywide development. Some adherents to this diversification philosophy spend much time and effort finding the perfect balance of stocks based on criteria such as an industry's sensitivity to interest rates and the cyclical nature of the business of each industry.

The protocol followed in these traditional diversification approaches is not valid for the insider investment strategy. First, the systemic-risk measurement is of no interest to us because that measurement is based on a company's past performance— or a crystal ball projection based on past performance as it relates to the stock market. Our insiders, however, are looking forward, and the event they are basing their investment decisions on will most likely change the company's past stock performance and its relation to overall movements of the market. The insiders are looking at upcoming company developments; they are not looking to general stock market trends or fashion to make them richer.

Since they are required to hold their shares for at least six months before taking a profit, insiders cannot "play the market" as other investors can and jump in and out to profit from short swings caused by overall market factors. That's why, as we've mentioned before, they are forced to view their potential investments as special situations. And if they don't see a special situation, then they won't invest. As any professional analyst will tell you, it is nearly impossible—if not impossible—to predict six months in advance the overall direction of the stock market. Our insiders are not stock market wizards; they are just people with a unique view of the special situation at their own companies. Since the insiders can't take market-risk factors into consideration, then we shouldn't either. It will make no difference on the final outcome of our investments.

Second, the struggle to perfectly balance a portfolio by industry also is of no interest to us because, again, the insiders are looking ahead to a *special* event that will affect that specific company. Often the event exploits an aspect of the company that has nothing or very little to do with its primary business. For instance, in the Alexander's department store example, the real value that the insiders were interested in had nothing to do with retailing; it was the company's underappreciated real estate holdings that made its stock a bargain.

Your insider portfolio should be diversified, but it should be made up of your best investment candidates without concerns about diversification in a traditional sense. At times, in fact, many of the best insider situations you discover will be concentrated in certain industries. For example, in late 1984 and early 1985 many banks and bank holding companies saw heavy insider buying. In mid-1985 several food retailing companies were favored by insiders. In late 1985 and early 1986, more than a few gas and oil companies saw a lot of insider activity. When faced with equally excellent investment candidates from the same industry, it would be wrong to discard them summarily just because they happen to be in the same business. Your best investment candidates—no matter how interrelated those companies happen to be at any one point—are still your best bets.

Similar and concurrent insider buying at companies within the same industry may suggest that similar positive developments may be affecting companies industrywide. But you shouldn't generalize and think that those developments will affect *all* companies in that industry equally. For example, the success that specific bank and bank holding companies had in late 1985 following heavy insider buying occurred when some other banks did very poorly. Don't, therefore, run out and invest in several companies within an industry that happens to see a great deal of insider buying. Keep focused on the *specific* companies that insiders favor. And finally, think of your diversified portfolio of insider favorites as a collection of stocks that hold great probabilities for future appreciation individually, not as interconnected entities that must be balanced to offset their inherent weaknesses and strengths.

Timing Your Buying

The green light goes on for your own investment when the situation fulfills two criteria:

- When the insider activity shows enough of a "consistent pattern of unusual behavior" to tell you that the insiders consider the company to be a good investment probability;

- When the current market price is in line with the prices paid by the insiders.

Of these two broad criteria, current market price dictates the timing of your own investment. It is central to your investment success. If you cannot purchase shares at about the same price as the insiders—with a 25 percent premium above the insiders' highest price paid as your maximum acceptable price—you do not have a green light.

This doesn't mean that you should throw away forever an investment candidate that *is* currently selling above an acceptable price level. Instead, keep an eye on the stock's price so that if it falls you will be able to buy. This happens fairly regularly. As we have mentioned before, the stock price of an insider favorite tends to slump following heavy insider buying because (a) insider favorites invariably are neglected rather than popular at the time insiders are buying—otherwise they wouldn't be the bargain that the insiders think they are; (b) given that a stock is not popular, the heavy insider buying itself provides unusual demand which temporarily pushes the stock's price upward; (c) after the insiders are finished with their own acquisition, the stock goes back to being neglected, which lessens the demand and causes the stock price to fall and (d) the stock will remain neglected until the corporate development on which the insiders made their investment decisions becomes evident to the bulk of stock market investors. Only then will the stock's price rise in any meaningful way.

Usually you will have plenty of time and plenty of opportunities to invest in your best insider candidates at (and even below) the prices the insiders paid themselves—if you have the patience to wait. The time you have available is, once again, a direct outgrowth of the function of the six-month rule that governs insider profit taking. This gives you at least six months— and usually more time—to invest following the *end of the insiders own acquisitions.* Of course you will never know when the insider acquisition actually stops. Insiders could buy heavily, be quiet for six months and then start buying again. That kind of acquisition pattern may go on for years. But the fact remains that you usually will have the time to invest at a good price before the corporate development that insiders are waiting for occurs. The time you have available is also caused by the long length of time it usually takes to work out the corporate development that the insiders are betting on. The wheels of corporate America turn very slowly when compared to those of Wall Street.

Many insider-watchers—including some professional insider analysts—miss this very important point and think that the faster they jump on insider coattails the better. Many who read insider advisory newsletters or financial media reports of insider activity often will eagerly leap on the news—with no regard to the current market price vis-à-vis the insiders' purchase prices—and buy stock, which creates more demand and pushes the price even higher. Then we see the "greater fool" syndrome at work. This concept holds that after this group of investors jump the gun, another group of fools becomes excited by the activity and often joins the foray which artificially (and temporarily) raises the price of the stock even more. These are the speculators who use charts and technical analysis as their guiding stars. As you may recall, technical analysts—and amateur investors who follow the technical philosophy—watch for signs of increased trading volume and rising prices to give them the clue that something is going on at the company that signals a continued future price rise. Since insider buying and the knee-jerk insider-watcher buying that often quickly follows show the technician a flurry of activity at the company, some technical people hop on the bandwagon without knowing why the stock is getting the attention it is. Worse still, these technical investors also will not pay any attention to the prices paid by insiders and will buy "at the market," creating even more demand and even higher prices.

All this speculative stock buying creates a price "spike" and can make the price pattern of your best investment candidates look like a roller coaster. Most of the time, when the overanxious insider-watchers and the uninformed technical people see that nothing happens quickly to the stock, they will dump it and that in turn will drive the price of the stock down—often to levels lower than the prices the insiders paid. But you can bet that the dumping that causes this "dishing out" did not include stock sales by the insiders themselves. They will continue to hold on to their shares until the *real* corporate development takes place. You, as a wise and unemotional investor, have the best opportunity to buy at the best prices during this dishing out period. And you will have a chance to steal a bargain from the trigger-happy. So, once again, remember this important Golden Rule: Don't jump with your investment dollars at the first twitch of an insider's movement. (Or a newsletter's recommendation.)

The final criterion that determines the timing of your own investment is the stock's current market price. And not only is current market price the *final* criterion, it is the *sole* criterion. Any other "market timing" formula or strategy that you may encounter in your journey through stock market investment advice has no application within the insider investment approach. Absolutely none. Here's why. With a "market timing" strategy, you assume that overall market forces will significantly affect your stock selections. The insider investment strategy, on the other hand, is a "situation timing" approach that looks only at the unique aspects of individual companies. The corporate development that the insiders are focused on will occur at some time in the future, and the value at that time will be totally unrelated to the market environment then. Also, since we can never know *when* the corporate development will surface, we cannot use current "market timing" criteria to help us predict any timetable for the performance of our selections.

You are, of course, free to apply any "market timing" techniques that you want. But you should recognize that it will not make any difference in the final outcome of the performance of your selections. The use of any other tactics beyond the green light that evidence of bullish insider buying and an attractive current market price gives is a game. While "market timing" can fit into your overall financial planning and relate to other stock market investment strategies (especially a technical one), the insider investment strategy agrees with the fundamentalist credo which says: Any time is a good time to buy a good stock at a good price.

Besides the consideration of timing, there are two other "rules" that you should follow when buying:

· Invest equal amounts of money in equally interesting insider situations—at least at first.

· When placing a buy order, always use a "limit order" that tells your stockbroker the maximum price you will pay per share.

It makes sense that if your final investment choices all share the same excellent qualities they all share the same probability of a final successful outcome. Since all is equal when you first take a position in an insider favorite, you should invest in it with an amount of money equal to your other insider "picks." Later, if you see further evidence of continued insider buying at any specific company you may consider investing *more* money into that company.

If you have the financial flexibility when you start acquiring stock in your insider favorites, you may want to take a partial position at the beginning—say, one half or one third the total amount you plan to put in—and then wait a month or so to see what happens to your selection before filling out the rest of your "equal" position. This approach is particularly compelling if your selection is currently selling at a premium above the insider's highest purchase price. By taking a partial position at the premium price you will have ensured that you have at least part of the action. In a month or so the stock's price may subside, allowing you to fill out your position at a lower price while at the same time "averaging down" to a level that is closer to the insiders' purchase price.

Since the price you pay for your shares is central to the success you ultimately achieve following the insider investment strategy, you should *never* place a "market order" for your buys. A market order allows your stockbroker to purchase shares for you at whatever the available price is at the time of the order. Instead, *always* use a "limit buy order." A limit buy order designates for your stockbroker the highest price you are willing to pay. If the stock is not available at that price or lower, your stockbroker will not buy it. This guards against unwittingly acquiring stock at a price higher than the attractive prices that the insiders have defined for you. Not paying attention to this rule could cost you significant losses.

There are times, however, when you may have to make a decision about whether to go over your price limit. For example, if you place a limit buy order for 200 shares of a company at $10 a share, you may get a call from your stockbroker telling you that 100 shares were available at $10, but the other 100 shares are available at $10¼. You probably would say to go ahead with the order in this case. But since stock prices can swing dramatically—particularly with stocks sold over the counter—you should stick to your guns and not buy when the shares are not available at the most attractive prices.

The Terrible Waiting Period

Now comes the hardest part of all. Waiting. The operative word during the time between your purchase of an insider favorite and the culmination of the corporate development that prompted the insider buying in the first place is *patience*.

Patience isn't currently a very popular investment mode for many Wall Street investors. In an age of computers when everything is supposed to happen fast, fast, fast—from fast food to a fast-track career to ten-day diets to one-minute management—

the delayed gratification that goes along with an investment approach that follows a "buy and hold" philosophy is almost quaintly old-fashioned. It seems that today more and more investors don't want to play the Wall Street game if they can't get a quick hit by the next morning or at least by the end of the next quarter. This attitude is fueled by glamorized stories of people who *have* been lucky enough to make big killings nearly overnight. It has also made big losers out of many small investors who have gotten caught up in this quick-hit pursuit.

The fast-moving image of today's stock market is also promoted by stories of large institutional investors who move their billions of dollars quickly from one company to another at the blip of a computer-projected signal. This type of trading, although often profitable, requires split-second timing and very nominal transaction costs. It unfortunately has given small investors the idea that this is the only way to play the market. For many investors the stock market now appears to be an investment alternative that is viable only if they can profit quickly— otherwise they fear being labeled losers. Other investment alternatives, such as real estate, savings bonds and zero coupon securities, do not have the time-pressure stigma that stock investing has acquired recently. Thirty years ago (even ten years ago) common stock investing was thought of more on the level of these other investment alternatives: An investor bought stock in a company because he or she had good reason to believe that the company's future performance would bring about an appreciation in the value of its stock. The stock was held—in a way similar to holding on to a savings bond—until the company had the opportunity to achieve the performance that would bring about that appreciation.

The insider investment strategy *requires* that you adopt this "old-fashioned" buy-and-hold attitude about your stock selections.

There are two things to remember when we invest in an insider favorite. We never know the real reason for the insider buying, except we do know from past experience that it most likely has something to do with a future corporate development that will greatly appreciate the company's stock price. And we can never predict the timetable for the corporate development or the appreciation of the stock's price.

The corporate development that we watch for may happen a few weeks after we make our own investment or it may not happen for several years. Ultimately, however, it *will* invariably happen—except in those relatively few instances when some disaster, unforeseen by the insiders themselves, cancels out the future opportunity that the insiders originally based their investments on.

For example, beginning in 1979 insiders at Beneficial Corporation, a financial services company listed on the New York Stock Exchange, started buying shares at prices in the low twenties. Most of the buying—which ultimately reached into the hundreds of thousands of shares—was carried out by Finn Casperson, chairman of Beneficial's board, and his mother, Freida, who was president. From 1979 through the first half of 1986, the Caspersons, and others, bought at ever-increasing prices. In the early 1980s they didn't buy very much stock. But in 1985 they bought over 80,000 shares at prices about $35 a share. In 1986 they paid up to $54 a share in new purchases. This off-and-on buying pattern went on for over six years before August of 1986 when Casperson announced that the board had decided to put the company up for sale at an asking price of $100 a share.

Casperson's publicly stated goal at that time was to bring the fullest appreciation and return for shareholders. (Of which, of course, he was a major one.) The market's reaction to this news quickly made the stock's price go up to about $78 a share, including a one-day jump of $28, or over 60 percent in price. Now, if you had been watching insider buying at Beneficial in 1979, you would have been justified in investing in this company at prices in the low twenties. But, it would have taken over six years before you could have garnered an "abnormal positive return" on your investment—if you had sold in late 1986. The Beneficial story, however, did not end with the proposed sale of the company. By the end of 1986, which was Casperson's target date for selling the company to take advantage of the changing tax laws on long-term capital gains, the best price the company could get was only $80 a share. This offer was rejected as not good enough and the company was taken off the auction block at the beginning of 1987. The market's reaction to this drove the price of the stock down to about $60 a share—just about where it was prior to the auction announcement back in August 1986.

For those insider-watchers who didn't take profits in the fall of 1986, this should not have been discouraging. We knew that

Casperson's publicly stated goal was to get $100 per share value out of the company. And we also knew that instead of selling the company he was going to use other tactics to bring about that value—perhaps by spinning off or selling only parts of the company. You can bet that as of this writing at the beginning of 1987, Casperson is working very hard to make his goal come true. As an "outside" investor into Beneficial at this time, he would have also been working very hard for you. The goal may be reached in 1987 or it might not happen until 1990. But here you have a highly motivated person—because of his huge holdings—working toward a publicly-stated goal and in possession of the power to make it happen.

The major point here is that if you had invested in this company in 1979 you would have had to wait six years and possibly more before you would have gotten a good return. During the holding period your shares would not have steadily and consistently risen in price to outperform the market. You would have had to wait until the final outcome to reap the abnormal profits.

The Beneficial story is an extraordinary case that involved a waiting period much longer than the average duration. But you will still have varying degrees of waiting to experience with your stock selections. A long wait is particularly prevalent in situations where insider buying continues beyond the point when you buy, which is because the corporate development that raises the stock's price will not occur until after the insiders have finished their own stock accumulation. In the examples cited in this book you will see many instances when insider accumulation continues over extended periods of time. When you first identify an interesting insider situation, you will never know whether you are viewing the insider buying at the start, the middle or the end of his accumulation. And you can't say that a long period of insider inactivity signals the end of the insiders' stock accumulation. Often the insiders will be quiet for months—and even a year or more—and then start buying again. Insiders, like the rest of us, can invest only when they have the funds to do it. We cannot expect that all insiders at different companies will invest with the same patterns. We can only identify the end of insider buying in hindsight after the corporate development actually happens.

Besides the patience you'll need to exercise during the waiting period, you will also have to keep the faith that your selection is the right one, even in the face of sometimes poor performance while your selection continues to "cook" prior to the final pay off. During this waiting period, your selection may be very volatile or it could appear to be simply dead. These are natural occurrences that are caused by the mere fact that your selection is a neglected stock that will remain neglected until a corporate development changes things. Before that happy ending takes place, the stock could be subject to market forces that, considering the rapid up-and-down swings the market as a whole has experienced in the last few years, could mean that your holdings will fluctuate in value for no specific reason. Other times the price of your stock may drop—and drop dramatically—as the absence of news coming from your company during the "cooking" period makes your selection even more neglected than ever or in disfavor from a technical analysis point of view.

If your choice *does* drop during this period, don't panic and sell. In fact, it may be an opportunity for you to *buy more* shares at a much lower price than your original purchase price, which allows you to "average down" the price per share of your holdings. (This is what Harold Oppenheimer at Oppenheimer Industries did in 1985.) Of course, it is a psychologically difficult investment technique to use at a time when everything looks bleak. But if you get nervous and sell prematurely, you could very well end up selling at an unnecessary loss to the insiders as they go back into the market to pick up more shares at bargain-basement prices.

There is a conventional stock-trading adage that says to sell when your stocks are dropping in price in order to "limit your losses." Often you will hear that you should give your stockbroker a "stop-sell order" to automatically sell your shares if they drop below 10 percent of your original purchase price. The person who created this concept must have been very insecure about the criteria originally used in his stock selection. To an insider-watcher, who has strong evidence of bullish insider buying, accepting a loss does not make sense—unless some major disaster happens at the company. Remember that the insiders—who told you through their buying that something good is going to happen at the company—also are affected by price volatility and price drops. And their investment stake is undoubtedly much, much higher than yours. They don't like seeing the value of their investments go down any more than you do. But they have the motivation and the opportunity to make sure that eventually the stock's price will go up. Remember the Golden Rule: To profit like an insider, you must stick with a stock just as an insider does, even through periods of bad weather.

There is one situation in which a "stop-sell order" *is* a valuable trading tool during this waiting period. If the price of your stock goes up substantially, say, 25 percent or more from your original purchase price, for no apparent reason—when there's no publicly available positive news about the company that would support such a price rise—you should protect this gain by using a *stop-sell* order at the 25 percent or higher level. When the stock's price starts going back down to its previous level, as it probably will if there is no news to validate the price increase, you automatically sell and take the profit. Then, should the price fall back toward your original purchase price, you are in a position to buy shares again in that price range and continue your wait for the corporate development outcome. If the price *doesn't* go all the way down to your original price level, you still would have gained an "abnormal return." And you can always decide to buy the stock back again at a higher price, if new insider buying evidence surfaces at that higher price.

Throughout the waiting period you can save yourself a lot of anguish by avoiding the temptation to "ride the tape," watching every little up-and-down movement of your stocks' prices. You don't need to know every hour how you're doing. You don't even need to know every day. Remember, in the insider investment strategy approach, you are a *value investor*, not a speculator. Being obsessed with price movements during the waiting period puts you in jeopardy of giving in to your natural instincts of fear and frustration. Instead, hold on to the strength of your convictions and let your selections play themselves out. If you monitor the news affecting your selections—through reading your advisory newsletter or general financial news sources or through periodic research using computer news data bases or printed business news indexes—you will have sufficient time to be alerted to the corporate development you are waiting for before selling your holdings.

Timing Your Selling

Timing your buying is somewhat easier than timing your selling. When you buy, the insiders give you all the signals for the go-ahead. Knowing when to sell hinges on your own reading of the situation at the company without any help from the insiders. But there are four scenarios that can tell you when it's time to sell. The first two, which occur when things go wrong, are happily the least likely to happen. The second two, which fulfill the promise of the insiders' investment decisions, are the most commonly encountered situations:

1. *Sell when a major disaster affects the specific company.* A major disaster is bankruptcy. Or a company's default on loans, or the discovery that the company's only product causes cancer, or the revelation that the company directors and/or management have been convicted of fraud. For our purposes, a major disaster is *not* a disappointing earnings performance last quarter or an announcement that the marketing of a new product has been delayed or a strike has been called on one division of the company. A major disaster also is *not* a rumor or a development that seems to affect your stock's industry. Keep focused on the specific events as they specifically affect your specific stocks. Only when all is proven to be lost with no possible turn for the better in the foreseeable future should you abandon your insider selections.

2. *Sell if nothing happens after three years following the last evidence of insider buying.* If no insiders have purchased any shares for three years and nothing has happened—the stock just remains dead—you can be fairly sure that something has gone awry with the corporate development that the insider originally anticipated. This doesn't mean three years from the time you first identified heavy insider buying and made your own purchase. Continued insider buying keeps the situation alive. The three-year measurement should be three years of no insider buying, no news from the company and no price movement.

3. *Sell part of your position if the stock's price rises dramatically for no apparent reason.* We think that if your stock's

price rises 50 percent from your original purchase price and
there is no supporting evidence for any specific reason for
the price increase, you should seriously consider selling 50
percent of your position. If the stock goes up another 50 percent, without good reason, sell another 50 percent of your
holdings. Following this selling pattern, you will have taken
nice profits without completely closing out your position in
case the price increase is being caused by positive events that
have not yet been publicly announced.

4. *Sell when a positive corporate development has been completely worked out.* This is the most common selling situation you will encounter. Since it is the event you have been
   waiting for from the beginning, you do not want to sell prematurely before the market has absorbed the news of a positive corporate development and raised the price of the stock
   to its fullest extent. For example, if there is suddenly a takeover announcement, don't sell at the first price jump when
   other investors become interested in your stock. Wait until
   the details have been ironed out and the takeover becomes a
   reality. That's when you'll get the full return on your investment. Or if your company shows evidence of turnaround performance and also announces that it expects to do even better
   in the future, don't leave it now. Hold on to it so that you will
   continue to profit. After your selections have proven to be
   winners, waiting with them—and basking in their glory—
   for a little bit longer can bring you the maximum returns. In
   the Beneficial example, most (75 percent) or all of the position could have been sold shortly after the $100 top estimate
   had been made, and before the price fall back.

The Central Human Factor

The insider investment strategy is not a get-rich-quick scheme.
You will not be able to take a thousand dollars and turn it into a
million dollars overnight. It is an *investment* strategy—and a
conservative one at that—that makes its selections based on
compelling common sense: Following the aggressive investments of the people who know the most about their companies
and have the power to make their own investments pay off.

Here's a warning: Your results may be slow in coming. But here's also a promise: The first time you identify a company as an insider favorite and then months later news of that company hits the business page headlines—because of an unexpected takeover, buy-out, performance turnaround, new product or some other development—and startles Wall Street, you will be hooked on the insider investment approach.

When you go through the process of identifying interesting insider favorites, you are not just putting check marks on a piece of paper or comparing columns of abstract numbers or counting the number of different insiders buying at your various investment candidates. You are assessing human behavior and the self-interests that motivate human behavior. This human factor permeates every level of business. Companies are more than numbers on a ledger sheet. They are not just factories or oil wells. Nor are they simply real estate or technological advances. Without the human factor nothing can happen. Our insiders are the people who are in a position to make it happen.

The stock market itself is not a list of stock price quotations. Those stock prices and their variations are merely reflections of the perceptions of the value of companies by people dealing in an auction parlor—the stock exchanges. The insiders are the individual people who are in the best position to promote or exploit a company's qualities and convert the values into cash. They do not need to change other peoples' perceptions of its value. They are the independent, professional appraisers of value—and the prices in the auction markets as compared to their "appraisal" determines whether or not they can buy a bargain.

So, when insiders invest in their own companies they are also investing, in a very real sense, in themselves. They are betting that they have the energy, talent, intelligence and ability to get things done to make their perceptions of their companies' value come true. Since they are human beings, they occasionally make mistakes. But because their motivation is based on their own financial self-interests, they will do their best to make their investments pay off. When you are looking at insider investments you are, in an almost literal sense, surveying their wallets and checkbooks to measure the degree of their belief in the future of their companies which will be in their own self-interest.

When you do this, remember that you are in possession of truly significant real-world facts: Official reports about what real people, in uniquely well-informed positions, are doing with their own real money in real situations, which is a particularly compelling thing to know following the crash of 1987. No charts. No theories. No guessing. Just hard facts and human nature at work. And if you become an investor because of what you find out, you will be standing shoulder to shoulder in line at the stock market ticket booth with the people who *are* American business.

PART FOUR:

Resources—Using Official Data and On-line Data Bases

Chapter 12

SEC Documents I: How to Read the *Official Summary*

GETTING your fingertips dirty with original SEC documents and printed sources of raw insider trading data will put you in the closest tactile contact with the insiders. These are the sources on which all other information about insider activity—whether it is found on a computer data base, reported in a specialized newsletter or in the general financial press—is based.

In the next two chapters we'll look at ways of sorting out raw insider trading data from government and nongovernment printed sources. In this chapter we'll look at the data from inside/insider reports—Form 3 and Form 4. In the next chapter we'll look at how to access information on outside/insider investments—Schedule 13D. The third chapter of this section describes the computer data base sources of insider trading information and strategies on how to use them. And the final chapter provides an evaluation test for sorting out likely investment candidates first identified by using original SEC documents or computer-assisted research.

The procedures presented in this section offer a very sophisticated and comprehensive approach to insider watching, but it is by no means a requirement for successful investing based on insider trading activities. You can find the "consistent pattern of unusual behavior" among insiders that signals investment opportunities with relative ease by carefully using advisory newsletters. The difference in following the guidelines described in this final section is that you will be able to find many, many compelling investment candidates—at least several hundred a year—that are *never* mentioned in advisory newsletters.

The problem with this process is that it can be very time-consuming, particularly if you don't have access to computer data bases and must rely solely on the printed sources of insider trading data. It could take you thirty or more hours a month to do it properly, although the techniques and guidelines are not difficult to understand or to carry through.

If you do have the time or inclination to do this kind of research, the key to keeping your time spent to a minimum is to focus tightly on the pieces of information that are important, while ignoring the irrelevant. Unfortunately, the original sources we must turn to were not designed for our convenience to use in the way we would like to use them. As a result, *most* of the data encountered is irrelevant for our purposes. All this irrelevant information can sometimes confuse and fatigue you. But if you take a methodical approach, with blinders on to block out the irrelevant, you will be able to stay on the track.

Tools You'll Need for Following Inside/Insiders

The cornerstone of printed source information about inside/insider activity is, of course, the *Official Summary of Security Transactions and Holdings*. You can subscribe to the *Official Summary* by writing directly to: Superintendent of Documents, U.S. Government Printing Office, Washington, DC 20402. You can also order it through one of the several Government Printing Office bookstores located in larger U.S. cities. The bookstores will not have copies of the *Official Summary* on hand; instead, your order will be sent to Washington and the subscription will be mailed to you.

As of this writing, the cost for a one-year subscription is $59 ($79 for foreign destinations). The order number for the subscription, which should be noted on your written order, is 746-001-00000-2. Payment by check or money order should accompany your order. Your subscription will begin with the first issue published after your order is processed, which may take several weeks. Back issues of the publication are also available at a cost of $6.00 per issue ($7.50, foreign). The order number for single issues is the same as the subscription. When ordering back issues, note which months you want.

Since you need at least six months of information from the *Official Summary* before you can make any really intelligent decisions about what the insiders are up to, you should order a full year's subscription and the six most recent back issues. Occasionally you may find that some back issues are sold out. The Government Printing Office does not reprint back issues. To fill in data from sold-out issues you may have to take a trip to a major public library or find the missing data through a computer data base supplier of insider trading information. If you want a subscription and the most recent past six issues, send payment of $95 ($59 for the subscription and $36 for the past six issues) and tell the Government Printing Office people that you want a subscription to begin with the next available issue and one copy of each of the most current previously published issues.

Six months of the *Official Summary* will comprise about fifteen hundred pages. If you think that would be too overwhelming to sort through, you can always start your insider search with the first issue of your subscription and follow along at a more leisurely pace for the next six months. But remember, don't get overzealous and make a hasty decision based on only one month's information—at least not at the beginning before you are familiar with the type of "consistent pattern of unusual behavior" that can signal a ripe investment.

To supplement the information you find in the *Official Summary* you may want to subscribe to either *Vickers Weekly Insider Report* or *The Insiders' Chronicle*. Both of these publications provide a fairly comprehensive weekly listing of the previous week's insider findings. This information can keep you up to date while you're waiting for the next issue of the *Official Summary*.

Another handy supplementary printed source of information you might consider is Standard & Poor's *Stock Guide* (Standard & Poor's Corporation, 25 Broadway, New York, NY 10004. Fifty dollars a year). Although this monthly publication doesn't provide any insider trading data, it does give you important information on about five thousand companies of the sort you won't find in the *Official Summary*. For example, it tells you which exchange the company is traded on, its price range, earnings and dividends and the total number of shares outstanding. For companies you are interested in that are not listed in the *Stock Guide*, you will have to turn to more comprehensive listings like Volume 1 of Standard & Poor's *Register of Corporations* or Moody's *Industrial Manual*. These reference books cost several hundred dollars but can be found in the business section of most large public libraries.

Deciphering the Official Summary

You may recall that in Chapter 2 there is an illustration of an actual Form 4. The information from Form 4, as well as that from Form 3, is printed in the *Official Summary* in a somewhat abstracted manner with different codes representing the different reported pieces of information.

The *Official Summary* is organized with the names of companies in alphabetical order with the details of all insider transacKtions reported to the SEC during the month covered by that issue appearing under the name of the company. There are fourteen items of information reported for each transaction entry.

1. *Issuer.* This is the name of the company that "issued" the stock that has been traded.

2. *Security.* This item tells you the type of security that has been traded. In most cases it will be common stock. But occasionally you will see insiders trading in other kinds of securities such as preferred stock, Class A or Class B. The important thing here is to make sure that when you invest based on an insider's actions you are buying the *same* type of stock the insider has chosen.

3. *Reporting person.* This, of course, tells you the name of the person (or company or investment group) that made the trade. Each individual is listed separately in alphabetical order by last name. If an individual—who is covered by the SEC's definition of corporate insider—invests as part of a group of investors or a company, a separate listing is included for *both* the group *and* the individual. This sometimes can be confusing. You have to be careful not to count the same transaction twice (or even three or four times if there are several "insiders" investing under the same group umbrella) since the same transaction will be repeated in the *Official Summary* under each individual's name.

4. *Nature of ownership.* There are two types of ownership status that interest us: "direct" and "indirect." Direct ownership means that the person reporting holds the securities in his, her or its (a company's) own name. Indirect ownership means that the securities are beneficially held by the reporting person, but that the securities were bought in someone else's name—usually a spouse, children or a company. There are three other types of ownership, but whenever you encounter them you can ignore the entire transaction as irrelevant. The three to ignore are "market maker," "indirect market maker" and "indirect proportionate interest." None of the people with ownership described by these three terms have a personal interest in seeing that the company's stock appreciates in value. Market makers are essentially brokers who buy a large block of stock—usually at the request of the company itself or a major shareholder—and then search out buyers for it. This is done so that the large block of stock is not dumped into the open market, which would probably depress the price of the stock unnecessarily. Since these market makers are not investors in the sense we are interested in, their activities are disregarded. Indirect proportionate interest describes a similar type of ownership that is of no interest to us.

5. *Relationship of insider to company.* This means the relationship of the reporting person to the issuing company. Each individual, group or company is assigned a relationship code in the *Official Summary* based on a specific list of possibilities. The *Official Summary* does not give the exact job title of the insiders, although that job title information is usually provided by the insider in the original public disclosure document he or she submits to the SEC. Because the *Official Summary* does not give us the precise job title, we must look elsewhere if we want to know the insider's position, such as president, chairman of the board, vice president and so on. Standard & Poor's *Register of Corporations* gives this information on all of the directors and top executives.

Here—in rough order of their importance to us based on our previous discussion of the hierarchy of insiders' access to information—are the codes used in the *Official Summary* and their definitions:

"H"—Officer, director and beneficial owner of more than 10 percent of any class of the company's equity securities. This means that the individual carries all three of the criteria that make him or her an "insider." We can assume that in most of these cases the insider holds a top position within the company and, of course, as an owner of more than 10 percent of the company probably has plenty of motivation to make its stock as valuable as possible.

"DO"—Director and beneficial owner of more than 10 percent of any class of the company's equity securities.

"OD"—Officer and director.

"D"—Director

"OB"—Officer and beneficial owner of more than 10 percent of any class of the company's equity securities. Here we get into a gray area. Since we don't know by looking in the *Official Summary* the title of the insider, an "OB" could be a chief executive officer and a beneficial owner. If so, that would put the insider on a higher level of interest to us than a director or an officer/director. There are cases—although rare—when a president or chief executive officer is not on the board of directors. On the other hand, an "OB" could be a major shareholder who has been given a token executive title, almost an honorary position, instead of being given a spot on the board of directors. Since this type of "OB" would have very little day-to-day involvement in the workings of the company and therefore little access to special information, that "OB" would remain low on our list of importance.

"O"—Officer. This, again, could describe a president, a vice president or a number of other possibilities. If the actual title describes a top position, this insider's importance would jump to the top of the list. If the position is just vice president, the insider would remain in this lower slot.

"B"—Beneficial owner of more than 10 percent of any class of the company's equity securities.

"AF"—Affiliated person. This is a catchall term used to describe someone who is connected with the company as an insider but doesn't fit any of the other categories. It is commonly used to categorize such special circumstances as a company's employee stock ownership program (ESOP) or a foundation closely connected with the company or even a trust fund. Transactions by "AFs" usually can be disregarded. Since the motivations for most of these purchases do not involve personal interests—the greed factor—they are usually of little interest to us.

"UK"—Unknown. This occurs when the filer fails to identify his or her relationship with the company or the SEC clerk who translates the data from the original form can't figure out how to classify the person according to the existing codes. A "UK" could possibly turn out to be a top executive. If you see interesting trading by a "UK," it is worth the effort to try to find out exactly what the insider's relationship is.

6. *Date of transaction.* This is the date of the actual trade. It is *not* the date that the insider submitted the report to the SEC. Watch these dates very closely. Don't be fooled into thinking that just because several transactions are clustered together in one issue of the *Official*

Summary that the insiders are making repeated trips to the market within a short time span.

7. *Character of transaction.* This refers to the type of trading transaction the insider carried out. When going through the *Official Summary* it is the first item of information you should look at to screen the potentially interesting situations from those that are not worth your time. Like the *Official Summary*'s "Relationship" category, the "Character" category uses codes to indicate the different types of transactions. But there are only five that are of primary interest:

"J"—Private purchase. This is, of course, purchases made outside the marketplace. And, as we've said before, if the price paid in a private purchase is at the same or a higher level as the then-current open-market price, it is a solid bullish vote for the company's stock.

"P"—Open-market purchase. This is of particular interest. Insiders who go to the open have decided that the full open-market price is a good bargain. How good a bargain they consider it to be depends on the number of shares they buy, the amount of money they spend and the aggressiveness of their acquisition—usually displayed in repeated instances of open-market purchases.

"X"—Acquisition by exercise (warrants, options, rights). This is the code that tells us that an insider has exercised his or her privilege under a company's stock option plan. If the insider has paid 50 percent or more of the then open-market price, we can apply some positive credence to his attitude about the company's future.

"K"—Private sale. This transaction is usually important, but the importance lies in who *bought* the stock and at what price rather than in the fact that it was a sale. If the sale price was made above the then open-market price we can assume that someone is buying and paying a premium for the privilege.

"S"—Open-market sale. Of the five, this is the least important, unless the pattern of sales overwhelms the buys significantly.

The other transactions reported in the *Official Summary*'s "Character" column are really of no interest to us at all. But for the record, here are their codes and definitions.

"3"—Initial statement of ownership. These transaction entries report the Form 3 filings, which we usually ignore because, as you may recall, we consider this type of transaction the fulfillment of an insider's political or public relations obligation to show the company's shareholders that he or she is loyal and optimistic about the company. Subsequent filings (Form 4) give us a better idea of his or her true feelings about the future of a company's stock.

"B"—Acquisition of shares accrued through a plan. Don't confuse this transaction with a purchase of stock under a stock option plan (code "X"). The shares acquired through a B transaction usually have been *given* to the insider as part of a compensation plan. The insider would not have paid anything for these shares.

"G"—Acquired by gift. "Gift" means free and therefore we can't tell what the giver or the receiver feels about the future of the company's stock.

"H"—Disposed of by gift. Like the receipt of gifts, the giving of gifts doesn't tell us much.

"T"—Acquisitions other than those separately listed. This catchall could mean things like stock given as a bonus that did not come under a specific company plan. Or it could mean a transfer from a trust to an individual. Or a change in "nature of ownership" status from "indirect" (in someone else's name) to "direct" (in the insider's own name) as may be encountered in a divorce settlement. Here, again, money rarely changes hands and therefore we cannot draw any concrete conclusions about the insider's view of the future value of the stock.

"U"—Dispositions other than those separately listed. Like a "T," money is usually not involved. Ignore this type of transaction.

"Z"—Stock split. If an insider finds himself with more shares on his hands because of a stock split, he has to report it to the SEC. But, again, the insider didn't take an active role with his wallet to acquire the stock and it is of no interest to us.

8. *Late, amended or inconsistent.* This category of information tells you if the insider has not been following the disclosure rules exactly. Code "L" means that the insider filed late. You're going to see many, many "Ls" as you read through the *Official Summary.* The SEC is very lax on letting insiders file late—sometimes several months after the transaction actually takes place. These "Ls" act as convenient reminders to look at the transaction dates to see when they actually took place. Code "A" means that the insider has submitted an amended report that corrects mistakes made on a previous filing. Be careful about amended reports and don't count them as new filings from an insider you have been following for several months. Code "I" means inconsistent with the previous filing. These alert you to possible mistakes in an insider's report that the SEC has discovered. For example, the SEC may apply an "I" to an insider's report when that filing shows that the total amount of the insider's holdings does not coincide with previous reports.

9. *Transactions: Bought or otherwise acquired—amount.* This is the actual number of shares *acquired* in each separate transaction through

any of the possible methods insiders get their shares—from gifts to options to open-market purchases.

10. *Transactions: Bought or otherwise acquired—price.* These are the prices the insiders paid *per share* in each acquisition transaction. If the acquisition didn't cost the insider anything—in cases such as receipt of a gift or stock split—this column will be blank. The price paid per share tells us three key items of information. First, by multiplying the price paid per share times the number of shares bought, we can find out the total amount of money the insider spent during the transaction. Second, if the buying transactions were done through a private purchase (code "J") or an open-market purchase (code "P"), it tells us the price at which the insider considers the stock to be a "bargain." Third, on option purchases (code "X") it tells us the price paid for the options. And if the options were purchased above 50 percent of the then open-market price, we can consider it a somewhat bullish sign; the closer to the market price the more positive.

11. *Transactions: Sold or otherwise disposed of—amount.* Just like the entries for purchases, this column tells you the number of shares disposed of in each separate transaction.

12. *Transactions: Sold or otherwise disposed of—price.* This column, of course, tells you the price the insider received for his or her sale of shares. If no money was paid for the shares—such as in the case of a disposition by gift—this space will be blank.

13. *Month-end holdings of securities.* This column tells you the total number of shares held by the insider at the end of the reporting month, *including the trades reported that month.* This information is provided only for those insiders who reported trades during that month. Other insiders who did not file any reporting forms are not listed even though they may hold shares.

14. *Option reported.* When a "Y" appears in this column it means "yes" that an insider has reported some type of exercise of options. This does not have meaningful significance for the insider investor approach.

What to Look For

Of the fourteen items of information we just described, only five are of real importance for you when you go through the *Official Summary.*

· Character of transaction

- Number of shares involved (Transactions: Bought or otherwise acquired—amount)

- Relationship of insider to company

- Price of shares (Transactions: Bought or otherwise acquired—price)

- Date of transaction

When looking at each entry in the *Official Summary*, you first look at the character of transaction. Don't bother looking at any other item if the character is not one of the signals that tell you something significant—primarily those that show an open-market purchase ("P") or private purchase ("J"). Through this initial screen you will eliminate the vast majority of the entries in any single issue of the *Official Summary*. If the character *is* either of these key indicators of insider buying, then look at the number of shares involved. If the figure is greater than 500 shares, then look at the relationship of the insider to the company. If you find that the insider holds an important position within the company—either as a top-level officer or a director—then you should look back at the entries in the previous five issues of the *Official Summary* to see if there is a history of continuing insider buying. (Looking back over the previous twelve months is even better.) After you have found evidence of a consistent pattern of unusual behavior, then look at the dates of transactions to determine the frequency and timing of the insiders' purchases. Then, finally, pay attention to the prices the insiders paid for their shares and compare that to the stock's current market price.

Setting Up an Insider File

The best way to keep tabs on an interesting insider situation as it develops over the months is to isolate the insider trading data in that situation from the irrelevancies surrounding it. A simple, but intelligent way to do this is to take a blank sheet of paper and copy down all the insider trading data that sparked your interest in the company in the first place. An easier alternative to writing the data down is to photocopy the insider transaction entry (or entries) and tape or glue them on a piece of paper in chronological order as they appeared in the different issues of the *Official Summary*.

This page of data is the core for all future information you gather about the company and the insiders' trading activity. As new insider data comes available, you add it to this sheet. Then you can quickly scan down the columns and get the full picture. Plus, by comparing one information sheet with others from other companies you can compare the strengths and weaknesses of each before making a final investment decision from among the alternatives.

In addition, your file might include news stories about the company that would give you the possible reasons behind the insiders' investments, or biographies of the insiders that may give you clues about the personalities or temperaments of the people you are looking to for your investment clues.

Chapter 13

SEC Documents II: How to Read a Schedule 13D

THERE are two types of information sources you must have in order to find out what the outside/insiders are up to.

One: A comprehensive summary of all recent Schedule 13D filings. With this source you first identify outside/insider investments that are of particular interest.

Two: Full copies of the original Schedule 13D report. Since the summaries of Schedule 13D filings that are currently available do not give you *all* the information you need about an outside/insider's investment, you must obtain a full copy of the original Schedule 13D as filed by the outside/insider for each of those investment situations that interest you sufficiently to warrant further study.

Unlike the government's publication of inside/insider trading data found in the *Official Summary*, there is no counterpart government publication for Schedule 13D filers. You must, therefore, go to nongovernment information sources to find comprehensive summaries of Schedule 13D filings.

Despite the extensive coverage you may *think* that the financial press gives to the activities of outside/insiders, don't believe that the information you read in the newspapers or any other general circulation publication about Schedule 13D filings is comprehensive. The opposite is the truth. Most of those Schedule 13D news reports focus only on initial Schedule 13D filings of newsy or well-known outside/insiders, or outside/insider trading activity in the stock of large or closely followed companies or when the initial filing makes news in announcing a takeover intention. Amendments to Schedule 13Ds are even less likely to be reported in general financial news media—except, again, when they involve major moves by well-known "players" or big companies or takeover moves. (An amendment to a Schedule 13D is required whenever an outside/insider changes stock ownership by 2 percent or when there is a change in any other investment status such as changes with the people who make up an investment group or changes in investment purpose, from, say, stock ownership for "investment purposes only" to "intention to influence management.")

Even when a general financial news source *does* print news of an initial Schedule 13D filing or an amendment, the information given is rarely complete. Usually the news report will leave out details identifying *all* of the people who are involved in the outside/insider investment (it will focus on the best-known people) and the amount of money the outside/insider paid for the holdings. All of this information can be found in the *original* Schedule 13D filing. But general financial news sources don't seem to want to bother to dig into it to find the *full* story. And without the full story you cannot make an intelligent investment decision for yourself based on the activities of outside/insiders. So, you must turn to specialized sources of outside/insider trading information.

To fill our first information need—a summary of all recent Schedule 13D filings—there are currently three regularly published printed sources that can be used.

SEC TODAY
Washington Service Bureau, Inc.
655 Fifteenth Street NW
Washington, DC 20005
(202) 833-9200
Published daily, Monday-Friday. One-year subscription: $280 (if mailed first class), $230 (if mailed second class).

SEC Today provides a daily tally of the previous day's Schedule 13D filings (as well as other required corporate filings that are of no interest to us as insider-watchers). For each filing the publication lists the name of the outside/insider, the name of the company that the filer has invested in, the amendment number of the filing (if it isn't an *initial* filing), the nationality of the filer, the class of security traded (common, preferred and so on), the actual date of the filing, an indication as to whether the filing reports an increase, decrease or no change in the filer's holdings, the total number of shares held by the filer and the percent of the company's outstanding shares the filer holds as of that Schedule 13D filing. The publication *does not* tell how many shares were involved in the outside/insider's trade or the amount of money paid for the shares (or the amount of money received if it was a sale). *SEC Today* is the least costly printed source of information on Schedule 13D filings and cannot be beat for timeliness.

SPECTRUM 5
CDA Investment Technologies, Inc.
11501 Georgia Avenue
Silver Spring, MD 20902
(301) 942-1700
Published monthly. One-year subscription: $405 plus postage.

This publication provides a comprehensive listing of Schedule 13Ds filed during the previous sixty days. It tells you the date of the most recent filing, the total number of shares held by the outside/insider as of that filing and the total of shares held by the outside/insider as of the previous filing. It does not tell you the amendment number of the Schedule 13D filing nor the amount paid (or received) for the purchase (or sale) of the outside/insider's holdings.

Spectrum 5 (which has an on-line computer data base counterpart) also provides a complete listing of every company in which an outside/insider has an active Schedule 13D on file at the SEC. This listing includes not only the filings made in the past sixty days but *all* filings by *all* outside/insiders—some of which go back several years but have not had recent amendments. The date of the most recent filing of each of these outside/insiders is given as is the date of the most recent previous filing—if there has been one.

Although *Spectrum 5* isn't as timely as the other two printed sources of Schedule 13D filings, the comprehensive listing of all outside/insider filings offers an excellent overview perspective on the holdings of all the different outside/insiders interested in the same company. This information is often difficult to piece together if you only know about the most recent outside/insider activity.

TRANSACTIONS & INTENTIONS REPORT
Vickers Stock Research Corporation
P.O. Box 59
Brookside, NJ 07926
(201) 539-1336
Published twice a week. One-year subscription: $495.

Like *SEC Today, Transactions & Intentions Report* provides almost overnight information on the latest Schedule 13D filings. And, like *SEC Today*, it tells you the name of the outside/insider, the amendment number (if there is one) of the filing, the total number of shares held by the filer as of the latest report and the percentage of the outside/insider's total ownership of the company's stock. In addition, the *Transactions & Intentions Report* tells you the exact number of shares involved in the trades that prompted the filing. And it also provides short annotations describing special announcements included in the outside/insider's report. For example, it will tell you if the filing was accompanied by a statement of takeover intent or whether the outside/insider is attempting to make changes in the way the target company is being run. (*SEC Today* and *Spectrum 5* do not tell you this.) The publication does not tell you the amount of money the outside/insider paid for his or her holdings, but the timeliness of the information and the descriptions of the special announcements in the filings make it a worthy subscription possibility despite its cost.

Besides summarizing the data found in Schedule 13Ds, the three sources we have profiled also provide details on other outside/insider forms that we ignore. For example, Schedules 14D, 13G and 13E-4. Schedule 14D is filed in situations involving tender offers. Schedule 13G is filed by investors, such as banks, brokers and insurance companies when they acquire a large block of stock, who have no intention of changing or influencing the control of the company they have invested in. Schedule 13E-4 is another form required by certain tender offer participants. The important thing to remember is that we are interested only in Schedule 13D filings; all others can be disregarded for our purposes.

After you have decided which of the three summaries of Schedule 13D activity is best for you (any of the three can be used successfully), you must find your source for obtaining full copies of the outside/insiders' reports. Both the Washington

Service Bureau (publisher of *SEC Today*) and Vickers Research (publishers of *Transactions & Intentions Report*) provide this service. You simply write or telephone the service bureau and order a copy of the specific filing or filings you are interested in seeing. A photocopy will be mailed to you, usually on the same day as the receipt of your order. And you will be billed for the service. The cost for this varies, but it is about 40¢ per page with a minimum order of about $20. Some of the Schedule 13D filings are many pages long—sometimes fifty or more, depending on the complexity of the filing. But it is a good idea to group together orders for copies of several reports so that you are sure to use up your minimum order charge to its fullest extent.

There are some other reputable companies that provide this service too.

BECHTEL INFORMATION SERVICES
15740 Shady Grove Road
Gaithersburg, MD 20877
(301) 258-4300

INFOSEC
Investment Banking Inside Trading Network
International Trade Building
P.O. Box 50109
Washington, DC 20004
(202) 429-6614

FACS INFORMATION SERVICE, INC.
157 Fisher Avenue
Eastchester, NY 10709
(914) 779-5314

All of these companies can also provide specialized services such as a daily watch for filings on specific corporations or by specific outside/insiders, and the services and costs differ among these companies. Each will send information on their capabilities on request.

A less costly alternative to using a nongovernment source for copies of Schedule 13Ds is to order directly through the SEC. The problem with this, however, is that it takes much longer to receive the copies. To order through the SEC, you first need official order forms, which you can obtain by writing (don't bother to telephone) to: Public References Branch, Securities and Exchange Commission, Washington, DC 20549. Ask for several copies of the "Request and Authorization for Records Services" form. The form's official number is "Form SEC-86." Each of these forms allows you to order up to five different SEC documents. If you think you will be ordering more than that number at a time, you should also request several copies of "Form SEC-86A Continuation Sheet." Also ask for the "Schedule of Fees for Records Services" (Form SEC 1237).

As of this writing, the SEC charges 10¢ per page for each request, with no minimum order. Postage costs are additional. There is also a $2.50 per half hour charge for locating the original document if it takes more than a half hour for an SEC clerk to find it. (The first half hour search is free.) Since most of the documents that we are interested in looking at are recent and are therefore easily available, you probably won't need to pay any extra search costs.

Sorting Through Schedule 13D Summaries

In any one day there are usually a dozen or more filings of initial and amended Schedule 13Ds. Like the trading activities of inside/insiders, outside/insider trading as reported in these dozen or so daily filings hold different degrees of interest to us as possible clues for our own investments. And like the standards we apply to inside/insiders, we are looking for a "consistent pattern of unusual behavior" among outside/insiders before we can even contemplate our own move.

We want to look at *who* is filing the Schedule 13D: Does this person or corporation or investment group have a solid history of picking winners or possess the ability to make things happen to appreciate a company's stock price? Is the filer a corporation investing into another company in the same or related business? And, most of all, is there any historical record of the "player(s)" style of play? We also want to judge the *aggressiveness* of the trading that is reported: Has the outside/insider shown repeated buying activity or, better yet, accelerated purchases of a company's stock?

Because we like to see *repeated* evidence of an outside/insider's belief in the future value of a company's stock—we want to make sure he really means it—we normally disregard *initial* Schedule 13D filings. Schedule 13D *amendments* are the documents that tell us the level of the outside/insider's aggressiveness. (It is common practice by outside/insiders to buy up to and hold at just under 5 percent—avoiding "going public" with an SEC filing—until they are comfortable with a decision to go ahead and buy more.) It's those fifth, sixth, seventh or greater number of amendments that show an outside/insider's stock accumulation growing from 5 percent to 8 percent to 12 percent and more of the company's stock that give us the clue that the investor is very certain of his investment decision.

Initial Schedule 13D filings, however, can be of interest in some situations. For example, if we had identified significant buying activity among *inside/insiders* and suddenly an *outside/insider* comes on the scene with an initial Schedule 13D filing, it would add further support to our positive reading of the actual corporate insiders' activities. Also, an initial Schedule 13D filing can be of interest when one or more outside/insiders have already shown 5 percent or more ownership of a company and another *new* outside/insider appears via an initial Schedule 13D. But, again, what we are looking for here is evidence of *repeated* bullish activity. Not by the same person or investing entity, but by similar ones. And all with the same motivation—financial self-interest.

We consider it very important to watch those Schedule 13D *amendments* that announce a *change* in the outside/insider's stated "purpose of transaction," which is one of the required parts of the SEC report. When the "purpose of transaction" goes from "for investment purposes only" to "in order to influence management" or "seeks representation on the board of directors," we can see that the outside/insider is getting more intimately involved with his investment. It is another obvious sign of aggressiveness. The outside/insider in these situations shows an investor who goes from a passive one to one who wants to protect and/or stir things up to appreciate the value of his holdings. It may even precede a later takeover attempt. This doesn't mean that an aggressive statement of "purpose of transaction" is a requirement before we can become interested in an outside/insider's investment. If the filer's buying actions show enough aggressiveness on their own but the "purpose of transaction" remains "for investment purposes only," it can still be a very, very interesting situation—as followers of Warren Buffett (one of the better-known winners) will attest.

The Original Schedule 13D

After you have gone through a summary of Schedule 13D filings and found one or more that interest you, you go on to the next step and get a complete copy of the original filing. Here let's look at one example of an actual Schedule 13D filing, which is particularly intriguing because of the players involved—none other than the principals of the world's largest investment advisory and mutual fund organization, Fidelity Management. If you had seen this example summarized in one of the printed sources, you would have found the following information:

Issuer:	Deltak Corporation
Date of filing:	11/18/85
Type & size of trade:	Buy—65,000
Total holdings:	267,700
Percent held:	24.6 percent
Beneficial owner:	Fidelity International Ltd, et al
Amendment number:	5

This summary clearly fulfills the criteria we use to screen reports of Schedule 13D filings. First, we find a filer who has a solid history of good investment choices—Fidelity International Ltd. This group, of course, is one of the investment vehicles used by the top management of the Fidelity mutual fund organization for its own personal investments outside its mutual funds. (Notice that the summary includes an "et al" to identify the name of the beneficial owner. Later, when we look through the actual 13D filing, we'll find out exactly who the "et al" includes.) Also, we see from the summary information that this is the fifth amendment, reporting on an additional acquisition of 65,000 shares which brings the investment group's holdings in the company to almost 25 percent—all very aggressive behavior by a group that definitely should know what it's doing.

Now the real excitement starts as we look into the original filing. With an actual copy of this Schedule 13D in hand, the first page you encounter—which is included with every Schedule 13D filing—tells you: (a) the date that the SEC received the filing, (b) the amendment number of the filing, (c) the name of the issuing company, which is the target of the filer's trades, (d) the type of securities involved in the report, which in this case is common stock, (e) the "CUSIP" number that the SEC uses to identify the issuing company, (f) the name and address of the person that the filer has designated to receive any notices or communications from either the SEC or the issuing company, (g) the date on which the latest trade occurred that prompted this filing—in other words, when the buying (or selling) changed the size of ownership by 2 percent from the previous filing and (h) the number of pages in this filing.

Page 2 of the filing gives the name of the principal filer—which is Fidelity International Limited—as well as the location, group status and share of ownership details. You'll find that the rest of that page of the form does not usually hold very much information. This is common because the information required in Schedule 13D filings takes up more space than is provided on the form, and, therefore, the form almost always includes attachments that explain the whole investment story.

For each different investment entity that files with the principal filer, another identical form must be filled out—even though the attachments explain the relationships among the different investment entities. In this example there were six other investment entities besides Fidelity International Limited involved in the Schedule 13D filing and therefore there were six separate pages filled out.

In this particular Schedule 13D filing, it is page 9 where the real meat is found. This begins the attachment that explains what is going on. In reading through a Schedule 13D, you are going to find that the most pertinent pieces of information are somewhat buried inside lawyer-style language. If you are not used to reading such documents, it will take some patience and practice and much rereading to make sense of all this.

The first item in any Schedule 13D—"Item 1. Security and Issuer"—identifies the company that issued the stock traded by the Schedule 13D filer. In our example, the company was Deltak Corporation, a Minneapolis-based manufacturer of heat recovery, steam generating and energy conversion systems, which makes things like waste heat boilers, wood- and coal-fired steam boilers and waste-to-energy boilers. The company's stock is sold over the counter.

The next item in a Schedule 13D—"Item 2. Identity and Background"—provides details on the participants in the investments: the names of the investment entities and the people behind them. In the Deltak example, we find that there are six investment vehicles reporting: Fidelity International Limited (FIL), American Values (AV), American Values II, American Values III, A.V. Investments III and Dorsey R. Gardner.

We also find out that FIL is a company that is incorporated in Bermuda—not the United States—and to which companies FIL focuses its energies on providing investment advice to:

> FIL is an investment advisor which, together with its subsidiaries, provides investment advice and management services to certain non-U.S. investment companies and other institutional investors.

Then, we are told the names, positions, addresses, principal occupations and citizenships of the officers and directors of FIL —including Edward C. "Ned" Johnson III, who heads FMR Corporation:

> Edward C. Johnson 3d, Chairman of the Board; *address:* 82 Devonshire Street, Boston, Massachusetts; *principal occupation:* Chairman of the Board and chief executive officer of FMR Corp., a financial services organization; *citizenship:* United States.
>
> William L. Byrnes, Vice Chairman of the Board; *address:* 25 Lovat Lane, London, England EC3R8LL; *principal occupation:* Vice Chairman of the Board of FIL; *citizenship:* United States.
>
> Charles T. M. Collis, Secretary; *address:* Clarendon House, Church Street, Hamilton, Bermuda; *principal occupation:* Partner of Conyers, Dill & Pearman (Barristers-at-Law); *citizenship:* Bermuda.
>
> Arnott C. Jackson, President and Comptroller and a Director; *address:* Pembroke Hall, 42 Crowlane, Hamilton, Bermuda; *principal occupation:* President of FIL; *citizenship:* Bermuda.
>
> James E. Tonner, Director; *address:* 25 Lovat Lane, London, England EC3R8LL; *principal occupation:* Managing Director of Fidelity International Investment Advisors (UK) Limited, an investment advisory company; *citizenship:* United Kingdom.

Quite an interesting group! Four of the people are involved in investment advice—at the Fidelity organization, no less—and one is a lawyer.

Next, we find that Ned Johnson owns the lion's share of the company:

A substantial portion of the capital shares of FIL is held by Edward C. Johnson 3d, and Mr. Johnson 3d may be deemed a controlling person of FIL.

We can surmise from this that Johnson has a sincere personal financial interest in making this company succeed. And since his expertise has helped make FMR Corporation—and its mutual funds—so successful, his personal financial involvement with FIL certainly suggests that he probably wouldn't take on an investment that would hurt him financially.

The next piece of information we discover shows that the American Values investment entities are incorporated under the laws of the Netherlands Antilles and that they share the same offices as FIL in Bermuda. Obviously the various investment vehicles are interrelated. We find out *how* interrelated they are when we are told the names of the officers and directors of the American Values companies:

Hisashi Kurokawa, Director; *address:* 4-26-25 Kichijojihoncho, Nusashino-shi, Tokyo, Japan; *principal occupation:* Chairman of the Board of Mitsubishi Petrochemical Co. Ltd; *citizenship:* Japan.

John M. S. Patton, G.C., C.B.E., Director; *address:* Church Street, Hamilton, Bermuda; *principal occupation:* Partner of Hallett, Whitney & Patton (Barristers-at-Law); *citizenship:* Bermuda.

James E. Tonner, Director.

Corporate Trust N.V., Director; *address:* 16-A Pietermaai, Willemstad, Curaçao, Netherlands Antilles; *business and citizenship:* a trust company organized under the laws of the Netherlands Antilles.

Charles T. M. Collis, Secretary.

In addition to the above, Dorsey R. Gardner is a Director of American II and American III. Mr. Gardner's business address, present principal occupation or employment, and citizenship are listed below in this Item 2.

Here we find familiar names from the list of people at FIL, with a few different names thrown in. Most notable is Hisashi Kurokawa, who is also chairman of the board of Japan's Mitsubishi Petrochemical Company.

It appears from this list that Johnson and FIL have put together a consortium of international high roller investors to invest in American companies. (Deltak isn't the only company that FIL has taken a large interest in.) The name that has been chosen for the investment companies—"American Values"—is telling, since these international investors are obviously looking for values among American companies.

Their selection of Bermuda and the Netherlands Antilles as the spots to incorporate their investment vehicles was most certainly not by chance. It probably has something to do with tax considerations. This does not imply, nor does anything else said here about these investors, that anything whatsoever is illegal or even remotely shady about this investment setup. All of the people involved have maintained an impeccable reputation in the past and will most certainly maintain it in the future. They have just found advantages to investing through these vehicles.

We also find out in this section that FIL "acts as investment advisor" to the American Values companies. And that "in connection with its obligations thereunder, FIL has the authority, for and in the name of each such investment company, to purchase Shares on its behalf and to dispose of Shares owned by it." FIL, therefore, has the power to buy and sell for the other companies. This seems somewhat of a moot point since some of the people heading FIL also head the other companies. But it does explain that FIL is only the advisor and the other companies are putting up the capital for the investments.

Next, a new name is introduced, Kelso Management Company. This Boston-based corporation, we learn, is owned by Dorsey R. Gardner. Its stated function is to supply "investment advice with respect to North American securities to FIL for its use in connection with American, American II, and American III." We also learn that a man named John R. Kountz is the vice president, secretary and a director of Kelso. (Remember that name; it comes up again in a different context later.)

Next comes a statement that is standard in all Schedule 13D filings telling you that no one involved has been convicted of any crimes in the last five years.

The third section of information in any Schedule 13D filing— "Item 3. Source and Amount of Funds or Other Consideration" —can be very telling. In the Deltak example we find that the American Values companies each purchased shares for cash and that all the funds used by each were its own funds and that no part of any purchase was from borrowed funds. But, we also learn that Dorsey Gardner *borrowed* at least some of his funds:

> Mr. Gardner purchased Shares owned by him for cash. The funds used by Mr. Gardner in purchasing such Shares were obtained through a margin loan facility maintained by Mr. Gardner with a securities brokerage firm.

Now, when you buy stock with a margin loan account you have to pay interest on that money. Gardner, then, must have thought that his investment into Deltak was such a good thing that he was willing to pay interest to get the money to be part of the game. This is very bullish and aggressive behavior. It probably wasn't an investment by someone who had excessive cash that he didn't know what to do with. It required a hard business decision. Gardner must have thought it was a good deal.

The next major section of a Schedule 13D—"Item 4. Purpose of Transaction"—is where the investors state the reasons for their investments. It is in this section that you would find notices about an intended takeover or a merger plan, for example. Most of the time, however, the filer says that the shares are purchased for "investment purposes only." This is the statement we find in the Deltak example. We are told that FIL and Dorsey Gardner bought shares to "acquire an equity interest in the company." And we are told that they "may purchase additional Shares...subject to a number of factors, including, among others, the availability of Shares for purchase at what FIL considers to be reasonable prices and other investment opportunities that may be available...."

This is also the section in which an investor who is buying shares for "investment purposes only" will state that he has no merger, reorganization, liquidation or sale plans for the company. In the Deltak example this is exactly what is stated. However, buried at the bottom of four long paragraphs stating that FIL and Dorsey Gardner have no aggressive designs on the company is this little bombshell:

> The Reporting Persons, however, have decided to seek representation on the Board of Directors.

It is an aggressive move that was not seen in the investors' previous Schedule 13D filings. And the group got its way. By

January 1, 1986, John Kountz—Kelso's only officer/director other than owner Dorsey Gardner—was listed as a director of Deltak. FIL and the others then had someone on the board to protect their interests!

"Item 5. Interest in Securities of Issuer" is the section on a Schedule 13D that tells you the exact size of the holdings of the investors and the amount of money they paid (or received) for their shares. In the Deltak example, the filers provided a table that illustrates the holdings—a nicety that is not often found on a Schedule 13D.

AMOUNT AND NATURE OF BENEFICIAL OWNERSHIP

Name of Reporting Person	Sole Voting Power	Sole Investment Power	Shared Voting Power	Shared Investment Power	Total Beneficial Ownership	Percent of Common Stock [1]
American	0	0	0	0	0	0
American II	145,000	145,000	0	0	145,000	13.3
American III	107,200	107,200	0	0	107,200	9.9
Dorsey R. Gardner	15,000	15,000	0	0	15,000	1.4
FIL	0	251,700	0	0	251,700	23.2
TOTAL					267,200	24.6

[1] Based on the number of shares outstanding as most recently reported by the company.
Source: Securities and Exchange Commission

Next we find out how much the investors paid for the shares they bought that prompted the filing in the first place:

On March 11, 1985 American II purchased 45,000 Shares in open market transactions in the over-the-counter market at a cost of approximately $345,375.

Divide 45,000 shares into $345,375 to find that this stock was bought at about $7.68 a share. Also:

On October 16th, 1985 American purchased 5,000 Shares at a cost of approximately $27,500 . . .

These shares cost about $5.50 a share.

The exact amounts and prices of Dorsey Gardner's shares are also given.

Date of Purchase	Number of Shares Purchased	Price per Share	Commission per Share
September 6, 1984	3,000	$7.25	$.09
January 25, 1985	2,000	5.50	.07
January 25, 1985	3,000	5.625	.07
February 22, 1985	2,000	6.75	.07
February 22, 1985	5,000	7.00	.07

It's interesting to look at the dates here. Gardner had purchased some of his shares more than a year before reporting along with FIL. In earlier amendments, Gardner is listed only as an investment advisor, not as part of the investment group. Here we see that he evidently wants to be aligned with FIL, perhaps because he wants to be part of this new direct involvement with Deltak, or because groups controlled by FIL want him and/or his associate John Kountz to be more actively involved.

The last section of this Schedule 13D amendment—"Item 6. Contracts, Arrangements, Understandings or Relationships with Respect to Securities of the Issuer"—is another standard statement found in such filings where there is more than one group involved. Essentially it says that everyone is friendly and there's no lying going on among the participants. And, finally, the Schedule 13D is signed, verifying that all is true.

You should recognize that the information gleaned from this Schedule 13D filing concerning Deltak stock displays a "consistent pattern of unusual" behavior that would have made Deltak Corporation a *very* compelling investment choice. The investing shown here is almost as good as getting a personal telephone call from Ned Johnson telling you that he, and several other investing cronies, considers this company to be an excellent investment.

FIL itself started investing in Deltak almost two years prior to this fifth Schedule 13D filing amendment. The *initial* FIL filing on this company was submitted on March 12, 1984, and showed 7.2 percent ownership. As we've just seen in the amendment, investing picked up speed. And the investors became more aggressively involved with the management of the company. By waiting to see *repeated* investing behavior on the part of the outside/insiders—and not jumping on the news of their *initial* Schedule 13D filing—the approach to following these investors is conservative. And it is no more speculative or risky an investment than Johnson and the others themselves consider it to be, whose consistency of buying implies that they believe the potential returns greatly outweigh the risks.

Throughout all the outside/insiders' investing and Schedule 13D filings—which continued into 1986, until by the end of July 1986, they had purchased a total of nearly 328,000 shares for a total ownership of nearly 30 percent—you could have picked up shares in this company at the same and lower prices than the outside/insiders paid themselves. By the spring of 1987, the Deltak Corporation "story" had not surfaced in the news, but the stock had advanced to well above $11 per share— already an excellent return on your investment if you had bought along with the outside/insiders.

It is impossible to know, of course, what these investors saw in Deltak or what they think will happen that will bring them the profits they most certainly expect. Deltak is a solid little company, but even in early 1987 there didn't appear to be anything exciting about it indicating that its stock would break away from the fairly steady $5–$7 a share price that it commanded over the previous few years.

But here's a prediction: FIL, American Values or Dorsey Gardner will not attempt to take over the company. This isn't the past style of these investors. More likely, the company will be promoted by its investors to some other investment entity—a larger corporation or individual investor—as an attractive acquisition property.

The Deltak story is just one example of the type of investment activity that should interest you as an insider-watcher. As of the beginning of November 1987, we do not know the outcome. But at the same time, as in all interesting insider situations, it should be evident that this has not been a "trading" or short-term play for these investors, but a long-term commitment that should pay off big enough to make the wait worthwhile for them—in their own self-interests.

SEC Schedule 13D filings resemble the sort of confidential report one would expect to get by hiring a very professional private investigator. But here you have the added benefit of being certain of the facts reported, because the SEC's enforcement procedures keep it that way. Thus, it is obvious that with this publicly available document in hand you can make some very concrete conclusions about the investment stance of these outside/insiders. And that, in turn, can become an influential factor in making your own investment decisions.

Chapter 14

On-line Data Bases

IF you have always wanted a personal computer system but could never think of a good enough reason to justify the expense, being able to access insider trading information via a computer on-line data base may be just the excuse you're looking for. It is truly a marvel. Using a small desktop computer and a telephone hookup, you can connect with a big computer thousands of miles away that holds billions of pieces of information. By typing in a key word (or a few key words), you instruct the big computer to sort through all those billions of pieces of information and display on your small computer's screen all the information that relates to your key word. In a matter of seconds—or at most a few minutes—you are able to glean through a mountain of data that could normally take hours if you did the same thing by using printed sources of information. The computer also can do it more completely and more accurately than doing it by hand because there is less chance of the human error that often accompanies searches through printed data.

Among the many financial data bases currently available are a few that contain information on insider trading activities. You can use them, for example, to find a detailed and comprehensive list of all the insider trading transactions at a specific company within the last six months, the last twelve months or even the last two years. This saves you from having to keep a shelf full of copies of the *Official Summary* and thumbing through many issues to find the information you need to make your own investment decision. Also, capturing the insider data about a certain company on your computer and then printing that information on paper saves you from cutting up bits of paper and pasting them on a file copy for each company you are following closely.

Despite the timesaving wonders that a computer hookup to insider data bases provides, it is not necessary for you to spend thousands of dollars to buy a computer system in order to access insider trading information. The data bases can be powerful helpmates, but they are not *essential* for following insider activities. As we have seen, advisory newsletters and printed sources can be used successfully for that purpose.

On the other hand, a computer is more than just a toy when used in insider information gathering. And if you already own a computer system, you should seriously consider subscribing to one or more of the insider data bases available. Since most of the data bases charge only for the amount of time you actually use the services, you will not be spending money except when you need the data base information.

Using Insider Data Bases—Opportunities and Limitations

Insider data bases have been available only since the early 1980s. However, the first use of the computer to help in the sorting and analysis of insider trading data started back in the early 1970s. In 1974 a few of us serious insider-watchers found out that the *Official Summary* was actually typeset from a computer tape on which the SEC had inputed all the data from the original Form 3 and Form 4 filings. Today you can subscribe to the computer version on a monthly basis. However, the use of on-line data bases is a much more convenient and less costly route for the average investor with access to only a personal computer. The government's magnetic tape is not available through the SEC (most people there don't even know that it *is* available) or through the Government Printing Office. Instead, you can get it by contacting: Machine Readable Reproductions Department, The National Archives, Constitution Avenue NW, Washington, DC 20005, (202) 523-3267. As of this writing a subscription to this tape costs $160 a month. It is available only in a magnetic tape version; it cannot be used on microcomputer floppy disk equipment, and you must design your own software to organize the raw data that the tape contains.

With the introduction of insider on-line data bases, comprehensive insider trading data has become available to anyone with a personal computer setup. The insider data base industry, however, is still in somewhat of a primitive stage. The data bases do not have as much flexibility for searching through the data as you would ideally expect. One of the reasons for this is that the data bases were designed to provide supplementary information to analysts following the traditional forms of fundamental and technical analysis strategies. These analysts use insider trading information to view insider "attitudes" about specific companies that have initially been identified through some other screening procedures. Therefore the data bases are set up to access the insider trading information by name of company and to display all the insider trading transactions (or holdings) at that specific company. Basically, you have to know the name of the company you wish to research. Also some data bases are set up to cross-reference the names of insiders to find their holdings in other companies. But, as an insider analyst looking to the actions of insiders as the *primary* signal to identify the names of companies as investment candidates, the currently available data base systems cannot be used efficiently to sort through the data.

Here's an illustration of an ideal data-sorting procedure for initially identifying the names of companies that is not possible using existing programs on currently available insider data bases: One of the basic sorting activities used at the Insider Reports Fund is a computer reading of the government's magnetic tape version of the *Official Summary*. (This tape, of course, contains only the trading information for inside/insiders—Form 3 and Form 4 filers. The computer application is only one of several used for analysis at the Insider Reports Fund.) Each month the data on the tape is sorted through the use of a specially created computer program to give a list of all insider transactions—organized by company—of 500 or more shares in the five "types" discussed earlier—"P," "J," "X," "S" and "K." This is the same type of initial sorting that you saw in the description of "How to Read the *Official Summary*" in Chapter 12. After this initial computer screening, each company on the list is examined more carefully. As you can imagine, the computer sorting saves an enormous amount of time by filtering out unimportant transactions while providing a comprehensive listing of all companies with even the remotest possibility of interesting insider activity. Although this ideal sorting process is not possible with existing data bases, there are ways that you can achieve the same result with those that are. Let's look at the data bases that are available, then learn a strategy for using them to the best advantage.

The Data Bases

The data base field is a very rapidly changing one. Descriptions of the insider data bases available as of this writing follow, but bear in mind that details on costs and features of these data bases may have changed.

CDA
CDA Investment Technologies, Inc.
11501 Georgia Avenue
Silver Spring, MD 20902
(301) 942-1700

The CDA data base is an on-line version of the company's printed directories, *Spectrum 5*—which provides monthly information on filings relating to 5 percent beneficial ownership (outside/insiders)—and *Spectrum 6*—a semiannual compilation of the total holdings by Form 3 and Form 4 filers (inside/insiders). The on-line version of the information is much more current than the printed versions since it is updated daily.

Using this data base, you can get an abstracted list of Schedule 13D filings on whatever date (or dates) you want. You can tell the data base to show you all the Schedule 13Ds filed yesterday, or in the last week or month, or the ones filed during a certain week last June or within any other time frame. The list provides information on the name of the issuing company, the class of securities involved in the report, the name of the owner, the date of the most current filing and total current share holdings as of that filing and the date and share holdings as of the most recent previous filing—if there has been one. By comparing the filer's current holdings with the holdings reported in the most recent previous filing you can tell whether the filer has bought or sold shares as well as the number of shares involved. As you saw in Chapter 13, this type of summary of Schedule 13D filings is essential for finding out what outside/insiders are doing. After a review of a listing of recent Schedule 13D filings, such as the one provided by the CDA data base, you can identify those filings that are of particular interest to you—either because of your familiarity with the name of the filer or the size of a buy transaction—and then take the next step by obtaining a copy of the *original* Schedule 13D filing for closer inspection to find out such details as the prices paid for the shares and the filer's "Purpose of Transaction."

Also, if you are interested in finding out the various holdings of a specific outside/insider, you simply type in the name of the person—or the name of that person's investment vehicle, if you know it—and you will be given a list of all companies where a stock investment has been made. This is helpful in determining the scope of an insider's total stock investment as well as for comparing the bullish attitude an insider has about his different investments. (This cross-referencing feature is *not* available for the Form 3 and Form 4 filers—inside/insiders.)

Another valuable capability of the CDA data base is the comprehensive listing of *all* insider holdings at a specific company. With this feature, you type in the name of the company you are researching and you will be given a complete list of all current holdings by Schedule 13D filers, inside/insiders and institutional owners. We ignore institutional ownership with the approach followed here, but the other information provides an overview of all the "players" at a specific company that is difficult to gather if you are looking at only the most recent activity at a company.

The only thing we would additionally wish was that the data base provided detailed information about the specifics of the insider's trading transactions. While an insider's total current holdings and the date of the last transaction are given, you do not know the amount paid for shares or the history of the insider's trades. To find out this information, you have to use the printed version of the *Official Summary* or turn to another on-line data base.

Subscription information. There is a onetime setup fee of $100 to gain access to the CDA data base. After that you are charged $45 per hour of connect time. Also, there is a $3 charge for each day of Schedule 13D summary that you request. And there is a $25 charge for each report. A report is the complete listing of all holdings at a specific company or the complete listing of all holdings by a specific outside/insider. The $25 charge is the same no matter how long the report is—whether it turns out to be three lines or ten pages. For a cost of $450 a month you can have unlimited access to the data base. Magnetic tapes are also available.

The CDA data base is also available through the Dialog Information Services, 3460 Hillview Avenue, Palo Alto, CA 94304, (800) 334-2564. Dialog carries hundreds of different data bases from a wide range of data base suppliers, including many data bases containing business and financial information.

INVEST/NET: INSIDER TRADING MONITOR
Suite 237
99 Northwest 183rd Street
North Miami, FL 33169
(305) 652-1721

This data base contains only the information about inside/insiders—Form 3 and Form 4 filers. However, every item of information found in the printed *Official Summary* is carried on the data base. And it is updated daily. (Outside/insiders are included on this data base when their holdings go over 10 percent ownership, because at that time an outside/insider is required to file a Form 4 as well as a Schedule 13D. But the data base does not identify those investors as dual filers.)

Using this data base you can find all the details on every inside/insider transaction for a specific company. The listing includes all the pertinent data we need: type of security, relationship of the insider to the company, the name of the insider, the nature of ownership (direct or indirect), the character of the transaction (with the same codes as used in the *Official Summary*), the date of the transaction, the number of shares involved in the trade, the price per share paid (or received) and the total holdings of the insider as of that report. The separate transactions are organized in reverse chronological order with the most recent transaction at the beginning of the listing and going back two years. Therefore you can select the amount of trading history you want to see.

The other choice you have in accessing trading data is to trace the holdings of a specific inside/insider. This cross-referencing feature displays the insider's holdings by individual company and tells you the date of the last trading transaction for each company and the size of the insider's holding as of that transaction as well as the nature of the insider's ownership. To find out the historical details on the trades, you must go back to the list of insider trades by company name.

These two capabilities—searches by company name and by insider name—are very valuable tools. But like all the other insider data bases, FCI-Invest/Net begs the question: Where do you start? Which of the thousands of companies should be investigated carefully? And which of the tens of thousands of insiders should be looked at?

The data base's designers have attempted to solve that universal problem. In a file called "Activity Ranking, All U.S. Stocks," the data base gives you a list of companies ranked by an insider activity weighting formula which shows the "best" prospects at the top of the list and the "worst" at the bottom. The formula counts the number of open-market purchases and the number of option plan purchases and considers each of those transactions as equally positive signals. Then, open-market sells are subtracted from the sum of the open-market and option buys to give a "net trend" rating. This means, for example, that if there were fifteen open-market buys, twenty-five option buys and twelve sells over a particular time period, the "net trend" would equal "twenty-eight" (15 plus 25 minus 12 equals 28). It also means that if there had been twenty-five open-market buys and no option buys and no sells the company would receive a "net trend" rating of "twenty-five"—lower than the rating at the company that is overwhelmed with option buying. But the company with the higher "net trend" rating would appear higher on the data base's rating list.

You probably recognize this rating "formula" as the type of configuration used in the early academic statistical studies of insider trading. Such a "formula" is not considered to have very much commonsense value in terms of the approach followed in this book. We wish that it included some special weights for considerations such as private transactions, the *position* of the person trading, the size of the transactions, frequency of transactions and the amount of money paid for shares.

Despite the current limitations, however, this "Activity Ranking, All U.S. Stocks" can be used with success in helping you initially to identify possible candidates of interest. Here's how: Have the data base give you the activity ranking for the last six months. When studying this list, ignore those entries where the high ranking was achieved through a large number of option transactions. Focus only on those companies where there has been a great number of open-market purchases. Often you will find that companies with a great number of options transactions are at the top of the data base's ranking list. Just bypass those, and watch for the names of companies with the largest numbers of open-market transactions.

Using this approach you will be able to "screen" a sizable list of possible candidates. Of course, don't forget this is an *initial* screening. You still must investigate each candidate carefully, following the criteria outlined in previous chapters as well as the criteria that you will read about in the next chapter.

Another feature of FCI-Invest/Net's data base is a weekly editorial summary of significant insider reports from the previous week, called "Weekly Periscope." This service tends to report on the largest individual trades—usually "sells." But it can be used to spark your interest in specific companies for further investigation. Also provided is an "Activity Ranking, by Industry" that follows the same insider trading "formula" as the company-ranking listing. This industry ranking does not fit into our approach since we focus on the insider activity at *specific* companies and not on industrywide insider trading.

Subscription information. There is no setup charge for this data base. Connect charges are $60 an hour, plus communication charges of $9 an hour during the prime hours of Monday through Friday from 9:00 A.M. to 5:00 P.M. and $6 an hour during other times. There is a $35 minimum monthly charge.

The data base is also available on Dow Jones News/Retrieval, P.O. Box 300, Princeton, NJ 08540, (800) 257-5114 [New Jersey residents: (609) 452-1511] and on ADP Network Services, 175 Jackson Plaza, Ann Arbor, MI 48106, (313) 995-6400. Both of these data base networks carry other business and financial data

bases that can be valuable to you in supplementing information
about insiders and the companies they invest in.

VICKERS ON-LINE
226 New York Avenue
Huntington, NY 11743
(516) 423-7710

The Vickers On-Line service comes from the people who also
provide two printed sources of insider data—*Weekly Insider
Report* and *Transactions & Intentions Report*. The most attractive feature of the Vickers service, which is unequaled by any
data base currently available, is the detailed information on
Schedule 13D filings. The data base's Schedule 13D feature displays information on three levels. The first is a very abbreviated
listing of filings by date and by name of filer. If you are familiar
with the names of the investment vehicles of different active
outside/insiders, you can quickly scan this list until you find
something of interest. The next level of the feature gives more
details on the specific filing. The information provided here is
the same as in Vickers-printed *Transactions & Intentions Report*: amendment number (if it is not an *initial* Schedule 13D
filing), name of the issuing company, date(s) of the transac-
tion(s) reported in the filing, the type of transaction, the number
of shares involved in the transaction, the total holdings as of the
filing, percentage of ownership and the name and address of the
filer.

The third level of the feature gives a textual summary of the
filing, which provides information on the "purpose of transaction" and other valuable details. But it does not provide details
on the prices paid for shares (or amount received for shares
sold). Therefore, you must still obtain a complete copy of the
original Schedule 13D filing to get all the information you need.
But reading Vickers's summaries can provide you insights and
help you decide whether it is worth obtaining a copy of original
documents.

Besides the daily updated Schedule 13D information, Vickers
also provides an overview summary of all inside/insider and
outside/insider holdings by name of company (similar to CDA's
summary service). And the data base allows you to cross-reference the holdings of specific people and companies. All the

necessary trading information on all insider transactions is available on this data base (similar to the information on FCI-Invest/Net's system).

Although Vickers can be used to quickly sort through Schedule 13D filings, it does not have a system that allows you initially to identify interesting inside/insider trading like FCI-Invest/Net's "Activity Ranking" feature. On Vickers you can get information on inside/insider trades, but you will have to know the name of the company you want to investigate before using the system effectively.

Vickers also provides detailed information on institutional investor activity, but following institutional trading is not used in our insider approach to stock selection and investment. On balance, however, this is a first-rate resource for insider investment practitioners.

Subscription information. Vickers charges a $50 annual subscription fee and a $1 per minute ($60 per hour) connect charge. There are no other additional fees and there is no minimum monthly charge. Vickers On-Line is also available on Quotron Systems, 5454 Beethoven Street, Los Angeles, CA 90066, (213) 827-4600. Like other data base networks, Quotron provides numerous different data bases, including several that have business and financial applications.

Using Data Bases Strategically

Clearly, gathering information via insider data bases can help you piece together the comprehensive data you need to make your own intelligent investment decision based on insider activities. If you use the data bases efficiently by limiting the amount of time you are actually logged on to any one system, you can keep your costs relatively low—low enough, in fact, to perhaps justify subscribing to all the different data bases. If you use data bases carefully and efficiently, you could do a comprehensive reading of insider activities for as little as about twenty dollars a month. With this capability you would be able to tap into the strengths of each of the data bases.

Assuming you have access to more than one of the data bases, here is a step-by-step strategy for amassing the data you need before making final investment selections.

Step One: Identify the names of specific companies that you feel warrant in-depth investigation. As you have already seen, there are several different methods and sources you can use to do this:

- Manual reading of printed version of *Official Summary* for evidence of interesting inside/insider trading

- Manual reading of comprehensive printed lists of all recent Schedule 13D filings for evidence of interesting outside/insider trading

- Insider advisory newsletter recommendations

- News of "significant" insider trades as reported in the general financial press or on FCI-Invest/Net's "Periscope" service

- Reading of recent Schedule 13D filings as reported on Vickers or CDA systems for evidence of interesting outside/insider trading

- Careful analysis of FCI-Invest/Net's "Activity Ranking, All U.S. Stocks" for evidence of interesting inside/insider activity

Step Two: For each company you are interested in investigating, obtain a comprehensive listing of *all* current outside/insider and inside/insider holdings by using either Vickers or CDA.

Step Three: If there are interesting outside/insider holdings (or if outside/insider trades sparked your interest in the company in the first place), identify the date or dates of the most recent Schedule 13D filings by using either Vickers or CDA. If you have access to Vickers, you can review the detailed summary of those recent filings of interest. Obtain copies of the *original*, complete Schedule 13D filings that are particularly significant by ordering directly through the SEC or through one of the nongovernment document retrieval services.

Step Four: If there are interesting inside/insider holdings, trace the details of *all* inside/insider trading for the last six months—or, better, the last twelve months—on either Vickers or FCI-Invest/Net.

Step Five: For all significant insiders, check their holdings in *other* companies by using the cross-referencing capabilities of either CDA (available for outside/insiders only), FCI-Invest/Net (available for inside/insiders only) or Vickers (available for both outside/insiders and inside/insiders).

Having completed these five steps, you can feel confident that you have a comprehensive "package" of all the insider information you need before applying the final selection criteria as outlined in the next chapter.

The plan of attack we have just described is useful for a company-specific approach. Another approach is person-specific, which you can use if you want to monitor the activities of certain people. For example, let's say that there are some outside/insiders whose investing personalities or track records are particularly attractive to you. You can find out where they have their investment money by following this strategy:

Step One: Identify the name of person you want to watch—either from the names you've encountered in this book or through news reports of big investors found in newsletters or the general financial media.

Step Two: Use the outside/insider cross-referencing capabilities of either CDA or Vickers to find all the holdings in that person's name from Schedule 13D filings. Or use the inside/insider cross-referencing services of FCI-Invest/Net or Vickers to find the names of the companies where the person holds 10 percent or more of the stock.

Step Three: Using CDA, FCI-Invest/Net or Vickers cross-referencing files, enter the names of the *companies* that the insider has holdings in and identify the other companies in which those companies have major investments. You will find that many major outside/insiders hold their investments in several layers. For example, Saul Steinberg is personally a major shareholder in several companies. But he uses Reliance Insurance as a vehicle for further investments. You must, therefore, trace through all the layers of each investing entity to find the *complete* picture of a person's investment activity.

Step Four: With the names of the companies in hand, go back to the company-specific strategy and repeat all the information-gathering steps starting with *Step Two*.

Remember that these two strategic approaches give you only the raw data. Your analysis starts after you have all this information together.

On-line Data Base Cost-cutting Axioms

When you "log on" a computer on-line data base you will be charged for the amount of time you are connected with the data base's computer. Obviously, the more time you spend on-line the more it will cost. Therefore, here are three basic principles for keeping your on-line time to a minimum.

1. Know exactly what you want to "ask" the data base before connecting. Make a list of the data you want to access and stick to that list. If you find some piece of information that takes you off your original planned track, log off the data base and think through your information needs. Then, you can go back on-line to continue your information search. Don't sit in front of a screen while the meter is running to figure out your next step.

2. Instead of reading every item of information as it appears on the screen, capture the data you request in the memory of your computer. Later, after logging off, you can review the information at your leisure without racking up those connect charge dollars. Also, you can print information captured in your computer's memory at a later time.

3. Use the highest transmission speed possible in capturing data. On all the existing insider data bases the charges for using a 1200-baud transmission is the same as using a 300-baud transmission. This means you can capture data at four times the speed by using the highest transmission possible, saving you a considerable amount of on-line time.

Chapter 15

Testing Your Candidates

THE initial screening you do of SEC printed or computer-generated data usually will lead to a dozen or more *new* interesting insider investment candidates every month. But now we want to apply some tests to find the *best* investment possibilities from among all our various choices. To begin this final selection process, you must have in hand *all* the essential insider trading information about each of your candidates. Without it you will be comparing apples with oranges when you examine your candidates to decide which ones offer the best investment opportunities.

The following checklist can serve as a reminder of all the information required on *each* company you are seriously considering. The information should be complete as of the last six months—preferably the last twelve months. If any of these information points are missing, you should go back to your data sources and fill in the gaps.

INSIDER INFORMATION CHECKLIST

I. Required inside/insider information

- Number of different insiders with open-market/private purchase buys

- Position of each insider

- Type of each transaction

- Date of each transaction

- Number of shares acquired through open-market/private purchase buys

- Prices paid for all open-market/private purchase/option buys

- Total amount paid for all open-market/private purchase buys

- Total increase in holdings by all insiders through open-market/private purchase buys in last six months (preferably last twelve months)

- Similar details on any selling transactions

II. Required outside/insider information

- Number of different outside/insiders reporting purchases in last six months (last twelve months if possible)

- Schedule 13D amendment number of latest filing by each outside/insider

- Prices paid for shares in these filings

- Percentage of company's stock ownership of each outside/insider

- Total amount paid for shares by each outside/insider

- Stated investment objective by outside/insider

- Evidence of involvement by outside/insider in company, such as directorship

- Investment history of the outside/insider

If your interest in a company was first sparked by outside/insider Schedule 13D filings, you must look to see if there has been any inside/insider activity. Often there won't be any, but don't overlook the possibilities of discovering some. The same thing goes, of course, for insider candidates that you first discovered by looking at inside/insider trading; you have to see if there has been any outside/insider activity at the company.

Besides the data on insider trading you also need to know the current market price of the company's stock—figures easily found in a daily newspaper. The first thing you should do in your final screening is to compare today's price with the highest price paid by insiders. If the current price is above 25 percent of the insiders' highest price, you can automatically dismiss that investment candidate—at least for now. At some time in the future, the stock's price may go down to a more acceptable level. When that happens—or if the insiders start buying at higher prices—you can look at the candidate again.

Another piece of information you should have about each of your investment candidates is the company's book value per share. Book value, as you may remember, is a traditional fundamental analysis measurement that tells you the value per common share of the company's assets minus all its liabilities. If an investment candidate's stock is currently selling at or below its latest published book value, you can consider that fact to be an extra "plus." The book value measurement, however, is not an overriding criterion that tips the scale in your final selection process. It's just an additional positive fact that you should incorporate into the rest of the data you have collected. Current book value figures can be found for about forty-five hundred companies in Standard & Poor's *Stock Guide*. Book value figures on other companies can be found in the more complete Standard & Poor's directories or in Moody's manuals or from data bases such as Dow Jones News Retrieval or at stockbrokers' offices. With all this information in hand, you can now compare your different candidates.

To help you rate your candidates, at the end of this chapter we have provided a scoring test to measure the aggressiveness of the insider trading you have found. Do not think of this as a definitive "formula" for selection. Instead, it can be used to grade broadly the different situations you may come across in your screening of raw data, the recommendations you find in advisory newsletters or the reports you hear about through the general financial news media.

The higher the score your candidate receives on this test, the greater the likelihood of a successful final outcome. This means, of course, that those candidates with high scores have a greater probability of achieving stock price appreciation in the future than the lower-scoring candidates. The reason for this is simple. The highest-scoring candidates will have the greatest number of participants investing in the most aggressive way. Both common sense and experience tell us that more people with more at stake have the strongest collective motivation to make sure that their investment turns out to be successful. It's just human nature at work, in this case in the stock market. Like our sorting of newsletter recommendations, this scoring test can help you predict the *probability* of a successful outcome from among your various choices. It cannot predict the *degree* of the successful outcome.

After you have compared the different investment possibilities and are satisfied that you have found insider trading situations that fulfill the criteria of a "consistent pattern of unusual behavior"—that the insider buying was large, repeated and aggressive—and if the current market price is good in relation to the insiders' purchase prices, you can consider that you have a green light for your own investment.

Scoring Your Insider Investment Candidates

1. Any inside/insider open-market/private purchase of five hundred or more shares in most recent month.

   YES = 1

2. More than two inside/insider open-market/private purchase transactions in last four months.

   EACH TRANSACTION ABOVE TWO IN LAST FOUR MONTHS = 1

   (MAXIMUM OF 4)

3. More than two different inside/insiders making open-market/private purchases in any one month during the past six months.

   EACH PARTICIPANT ABOVE TWO IN ONE MONTH = 1

   (MAXIMUM OF 4)

4. More than one month in last six months with two or more different inside/insiders making open-market/private purchases.

   EACH MONTH WITH MORE THAN TWO PARTICIPANTS = 1

   (MAXIMUM OF 4)

5. Number of different inside/insiders making open-market/private purchases in last six months with top executive titles or director positions.

   EACH PARTICIPANT WITH EXECUTIVE/DIRECTOR POSITION = 1

   (MAXIMUM OF 3)

6. Any incident of inside/insider private purchase in last six months.

   YES = 2

7. Any inside/insider private purchase made above open-market price.

   YES = 3

8. Any options exercised in last six months at prices equal to more than 50 percent of open-market price.

   YES = 1

9. Any inside/insider sales in most recent month.

   NO = 1

10. Any inside/insider sales in last four months.

    NO = 2

11. Total amount of money paid by all inside/insiders in open-market/ private purchases in last six months.

> ABOVE $200,000 = 1
> ABOVE $600,000 = 2
> ABOVE $1 MILLION = 4

12. Total percentage of increase in holdings in last six months acquired through open-market/private purchases by all inside/insiders.

> MORE THAN 50 PERCENT INCREASE IN HOLDINGS = 1
> MORE THAN 100 PERCENT INCREASE IN HOLDINGS = 2
> MORE THAN 300 PERCENT INCREASE IN HOLDINGS = 4

13. Any outside/insider Schedule 13D filing reporting purchases in past nine months.

> YES = 3

14. Number of different outside/insiders filing Schedule 13Ds reporting purchases in past nine months.

> EACH OUTSIDE/INSIDER FILING IN PAST NINE MONTHS = 3

15. Any outside/insider Schedule 13D filing reporting purchases in last nine months that adds to holdings purchased prior to current nine months.

> YES = 2

16. Percentage of company's stock owned by outside/insider.

> EACH OUTSIDE/INSIDER OWNING 10 PERCENT OR MORE = 3
> EACH OUTSIDE/INSIDER OWNING 20 PERCENT OR MORE = 5

17. Total amount of money paid by outside/insiders for shares.

> ABOVE $1.5 MILLION = 2
> ABOVE $10   MILLION = 3
> ABOVE $20   MILLION = 4
> ABOVE $100   MILLION = 5

18. Amendment number of latest Schedule 13D filing by most active outside/insider which reports additional purchases.

> SCHEDULE 13D AMENDMENT NUMBERS 3 OR 4 = 3
> SCHEDULE 13D AMENDMENT NUMBERS 5–9 = 4
> SCHEDULE 13D AMENDMENT NUMBERS 10 OR MORE = 5

19. Any outside/insider with a seat on the company's board of directors or acting as an executive.

> YES = 3

20. More than one group of outside/insiders with active role in management of company.

> YES = 5

21. Outside/insider with no historical record of private sell-back to company ("greenmail").

YES = 4

22. Outside/insider with history of private sell-back ("greenmail").

ONE INCIDENT IN PAST TWO YEARS = MINUS 3
TWO OR MORE INCIDENTS IN PAST TWO YEARS = MINUS 5

23. Outside/insider with history of moving into active management of company.

YES = 3

24. Outside/insider is non-U.S. citizen or company.

YES = 3

25. Outside/insider filing Schedule 13D amendment giving notice of change of "intention" from passive investor to activist.

YES = 4

26. Current market price same or below latest published book value of company.

YES = 3

27. Current market price same or below highest open-market/private purchase price paid by any insider in last twelve months.

YES = 3

28. Current market price below 10 percent above highest open-market/private purchase price paid by any insider in last twelve months.

YES = 2

29. Current market price below 25 percent above highest open-market/private purchase price paid by any insider in last twelve months. (If current market price is above 25 percent of highest insider price, automatically discard candidate.)

YES = 1

SCORE RESULTS

For practical purposes, we assume that the maximum number of points your insider investment candidate could receive from this scoring test is "100." However, you will probably never see this "perfect" score. But here's how you might view the investment possibility of the score your candidate *does* receive:

above 55   Buy today! Even if you have to pay a premium of up to 25 percent over the highest insider purchase price. To get a score this high your investment candidate will show heavy buying by both inside/insiders and outside/insiders.

35–55 A very strong buy signal. If you can purchase shares at prices very close to the insider's prices, you can consider this score to be a green light. To achieve this score there is either very heavy buying by inside/insiders alone or outside/insiders alone. Or there could be moderate buying by both groups.

25–35 Good, but not overwhelmingly compelling. Here you probably will find evidence of aggressive buying by only one of our two groups of insiders—with few members of that group participating and buying relatively low numbers of shares at a relatively low total cost. Subjective analysis of the situation is necessary before making a final investment decision. You will need to look more closely at *who* is buying and the size of the company—with larger companies requiring more stringent fulfillment of a display of aggressive insider behavior than will smaller companies. Most of the candidates you identify through your initial screening of insider-trading data will fit into this scoring category. Don't summarily dismiss the possibilities of these situations. Just approach them with more caution than you would with higher-scoring candidates.

15–25 Marginal. The candidates getting this score will have some attractive-looking activity, but you should probably wait to see further evidence before making an investment move. This score could, however, include heavy "lone wolf" investments which should not be ignored.

BELOW 15 Discard all these—at least for the present time—unless the score was achieved by a very aggressive, top-level "lone wolf" investor who has spent millions of dollars in constant trips to the open market over several months.

Epilogue

When you've spent as many years working on Wall Street as I have—thirty-four at last count—you can't help learning a few things. One of Wall Street's hardest lessons, a lesson that can be learned in other arenas as well, is that no matter how hard you work or how clever you may be, you can always find someone who is smarter, faster, more insightful, better connected and who enjoys a better ratio of results to personal effort. If a stock selection strategy based on insider investment activities seems to give in to this point of view by conceding that insiders are clearly better connected and historically enjoy a very good return on their stock market actions (if not being smarter, faster and more insightful than nearly anyone else), then I must plead guilty. But this conviction is based on personal experiences during the first twenty-plus years of my career as an enterprising "fundamentalist" analyst when I concentrated on close, direct contact with the insiders themselves in their roles of management and/or controlling interests.

For me, since I am not now a corporate insider at any publicly held company (except one mutual fund) and therefore don't have access to the kinds of special information that the insiders use, the second-best thing is for me to keep an eye on those SEC public disclosure reports and to identify the types of "consistent patterns of unusual behavior" we've been discussing for the past couple hundred pages. Perhaps you recognize the opportunities as well.

Another lesson I've learned over the years is that the people who ultimately "win" are those who maintain a long-term investment perspective by concentrating on "value situations" while resisting the lure of currently fashionable attitudes about stock investing. There have been all kinds of investment ideas that have had their place in the sun and subsequently disappeared. There was "nifty fifty" investing, for example. "Concept stocks" were favored for a while. An obsession with "beta-risk measurement" for portfolio management took hold for a few years. Every cycle saw "new issues" enjoying a frenzy of popularity when it was believed that any new company would bring big future stock price increases no matter how strong (or weak) the company's operations were. The "winners" who survived these different ideas have learned to focus not on how much money is "made" (on paper), but on how much is "kept" (in real terms) after the fashion changes.

Throughout all these fashionable investment approaches—and there have been many others—there has been a constant: The insiders keep plodding along year after year, decade after decade, watching the special circumstances at their own companies, buying stock when they see that the price is a "bargain," holding on to it until the price goes up or until they are able to convert their stock to cash, and profiting from their investment decisions. While others have been looking under every rock to find a new gimmick for making a quick hit, the insiders have focused on the value of their companies that they *know* is for real, and they have just gotten richer and richer. Now it's your chance. And, if you are new to the insider investment strategy, a bonus opportunity was created by the crash of 1987. As the bulk of investors scrambled to make sense of the new investment atmosphere, the insiders have provided the clearest route for identifying sound stock market choices.

AARON B. FEIGEN
  New York
  November 1987

Bibliography

STATISTICAL STUDIES

If you are interested in examining the reports of statistical studies of insider trading performance, here's a list of the most important ones.

Baesel, J. B., and G. R. Stein. "The Value of Information: Inferences from the Profitability of Insider Trading." *The Journal of Financial and Quantitative Analysis* (September 1979): 553–71.

Finnerty, Joseph E. "Insiders' Activity and Inside Information: A Multivariate Analysis." *The Journal of Financial and Quantitative Analysis* (June 1976): 205–16.

———. "Insiders and Market Efficiency." *Journal of Finance* (September 1976): 1141–48.

Givoly, Dan, and Dan Palmon. "Insider Trading and the Exploitation of Inside Information: Some Empirical Evidence." *Journal of Business* (January 1985): 69–87.

Glass, Gary A. "Extensive Insider Accumulation as an Indicator of Near-Term Stock Price Performance." Ph.D. diss., Ohio State University, 1966.

Holderness, Clifford G., and Dennis P. Sheehan. "Raiders or Saviors? The Evidence on Six Controversial Investors." *Journal of Financial Economics* (December 1985): 555–79.

Jaffe, Jeffrey F. "The Effect of Regulation Changes on Insiders Trading." *Bell Journal of Economics and Management Science* (Spring 1974): 93–121.

———. "Special Information and Insider Trading." *Journal of Business* (July 1974): 410–28.

Kerr, Halbert S. "The battle of insider trading vs. market efficiency." *Journal of Portfolio Management* (Summer 1980): 47–56.

Lorie, James H., and Victor Niederhoffer. "Predictive and Statistical Properties of Insider Trading." *Journal of Law and Economics* (April 1968): 35–53.

Mikkelson, Wayne H., and Richard S. Ruback. "An Empirical Analysis of the Interfirm Equity Investment Process." *Journal of Financial Economics* (December 1985): 523–53.

Nunn, Kenneth P., Jr., Gerald P. Madden, and Michael J. Gombola. "Are some insiders more 'inside' than others?" *Journal of Portfolio Management* (Spring 1983): 18–22.

Penman, Stephen H. "Insider Trading and the Dissemination of Firms' Forecast Information." *Journal of Business* (October 1982): 479–503.

———. "A Comparison of the Information Content of Insider Trading and Management Earnings Forecasts." *Journal of Financial and Quantitative Analysis* (March 1985): 1–17.

Pratt, Shannon P., and Charles W. DeVere. "Relationship Between Insider Trading and Rates of Return for NYSE Common Stocks, 1960–1966." In *Modern Developments in Investment Management*, edited by James H. Lorie and Richard Brealey. New York: Praeger, 1970.

Rogoff, Donald L. "The Forecasting Properties of Insiders' Transactions." D.B.A. diss., Michigan State University, 1964.

INSIDER INVESTOR PROFILES

Articles and books covering the personal and business lives of prominent insiders are useful when you are following their investment activities. Here is a list of articles covering most of the important people actively investing as of this writing.

Ames, Elizabeth, and Marc Frons. "There Are Two David Murdocks—Both Are Used to Getting Their Way." *Business Week*, January 28, 1985, 88–90.

Angrist, Stanley W. "The Up & Comers: The Terminators." [Irwin Jacobs] *Forbes*, September 16, 1985, 67–70.

Bianco, Anthony. "Why Warren Buffett Is Breaking His Own Rules." *Business Week*, April 15, 1985, 134–35.

Boland, John C. "Clyde Engle Wants to Be Friendly." *Fortune*, April 30, 1984, 185–200.

Briloff, Abraham J. "Saul Steinberg's Pyramid: It Raises Some Critical Questions." *Barron's*, November 12, 1984, 16–24.

"Carl Lindner Wields His Clout in the Boardroom." *Business Week*, July 2, 1984, 66–70.

Cooper, Wendy, and Erik Ipsen. "The New Generation of Corporate Raiders," *Institutional Investor* (January 1986): 55–59.

Crudele, John. "A Canadian Raider Does It Again." [Samuel Belzberg] *The New York Times*, April 6, 1986, 6F.

Dewar, Elaine. "Takeover." [George Mann] Parts 1 and 2. *Canadian Business* (November, December 1985): 26–56, 159–83; 53–63, 152–54.

Field, Alan M. "A Sheep in Wolf's Clothing?" [Harold Simmons] *Forbes*, May 5, 1986, 127–28.

Gray, Patricia Bellew. "Unlikely Mogul: Breezy and Irreverent, Raider Sam Zell Runs a $2.5 Billion Empire." *The Wall Street Journal*, November 7, 1985, 1.

Gubernick, Lisa. "Raiders in Short Pants." *Forbes*, November 18, 1985, 54, 58.

"How Bob Pritzker Runs a $3 Billion Empire." *Business Week*, March 7, 1983, 64–69.

"How the Fast-Moving Belzberg Brothers Are Building a Financial Empire." *Business Week*, December 5, 1983, 134–35.

Javetski, Bill. "The Power of Canada's Economic Elite." *Business Week*, December 2, 1985, 50–51.

Lecky, Robin. "How Peter Cundill Beats the Market." *Canadian Business* (January 1980): 44–49.

Leinster, Colin. "The Second Son Is Heir at Seagram." *Fortune*, March 17, 1986, 28–31.

———. "Carl Icahn's Calculated Bets." *Fortune*, March 18, 1985, 142–48.

Loomis, Carol J. "The Comeuppance of Carl Icahn." *Fortune*, February 17, 1986, 18–25.

Miller, Gregory. "Irwin Jacobs' Quest for Respectability." *Institutional Investor* (February 1985): 128–35.

Morgello, Clem. "Spotting the Value in Chapter 11s." [Max Heine] *Dun's Business Month* (December 1984): 105–06.

Moskal, Brian S. "Nuts-and-Bolts Profits: Robert Pritzker's Winning Smokestack Formula." *Industry Week*, January 6, 1986, 51–52.

Partridge, John. "Empire Builder: George Mann Sets Unicorp on the Fast Track to Riches in US Real Estate." *Canadian Business* (February 1984): 22–29.

Phalon, Richard. "Ned Johnson of FMR: Watch Your Flank, Merrill Lynch." *Forbes*, October 26, 1981, 158–62.

"Professional Profile: The Patient Value Hunters." [Max Heine and Michael Price] *Financial World*, July 15, 1983, 32–33.

Quirt, John. "The Man Who Collects Companies." [David Murdock] *Fortune*, March 26, 1979, 78–82.

Rennie, Philip. "Brierley's On-Going Joust with Officialdom." *Rydges* (January 1984): 10–13.

Rosenberg, Hilary. "Newest Kid on the Takeover Block: Boone, Carl, Vic— Make Room for Asher Edelman." *Barron's*, March 11, 1985, 8, 9, 49.

"Seagram: Its Cash Hoard Is Spent, and Its Future Is Up in the Air." *Business Week*, December 21, 1981, 98, 100, 102.

Sherman, Stratford P. "The Belzbergs; 'They Like to Kick the Tires.'" *Fortune*, March 4, 1985, 128–34.

Sloan, Allan. "Victor's Smiling Face." [Victor Posner] *Forbes*, December 16, 1985, 42–43.

———, and Mary Kuntz. "The Hunt Is Better Than the Catch." *Forbes*, December 2, 1985, 38–40.

———, and Harold Seneker. "How Posner Profited Even Though His Companies Didn't." *Forbes*, April 8, 1985, 42–46.

Stauder, Kathleen. "How the Bass Brothers Do Their Deals." *Fortune*, September 17, 1984, 144–54.

Stern, Richard L. "Cash and Cachet?" [Marshall Cogan and Stephen Swid] *Forbes*, February 14, 1983, 146–47.

Taub, Stephen. "Shark Alert: A New Generation of Corporate Raiders Has Come of Age." *Financial World*, April 1, 1986, 22, 24, 26–29.

Thackray, John. "Odyssey Partners' Independent Odyssey." *Institutional Investor* (November 1983): 191–99.

Tompkins, John. "The Strategy of a Takeover Artist: What Goes on Inside Asher B. Edelman's Head." *Management Technology* (April 1985): 19–20.

Trian, John. *The Midas Touch: The Investment Genius of Warren Buffett*. New York: Harper & Row, 1987.

———. *The Money Masters: Nine Great Investors*. New York: Penguin, 1981.

"What Carl Icahn Wants: 'Full Control of Companies.'" *Business Week*, December 12, 1983, 116–17.

BOOKS DISCUSSING INSIDER TRADING

Most of the words printed about insider activities deal with *illegal* trading. The books listed here, however, give at least some attention to the legal aspects of insider stock investments.

Band, Richard E. *Contrary Investing*. New York: McGraw-Hill, 1985.

Boland, John C. *Wall Street's Insiders*. New York: Morrow, 1985.

Fosback, Norman G. *Stock Market Logic*. Fort Lauderdale, Fla.: Institute for Econometric Research, 1976.

Manne, H. A. *Insider Trading and the Stock Market*. New York: Free Press, 1966.

Rider, Barry A. K. *Insider Trading*. Bristol, England: Jordan, 1983.

Shapiro, Susan P. *Wayward Capitalists: Target of the Securities and Exchange Commission*. New Haven: Yale University Press, 1984.

Wysong, Perry. *How You Can Use the Wall Street Insiders*. Fort Lauderdale, Fla.: Wilton House, 1971.

Zweig, Martin E. *Martin Zweig's Winning on Wall Street*. New York: Warner Books, 1986.

OTHER INVESTMENT BOOKS OF INTEREST

While hardly a word of insider trading is mentioned in any of these books, they provide general stock investment advice, differing stock selection approaches or portfolio management techniques that can be applied to the insider investment strategy.

Dreman, David. *Psychology and the Stock Market: Investment Strategy Beyond Random Walk*. New York: Anacom, 1977.

———. *The New Contrarian Investment Strategy*. New York: Random House, 1979.

Engel, Louis, and Brendan Boyd. *How to Buy Stocks*. 7th ed. Boston: Little, Brown, 1983.

Glossbrenner, Alfred. *The Complete Handbook of Personal Computer Communications*. New York: St. Martin's, 1983.

Graham, Benjamin, David L. Dodd, and Sidney Cottle. *Security Analysis: Principles and Technique*. 4th ed. New York: McGraw-Hill, 1962.

Meyers, Thomas A. *The Dow Jones-Irwin Guide to On-Line Investing: Sources, Services and Strategies*. Homewood, Ill.: Dow Jones-Irwin, 1986.

Pessin, Allan H., and Joseph A. Ross. *Words of Wall Street: 2000 Investment Terms Defined*. Homewood, Ill.: Dow Jones-Irwin, 1983.

Rolo, Charles J. *Gaining on the Market: Your Complete Guide to Investment Strategy*. Boston: Atlantic-Little, Brown, 1982.

Rosenberg, Claude N., Jr. *Stock Market Primer*. New York: Warner Books, 1981.

Sobel, Robert. *Inside Wall Street*. New York: W.W. Norton, 1977.

Woodwell, Donald R. *Automating Your Financial Portfolio*. 2nd ed. Homewood, Ill.: Dow Jones-Irwin, 1986.

Index

D0971556

american pie

american pie

slices of life (and pie)
from america's back roads

PASCALE LeDRAOULEC

HARPERCOLLINSPUBLISHERS

FIRST EDITION

Designed by Claire Vaccaro

Printed on acid-free paper

Library of Congress Cataloging-in-Publication Data

LeDraoulec, Pascale.
American pie : slices of life (and pie) from America's
back roads / Pascale LeDraoulec.
p.   cm.
ISBN 0-06-019736-6 (hardcover)
1. Gastronomy.   2. Pies—United States.   3. Food habits—United States.
I. Title.
6/14/02
TX633 .L5 2002
641.8'652'0973—dc21
2001051936

02   03   04   05   06   ❖/RRD   10   9   8   7   6   5   4   3   2   1

To my parents
who fed me stories with every meal
and who see beauty and truth in small things . . .

ACKNOWLEDGMENTS

I wish to thank all the people I met on America's pieways who took the time to share a slice of life and/or pie with me. Thanks, also, to all those who pointed me toward pie and to the bakers who contributed recipes. Together, we've assembled quite a collection.

I can't thank Kris enough for sticking with me through twenty-four states, for her beautiful photographs, her sense of humor, and for scraping the bugs off the windshield at every fill-up.

Thanks also to my other co-"pie"-lots: Nicole, for her lean and keen observations and for turning me on to BBQd corn chips in South Carolina; Teri, for running away to eat pie with me a month before her wedding; Liz, though Maine didn't make the cut—I will never forget your waking up at 4 A.M. to go lobstering for pie.

Thank you, also, to friends old and new, in Livingston, Montana, Houston, Texas, Thornton, Iowa, Hammond, Louisiana, Ripon, Wisconsin, Traverse City, Michigan, and Orleans, Massachusetts, who took road-weary pie travelers in for the night and fed them something other than pie.

Thanks also to my mechanics, Tim, in Yonkers, New York, and Clay, in Marin County, California, who made sure Betty and Betty Blue were ready to rumble. Thanks to Rodney, the shy cowboy in the pepper-red jumpsuit who stopped to fix my thermostat near Roswell, New Mexico.

I am grateful to my editors at the *Daily News* for their patience while I baked this book. Hanna O'Clair: thank you for testing all those recipes and making the pies look so pretty.

Elena, thank you for coming into my life at the tail end of yours. Thanks for my bowl and for Judy's number. Nancy Bronstein and Olivia Barker, thank you for being such caring friends and back readers.

Thanks to Mike and Andrea for introducing me to Gordon Kato, my agent, who "got it" right away and who gave me great tunes for the trip; and to Larry Ashmead and Krista Stroever, my editors at HarperCollins, for their insights and for understanding that writing a first book is a lot like making pie: you just can't rush it . . .

Un grand merci to my family for their constant cheerleading and, finally, to Ty, for patiently working on "dough" with me until we got it just right.

CONTENTS

part one

"Everything in life is somewhere else,
and you can get there in a car."

—E. B. WHITE

"Fro-Joy," ONE MAN'S MEAT

my huckleberry friend

> *. . . Two drifters,*
> *Off to see the world,*
> *There's such a lot of world to see.*
> *We're after the same*
> *Rainbow's end*
> *Waitin' round the bend,*
> *My huckleberry friend,*
> *Moon River*
> *and me.*

—JOHNNY MERCER, "MOON RIVER"

On November 16, 1982, a state bear trapper named Dave sat in his living room in Whitefish, Montana, with a loaded .357 Magnum in his lap and his dog, Pip, curled at his feet.

Most marauding bears can be snared and relocated, never to be seen again. But some pesky bears keep coming back.

On that icy November night, under the cold, stern eye of the Northern Rockies, Dave knew his personal grizzly had returned one too many times. He reckoned he had only two choices: live dry or die drunk.

The state fish-and-game warden, a hardened bachelor of 43, stared at the gun in his lap. His thoughts drifted to those endless nights frittered away on bar stools. The way Pip cocked his head at the sight of him teetering home through knee-deep snow. So many boyhood dreams, dissolved, like ice in whiskey.

Then Dave passed out.

When day broke, he cracked open his slate eyes. The gun had not moved. Neither had Pip, a Saint Bernard mix, named for J. R. R. Tolkien's most statuesque hobbit.

Dave pushed himself up from his easy chair knowing that nothing about the days and months ahead would be easy. He'd have to keep busy. No idle hands.

With Pip at his heels, he marched into the kitchen to look for a rolling pin.

And he made a huckleberry pie.

And then he made another.

Growing up in the foothills, in Choteau, Dave used to watch his mother make pie. He'd lay his head on the kitchen table and stare as she'd roll out her dough, pushing the large rolling pin away from her belly with the sure, even strokes of a rower. From this cheek-to-flour angle, the rolling pin came straight at him.

He must have picked up a lot this way, because those first pies came pretty naturally to him. He tried all sorts of recipes. Bourbon pecan made him want to lick the slope of his wooden spoon. But huckleberry quickly became his favorite.

"Another trait I share with the grizzlies," he says with an impish grin.

A huckleberry, the grizzly's late-summer snack, is a wild bluish-black berry that is often confused with the tamer, sweeter blueberry. Only found in the wild and at high elevations, the huck has a thicker skin and packs ten small hard seeds. Grizzlies gorge on the berries to fatten up for winter's long hibernation.

Since it was the dead of winter, Dave used frozen huckleberries for those first pies and, after all these years, he insists that frozen hucks make just as good a pie filling as fresh. Dave baked pies as gifts for the town bartenders and waitresses who'd kept him company all those years. The companionship, it turns out, was a lot harder to give up than the beer and bourbon.

When Pip died a year later, Dave didn't think he'd bounce back. Pip had saved him from scrapes with mountain lions and armed poachers, but Dave was most grateful the dog had stuck it out through the toughest part of his recovery.

A year later, a waitress in town surprised Dave on his birthday with a six-week-old golden retriever pup wearing a red bow. Pretty soon, Dave graduated to seven goldens, most of them rescued. He called them "The Magnificent Seven."

The dogs liked nothing better than to watch Dave make pie, he says. They'd lie down in the kitchen, muzzles resting on crossed forepaws, and wait for a stray scrap of dough. By then, Dave was baking nearly every night. Friends who owned a popular café in Whitefish had asked him to bake for the restaurant. Eventually, Dave was making fifteen covered pies a day and putting an extra $12,000 a year in his pocket.

Tourists who had discovered Dave's crimped huckleberry pies while skiing in Whitefish had them FedExed to their homes as far away as London, Australia, and Japan. But Dave says the compliment that meant the most came straight from his mother—a woman of few words and, I gather, even fewer displays of affection. She had come from Choteau to visit him in Whitefish, and he had invited a few friends over for dinner. He made a huckleberry pie. "This is as good as Mom used to make," a guest said after tasting the tart pie with a sturdy crust, to which Dave's mother replied:

"I never made a pie *this* good."

Dave eventually retired from his state job and moved with his pack of dogs back to Choteau, a town of 1,800, where he now builds and sells aluminum bear traps. Something about growing older made Dave, now 62, want to be close to his flatland roots. "As a kid, I couldn't wait

to get out of here . . . but something drew me back. I guess I needed to complete the circle," he muttered under his breath, the night I met with him, and his dogs, to talk about Zen and the art of making pie.

He was working on his truck when we pulled up at dusk after driving across the same wide Montana prairie where dinosaurs once came to breed, using Ear Mountain as our beacon.

"I hear you make a mean huckleberry pie," I said.

"Well, that depends on what you mean by mean," Dave growled.

"I mean damn good."

"Damn right."

Dave was gruff at first. But when he saw how I took to his dogs, letting them lick my face and my toes, and when he saw the rolling pin attached to the front grille of my car, he opened the screen door and invited us inside.

"This is their home. I live here but by their grace," he said, as each of the dogs took its respective spot.

All pie bakers will tell you that the real trick to crust is knowing exactly when to stop working the dough. Overworking the dough makes for a tough, plaster crust. Once you've reached that point, there is no turning back.

"It's a make-or-break point," said Dave, "and I had reached that point in my drinking."

He recounted the details of that November night and, with his chin, pointed to my chair. "That's the chair I was sitting in," he said.

Silence.

I asked Dave if baking pie was a form of therapy. He winced.

"Baking pie was just a way to keep me busy—and away from the bottle"—on those long, lonely nights after trapping, he said.

Dave had trapped about five hundred bears in his lifetime, a third of them grizzlies. Dave hated to see bears cozying up to civilization, and was always happy to return a bear to its natural element—even if it meant fewer huckleberries for pie.

For all of his bluster, Dave clearly had a gentle heart, and I asked him why he'd never married. He drew back in silence. And, as if they knew something I didn't, the dogs stopped their panting. There had been one woman, Dave said. She was married to someone else.

And he left it at that.

It was as good a time as any to turn to the rules of pie. Dave prefers shortening to butter or lard. He always adds a touch of vinegar to his dough and he never makes a pie unless all of his ingredients are very cold. He slips his rolling pin in a cheesecloth glove to prevent the dough from sticking. He's a crimper, though not a fussy one.

Had he not been leaving town so early to deliver a bear trap in Arizona, he would have baked me a huckleberry pie for sure.

"Will you settle for the recipe?" he asked.

Dave pulled the recipe from a dented *Ladies' Home Journal*

index-card box decorated with daisies, which, I presume, had once belonged to his mother.

It was past midnight when we finally found a room for the night at the shabby Wagons West Hotel just off the highway in Augusta, near the Scapegoat Wilderness Area and the Continental Divide.

It had been a long day but I wasn't ready to sleep, so I threw on a sweater and sat on the wooden bench directly outside my room. A low maple moon popped out of the black sky like a gold button.

The motel manager, a tall, tumbleweed blonde, stepped out for a smoke. She propped herself against one of the decorative wagon wheels, facing the desolate highway, one leg in a flamingo tuck.

"So you're driving across America looking for pie," she said matter-of-factly. She paused to blow smoke at the moon.

"Bet you're finding *a lot* more than pie . . ."

DAVE'S HUCKLEBERRY PIE

CRUST

1¼ cups of butter-flavored Crisco

3 cups of flour

1 teaspoon of salt

1 raw cold egg

1 tablespoon of ice-cold vinegar

6 tablespoons of ice-cold water

FILLING

3 cups of fresh (or frozen) huckleberries rinsed and picked clean

1 cup sugar

¼ cup flour

⅛ cup of heavy whipping cream

Cut your shortening into your flour in a mixing bowl. Incorporate the fat into the flour, add the egg, vinegar, salt, and water and mix until the dough holds together. Place the dough on a work surface covered with cheesecloth. Work it a little more with the heel of your hand before separating the mound into three equal parts. Slip some cheesecloth over your rolling pin and roll out each piece of dough, gently applying pressure. Lay the dough into the bottom of a 9-inch pie pan.

    Combine all ingredients for the filling in a mixing bowl and mix gently. If the filling is too runny, add more flour. Set aside, high on a shelf, away from dogs. Fill with huckleberry mixture. Lay top crust on top of pie. Crimp edges. Cut slits into top crust to release steam. Bake at 425 degrees for 15 minutes, then reduce heat to 350 degrees and bake for 35–45 minutes longer.

why pie?

*"A lot of people have never really had the chance to taste
a decent apple pie, but after a minute's sensual reflection will know
positively what they would expect if they did. They can taste it on
their mind's tongue . . ."*

—M. F. K. FISHER, "MOM, THE FLAG, AND APPLE PIE"

I never set out to find the *best* pie in America.

I was moving from San Francisco to New York for a newspaper job and decided to drive, rather than fly, into my new life.

It occurred to me that in switching coasts, I was trading one extreme for the other and it seemed important that I spend some time in the middle getting there.

Truth is, I've always wanted to take a back road across America.

As a journalist, I was all too familiar with the America that makes headlines. I'd often wondered about the America that wakes up to them. Not the slick USA packaged in sitcoms and strip malls, but the America that still buys eight-penny nails at hardware stores, shucks peas on a weather-beaten porch, and boxes Little League scores on the front page of the local paper.

I bought a map of the United States and for weeks it sat splayed on my kitchen table. The bold blue interstates, thick as veins, jumped off the map with the subtlety of a cheesy come-on line. They could get you from A to Z all right, no exploration necessary. But the myriad "two-lanes," faint filaments of muted gray and red, they offered miles and miles of mystery.

I considered each squiggly line on the map with the same gravity with which I'd considered some of the men in my life. I didn't have much time for the trip, less than three weeks, so I'd have to choose my route carefully. I knew that whichever route I chose, it would offer a completely unique scenario. I had never given Nebraska much thought, but it suddenly looked sexy there, sandwiched between Kansas and South Dakota.

Too many options can be paralyzing. Rather than choose a route, I wanted it to choose me. I needed some sort of peg, a thread, to pull me from one coast to the other and, at the same time, deliver the raw America I was seeking.

As a news reporter turned food writer, I thought it made sense to turn the journey into a culinary quest. I flirted with barbecue, but that sounded geographically limiting, not to mention leaden.

Then it hit me one night as I sat at the kitchen table, staring at the map. Pretend it's a cake or a pie, I told myself. Just make the first cut; the rest of the journey will follow.

Pie.

Although the Egyptians first imagined it and the British brought it across the Atlantic, pie—the sweet staple of pioneers—is *the* quintessential American dessert. There isn't a state in the union that doesn't boast a signature pie, from Georgia peach to Florida Key lime to Pennsylvania shoofly. Pie transcends all lines of race, color, and class. A rhubarb pie feels as much at home in a blue-collar diner in Flint, Michigan, as it does in a lacy autumn inn in Vermont.

And while no two Americans bake their pie exactly the same way, most would agree that nothing screams USA better than a wedge of apple or sweet-potato pie served warm on a plate.

My grail would be pie.

Just saying it out loud made me surrender a smile. I would drive to small towns looking for pie bakers, pie recipes, and pie lore. I'd seek out pies with character and characters who love pie.

Perhaps examining the state of pie in America would also take me back to the essence, the roots of this country, and just maybe help me get to the bottom of mine.

As a first-generation American born to two faithfully-French immigrants living in Los Angeles, I had straddled two cultures most of my life. The plan was that we'd move back to France someday. So, I attended a French school, spoke only French at home, and ate smelly cheese after dinner. When it rained, we'd dive into the back-yard laurel bushes for snails, which my mother would prepare *à la bordelaise*. We celebrated Bastille Day and played petanque on the Fourth of July.

I still don't know the words to the "Star-Spangled Banner," and my mother never learned to make pie.

"A pie is not a *tarte*," she would say, shrugging her slight shoulders in that typically French way that suggests a conversation has no place to go. I never questioned it, just as I never questioned the dictum that a baguette placed on its back brings bad luck or that all French women "just know" how to wear a scarf.

My parents never did move back to France, though we visited often. And, on either continent, I always felt like an extra, never part of the main cast. I look like an Easter egg whenever I try to wear a scarf *and* I missed out on all those family debates pitting lard against butter, Pyrex against pie tins.

I didn't even taste my first slice until I was in college. It was pecan. Store-bought. Uneventful.

I had a lot of catching up to do.

Some of my more jaded San Francisco friends didn't understand my quest. They deemed it frivolous—and, God forbid, fattening.

"Who bakes pies from scratch anymore?" asked a colleague. "Who has that kind of *time?*"

Was she right? Had the spirit of pie gone out with the old kitchen guard, the pin-curled grandmothers with their wooden potato mashers and ceramic mixing bowls? Had working mothers everywhere traded their pastry cutters for briefcases and panty hose? Maybe I had missed the boat entirely on pie, and, like Don McLean who mourned the death of rock 'n' roll in the song "American Pie," I, too, was "out of luck."

I knew I was on the right quest when I floated my idea past the couple seated next to me on the plane during a last-minute business trip. The woman nearly choked on her honey-roasted peanuts. "Our entire relationship was based on a shared passion for pie," she said. Her beau grabbed her hand. "I recently proposed to her," he said, "and before she said yes, she asked if we could have pie at the wedding."

As I dismantled my California life, I reread books by other road-trippers. Skimming Alexis de Tocqueville's *Democracy in America*, I was struck by how contemporary some of his observations were. Americans had, in fact, changed little in the two centuries since the Frenchman took to the road with his traveling partner, Beaumont. The following passage, about the purely American notion of "drive," seemed particularly apt:

> *An American will build a house in which to pass his old age and sell it before the roof is on. He will plant a garden and rent it just as the trees are coming into bearing; he will clear a field and leave others to reap the harvest; he will take up a profession and leave it, settle in one place and soon go off elsewhere with his changing desires. . . . Death steps in in the end and stops him before he has grown tired of this futile pursuit of that complete felicity which always escapes him.*

As a woman in her mid-30s who wanted children but hadn't yet paused long enough to have them, I knew all too well about how time, and drive, can play tricks on you. And maybe my thirst for a two-lane slice of America, for a place where people still took time to bake pies from scratch, spoke to something deeper.

In the days before my departure, I cast my pie line out at dinner parties, at my mechanic's, even in line at the post office, to see what I could reel in.

My doctor told me it wasn't a real pie quest if I didn't stop in Montana, his wife's home state, for some huckleberry pie. Everyone had a pie-baking relative named after a leafy plant (Fern, Iris, Rose) in some small town that I just *had* to add to my route.

At my office going-away party, several coworkers scribbled favorite pie stops on business cards. A group of men argued over whether strawberry had any business shacking up with rhubarb, putting to rest all theories about this being a purely feminine quest.

"Nothing is more honest than pie," said Scott, the photo editor at the small Marin County newspaper that I was leaving. "Pie," he said, "is like a comfortable pair of shoes."

"And no cross-country pie journey would be complete without a stop in Hurricane, Utah, for their famous bumbleberry pie," he added. His wife bakes him a pie every year on his birthday. I had worked alongside Scott for four years and never knew of his passion for pie. What had I tapped into here?

The next day, I drew a red pie dot on the town of Hurricane and other "must-hit" towns. For the rest, I'd rely on intuition.

That made sense, since intuition—knowing exactly when to stop working the dough or when to pull a pie out of the oven—is a large part of baking pie.

I knew this intuitively because I had never baked a pie.

I had baked a handful of tarts but had somehow managed to live 35 years dodging the trauma of the all-American pie crust. Many of my friends confessed to the same subterfuge. They, too, had mastered profiteroles and tiramisu, but pie? Well, pie was too intimidating.

Pie stands for "motherly love," and who wants to fail at that?

My plan was to turn up in small towns, seek out the most typical locals, and ask them where they'd go for a good slice of pie. I promised myself that, to stay true to my mission, I would go wherever they sent me, which is how I landed deep in the Ozarks one night when the locusts were running.

Since the berries in the northern states were two months shy of ripe, I decided to stay on the lower half of the country, in the belly and legs of the beast.

I went to the Automobile Association of America to pick up some state maps. The woman behind the desk tossed her head back in laughter at my quest—a sweet deviation from the "Route 66" itineraries she usually prepares for members.

"Pie route? We don't have a *pie* route," she said, "but if you find a good cherry pie on the road, will you bring me back a slice?"

She leaned back into her chair and, within seconds, was taking a little pie trip herself, stirring up memories of the latticed cherry pies her former mother-in-law used to bake for her on her birthday. The pie, she confessed, was the sweetest memory she had of that marriage.

Pie does that: loosens tongues and inhibitions. Tell someone you're looking for a good slice of pie and their countenance changes: shoulders sigh, brows soften, eyes open wide as a barn door. Memories drift to a spiced sweet-potato pie cooling on the kitchen sill, to backyard picnics and church bazaars and Ma's favorite rolling pin, worn handles faded artichoke-green.

Pie brings even the crustiest people out of their shells.

All lovers of pie can remember exactly where they ate their favorite slice as clearly as they remember their first kiss.

And all pie lovers, I would soon discover, have a story to tell.

De Tocqueville had his Beaumont, and as my departure date neared, I realized I needed mine. What a shame to discover a great slice of blueberry pie and have no one to share it with. Who would warn me about gruesome roadkill up ahead or play the state-capital game on those long stretches between pie stops?

I called my friend Kris to see if she would join me on the American pieways. A producer of commercials, Kris is always game for adventure. She, too, has traveled the world, from Dar es Salaam to the Australian bush, but had yet to explore the American outback. And, like me, who had just broken up with someone serious, Kris was untethered. She had grown disenchanted with advertising and was tiring of San Francisco, where, she insisted, she would never find a man. She could use a good road trip to clear her head.

Kris had one concern.

"I'm hypoglycemic and can't eat too much sugar," she said. "Is that going to be a *problem?*"

We made a pinkie pact to run every day on the road to keep pie thighs at bay. We tossed our running shoes in the trunk—and that's exactly where they stayed for the next three weeks.

dawn

"Morning is when I am awake and there is a dawn in me."
—HENRY DAVID THOREAU, *WALDEN; OR*
LIFE IN THE WOODS, 1854

Any veteran of the road will tell you it's always best to get an early start. There's nothing like beating the sunrise on a desert highway with that first cup of steaming coffee coaxing your senses back to life.

A dawn departure makes the day's possibilities seem endless. It means you will be able to "motor" instead of just drive. "Driving" means you will be efficient: you will stop to relieve yourself at the same place you stop for gas. "Motoring" means you can dawdle: you can pull over when you see a sign for a tag sale or poke around a cool rock shop. Motoring means leaving yourself enough time to get lost and secretly hoping that you will.

Most veteran pie bakers will also tell you it's best to bake a pie first thing in the morning, before the house, or the day, have come to life. There's a stillness to dawn that keeps your dough from acting up. Maybe it's a stillness of spirit that radiates right down through to your fingertips. Before that first telephone call, that first glance at the morning headlines, your mind hasn't started racing yet, hasn't filled up with lists.

Similarities end where temperature is concerned. While it's best to let your engine warm up before you clock that first mile, the opposite is true for pie ingredients. "Chill" is the pie-baker's mantra. Your fat of choice—butter, lard, or shortening—should be as hard and cold as the slate floor against your bare feet. Whether you use milk or water in your dough, it, too, should be ice-cold so that when your knuckles bear down on the mealy mound in your bowl, you'll be reminded of the earth in your geranium pots when it's time to bring them in for the winter.

Even your mixing bowl should be as cold as your ears when vanity prevents you from wearing a hat in winter, and some bakers even refrigerate their mixing bowls overnight before making a pie. All this requires some forethought, of course, something that went out of style when we learned to point and click. But the number-one rule of the art of pie—and there *are* rules, I learned—is that you can't rush a pie any more than you can hurry on a two-lane road with a tractor hauling hay up ahead . . .

on the road

"There is a time for departure even when
there's no certain place to go."
—TENNESSEE WILLIAMS, *CAMINO REAL*

Jack Kerouac had no trouble finding pie when he was on the road. His daily dose of apple pie à la mode was a steadfast source of nutrition, he wrote. No doubt that familiar wedge of pie also had a grounding effect on the rambling poet.

It seemed like a good omen to begin my journey by driving past the small unassuming house on Russell Street where Kerouac is believed to have penned a draft of *On the Road*.

I lived in a sunny studio right around the corner, on Russian Hill, so it wasn't much of a detour.

Pescadero, a two-hour drive south of San Francisco, now *that* was a detour. But it was where Richard P., a seasoned cable-car operator, had suggested we go for good pie. In the spirit of the hunt, Kris and I had set out to find a cable-car operator for a pie recommendation in San Francisco. What could be more typical than a grip man?

We'd found Richard at the Bay Street turnaround. He was on a break, in his empty trolley, eating a Fuji apple. Behind him, the Golden Gate Bridge's twin vermilion towers were being swallowed up by a meringue of dense fog.

"Do you know where I could find some good pie around here?" I asked, testing my pie handshake for the first time.

Richard seemed relieved that we weren't asking for the nearest rest rooms. He smiled.

"Pie? San Francisco isn't a pie town," he croaked. "Pie's too pedestrian. For a good pie, I'd get out of the city and go down the coast south a ways, to Duarte's in Pescadero," he said. "Try the olallieberry pie. They grow the berries right there behind the restaurant."

I had heard of Duarte's Tavern (pronounced Do-Arts), a roadside diner in San Mateo's coastal farming community, famous for its buttery artichoke soup, but had never been there. We weren't crazy about backtracking from the get-go—but going where we were told was part of the pact. Besides, neither one of us had ever heard of olallieberries.

A crowd of Japanese tourists gathered around the cable car. Richard looked at his watch and reached for the grip.

"Hey, you two ladies have a safe trip now," he said above the sound of clanging bells. We didn't know it yet, but this farewell, thrown out as casually as a banana peel, would become a leitmotif of the trip. There wasn't a person we met on this journey, from the woman who ran the rock shop in Springdale, Utah, to the 79-year-old antiques dealer in Russellville, Arkansas, who didn't send us off with that singsong road-luck blessing.

So, the next morning, we pointed the piemobile south instead of east. On U.S. 280, we rode alongside latte-sipping commuters bound for Silicon Valley. We left them at the Half Moon Bay turnoff and followed the seven-mile narrow road past sleeping Christmas-tree farms to the water's edge. For the next 15-mile stretch of Highway 1, the Pacific ocean sprayed the tall bearded iris lining the road.

Pescadero, "fisherman" in Spanish, is a small, one-street town with old frame houses whose roots date back to the pioneer Yankees who made their way west. Duarte's Tavern is right on Stage Road, once the main artery along the California coast. Ron Duarte himself was out sweeping the sidewalk when we parked beneath the tavern's retro neon sign.

Barely taller than his broomstick, Ron was tickled that Duarte's was to be the first stop on our pie tour and that a longtime cable-car operator had urged us to try the olallieberry pie his mother, Emma, made famous.

"Have you girls ever seen an olallieberry vine?" he asked.

We shook our heads.

Broom still in hand, Ron escorted us to his home, directly across the street, and opened the latch on the white picket fence brimming with peonies, delphiniums, and daisies. He led us to the rear, where trained olallieberry vines, dotted with white star-shaped flowers, stood tall on the verge of summer ripeness.

An olallieberry is a cross between a loganberry and a youngberry. It grows primarily on the West Coast and has a distinct fruity flavor, much sweeter than its blackberry cousin. Ron, a dead ringer for Mickey Rooney, said his family had planted several vines "as an experiment" years ago and that they took remarkably well to the foggy coastal climate.

Indeed, ruthless El Niño storms had just pummeled the California coast, wiping out his strawberry crop and toppling cliffside homes, but the olallieberry vines were thriving.

Kris and I were eager to taste our very first pie of the trip, particularly since neither one of us had eaten breakfast. But Ron wanted to show us the artichoke patch behind the restaurant. He explained the difference between a tubular artichoke, which has more heart and more flavor, and the more common seed variety. Then he took us to see a batch of baby goats, still wobbly on their Q-tip legs, that his son was raising to make cheese.

I was wondering why Ron was being so friendly when he pulled me aside and extracted a small, tattered, spiral-bound notebook from his chest pocket.

"I really understand what you girls are doing," he said, handing it to me. Every page had a recipe or a description of a meal. Turned out Ron and his wife traveled extensively and Ron liked to collect recipes as souvenirs. He made me look up the rhubarb-and-marionberry pie he'd tasted in Alberta, Canada, and still woke up some nights dreaming about.

"I'll give you the recipe for your collection, if you'd like," Ron said. I told him thank you, but I had to *earn* mine, as he had his.

Maria Huerta, one of thousands of Mexican immigrants drawn to this fertile, agricultural area for work, had just pulled a batch of pies out of the oven when we entered Duarte's kitchen through the back door. She usually bakes between fifteen and thirty pies a day, depending on what's in season and on the time of year. In broken English, Huerta said she'd never eaten pie as a child, but here she was, whipping them out with no apparent stress.

In the kitchen, two younger women with long, flowing ponytails, also from Mexico, were cracking steamed Dungeness crab for the cioppino, and the milky smell of sweet crab competed with the aroma of just-baked olallieberry pies.

By the time we sat down at the counter, it was lunchtime, so we ordered some creamy artichoke soup before our pie. Kathy Duarte, Ron's daughter, told us the Duarte's story, which began in 1894 when Ron's grandfather, Frank, brought a barrel of whiskey up from Santa Cruz, placed it on top of the wood bar, and sold shots for ten cents a pop. In 1934, Ron's parents took over the tavern and added a barbershop and a sandwich parlor. Ron's mother, Emma, baked pies every morning from 7 A.M. till noon. Old-timers still talk about Emma's way with pie.

Kris and I had decided that we'd share each and every slice of pie on this trip to keep her hypoglycemia and our waistlines in check. Kathy understood, but her father would hear nothing of it and sent out two thick slices of olallieberry pie. Maria had not skimped on the deep-purple filling, which spilled out on either side of the wedge like the flowers in Ron's garden. The crust was on the tender side. Flaky, fragile, and slightly sweet.

"The secret," Kathy said, leaning across the counter, "is to put milk in the dough instead of water."

Ron was happy to give me the recipe for his mother's pie, my first.

I still had olallieberry seeds in my teeth when we took the mind-numbing I-80 toward Reno, and Kris could feel a sugar rush coming on. But we both had a very good feeling about our first pie out. That night, we passed several truck-weigh stations on the road and toyed with the idea of getting weighed at the start of the trip.

Naaaaaaaah.

THE LATE EMMA DUARTE'S OLALLIEBERRY PIE, FROM DUARTE'S TAVERN, PESCADERO, CALIFORNIA

DOUBLE CRUST

¾ cup of shortening

2 cups all-purpose flour

1 teaspoon salt

⅓ cup of cold milk

FILLING

1 quart olallieberries (raspberries or boysenberries will do)

1¼ cups of sugar

a handful (approximately ¼ cup) of flour

With a pastry blender, cut the shortening into the flour. Add salt and milk. Stir well; if too dry, add more milk. Roll out half of the dough and use it to line the bottom of a 9-inch pie pan. Roll out the remaining dough for the top crust. Set aside. In a heavy bowl, mix 1 quart berries with 1¼ cups sugar and the flour. Fill the pie shell and rest the remaining dough on top. Seal it well and bake at 375 degrees for an hour or until brown. Put a pan underneath the pie while it's baking, to catch the drippings. Serve warm with fresh clotted cream or vanilla ice cream.

no-luck nevada

*pie-alley: a bowling term which refers to a
lane where strikes are easily made.*

In the early morning sun, the parched earth—orange and pockmarked along Highway 50, better known as the Loneliest Highway
in America—looked like baked corn bread. Up ahead, in the faded-
denim sky, snow-capped Pinto and Pancake summits kept a watch-
ful eye on the valley's alkaline flats.

Not much to see out here but the occasional shuttered brothel
and tufts of wiry sagebrush skedaddling across the highway. When
we saw a sign for the Loneliest Phone on the Loneliest Highway, we
pulled over to check in with the parents (had to). "Had any pie yet?"
my mother asked in French. I tried to describe an olallieberry to the
best of my ability.

"*Très intéressant* [Very interesting]," she said. "*Sois prudente!*
[Be safe!]"

We had purchased a CB radio for the trip so we could ask truckers for their pie recommendations on the road. This was as good a
place as any to install it. The more-mechanical Kris tackled the job
while I ducked behind some sagebrush to answer nature's call.

A series of big rigs thundered past and honked. Back in the car,
we immediately set the CB on channel 19, the truckers' channel, to
see what we'd retained from those late-night reruns of *Smokey and
the Bandit*.

We heard a couple of truckers having a good chuckle at my expense.

Loneliest Highway in America, my foot!

We'd been driving for about an hour, listening to a local country station, when Kris, who was sunning her legs out the window, straightened up and asked:

"What are we going to call her?"

"Who?" I asked, turning down the radio. "Your car," she said.

"We can't drive a nameless car across America. It's bad car karma.

"All of *my* cars have had names," she said. There was Felix, her first, a brash and speedy Datsun B-210, and Günther, a spiffy, hunter-green Karmann Ghia, and, finally, Rowdy, her new Audi A4, named after Olympic swimmer Rowdy Gaines.

All of her cars were named after men, and I was thinking about the psychological ramifications of this when she said: "What about Betty?"

I liked it immediately.

Betty is a '50s kind of name that, for me, has always conjured up images of curvy women with broad hips and wide girth . . . signature traits of the 240 Volvo sedan. Plus, there was the whole Betty Crocker connection.

We agreed to make it official by running Betty through a baptismal car wash at the first opportunity. We patted her dash and, from that moment on, Betty became a character, not just a car.

At around 2:30 P.M., we pulled into Austin, a scruffy little town that has experienced a steady melancholy decline since 1873, the year a silver ore mining boom ended. Three hundred people live in Austin, which boasts three cafés, three gas stations, and three motels.

"Maybe we'll find three pies," I said. Our first day out had been so successful, I was feeling confident. In Nevada, I'd made the executive decision to bypass Las Vegas. I told Kris I wanted to find a slice of real desert pie. Not some mass-produced Caesar's Palace pie served up by a chain-smoking waitress in a toga.

We got gas and I walked over to a sheriff's deputy sitting in his parked black-and-white sedan, bronzed forearm dangling alongside the door. "Can you recommend a good place for pie around here?"

Deputy Pete Hegge was young and handsome in a "crunchy" sort of way, a striking contrast to the decaying town he was paid to protect. He rubbed his chin.

"I'm kind of new in town but, you know, who can help you is Darla, our dispatcher. Why don't you follow me to headquarters."

Darla came out of her hutch of an office and icily asked us what our business was. She thawed as soon as we explained our mission.

"I wasn't going to give you two the time of day, but now that I know what you're looking for, I have all the time in the world," she said, taking a seat next to Kris. "I *love* pie."

Two German tourists had just walked in with some serious car trouble. But Darla told them they'd have to wait.

"I have some bad news for you girls, though," Darla said. "There is no good pie in Austin. No good pie at all."

"What about that International Café down the street?" Hegge asked. She shot him a pistol with her eyes.

"I can defrost a pie as well as they can," she said, curling her upper lip. "Which way you two girls headed?"

Hurricane, Utah, for bumbleberry pie, we said. Darla couldn't think of any good pie between Austin and Hurricane. But she was most curious about bumbleberry pie, surprised, even somewhat embarrassed, that as a pie connoisseur and a woman of the law, she hadn't heard of it. She scribbled her address on an office memo pad and wrote in big letters: PLEASE SEND ME INFORMATION ON BUMBLE-BERRY PIE.

Officer Hegge walked us back to the car. "Sorry she wasn't much help," he said. "Say, what are you ladies calling yourselves?" He'd spotted the CB antenna.

"We're thinking the piemobile," said Kris.

Hegge winced. "I don't think you want to go with that," he said. "Two redheads driving across America in a piemobile? That could get you into a whole lot of trouble."

We blew through Eureka and Ely and Connor's Pass where, at dusk, we headed south on desolate US Route 93 toward Utah, with no pie in sight.

"Maybe Nevada isn't a pie state," I sighed. "Maybe we *should* have gone through Vegas."

In the dusty, barren Panaca, a wild mustang came barreling down the highway, headed straight for our car. Kris swerved just in time. Sunflower seeds and baby-carrot sticks—our pie-thigh antidote—flew everywhere. The nervy, dark-chocolate horse bolted, running slanted, as only wild horses can, then disappeared into someone's backyard.

Eerie. A few miles down the highway, we noticed a sign touting the state's mustang protection program. The wild horse had bucked us right out of our funk. I found The Rolling Stones' CD with the "Wild Horses" cut on it and popped it in the player. Kris was cruising at eighty-five, or that's what the clenched state trooper told us he clocked her at when he pulled us over and shined a flashlight in our faces.

"Do you know where we can go for some good pie around here?" I asked the badge as he examined Kris's driver's license. I saw his jaw slacken ever so slightly.

Tammy at the de Veyo Mercantile

"Nope," he said. "Nothing around here for miles."

He handed Kris her license. "This is your lucky day, ladies. I'm going to let you go this time, but you slow down a bit, OK?"

We thanked him profusely and continued on south on state Route 18 toward the Utah border. Lucky? It was 9 P.M. and we still hadn't found any pie in Nevada.

We were both parched from the sunflower seeds, so around 10 P.M. we pulled into the Veyo Mercantile, which is connected to an RV camp and seemed to be the nerve center of a hamlet called Veyo. Kris stayed in the car, and, when I spied the gleaming display case behind the register, I was sorry she had. Wedged between bug repellents and cans of chewing tobacco was a veritable oasis of cream pies: banana cream, lemon meringue, and coconut cream, all lined up like Vegas showgirls.

"I'll tell you what, the pies will kill you here," said Tammy, the long-haired woman in a Harley Davidson T-shirt behind the counter. "People come all the way from Vegas to buy them."

Redeemed, I ran outside to get Kris, who was methodically picking sunflower seeds out of the gear box. "Jackpot!" I said.

The baker, Evaline, 79, wasn't in at this late hour, but Tammy gave me her phone number—after selling a fishing license to a guy in tip-to-toe camouflage.

We shared a generous slice of banana cream in the car, right there in the parking lot. The thick-cut banana slices sat plump and cold on my tongue while folds of freshly whipped cream tickled my palate. I didn't know what was sweeter: the pie or the success of finding pie just when we'd lost hope in Nevada.

Either way, it was a wondrous thing to be tasting my first slice of banana cream pie on a warm spring desert night under a rhinestone sky.

"They all call me the pie lady around here," Evaline said when we spoke. She'd moved from Connecticut to the desert to be near her son. She was only five when she made her first pie—apple. Growing up, she'd had pie for dessert every single day. Making pie was second nature to her. Not so for today's generation of women, she said.

"I have young girls who come into the bakery looking for work and they've never even seen a rolling pin, let alone roll out a crust," she sighed. "Everybody wants everything ready-made and out of the freezer these days."

I was too embarrassed to tell her I had never made a pie myself. I did tell her that her banana cream pie was an inspiration.

"The secret is the *touch*," she said. "I've given my recipe, ounce for ounce, to lots of people and they tell me it never comes out as good."

"I'll take my chances," I said, and I took down the recipe.

The sugar buzz from the pie gave us enough energy to drive on to Hurricane, to find a motel. As I sat up in bed tracing our day's route on the map with a yellow highlighter, I realized that Veyo was technically, though just barely, in Utah—not Nevada.

Oy Vey-o.

EVALINE'S BANANA CREAM PIE

CRUST

1 9-inch pie crust

FILLING

½ cup sugar

¼ teaspoon salt

3 tablespoons cornstarch

1½ cups milk

½ cup light cream (half-and-half)

3 egg yolks, lightly beaten

2 tablespoons butter

1 teaspoon vanilla

¼ teaspoon banana extract

1–2 bananas, depending on size

WHIPPED-CREAM TOPPING

¾ cup heavy cream

½ teaspoon vanilla extract

1 tablesoon sugar

pinch of salt

Combine sugar, salt, and cornstarch in a small mixing bowl and set aside.

Scald milk and cream and slowly beat in the sugar mixture. Cook on low flame until filling thickens.

Beat a small amount of this filling into your 3 beaten egg yolks. Mix thoroughly, then incorporate egg mixture into the filling. Cook at low temperature, stirring constantly, until thick, about 3-4 minutes.

Remove from heat. Add butter and flavorings. Pour ⅓ of filling into prebaked pie shell. Slice bananas on top. Add remainder of the filling.

Let cool. Beat topping ingredients together until thick. Slather on pie.

fumbling toward bumbleberry

"Snozzberry? Whoever heard of a snozzberry?"
—LITTLE MIKE TEAVEE, *WILLY WONKA AND THE CHOCOLATE FACTORY*, BOOK AND SCREENPLAY BY ROALD DAHL

The first thing we learned when we woke up in Hurricane, Utah, was that it was pronounced *Hurry-cun*. The second thing we learned was that it was *not* the home of bumbleberry pie.

My friend and colleague Scott couldn't remember the name of

the café where he'd allegedly tasted this pie, but he'd told me we couldn't miss it: "There are signs for bumbleberry pie all over the town."

Here we were, in the eye of the Hurry-cun, surrounded by strip malls, and there was no such sign in sight. In fact, the only sign that caught our eye was one for a GIANT YARD SALE. Naturally, we pulled over.

Donna P. was trying to clear some space in her 1920s Mission-style home, a refreshing architectural gem in this sea of 1960s stucco. Donna was smiling. She had just sold an old wooden carriage for $100 and two old friends, Vi and Lloyd, had dropped by in their RV to visit and rummage through her toss-aways.

The seventy-something Vi wore a tight T-shirt with these words stretched across her bust: "If you don't like my attitude, quit talking."

She was as plucky as that wild mustang we dodged in Panaca. Surely, she'd tried the local bumbleberry pie, I thought.

"My full name is Violet Rosela," said Vi. "My mother named me after a flower; she'd be whirling in her grave if she knew I'd turned into a weed."

Indeed, Vi had tasted the famous bumbleberry pie, and it was in Springdale, Utah, about 20 miles east, near the entrance of Zion National Park.

"I don't know what the big deal about bumbleberry is," she harrumphed. "Lloyd and I like the coconut cream pie at Grandma Bishops right around the corner much better. Don't we, Lloyd?"

Lloyd, a retired old driller, who wore one of those mesh baseball caps that could double as a pasta drainer, agreed with his wife, which, I imagined, he did often. Neither Kris nor I had ever tasted coconut cream pie, so we decided to stop at Bishops on our way out of town. It looked like it was going to be a two-pie day, and that made me happy. Three Utah pies would surely make up for striking out in Nevada.

Mel, our waitress, had an attitude and eyes layered thick with powder-blue shadow. We'd barely ordered our eggs when she slapped the check on the table facedown. We took the hint and our slice of coconut cream pie to go and were glad we did. There was enough sugar in this pie to choke every weed from Hurricane to Springdale.

We tossed it in the first trash receptacle we could find and coined the term "Dumpster pie."

Springdale is one of the main gateways to the national park, and holiday traffic was already heavy through town. An outdoor table filled with blue-lagoon calcite rocks caught our eye. We ducked inside the rock-and-gem shop to ask the owner, Sherry, where we could find this bumbleberry pie we'd heard so much about. She tried to suppress a laugh.

We explained that our mission was loftier than merely satisfying a sweet tooth. We were after pies with geographic significance.

"Well, this is Mormon country, ladies," Sherry said. "Mormons rarely go *out* for pie. *Home* is where you go for good pie around here."

Was that an invitation, we asked. "Goodness, no," said Sherry. "I don't bake. But Elva Twitchell, who lives right across the street in that little house, makes great peach cobbler and pie. She sometimes brings some over. Let me give Elva a call and see if she's home."

It was mighty nice of Sherry whose husband had left her for a California tourist who had wandered into the shop one afternoon looking for rocks.

"She says to just go on over," said Sherry, hanging up the phone and pointing to a white clapboard house across the street.

Elva Twitchell's daughter, Sharon, opened the door with a bucket of aqua curlers in one hand. Elva, 88, was sitting in a worn velvet

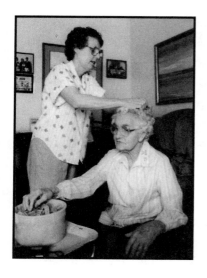

recliner in the living room. We'd interrupted a Cliff Robertson movie.

"Do you mind if Sharon sets my hair while we talk?" Elva said, muting the television. "We're going to my great-grandson's eleventh birthday today and I want to look my best."

She had a calm, peaceful expression on her face and a slow, deliberate way of blinking that reminded me of the Thumbelina doll I had as a child. She didn't seem the least bit surprised that two strangers would land on her doorstep to talk pie.

"I'm not sure why Sherry sent you over here, though," she said. "Everyone in town knows that my sister Beulah's pie is better than mine."

It was the way she said her sister's name that suggested Beulah was the elder sister. And while the pie seeker in me did want to speak to the better baker, the little sister in me wanted to stay exactly where I was.

She told us that her family had homesteaded in Zion canyon before it became a national park in 1931. She described the days she spent chasing polliwogs in the streams ("we always put them back") and climbing over the park's famous jagged red rocks.

The word "Zion" means a peaceful resting place. But Elva's life didn't sound all that restful. As a Latter-Day Saint, she was raised to be completely self-sufficient, which is why she made all of the clothes for her seven children by hand ("I didn't make the boys' overalls, though") and baked two fresh pies every Sunday. The secret to her peach pie, she said, wagging her curved index finger for emphasis, is to "thicken the filling with a little tapioca."

Elva told us that Mormon pioneers first began to settle in southern Utah in the 1850s. They grew crops, planted fruit trees, and raised livestock in Zion canyon where they lived in dugouts and small log cabins.

"I only wish my own children could have known what it was like to grow up there, too."

When her hair was set in white lamb curls, Elva asked if we wouldn't mind moving into her kitchen. She was more comfortable there, surrounded by all her knickknacks, her collection of porcelain salt-and-pepper shakers, her teapots, the wooden sign that said "Elva's Kitchen." She was crushed that she didn't have any ready-made peach pie for us to try. The peaches in the backyard weren't quite ripe, she said.

"Can you come back in a month?" We told her this was a one-way trip. "My, my, you girls must be having fun," she said.

Elva wondered why we were so fascinated with pie.

"It's really not difficult to make a pie," she said. "You just have to practice until you get that first one right." Then, after a moment's reflection, she said:

"I guess I do feel a sense of pride and accomplishment when I've made a pie first thing in the morning."

Careful not to muss up her new 'do, we gave Elva a big hug on her doorstep and thanked her for her peach pie recipe.

"I sure wish you had time to talk to Beulah," I heard her say from the end of the walkway.

Scott may have been wrong about the town, but he was not wrong about the signs. The Bumbleberry Restaurant was attached to the Bumbleberry Inn, which hosts the Bumbleberry Theater. The owners of the bumbleberry compound were sitting down to a late lunch, and invited us to join them for a slice of pie and a lesson on the mysterious berry.

"The bumbleberry is a cross between a binkelberry and a burpleberry," owner Ken Smith said with a perfectly straight face. "It grows on a giggle bush and can only be picked by a happy, kindhearted person."

Kris and I laughed politely. Pen to pad, I waited for something useful to jot down.

"The size of the berry is determined by the heart of the picker," Smith went on to say. "It grows only where nothing else can grow. At the precise moment it becomes ripe, the bumbleberry giggles. And if you're eating a bumbleberry at the right time, you will spend the rest of your life giggling."

I put my pen down. Clearly, this was *not* a recipe they were willing to part with, although many food writers—and investors—have tried to pry it out of them. Smith explained that the secret recipe came with the restaurant, which his family, also Mormons, bought from a frugal woman of pioneer stock who often mixed her leftover fruit-pie fillings.

"One day, she came upon this combination of berries that was particularly magical," Smith said. "When the customers asked the waitress what was in the pie, she came up with the word 'bumbleberries' and it stuck."

According to the Smiths, the recipe does not exist on paper. The current pie baker, Tracie, was whispered the recipe in her ear by her mother, who'd baked for the restaurant for years and had recently retired.

When the pie arrived, the Smiths derived obvious (and, may I say, not very spiritual) pleasure in watching us try to divine the berries in the filling. The beet-purple color and the tug-of-war between sour and sweet made us guess it was a combination of blueberry, blackberry, and maybe rhubarb.

The crust was puff-pastry light and dusted with powdered sugar. Our teeth stained purple, we laughed our way through the ochre sandstone cliffs and shaled slopes of the national park where the cacti were in peacock bloom. The moon lilies were wilting in the heat like a belle at a barbecue. These can be hallucinogenic, I told Kris, and we wondered if the Smith family didn't have its own private patch.

When we emerged on the other side of the park, we bought some buffalo jerky from a roadside vendor to satisfy a serious craving for salt.

HERE'S HOW ELVA TWITCHELL MAKES PEACH PIE:

CRUST

"I usually make enough dough for three pies at a time, and freeze any pie I'm not going to eat. For five cups of flour, I use about two cups of shortening, but that's rough because I usually don't measure anything. I like the butter-flavored Crisco because it seems to come out flakier. My sister Beulah uses lard and, like I said, her pies are *very* good. I add a little bit of ice-cold water to the dough, and a teaspoon of salt. I also put in a spoonful of vinegar and beat up a whole egg into the dough. It just seems to make the dough handle better and makes it less sticky. I bake it until the crust is brown on top, in a 400–425 degree oven. Careful, if the temperature is too high, the fruit will boil over."

FILLING

"For a nine-inch pie, I peel and cook about three LARGE peaches just until they're tender. But you really don't have to cook them, you could just cut the sliced peaches and lay them in the crust. I usually sweeten them with a little bit of sugar (about two tablespoons, I guess) and season them with cinnamon and nutmeg and throw a bit of tapioca in there, too."

fumbling toward bumbleberry · 37

a pie is not a tarte—
vive la différence!

Piebald: *having irregular patches or spots of colors, particularly black and white, as in a piebald cow.*

I've done my share of foolish things for love. And on those long stretches between pie stops, Kris heard about most of them.

The craziest, Kris agreed, was spending a year on a dairy farm in northern France, in a village named Warlus, with a population of 200 and a median age of 72.

I was 23 then, and in that carefree space between college and graduate school. My love interest at the time—an older Frenchman—had been asked to teach at an experimental language school there.

Housing was limited. We landed in a two-room cottage attached to a dilapidated barn. I agreed to simply "play house" for a year in the French countryside.

That meant learning to wash clothes in a tiny portable washing machine and getting used to the occasional piebald cow poking her head through our bedroom window.

When I tell people about my year in Warlus they imagine a bucolic, under-the-Tuscan-sun experience. But Warlus didn't have any of the obvious charms of Cortona. The town was so small, there was no bakery for croissants or even a village grocery or a café. To the villagers, Paris, where we, thankfully, spent most weekends, may as well have been the end of the earth.

Although I spoke French fluently, I stood out like a sore thumb for what the villagers called my "American eccentricities." A few days after moving in, for instance, I decided to wash our muddy Fiat in the open barnyard. I was scrubbing the hubcaps to the beat of Madonna's "Papa, Don't Preach" on my boombox when I sensed I was being watched. I stood up and saw a dozen villagers standing in a half moon around the car, staring.

"We let the rain do that here," a beret-clad farmer said, arms folded across his barrel chest. "Are you gonna wash my tractor next?"

To try and ingratiate myself to the farmers and because I was curious, during calving season, I asked if I could watch the next time a cow gave birth. Two days later, a teenage boy rapped on our bedroom window at 5 A.M. I dressed quickly and followed him to the main barn. Two of the older, red-nosed farmers were standing directly behind the cow, facing each other. Each had one gloved arm buried deep inside the cow's privates, and was trying to pull the calf out by its legs.

Next I knew, I was lying faceup in a pile of hay with four old, whiskered Frenchmen hovering over me. "Quick. Someone get some calvados for *l'Americaine*." The farmers walked me home, my legs wobblier than the newborn calf's.

I stayed indoors a lot after that. I passed the time by writing long, detailed letters to my parents. And I learned how to make a *tarte*.

In fact, this *Americaine* learned to make a *tarte* long, long before she ever tackled her first pie. And there is a difference.

"*Une tarte ne cache rien* [a *tarte* hides nothing]," my mother said when I called her long-distance before my first attempt: a *tarte aux pommes* with Normandy apples and a recipe I'd clipped from *Elle* magazine.

A *tarte* is always topless, or open-faced. Pies, more often than not, are covered, if not with a top crust, then with a mound of meringue or a blanket of whipped cream, making pie slightly more forgiving. Generally speaking, a *tarte* crust is sweet, buttery, and has a crumble to it. It could easily stand alone if it had to. Pie crust, on the other hand, is less sweet, and has a crisp, not crumbly, texture. On its own, pie crust is rather uninteresting.

A *tarte* pan is already fluted and has shorter, non-sloping sides, so the filling-to-crust ratio is larger. *Tarte* pans also have a removable bottom, which makes for a more elegant presentation.

I don't remember the details of making my first *tarte,* but I do remember taking my time and not being stressed. I didn't own a rolling pin, and I used a bottle of Sancerre to roll out my dough. I remember that the Frenchman found it delicious and that we dunked leftover slices in our café au lait the next morning.

The ignorance of youth? Perhaps. But I just don't think making crust is grounds for trauma in France, where a cook is more likely to be judged by her coq au vin or the balance in her vinaigrette.

In America, pie crust is the barometer of a cook's mettle. Susan Westmoreland, food editor at *Good Housekeeping* magazine, says all candidates applying for jobs in the test kitchen must roast a chicken *and* make a pie from scratch.

"Making a pie is the ultimate test of a good cook," she says. "It shows technique *and* heritage."

Emboldened by my first effort, the following week I made a pear tart for my neighbor Monsieur Poulet.

Poulet was the only person in Warlus who didn't make me feel like an outsider. I spent many an afternoon in Poulet's barn, both of us on low-slung stools, me watching him dunk then pluck chickens at record speed.

"*Bravo, la tarte!*" he said with a thumbs-up sign, when he came by two days later to drop off my weekly order of a just-skinned roasting rabbit.

I'd raised rabbits as pets but I had no compunction about cooking rabbit, having been weaned on my mother's country cooking. One thing, however, made me squeamish—Poulet's habit of leaving one back paw on, its fur still intact.

"*Ca porte bonheur,* [it brings good luck], *Mademoiselle,*" he'd say whenever I peeled back the *torchon* [damp kitchen rag] and cringed.

I finally told him I had enough good luck to last several lifetimes, but by then the Frenchman and I were headed stateside.

The relationship ended a few years later, and I never heard from Poulet again. But there have been many moments in my life, and on the pie trip in particular, when I was grateful for all the luck those rabbit feet kicked my way.

rocky mountain pie

"The rule for overcoming fear is to head right into it."
—ANONYMOUS

Two days into the trip, we had already logged 1,236 miles, eaten four pieces of pie, dissected the men we'd dated, extolled the virtues of navy-blue toe polish, compared biological clocks, and examined our respective relationships with our fathers.

Could we keep up the pace—calorically and conversationally?

In Colorado, the plan was to head toward the canyons above Boulder, but not without stopping to visit our respective families first.

My sister Valerie, and her husband, Jerry, live in Steamboat Springs, in a small house nestled against the mountain, with their daughters, Natalie, 8, and Allison, 5.

I hadn't had a chance to explain the pie quest to my sister before leaving California. With two small children in the house, phone conversations are usually clipped.

She seemed surprised I'd chosen pie as my grail since, like me, she felt pie was a stranger. Although her husband is American, she'd never made a pie either. Still hasn't.

"I don't think it's right to make a pie with a frozen crust," she said defensively. "And since I'm scared of crust, I've never made a pie."

I didn't know my big sister was afraid of anything.

Jerry thinks a frozen-crust pie is better than no pie at all, and so, once a year, for Thanksgiving, he makes pies with the girls using store-bought crusts.

So, is it any wonder that when Natalie handed me an apple pie recipe as we headed out of town, it went like this:

PERFECT APPLE PIE BY NATALIE PEARL

"You get some crust at the store. When you're at the store, you get twelve yummy delicious apples. Peel them and cut them up into triangles. Put a plate under the crust. Put apples on top of the crust and pour ¼ teaspoon of sugar and ¼ teaspoon of cinnamon and then put another crust on top and bake at eighty degrees for twenty minutes."

Kris's parents had prepared a homespun Italian meal for us in Denver. Her father was also perplexed by our journey, though the simple logistics of it were what threw him.

"You mean you just go up to complete strangers and talk to them about pie?" he asked, his spaghetti fork poised like a question mark. "And they talk back?"

Earning the trust of strangers, getting them to talk is key to my job. Maybe to a civil engineer like Kris's dad, I realized, such behavior is as odd and mystifying as Emma Duarte adding milk to her dough.

We rose at dawn, hoping to make up for our lazy Sunday. Kris's dad had been thoughtful enough to pack a few Frank Sinatra CDs for us.

"You can't drive across the country without the Chairman of the Board," he said. Maybe he was telling us he wanted to come along.

On the Peak-to-Peak Highway, bordered by shimmering aspens, a jet-black wild pig lurched in front of the car, sending me into the other lane. We missed the pig—and an oncoming Jeep—by a bristle.

Our nerves jangled, we stopped at the Sundance Café and Lodge for breakfast. One table over, a cool middle-aged couple—cool in that they seemed to genuinely enjoy each other's company—shared a stack of buttermilk pancakes. I leaned over to borrow some syrup and ask where we could get some good mountain pie. Karen, the director of cultural programs at the Boulder Public Library, and her partner, Tom, a contractor, were building a home in nearby Coal Creek Canyon. They liked to carbo-load on pancakes every weekend before pounding nails, they said. They didn't hesitate when we asked them for a local pie recommendation. "You've got to go to the Gold Hill

Inn," they said. Gold Hill, which has no stoplights or pavement, we learned, is the oldest mining town in the Nebraska Territory.

On a sticky napkin, they drew me a map with lots of little fingers for canyons. We followed the rippled index finger for some time until the road switched from pavement to dirt without warning.

I saw a strapping young man in khaki shorts and a T-shirt working in his garden, and pulled over to ask if we were on the right path to Gold Hill and good pie.

He wiped his brow and shook his head.

"Oh, you're headed for Gold Hill all right," said the man, whose name was Bill. "You're also headed straight for pie heaven."

We sat on a boulder and let him explain. It turned out, he too had recently gone on a quest for pie. Banana cream pie. He'd begun the quest as a game, with his ex-girlfriend who shared his lifelong passion for this vintage dessert. They broke up before finding the perfect pie.

Maybe it was his way of keeping the relationship alive, said Bill, an organic herb farmer, but he'd never stopped searching. He had almost given up hope. Then, one day, that previous winter, he was coming down the mountain after a day of cross-country skiing in the Arapaho Recreation Area and he stopped at the general store in Gold Hill for a quick sugar fix.

"There, right in my own backyard, was the most wonderful banana cream pie I'd ever seen," he said. "I sat down and ate it, and I knew I'd found my pie. It's funny, but when I needed it most, that's where it was."

We offered to take him up the dirt hill, known as Lick Skillet, for a slice of this perfect pie, but he declined.

There are 160 people who live in Gold Hill year-round and, at last count, 57 dogs. But on weekends, the town, a maze of low-slung log cabins with flowerpot porches, triples in size as Boulder residents, bikers and hikers, head up the hill for good food and bluegrass.

It was Memorial Day, and the Gold Hill Inn was closed. So we headed straight for the general store to find Bill's banana cream dream.

No one knows for sure when the general store was built, but Hugh Moore, who bought it a few years ago, has a copy of an early bill of sale for $4.25 dating back to the 1880s. The store used to sell hardware, as evidenced by the metal bins lining an entire side wall. Today, it serves as a community center of sorts: video store, fax service, post office, consignment store, grocery store, and café.

Moore said they got many of their pies delivered from a bakery in Boulder—but the banana cream pie is the only one that's made in-house by a young woman on his staff.

On cue, she emerged from the kitchen balancing a hot tray of twice-baked potatoes. Susan, in her early 30s, was wearing a full-length apron with a red-chili-pepper motif over a peasant blouse and a pair of shorts and Birkenstocks. With her mane of floppy curls and her sad, deep-set eyes she reminded me of a cocker spaniel.

She was flattered—albeit surprised—that someone had raved about her pie.

"Did he really say it was the best he'd ever had?"

When we asked her her secret, she blushed.

"I cannot tell a lie," she said. "I got the recipe from the back of a Jell-O pudding box."

Susan never ate pie made with box mix when she was growing up in North Carolina.

"My nana used to make boysenberry pie from scratch when I was a little girl," she said. "All the kids and cousins would go pick the berries on her farm and then we'd bring them to her kitchen and she'd get to work and we'd all watch and wait for the pie to come out of the oven.

"What would my grandma say if she knew I was making pies from a box?" We told her that Nana would just be glad she was still making pie. So few people her age seem to take the time anymore.

There were only two slices of banana cream pie left, so Kris and I shared one on the spot and had the other slice wrapped for Bill. It was much sweeter than the one we'd had in Veyo, and the banana chunks weren't as firm or single-minded. But it had big fluffy mounds of whipped cream worthy of a double-black diamond powder day in the Rockies. Perhaps it was the pure mountain air, Susan's freshness of spirit, or that her nana had somehow passed on "the touch." But the pie didn't taste box-made at all.

Handsome Bill was relaxing on the porch when we pulled into his driveway to deliver his pie. He was grateful, took a bite, then said he'd save the rest for later. We decided it was best not to tell him that it was pudding-mix pie. In the end, did it really matter?

On deadly quiet and arrow-straight Highway 36, going toward Kansas, we passed eerily quiet and flat Colorado towns with names like Last Chance and Cope. We saw our very first silos of the trip that night. In the dusk hour, they glistened like the handlebars on a new bike.

"I think I'm going to move back to Colorado and find myself a man like Organic Bill," said a wistful Kris.

P.S. About a year later, I was in a restaurant bar with a friend in Irvington, just north of Manhattan. We were talking about the pie trip, and a woman three stools down overheard our conversation and wandered over.

"Are you the Pie Lady?" she asked.

(Ever since my articles about my search for American Pie had run in the local Westchester paper along with a picture of me and Kris and the piemobile, readers would often corner me in the supermarket or at the bank and ask me if I was the "Pie Lady" from San Francisco.)

"You interviewed my brother in Colorado," the woman said. "Bill, the herb farmer."

Sometimes the world seems no bigger than an eight-inch pie pan.

Kris still hadn't met anyone and, on her behalf, of course, I asked if Bill was still single.

"I'm not sure, but I think he started dating that gal you mentioned in Gold Hill who made the banana cream pie," she said.

I have both Susan's and Bill's phone numbers in my pie journal. I've considered calling to see if it's true. The romantic in me keeps me from dialing. Best to keep on believing instead.

kansas

"You dare to come to me for a heart, do you? You clinking, clanking,
clattering collection of caliginous junk!"
—WIZARD TO TIN MAN, *THE WIZARD OF OZ*

The sky was streaked purple and gray, like a shallot, when we passed
the WELCOME TO KANSAS sign around 8:30 P.M. With its beaming
sunflower set against a violet backdrop, it was the prettiest state sign
yet, so we stopped alongside the highway and took pictures.

Maybe it's because we were leaving the West and entering unfamiliar territory, or maybe we were curious to discover pie in the
Land that inspired Oz, but Kris and I, barefoot since Boulder, were
feeling giddy.

The dusk air felt warm and wheaty. Neither one of us wanted to
get back in the car, which was starting to feel crowded and was
strewn with soggy sunflower-seed shells. Suddenly we were doing
cartwheels in the middle of the highway, trying to land square on the
dotted yellow line.

Kris clicked her heels three times.

Our goal was to make it to Oberlin, in the northwest pocket of
the state, where our AAA guidebook promised a clean budget motel
and a monument to the nineteen settlers who'd been killed in the last
Indian raid.

For a long time, it was just us and the silos on Route 36, then a fleet of June bugs came out of nowhere and slammed their green bulbous bodies against Betty's windshield.

The windshield was so littered with bug goop, we almost missed the sign for the Frontier Motel in Oberlin. The fiftysomething woman behind the counter seemed daisy-fresh at this late hour. "You're lucky we have a room, because there's a fiftieth high school reunion in town," she said, handing us a cartoonish wind-up alarm clock on three legs. (When I picture my biological clock, I picture one just like it.)

We asked her about the June bugs.

"In the Midwest, kids like to tie a string around their legs and fly them like a buzzing kite," she said.

"But I just hate those buzz bombs," she said. "Tell you what: if I get one of those down my blouse, I don't care who's standing in front of me, I'll just rip my clothes off."

The alarm buzzed us awake at 6 A.M. We used a dull plastic knife to scrape dead-bug residue off the windshield before hitting the road.

In 1878, an Indian by the name of Chief Dull Knife led a band of Cheyennes across Kansas, leaving a path of destruction in their wake. Oberlin was the site of their last battle. Neither one of us was keen on seeing the monument, so we headed south on Highway 83. I'd promised Kris that we'd make a stop in Liberal at the very bottom—or stem—of the corn state to visit the Dorothy Museum. Liberal is where Frank Baum is believed to have written *The Wizard of Oz* and where Dorothy Gale allegedly lived. Kris has seen the movie twenty-eight times.

There are 4,606 John Deere retail outlets in North America and my guess is, two-thirds of them are located right along Highway 83, where one mile feels like three. The map had promised "scenic," but only a Kansas farmer could consider the flat, dull promise of corn picturesque.

No wonder Frank Baum had such an active imagination.

For a much-needed diversion, we stopped at Prairie Dog Town petting zoo and freak show. The zoo is home to the world's largest prairie dog (8,000 pounds) and such bizarre attractions as caged city pigeons and a cow with an extra leg coming out of its rear.

We talked to truckers on the CB radio more often in Kansas than in any other state—out of boredom, really. A trucker named Norman waxed "pie-etic" about his mother's peanut butter pie. Norman couldn't recommend any local spots for pie, but he suggested we stop in Oakley to get a feel for a typical small Kansas town.

"OAKLEY?" Kris nearly slammed into Norm's rig filled with corn feed.

Several years back, a woman Kris knew from college had surprised all of her friends by moving to Oakley to marry a farmer. Oakley had always seemed like a mythical place to Kris, even after she'd heard that the friend had dumped the farmer and moved back to Denver. We were so close it was a shame not to stop and visit, she said.

Norm honked and left us at the Oakley exit. It was odd, having spoken to him for so many miles without seeing his face.

The main drag was so quiet, I wondered if the whole town had picked up and gone fishing.

"I can't believe Sabrina lived here," said Kris, scanning the lifeless town. The Carrell Variety Store had a pulse, so we stepped inside where it was nice and cool.

Louise, the cashier, turned from her register to greet us. She had long gray hair and wore glasses that were twice too big for her face, but her skin was translucent and her smile broad.

She was eager to help a new face in town, she said, but couldn't think of any place between Oakley and Liberal that had any good pie.

"You wouldn't consider backtracking, would you?"

Backtracking in Kansas? I went as limp as the Scarecrow.

"Because you just passed the best pie in Kansas about 50 miles northwest of here, in Colby. My husband and I drive to Colby at least once a week just for their pie at the Deep Rock Café."

And then there was no stopping her.

"My husband is a pie connoisseur," she said. "Every time we go on vacation we stop at little cafés to try their pie. He grew up with pie every day, on a farm in Seldon. His mother used to bake them for the church. He doesn't like to go anywhere except to look at and taste pies. He likes coconut cream, I like mincemeat."

By now, a long line of customers had formed at the register—a woman buying beads for a wedding quilt, a girl who looked like a wax bean in cutoffs clutching some Chupa Chups, a man in overalls buying mothballs.

Louise kept talking to us as she rang them up. From Michigan originally, she had moved to Oakley because "I like small towns where everybody knows everybody's business." Louise's husband, Dean, was a retired wheat farmer. On their first date they stopped to check on his crop on their way to dinner.

"I think what he liked about me was that I was willing to go traipsing through the fields in my high heels and panty hose."

I didn't know which vision was more entertaining: the one of Louise running through wheat fields in her panty hose or of the Frontier Motel lady stripping in public to free a buzz bomb from her bra.

"Well, it certainly wasn't my baking skills that won his heart," Louise said, rescuing me from my own thoughts. "I've always been intimidated about baking pie . . . I guess it's because pie has such emotional baggage.

"My mother is a superior pie baker and I wouldn't dare attempt a pie with her around," said Louise. "Whenever she comes to visit she makes her famous apple pies and the smell of warm cinnamon apples just fills up the house."

The people standing in line nodded knowingly.

Interesting, I thought, that after everything we've accomplished as women, it's often their domestic aplomb we admire most about our mothers.

If Louise and Dean braved the drive to Colby every week for pie, then surely we could make the drive just once, I told Kris.

To amuse ourselves on the drive there, Kris made several phone calls to track down her girlfriend Sabrina in Denver.

Sabrina couldn't believe that we'd found Oakley. What drove her out, she said, was exactly what had attracted Louise: "Everybody knew everyone else's business," she said. And we laughed, because she remembered Louise.

It was lunchtime, and the regulars were keeping the waitresses dressed in pink shorts, pink blouses, and matching pink hairbows, hopping at the Deep Rock Café. Between ads for a local muffler shop and auto parts store, the menu boasted no fewer than thirty-five pies.

Pauletta, the pie baker, had just left. "She has a side job pulling wells with her husband," a friendly waitress named Grace explained. Grace was more than happy to sing Pauletta's praises, though.

"When Pauletta makes the meringue, if there's so much as a dot of yolk in the bowl, she'll toss the whole thing out," she said. She turned to greet a customer. "Hey there, I didn't recognize you without your suspenders."

Then she leaned in to our table and whispered:

"You can set your clock by Frank," she said. "He's a corn-and-wheat farmer who comes every day for his fix of Dutch apple pie." Although Pauletta has trained other members of the staff to make pie, Grace said, "we think there are secrets she holds back."

In honor of Louise's husband, Dean, we gave coconut cream another shot. The crust was unusually flaky. But the filling did nothing for me. This had little to do with execution. I just realized right there in Colby, Kansas, that I was not a coconut cream kind of gal. Neither was Kris.

The Colby stop had delayed us, and by the time we arrived in Liberal, the Dorothy Museum was closed. Kris was crushed. There's nothing else to see in Liberal. So, having found pie in Kansas, we wandered into an antiques shop where we had fun looking at old cookbooks before hitting the road.

"Knowing how to make a pie is a certain means to a man's heart," I said, reading aloud from a farm journal cookbook.

"That's it," said Kris, "I'm getting myself a rolling pin."

She bought the book. I bought Ruth Wakefield's 1930 *Toll House Cookbook*.

We ran Betty through an automatic car wash and washed those June bugs right out of her grille.

TREASURE IN THE BARGAIN PILE

Ruth Wakefield's book turned out to be the best $1 I ever spent. In this excerpt, Ruth examines common "pie failures" and their causes. No mention of "the touch" anywhere.

If your pie burns around the edges:

    a. oven too hot

    b. pastry too thin on rim of plate

    c. pans placed too close to oven side or to other pans on same rack

If your top crust is too light in color:

    a. oven not hot enough

    b. insufficient baking time

c. oven too full, cutting off proper circulation

d. pie set too low in oven

If your pastry is tough:

a. not enough fat

b. handled too much when it was rolled out

c. too much flour in dough

d. too much flour used on rolling board

If your pie is soggy on the bottom:

a. set too high in oven

b. shiny tin or aluminum pans intensify condition

c. oven not hot enough, especially during first part of baking

d. pie stood too long before being placed in oven

e. too much liquid in filling

If your double-crusted fruit pies boil over:

a. too much fruit for depth of pan

b. edges not firmly sealed

c. crust punctured near edge of pan

d. oven too hot

e. baked too long

o-k-l-a-h-o-m-a!

"Away from the superslab, you can still order a piece of pie from the person who baked it, still get change from the shop owner, still take a moment to care and to be cared about, a long way from home."
—MICHAEL WALLIS, *ROUTE 66, THE MOTHER ROAD*

My favorite picture of my parents is the one of them standing cheek-to-cheek on the top of the Empire State Building. It was taken forty years ago, when they were both 26, shortly after they moved to America.

My mother is wearing a strapless cream dress with navy polka dots big as balloons. My father is clutching her thimble waist tightly, lest she fly away.

My parents really tried to make a go of it in New York. My father worked as a waiter in a fancy French restaurant and they rented a dirt-cheap basement apartment in the heart of Hell's Kitchen. But after their first snowy New York winter, they decided that perhaps California was the America they'd dreamed about back home. So they scraped together enough money to buy a 1957 Chevrolet Bel Air and drove there.

Funny, the things they remember about the twenty-one-day road trip along Route 66. The motel swimming pools shaped like kidney beans. The "Soft Shoulder" road signs, which, they thought, were there as a gentle reminder to relax their shoulders while driving.

They picked Santa Monica as their final destination, because "it had a pretty ring to it," my mother says. Santa Monica was also where Route 66 came to a full stop, on a palmed bluff overlooking the Pacific Ocean.

It was important to me that we hook up with the historic highway at some point on the trip. Though Route 66 was finally put to pasture, "decommissioned," in 1984, sections of it still remain, often paralleling the superslab that replaced it. Such is the case in West Oklahoma, where we met up with the historic highway in Clinton.

It was late, we needed a room. The sign at the Best Western Trade Winds Inn beckoned shamelessly: SLEEP WHERE ELVIS SLEPT.

Neither one of us were big fans of the black-velvet crooner, but we asked for the Elvis room anyway.

The woman at the front desk, Kay, wore a sherbet-green pantsuit and eye shadow to match. She was sorry but room 215, where Elvis slept four times, was already taken. Would a ground-floor room by the pool do?

Sure, but we wanted to know more about the Elvis connection. Walter Mason Jr., also known as "Doc," owns the franchise and took care of Elvis personally.

Doc told us that Elvis was afraid to fly. So, during the '60s, when he was making movies in Hollywood, Elvis and his entourage would take long road trips between Los Angeles and Memphis, stopping at the Trade Winds for some shut-eye. At The King's request, Doc never told a soul.

Sadly, Doc said, on what turned out to be Elvis's last visit, a maid delivering food to room 215 glimpsed The King through the cracked door.

"She made a Paul Revere ride through the downtown area," said Doc, "and pretty soon all of Clinton was in the hotel parking lot chanting his name."

Elvis stepped out onto the balcony and waved to the crowd. He even tossed a ball with some of the kids but, Doc sighed, "he never came back after that."

After all these years, Doc had kept the Elvis room just the way it was. He said "corporate" had been pressuring him of late to bring the outdated room furnishings in step with the rest of the hotel chain. He wasn't budging.

We asked Kay and Doc if they had any local pie recommendations for us.

"I'll tell you, I fell in love with that pecan delight pie at the Flamingo Restaurant in Elk City," said Kay. "I used to go there all the time with my grandmother. I think it's the best-kept secret in Oklahoma.

"It's been years since I've been there, but I still think about that pie every now and then," she said. "The baker was a sweet old woman with white hair." Elk City was 20 miles behind us, but backtracking seemed to be becoming a habit. Besides, I liked the image of a young Kay sharing pie with her grandma, so we decided to go there after breakfast.

Our 7 A.M. wake-up call the next morning came courtesy of twenty-five Harley hogs being revved up one at a time. A posse of leather-clad German tourists, all Route 66 junkies, had shipped their Harleys stateside for a late-spring ride from Chicago to California. We were grateful for the early start because we had a lot of ground to cover, and finding pie, even bad pie, was proving challenging.

Kerouac didn't know how good he had it.

We walked over to the Route 66 Café connected to the hotel and, going past the Dumpster, we noticed an old, yolk-yellow Best Western sign resting on its side. It bore the hotel chain's former corporate logo—the sparkling royal crown. So much more whimsical and certainly more inviting than its bland replacement, better suited for a bank.

Jimmie, Ferd, and Darrell

We ordered coffee and eggs and dived into our journals to catch up on the events of the last few days.

A brawny man with a polka-dotted scarf wrapped around his black straw hat sauntered in holding a bouquet of fresh-cut roses, yellow and peach, straight out in front of him.

"These are for you," he said, handing them to the waitress behind the counter where he took a seat. "They're from my garden. They're for putting up with me every day."

"Oh, Jimmie, you shouldn't have," the waitress said, flipping his cup over to pour his coffee.

"Now, where are my grits?" he barked.

A few minutes later, an elderly, thin-lipped toothpick of a man climbed right up on the stool next to Jimmie's and also ordered grits.

"Hello, Ferd," Jimmie said, his head buried in his crockpot o' grits. "Hello, Jimmie," Ferd replied. Five minutes later, Darrell arrived and took his seat to the right of Ferd. "Hello, Ferd. Hello, Jimmie," he said.

"Now the trio's complete," said the waitress of the three friends who looked ready to trade Clinton news of the day.

I slid on the stool next to Jimmie and asked him about the flowers.

"Aw, that's nothing. These ladies put up with a lot from regulars like me," he said. "Sometimes I bring horny toads in for their kids."

Surely such a generous soul would point me toward some fine pie.

"Pie?" said Jimmie, pulling on his long beard. "My mama used to make the best rhubarb pie. I can't tell you how good that pie was."

"Rhubarb?" the waitress groaned from behind the counter. "Yuuuuk."

Jimmie sat up straight and wagged an angry finger. "Anybody who don't like rhubarb pie just get out of here right now," he said. He was 12 again; a classmate had just dissed his mama in the schoolyard.

Ferd told his friend to settle down.

"Well, OK, then, not everyone likes rhubarb," Jimmie said. "I'll admit even *I've* grown more fond of coconut cream in my old age."

Indeed. Jimmie told us he often drove the 80 miles or so up Highway 40 (the new Route 66) to the Cherokee in Calumet, a truck-stop chain, "for a slice—or two." He rubbed his taut, protruding belly as evidence.

Ferd, who made us guess his age (86!), pooh-poohed Jimmie's recommendation. "My wife Leoda makes the best coconut cream pie in the world," he said. "That's why I married her.

"Yes, sireee, it was her coconut cream pie that done me in."

Neither one of them had eaten the pecan delight pie in Elk City, which worried me a little, but at least Darrell, the quiet one, had heard of the place.

Ferd, who works at the car wash across the street, reached into his blue work shirt pocket to give us a token for one free wash.

"You've got to get to West Oklahoma to find Southern hospitality," Jimmie said. "The best people in the world live in this little town of Clinton, which, incidentally, ladies, was named long before that guy ever made it to the White House."

As we loaded the car, one of the maids called out to us from the upstairs balcony. She was outside the Elvis suite, balancing a stack of sheets in the crook of her arm.

"You girls want a peek at Elvis's room?"

The tacky room was exactly as I'd imagined. King-sized bed with a white scalloped headboard, a white vanity, a divan, smoked-glass mirrors, and Viva Las Vegas bathroom fixtures. We took turns, posing on the bed, for a Polaroid picture. The maid giggled, declined our offer to take one of her.

Betty had just gotten a scrub in Liberal, but since we had no plans to return to Clinton in the near future, we used Ferd's token and gave Betty a rinse anyway.

"Pecan delight pie, here we come," I said as we pulled out onto Route 66. Kris had high hopes for this pie, but the word "delight" attached to anything edible always makes me nervous.

I took one look at the refrigerated pie display and, once again, saw only tufts of meringue and cream. This display case had angled mirrors on each shelf, so you could see the top of each pie. Kind of kinky. We asked if we could meet the elderly baker we'd heard so much about.

A woman in her late 50s stepped gingerly out of the kitchen. She seemed too young to be the veteran baker Kay had described, but, then, there was the pecan delight pie in the case, in all its burnt-orange bouffant splendor.

Carla was extremely shy. Like Elva, she failed to grasp the meaning of our mission. Pie was pie. She was too close to it to appreciate its worth or imagine life in America without it. She'd learned to bake when she was only four, using a miniature rolling pin her aunt Cissy had given her.

Tactfully, we asked her if she was the baker Kay had described.

Carla at the Flamingo Restaurant, Elk City, OK

"Oh, no," she said. "That's Gloria. She retired a few years back. She's in a nursing home just north of town. But we still use a lot of her recipes." Still full from breakfast, we bought our slice of pecan delight to go, and slid it in the glove compartment for later.

"Something tells me we should try and find Gloria," I told Kris who knew better than to argue with my instinct.

Elk City is the kind of town where the local newspaper lets parents know on the front page when report cards are ready, so it was easy to find the nursing home on the outskirts of town. Gloria was slumped in a wheelchair, waiting for a nurse to come change her soiled clothes. She was not completely lucid, and it took a while for her to realize that two strangers were in her room.

She caught me admiring a decorative, three-tiered pie stand on her nightstand.

"My son gave me that," Gloria said, her speech slow and slurred. "It's a jewelry box."

I heard myself saying that we were researching the best pies in America and we'd heard from several pie experts that her pies had been voted the best in the state. It was a stretch, especially since we hadn't even tasted the pie yet. Kris looked at me and smiled. "Congratulations, Gloria," she said, shaking her hand.

"That makes me very proud," Gloria said. "Thank you for telling me." A nurse arrived at that moment and wheeled Gloria into the bathroom to change her. We slipped out.

And for the first time since leaving California, Kris and I had nothing to say.

Lucille Hamons was just the gal we needed to see to lift our spirits. If John Steinbeck called Route 66 the Mother Road, then the plucky Lucille, who ran a Route 66 gas station just south of Hydro for sixty years, had to be the mother of the Mother Road.

Lucille and her husband, Carl, bought the gas station in 1941. When World War II erupted, Carl started hauling hay to the northern states to pay the bills. Lucille learned how to pump gas and fix flats. When Route 66 gave way to I-40 in 1985, many businesses tumbled, but the by-then widowed Lucille hung on, selling cold drinks and highway memorabilia.

A stop at Lucille's eventually became a rite of passage for all those cruising the historic highway. A slip of a woman, Lucille was sitting at her kitchen table, showing her beloved scrapbook to three hard-core bikers when we strolled in. One of the bikers wore a Daniel Boone–style hat. The head of a fox was still attached, and its muzzle lay flat on his forehead.

He asked us if we were "66ers," too. We had to tell them the truth, that our quest for pie had only intersected with Route 66. Lucille had zero interest in pie and she made that very clear, immediately bringing the conversation back to the famous highway and her place on it. So we sat down and listened quietly as she made it through to the very last page of the scrapbook.

When she was finished, "Daniel Boone" recommended an unforgettable pie in Hamden, Connecticut, where he grew up. "I've traveled the country," he said, "and it's still the best pie I ever had."

"Any pie in particular?" I asked. "No, they're all good," he said. That should have been a tip-off.

We took pictures of Lucille with the bikers next to the gas pumps and then we rode off in search of Jimmie's Cherokee restaurant off the interstate in Calumet.

Amy, the 18-year-old hostess, sat on a stool, directly under the chin of a wall-mounted bison head, ringing up customers who mechanically handed her the check, then grabbed a toothpick.

Amy has a soft spot for the lemon meringue.

We looked at the pie case and saw only cream pies. My heart sank. Was I ever going to see a fruit pie again?

I couldn't bear to eat another slice of coconut cream. Amy said she had a soft spot for the lemon meringue.

"When I was little, I'd always buy my grandmother lemons at the store and then bug her to make me a pie," said Amy.

Lemon meringue was another first for me. Sadly, the only words I scribbled in my pie journal were: "foamy, yellow, practical."

A trucker we talked to in the parking lot said he stopped for pie at the Cherokee whenever he started to nod off at the wheel. "The sugar picks me right up," he said. So did, I suspected, the fresh-faced Amy.

Exhausted from our pie-packed day, we barreled down a quiet

two-lane back road toward the Arkansas border. As night fell, the first fireflies of the trip flickered around Betty as if to say: "What are you doing way out here?"

"It's like a scene from *Fantasia*," said Kris.

And then we remembered the pecan delight in the glove compartment, which, since it was mostly whipped cream, was no longer delightful or safe to eat.

We tossed it somewhere between Eufala and Spiro on US 9. It was on that lonely stretch of road that we noticed a ramshackle "liquor shack" and pulled over to buy a small bottle of Maker's Mark bourbon, so that we could pour a civilized drink if and when we found ourselves a room that night. We were due.

The store was connected to the owner's living room and we glimpsed him, a bear of a man, watching television in his Barca-lounger with a poodle on his lap. He shuffled into the store in his muscle T-shirt and overalls, the yapping poodle running circles at his feet.

The poodle wore a spiffy pink bow, and when it jumped into its owner's arms, we noticed that its tiny claws were painted fire-engine red. We suppressed a giggle.

"They paint her nails at the beauty parlor," the man said defensively. We paid for our bourbon and backed out of the store.

Lucille Hamons died a few months after our visit. The funeral procession crawled from Weatherford, Oklahoma, down Route 66 to her old store, where she was once photographed kicking up her heels for a "Get Your Kicks on Route 66" postcard.

· · ·

Here's the recipe for Ferd's wife's pie—the one that made him weak in the knees.

LEODA MUELLER'S COCONUT CREAM PIE

FILLING

½ cup sugar

½ cup sifted flour

¼ teaspoon salt

3 cups of milk

3 egg yolks, lightly beaten

¾ cup shredded coconut

1 tablespoon butter

1½ teaspoons vanilla

CRUST

1 prebaked pie shell

MERINGUE

3 egg whites

¼ teaspoon cream of tartar

6 tablespoons sugar

¼ cup of shredded coconut

Mix sugar, flour, and salt in a saucepan over low heat. Add milk gradually and keep stirring until smooth and mixture comes to a boil.

Remove from heat and incorporate the hot mixture, in small

batches, into a bowl with the lightly beaten egg yolks. Return this mixture to a saucepan, let boil for two minutes, stirring constantly. Remove from heat, add coconut, butter, and vanilla. Let mixture cool, then pour into a prebaked pie shell.

For the meringue, beat egg whites and cream of tartar until frothy; gradually add sugar as you continue beating until egg whites form stiff peaks. Spread over pie filling, sealing the edges of the pie to prevent shrinkage. Sprinkle coconut over meringue. Bake at 425 degrees for about 5 minutes or until meringue is delicately browned and the coconut is toasted.

# of bowls, buford, and pine bluff

"Flyspecks! Flyspecks! I've been living my life among flyspecks, while miracles have been leaning against lampposts on the corner of 18th and Fairfax."

—DR. WILLIAM CHUMLEY TO ELWOOD P. DOWD
IN THE PLAY *HARVEY* BY MARY CHASE

I have a collection of old ceramic mixing bowls, which I did not have before I drove across America.

Most are displayed in my kitchen, but I keep a butter-yellow bowl I bought in Virginia on my desk as a round reminder of my journey— and as a handy receptacle for divorced pen caps and stray paper clips.

Its sides are scalloped like an Esther Williams swim cap. The interior is crackled, and I like to believe this bowl was a workhorse in its day.

Maybe it was a woman's wedding ring, hitting the side of the bowl as she whipped egg whites, that cracked the glaze. Something tells me this bowl has played a starring role in many lemon meringue productions.

The wide-openness of a worn bowl invites such wanderings.

Although my mother was never a baker, she had—and still has—such a bowl. Hers is sage-green, wide, deep, and remarkably heavy.

For as long as I can remember, my mother served our tossed green salad in that bowl every night. And on special occasions it was the vessel of choice for my mother's famous *îles flottantes*, or floating-islands dessert.

My mother would make this dessert whenever we were invited to a dinner party. I remember her sitting in the passenger seat with the green bowl lodged between her bird legs, cautioning my father to slow down so that the frothy egg-white islands floating on crème anglaise didn't jump ship.

The urge to buy bowls that had once been cradled by our nation's grandmothers surfaced somewhere in Colorado, where, incidentally, more dinosaur fossils have been found than anywhere else on earth. The urge intensified as the journey progressed. Just as in pies, I wasn't looking for pottery with a pedigree. Yellow ware, for example, once deemed utilitarian, is now the ultimate in kitchen chic.

No, I looked for bowls that spoke to me, like poppy-orange and pool-bottom blue bowls that had seen a ball of dough or two in their prime.

Burrowing through dusty, cluttered "antiques" shops was, I realized, a good way to get a fast feel for the history and personality of a region. In Kentucky, for example, much of the antiques were horse paraphernalia: old bridles and bits. In Russellville, Arkansas, antiques shops were cluttered with locally manufactured pottery, and also became a great—albeit convoluted—source for a most memorable lemon pecan pie.

"Pie? You're asking me where to go for pie? Why would anyone go out for pie? Pie is something you should bake at home," Mary B. sputtered as she carefully wrapped in yellowed newspaper a green, thickly ribbed mixing bowl I had just purchased. Mary is a tall woman with Farrah hair and more glitz than, I'm sure, is legal in Russellville, which boasts sixty churches for a town of about 25,000. Mary was running things at the This n' That and Something Else antiques shop, to help out the vacationing owner. It was a good distraction, she said, as she had recently gone from wife to widow and was still adjusting to the emptiness in her life.

"I would never eat pie out because I make the best strawberry pie," she declared. "What do *you* think, Buford, you've had my strawberry pie. Isn't it goooooooooooood?" Buford Smith, a dapper vision in a cream linen suit with a cherrywood cane, had just snuck in the back door. Although a "retired" antiques dealer, Buford still made the rounds at the local shops in town to keep an eye on the lucrative pottery market, she whispered.

Mary explained our situation to Buford and, after some brainstorming, they came up with an artisan bakery in Leslie, in the Ozarks, which mutual friends had recommended to them. They weren't sure if the bakery made pie, but the friends said their bread was "out of this world," said Mary. It wasn't our modus operandi to follow a pie lead once removed, especially one as tenuous as this one. But Kris and I had both expressed a desire to see the Ozarks, and my journalistic nose was all in favor.

Buford wandered about the shop, slow and cautious as a heron, turning his head once in a while in our direction to examine us up and down. So many years in the cutthroat antiques business had made him wary.

When he was convinced that all we wanted was pie, he pulled up a stool next to Mary, planted his cane firmly between his bent knees, and wrapped both hands over the burled handle. For the next half hour words poured from his mouth slow and sure as sap. His father, as it turned out, owned the Little Model Café, one of the first bakeries in Russellville, which opened at the turn of the century. "So I know a thing or two about pie," he said.

"My father's egg custard was so good that all the bakers in Little Rock would come down to Russellville to watch him bake," he said. His father had started out as a sweet-potato farmer, but a series of devastating crop failures led him to open the bakery. "I've seen him bake a hundred pies at a time. He would sell four hundred slices of pie between 11 A.M. Saturday and noon on Sunday. Pie was 10 cents a slice back then."

I don't know if Buford and his father were close, but I could tell by the way he talked he would have liked them to be. I told Buford that listening to him talk was like reading a period novel.

"You should see his house, honey," Mary said. "Buford, why don't you let them take a peek?"

We followed Buford in his white Bentley into a quiet, peaceful neighborhood where majestic magnolia trees in full fragrant bloom offered a real Southern welcome. A large boulder at the start of the walkway was once used by Buford's grandfather to hoist himself upon his horse. "I had to fight tooth and nail to retrieve it from the family estate when my grandfather died," he told us, tapping the rock with the tip of his cane.

Hard to imagine blood relatives fighting over a rock.

Buford gave us a tour of the house, and his suspicions suddenly became clear. Rarely had I seen such opulence, outside of eighteenth-century chateaux in the Loire Valley. Room after room was cramped with gilded mirrors, French and British portraits from Napoleonic times, tapestries, golden mantel clocks, and ballroom chandeliers.

A man much younger than Buford was stretched across a couch in one of the more casual rooms, watching television. Buford introduced him as a fellow antiques buff and "my traveling companion."

Buford finally relaxed, took off his jacket, and pulled out a long nutty cigar, which he smoked on the porch. The two men regaled us with tales of their cross-country escapades visiting antiques fairs, historic cemeteries, and estate sales and eating pie and turtle soup whenever, wherever possible.

We talked until Buford got to the sweet part of his Cohiba, and then we had to push off to the Ozarks.

Arkansas back roads treated us to the most interesting church "message" signs of the trip. WAL-MART: IT'S NOT THE ONLY SAVING PLACE was my favorite. It was also in Arkansas that people started waving to us from their porches. People who seemed to have all the time in the world, sunken in overstuffed recliners with a dog at their terry-cloth slippers. Grand marshals at a parade, we waved back in slow motion.

When we got to the Ozark mountain range in the late afternoon, we could hear a loud crackling sound, like bacon frying in a skillet.

"It's the locusts," a construction worker on the main drag in Leslie said. "They come every seven years."

Locusts are short-horned grasshoppers that migrate in swarms so dense they can sometimes block out the sun. This year's infestation, although raucous, was relatively mild, and we were the only ones who seemed to pay any mind.

The bakery our Russellville friends had recommended in Leslie did indeed make pillowy bread in a wood-fired oven, but, to our chagrin, no pie. We needed to get to Mississippi later that night to stay on schedule, but we couldn't leave Arkansas without finding pie.

"What should we do now?" Kris said, hands on her hips.

Martha and Curtis Purvis

That's when Martha and Curtis Purvis walked through the door, holding hands. They were from Harrison, north a ways near the Missouri border. They were driving to Greenville, Mississippi, to visit family, they told the baker. They'd read about the new bakery in their local paper and had popped in for some fresh bread to snack on while driving. Since Greenville was also where we had planned to rest our heads that night, I butted in and told them so.

Within minutes, we were telling them about our pie plight and Martha squealed. "I know *just* the place for Arkansas pie," she said in a voice sweeter than any pie we'd had thus far. "And it's on your way to Mississippi."

I wanted to kiss her.

"Pie is *the* dessert at Jones Café in Pine Bluff," she went on. "They make it from scratch, don't they, Curtis?" Martha and Curtis had been married for twenty-one years but you'd think it had been twenty-one hours by the way they clung to each other. Curtis, a sales contractor, agreed with her, of course, but he was quick to point out that no restaurant pie in the state could match Martha's.

"Martha can put a chocolate pie together in thirty minutes and then we'll sit down and eat the whole thing in one sitting," Curtis said, pulling Martha closer into him.

"Curtis makes a very good pecan pie himself," she countered, "his mama's recipe."

Then Curtis confessed that it was Martha's delicate ankles, not her pie, that won his heart.

Martha blushed.

She works at the cosmetics counter at Wal-Mart but she once dreamed of being a journalist, she said. She was crushed that we weren't going to drive through Missouri, because a restaurant there called The Sugar Shack had the most dizzying array of fresh-baked pies she'd ever seen.

"The first time we went there I ran back to the car to get my camera to take a picture, didn't I, Curtis?" she said. "Give me your address and I'll send you the picture."

The Purvises, who were driving a rambling baby-blue Ford pickup truck with a huge bugle horn on top of the cab, offered to lead the way to Pine Bluff, but we knew we'd be making some stops at antiques shops and fruit stands, and maybe even to walk a bit, so we declined.

Five hours later, after having done all of the above, we pulled into the Jones Café parking lot in the dark. We were making our way toward the front door when we heard a loud nasal honk coming from southbound Highway 65. Martha Purvis was hanging out her open window. "Yoo-hoo! Girls! Yoo-hoo! Enjoy your pie!"

You could have knocked us over with a pastry brush.

Ruby Jones was only 15 when she started cooking in Mrs. Walter Harper's boarding house—four boxcars pulled together at Stoudemire's lumber camp. The camp furnished the timber to the crew building railroad bridges. In 1925, at 23, she married Henry Jones, a Pine Bluff fireman. They opened the Central Grill right near the depot in town. She made from scratch dozens of pies, which she sold for 75 cents whole.

During World War II, Ruby fed lots of pie to the troops that pulled through town by train. When her husband retired, they bought a farm and Ruby opened the original Jones Café at nearby Noble Lake. All the fruit for the pies were grown at the farm. In 1985, the café moved to its current location, in Pine Bluff proper. When she was 90, Ruby would still turn up at the restaurant at 6 A.M., six days a week, to bake eighteen dozen rolls and make forty to fifty pies!

Ma Jones was 93 and living in a nearby nursing home when we dropped by the café, but her son W. R. "Wimp" Jones told us she was still calling daily "to make sure those pies are coming out just right," and that "those girls in the kitchen aren't using too much sugar and making that meringue weep" like those Arkansas willows we'd seen on our drive.

Several years ago Wimp convinced his mother to write a cookbook.

"It was really difficult to put it together because Ma's a *pinch* lady," he said. "You know, her recipes are full of a pinch of this and a pinch of that." Before she retired, Ruby passed on her baking secrets to Lizzie and Tootsie, the two gals in the kitchen.

Tootsie, 46, had just whipped up dinner for thirty, a party for a beloved teacher who was retiring from the Pine Bluff school district. The last customers in the house, we dined on broiled catfish, purple-hull peas, and corn bread. We left room, of course, for pie. The ten pies of the day were listed on a borderless blackboard hanging on the wall, with a piece of chalk tied to a string. Given the late hour, certain pies had already been scratched out—though not erased. We ordered a slice of lemon pecan and a slice of chocolate pudding pie.

How refreshing not to have to excavate through mounds of whipped cream or meringue to see the face of a pie, as we'd had to do in the last three states. The lemon pecan—predictably, another first for me—combined two of my favorite flavors and textures: a tart soft yellow filling capped with a sweet crunchy layer of pecan halves. Kris swooned over the chocolate silk, a smooth layer of milk-chocolate velvet pudding encased in a firm, no-nonsense crust.

Martha and Curtis Purvis were already spooning, ankles locked, in Greenville. No doubt our names came up that night. I wasn't sure why, but Martha Purvis got to me in some way. As naive as her airs were, she had one big secret over all of us, I'm convinced.

And it had nothing to do with chocolate pie or a well-turned ankle.

Tootsie came out of the kitchen to say hello after her shift.

"Miss Ruby taught me everything I know," said Tootsie, a big-boned gal with full lips, a beautiful smile, and ebony skin as dark and smooth as her silk pie. We asked her if she had any pie tips she could pass on to two novices like us.

"Make sure you work your dough real good just until you add the water," she said. "Real good." Hmmm. Kathy Duarte had told us she's careful not to overwork her dough, once she adds the milk. That's the thing with pie, we were learning. Everybody's got their own rules.

FIKE'S LEMON PECAN PIE
FROM THE JONES CAFÉ,
IN PINE BLUFF, ARKANSAS

(straight from *The Best of Ruby Jones* cookbook)

RUBY'S PIE CRUST

2 cups flour

½ teaspoon salt

⅔ cup shortening

6 tablespoons ice water or just enough to moisten and hold together

FILLING

3 whole eggs (unbeaten)

⅓ cup of melted margarine

1½ cups of sugar

¾ cup of pecan halves or pieces

1 teaspoon of lemon extract

juice of ½ lemon

a pinch of salt

Sift flour and salt. Do not measure flour until after it's been sifted. Mix shortening with flour mixture. Add ice water. (NEVER add more flour to mixture once water has been added, because pastry will become tough.) Makes 2 pie crusts.

Mix ingredients for the filling with fork. Do not use an electric mixer. Pour into unbaked pie shell. Bake at 300 degrees for 45 minutes.

BUFORD'S DAD'S
BUTTERMILK PIE

CRUST

1 prebaked pie shell crust

FILLING

3 eggs
¼ cup sugar
a pinch of salt
1 cup whole milk
1 teaspoon vanilla
nutmeg to taste

Mix filling ingredients (except nutmeg) together in as pretty a bowl as you can find. Fill a prebaked pie shell with the mixture. Bake at 325 degrees for 45–50 minutes. Sprinkle nutmeg on top midway through cooking time.

π r round

Colonial women used round pans, literally, to cut corners and stretch out scant ingredients as much as they could. That's also why they baked shallow pies. Plump, juicy, deep-dish pies didn't emerge from

American kitchens until newly planted orchards and berry patches finally bore fruit.

By the turn of the twentieth century, it was not unusual for an American to eat a slice of pie daily. In 1902, when an Englishman suggested this was gluttony and that, perhaps, two slices a week would be plenty, the *New York Times* responded thusly:

> *"It is utterly insufficient . . . as anyone who knows the secret of our strength as a nation and the foundation of our industrial supremacy must admit. Pie is the American synonym of prosperity, and its varying contents the calendar of the changing seasons. PIE IS THE FOOD OF THE HEROIC. No pie-eating people can ever be vanquished."*

mississippi mammies

"Marriage pie is a pie made with two different types of fruit. In an ideal marriage pie, the fruit enhance one another while maintaining their respective flavors, textures and independence."
—PAT WILLARD, *PIE EVERY DAY*

I woke up in Greenville, Mississippi, wondering who had draped a wet blanket over me in the middle of the night.

I sat up, looked in the mirror across the bed, and shrieked at my Brillo-pad hair.

"It's the humidity," said Kris, who was already up and frantically searching for a scrunchie to tame her unruly curls.

Hair slicked down, we headed south on narrow State Route 1, toward Natchez. We had picked Natchez (pronounced Natch-isssssssss) for our next pie stop, because it's the oldest settlement along the Mississippi River, and like pie, noble yet humble, it was full of contradictions.

Even though the cotton-rich city boasted the most millionaires and brass-button waistcoats per capita, Natchez was staunchly opposed to the Confederacy and Mississippi's secession from the Union. In its heyday, Natchez was as famous for its frilly antebellum mansions as for its steamy red-light district.

State Route 1 is a gangly road that slithers alongside the Mississippi River through spotty, forlorn towns where houses that had once stood proud are boarded up and left to the mercy of the oppressive, uncontrollable kudzu vine.

We passed lots of "shotgun" houses. From the road, you could see clear through the front-door screen to the barbecue smoker in the backyard.

The wet, taxing heat, the voracious vine, contributed to a sense of physical and psychic abandon in the air. For a change of scenery, we cut over to wider Highway 61 and saw our first fields of old King cotton, fields where the sweat and blood of blacks had paid for the fine filigree on those mansions still intact in Natchez.

Near Hollandale, a low-riding rusted-out Cadillac in front of us slowed way down. The driver opened his door and tossed the remains of his fast-food breakfast onto the highway. A foil wrapper flew onto my windshield and clung there to grease our disgust. After only a few days of driving, we were starting to feel a sense of ownership over these back roads.

At Vicksburg, we switched to the Natchez Trace Parkway, once a pre-Columbian Indian path, and that immediately lifted our spirits. The Trace, as it's called, was as forested and self-contained as Narnia: a shaded tunnel of kudzu vine, towering oaks, and Spanish moss. From the 1780s to the 1820s, the road was popular among farmers and craftspeople who would transport their goods downstream by raft and take the Trace home, watching for roving bands of thieves.

Natchez was ringed by the usual generic suspects: chain hotels and Jiffy-Lubes. But the generic quickly gave way to the genteel, when we drove into the old part of town, barely changed, it seemed, since before the Civil War.

In fact, Natchez, which sits on a high bluff, had been spared the ravages of the war, and when a boll-weevil infestation pillaged local crops in 1908, developers lost interest in the pretty town. Each garden was prettier and more fragrant than the next, brimming with azaleas, glossy-leafed camelias, jasmine, and dogwood.

We wanted to see the mighty Mississippi up close, so we made our way down to Natchez-Under-the-Hill, a spirited part of town with lots of restaurants and shops, which flanks the river. At an outdoor restaurant and bar we took in a Mississippi sunset and a mint julep.

A handsome married couple in shorts and flip-flops came to sit next to us. Braxton and Carol, both locals, both in the insurance business, said juleps by the river was a Friday-night ritual. They had lived in Natchez all their lives and they couldn't say enough about their hometown.

I had planned to ask one of the tour guides at the antebellum mansions where in Natchez to go for pie, but since neither Kris nor I wanted to leave this magical spot, we decided to stay put and ask Braxton and Carol instead.

"Mammy's Cupboard," they said without hesitation. "It's a restaurant shaped like an old black mammy and the dining room is inside her hoop skirt," they explained. "Doris, the owner, makes pies just like our grandmas did," said Carol. "We love the banana caramel."

A restaurant shaped like a mammy? Was that not considered insensitive, we asked. They laughed.

"Welcome to the South. . . . People don't get ruffled about things like that as much as they do in California," said Braxton. "But we all get along better than you think."

Just then, the *American Queen*, the largest paddlewheel steamboat in the country, crawled upriver, docking directly in front of the restaurant. With her delicate gingerbread filigree and two towering smokestacks, she looked like a floating wedding cake capped with a decorative bride and groom. Perhaps it was the julep working its mint-mash magic, but I half expected Mark Twain to come strolling down the gangplank, tamping his pipe.

When we stepped out under the canopy of stars, the paddleboat's thousand small lights beckoned. "They'll never let you on board without a passenger ticket," said Carol, who caught me eyeing the gangplank.

What Carol didn't know was that pie takes you places you never thought you'd go, from the artichoke patch at Duarte's in Pescadero to Elva Twitchell's living room to the king-sized bed Elvis slept on four times.

A grumpy guard at the top of the plank was about to prove me wrong, when an engineer named Mike, who just happened to be walking past, interjected.

"Did I hear correctly? You two ladies are driving across America looking for pie?" He unhooked the security rope to let us through.

We turned and waved good-bye to Braxton and Carol.

Mike had been an engineer for the touring steamboat company for years, and Natchez was his favorite stop along the Mississippi.

"Do you know *why?*" he asked. "Because there's a black mammy named Sophronia who sells delicious sweet-potato pies right on the lawn there," he said, pointing to the spot where, just moments earlier, we'd said good-bye to our new Natchez friends.

We asked him if he had heard of Mammy's Cupboard.

"Sophronia is the *only* mammy you need to know in Natchez," he said resolutely. Mike gave us a tour of the stately ship, from the turn-of-the-century opera house to the Mark Twain Gallery with its reading and writing nooks. Then he led us to the bow of the Texas Deck, where he invited us to sit on any one of an assortment of empty rocking chairs and porch swings.

"We call this 'the front porch of America.' Make yourselves at home," he said. "I'm going to go to my room and dream about that sweet-potato pie."

We sat quietly for a good hour on this "porch," watching the moon dance in the glossy licks of the river. I was 7 again, learning to jump rope on the front lawn of our Santa Monica duplex. With my arms shooting straight down either side of my body to keep my dress from rising up, I was chanting "M-I-SS-I-SS-I-PP-I."

Doris Kemp was about 7 years old when she got caught stealing an egg-custard pie from her aunt's windowsill.

"It was my cousin who put me up to it. We ate the whole thing to hide the evidence," she remembers.

"Children don't get caught stealing pies anymore, because there are no pies left on the sill to steal."

That's why they line up at Mammy's Cupboard on Saturday. Busy working people all longing for a slice of homemade pie. A slice of remember when. A slice of slow.

The sky-high café, truly shaped like a slim-waisted Aunt Jemima, is hard to miss. Mammy's head, adorned with hoop earrings and a knotted head scarf, towers above the oaks, themselves draped with scarves of Spanish moss.

The restaurant wasn't open yet, so we peeked through the front door and saw Doris, her white hair pinned in a loose bun, bringing her pies out of the kitchen one at a time until there were about fifteen on display. She carried each one with two hands and carefully placed it on a three-tier stand. Sometimes she'd take a step back to admire her handiwork. The coquettish tilt to her head suggested she was pleased. I felt guilty catching her in this moment of self-admiration.

The place filled up the moment Doris opened the door. First in line, we scored a table right next to the pies. We couldn't believe how many people ordered their pies at the same time as their lunch.

They didn't want Doris to run out of their favorite, they told the waitress.

Doris's pies were, hands down, the prettiest we'd seen so far, so we agreed to break our "share one slice" rule, just this once. Banana caramel sounded too sweet for this heat. Craving fruit, we both picked blueberry apple.

Some of my married friends tell me that they knew the moment they met their husbands that these were the men they were going to marry. I wouldn't know, but I can tell you that I looked down at the buckling slice of apple blueberry pointed directly at my heart, and I knew it was going to be the pie against which all others would be judged.

The tawny crust had a strong backbone but a tender touch. My fork slid through the filling but met only a touch of resistance at bottom crust, itself firm but pliable. The tart apples were rounded out by sweet, plump berries that managed to stay whole and independent in mind and in flavor. Doris had been gentle with the sugar, letting nature work its chemistry.

I took a bite, and it was one of those rare moments where substance and style come together with the grace of synchronized swimmers. It tasted deeply familiar and right. I shut my eyes to seal in the flavor and the feeling.

"You like it then," said a pleased Doris, pulling up a chair at our table. We asked how she had come upon this unlikely combination. And that's when she told us about her late husband who had died of cancer a few years earlier.

He started planting blueberry bushes right after the diagnosis, she said, "to keep his mind off how sick he was." He died before he got to see his blueberry bushes bear fruit. When she opened the café, she promised herself that she would have at least one special blueberry item on the menu each day, in his memory. Hence the tart-meets-sweet blueberry lemonade, which she serves in glass Mason jars.

One morning, she was making an apple pie and ran out of apples. It was only natural that she should grab for some blueberries to fill it out, meeting two challenges with one batch of berries.

"I tasted it and thought it was a real good combination, so I kept on making it," she said. "People love it."

We asked her what the secret is to making pie.

"Practice, practice, practice," she said. "When making the dough, don't stretch it. Don't work it too hard. Be gentle. That's the big trick. Be gentle."

Although most people like her meringues—Doris admits she's just a big showoff when it comes to getting her meringue as tall as a ship's prow—she has a soft spot for her fruit pies, especially blueberry.

"Next to mashed potatoes and gravy, I can't think of a better comfort food than pie, can you?" she said.

Doris learned to make pies from her mother, who learned to

". . . *sweet potato, now that's* Southern *pie.*"

make pies from *her* mother. With working mothers on the run, and home-economics classes on the outs, who is teaching today's children to bake, she asked.

"It's not a judgment on working mothers," she hastened to add. Her own daughter has no time to bake with her children. "It's just the state of our society."

She was right. In every state so far, the pie trail had invariably led us to the kitchens of gray-haired women who feared that they were the end of the pie line.

Sophronia Dyson—Natchez's other pie mammy—was no exception.

Sophronia was leaning against an oak tree, making cardboard boxes from flats for her pies and candy, when we showed up about 12:30.

Sophronia's pies were tiny, but we could smell the nutmeg from ten feet away.

"You can get a cream pie anywhere, but sweet potato, now that's *Southern* pie," said Sophronia, who wore a blue bandanna scarf around her head. Some have argued that sweet potato—not apple—is the true American pie, and Sophronia would agree. Sophronia, who had the long, outstretched fingers of a cellist, used locally grown sweet potatoes.

It was impossible to put an age on Sophronia. Fifty? Seventy?

As for her beautiful name, "I always thought it was an old lady's name," she said. "But I've grown into it."

To sell her pies to tourists, she positions herself on a small folding chair, her back turned to the thick belt of churning water that is the Mississippi. She has mixed feelings about the river. River tourism butters her corn bread. But she was raised on haunting tales of ancestors being swallowed by its murky currents.

"I call it the baaaaaad Mississippi River," she said, turning to face the river head-on, squinting like a crocodile coming up for air. I decided not to ask Sophronia for her recipe, much as I wanted it for my collection. Something told me she might take it the wrong way.

Some elderly tourists in seersucker shorts and crisp white polo shirts walked past, and Sophronia immediately switched currents: "Come try Sophronia's homemade sweet-potato pies," she said in a high-pitched and singsong voice. "It's homemade and it's so good, it comes with a money-back guarantee."

We took our sweet-potato pies on the road with us for the long drive toward Memphis, Tennessee. In deserted Tutwiler, the birthplace of the blues, we sat on the stoop of an abandoned junk store and inhaled Sophronia's sassy pies in three bites. A group of spindly girls in braids and hand-me-down dresses dreamed up a dance routine in front of a faded mural of B. B. King.

DORIS KEMP'S ACCIDENTAL
APPLE-BLUEBERRY PIE FROM
MAMMY'S CUPBOARD
IN NATCHEZ, MISSISSIPPI

CRUST

2 unbaked pie crusts

FILLING

2 cups of blueberries, preferably fresh, but frozen will work

3 Granny Smith apples, peeled and thinly sliced

1½ cups of sugar

½ cup of flour

1 tablespoon of lemon juice

½ teaspoon of nutmeg

1 teaspoon of cinnamon

2 tablespoons of butter

Combine the filling ingredients, except for the butter, in a mixing bowl and mix gently with a wooden spoon. Pour the mixture into a 9-inch pie pan lined with a basic pie crust. Cut butter over top of mixture. Cover with a top crust. Crimp edges together to seal. Cut slits into crust to allow steam to escape. Bake at 375 degrees for about 45 minutes.

salvation and a sax in memphis

*"I'm trying to get people to see that we are our brother's keeper,
I still work on it. Red, white, black, brown, yellow, rich, poor,
we all have the blues."*

—B. B. KING

Our drive through the Mississippi Delta, birthplace of so many
blues legends, had given us dancing feet, so, when we pulled into
Memphis around 11 P.M., we freshened up and made a beeline for
Beale Street.

We ducked for a late snack into the Southern Cultural Center
where an old, thin black man with a salt-and-pepper, philandering
beard wailed on a saxophone. When it was time for a break, he
stepped outside to get some air back in those lordly lungs. I followed
him and, after paying my humble respects, asked him if he could recommend a Memphis pie.

He didn't have much meat on his bones, but it was hard to imagine that good pie hadn't passed those amazing sax-blowing lips.

He smiled, massaged his beard, thought about it for a while.

"I gotta say Piccadilly over there on Elvis Presley Boulevard," he
finally said. "Piccadilly has all kinds of good pie. Sweet potato. Custard. Cherry. That's where everyone goes for pie after church."

I was glad he brought church up, because Kris and I had a hankering for some live, soul-searing spirituals. Mr. Saxophone suggested the Greater Harvest Church of God in Christ Ministries for gospel, and then he shuffled back inside for another set. What's your name, I asked as he walked away.

"Fred Ford," he replied without turning back.

With our Sunday-morning strategy all squared away, Kris and I moved on to the B. B. King Blues Club up the street to shake a leg, or a pie thigh, as it were. We danced until closing, and when the last blues band was packing up, the keyboardist, who had to be 70 at least, stepped down from the raised stage to compliment Kris on her fine moves. He joined us for a drink and some reminiscing about the "old Beale Street." The keyboardist was touring the country and bound for New York City.

"Well, since we're going the same way, why don't I hitch a ride with you," he said. "I'm so sick of those damn buses and trains. I could use a stretch on the open road with the windows down."

Betty's backseat was loaded with mixing bowls.

He didn't mind, he said, he knew a thing or two about cramped spaces. He popped open his leather traveling case, battered like a thrift-shop shoe. All of its contents, razors, paperbacks, plastic combs, were disposable. We outlined our plans for Sunday: church for gospel, Piccadilly, and then Graceland. Was he up for it?

"Church?" he said, his voice cracking.

He grabbed his case, bade us farewell, and headed down Beale Street.

Greater Harvest is a futuristic church built like a modern fort. It has none of the charm of the intimate, whiteboard chapels we'd passed on some of the smaller country roads. The parking lot was packed with fancy cars.

We were late since we got lost getting there, but the two smiling ushers who greeted us at the door made us feel instantly at home as they showed us to the only vacant pew. From what I could tell, ours were the only white faces here on this sunny June morning. We'd missed most of the spirituals, but the impassioned sermon more than made up for it. It was all about "finding one's place" in the world, a tailor-made message for peripatetic pie seekers like us and, I thought, for a lonely, nomadic musician.

The crowd was pretty worked up. People burst out of their seats like geysers, shouting "Hallelujah! Amen! Uh-huh!" Then members of the deliverance team poured into the pews to seek out sinners. Naturally, they headed straight for the two redheads in the house. Minutes later, we were standing before the congregation, our heads buried in the salvation team's ample breasts, being saved for all to see.

As soon as the service ended, a group of women gathered around us and welcomed us to their church. They could not have been nicer. And we wondered how many churches with white congregations would be as welcoming to two new black faces in the pews. We told them we were just passing through, on a cross-country sojourn for pie. "Have you been to Piccadilly's yet?" they all asked.

"It's right near the house where Elvis lives," said a young lady in a flower-print dress. Her use of the present tense was sweet. The senior pastor stepped up and inquired about the commotion. Although ours wasn't the type of quest he was used to, he smiled. He dug in his pocket and pulled out a crisp twenty-dollar bill. "Have lunch at Piccadilly's on Greater Harvest," he said. Now, I haven't spent much time in church, but I did know this wasn't how things usually worked. We refused, but the pastor would not take no for an answer.

So, on divine orders, we headed for a free lunch at Piccadilly's, where we hoped to treat some locals to pie. The restaurant, one of 140 from coast to coast, was packed with families in their Sunday best, who had caravanned there from churches all over Memphis. Women in stylish plumed hats fanned themselves with church programs as they waited in the cafeteria line. Little girls with knobby knees and lemon-yellow tulle dresses stood on their patent-leather toes to glimpse pans of fried chicken and ribs and glistening sweet potatoes.

I scanned the room for someone who needed a piece of pie, and my eye fell on Sarah Webster—or, rather, her hat: a box-style black number with satin trim and two black feathers that shot straight up like a "peace" hand sign. She was sitting in the back of the room with three friends, gnawing on a chicken bone.

First, we complimented Sarah on her chapeau.

"This isn't my best," she said coolly. Sarah owns about fifty hats, we learned, one for nearly every sermon of the year. We asked Sarah if she wouldn't mind some company and conversation in exchange for some free God-given pie for her and her friends.

Her friends nodded, but Sarah looked us up and down, nostrils flared.

She'd been eating at Piccadilly every Sunday after church for twenty-five years. She thought she'd seen it all, she said.

We enlightened her about our quest, and it was obvious she deemed it frivolous. Pie was common, of the earth, almost heathen in its simple pleasure. It was not the noblest of grails. All this she said with the lift of an eyebrow. Still, Sarah did not say no to the slice of pecan pie I brought her back from my trip to the cafeteria line. And what a trip that was. There were at least eighty slices of pie stacked so close, the edges of their plates overlapped. It reminded me of that whimsical Wayne Thiebaud pie painting, though this display was messier and darker hued. These were working-class pies.

I held up the line for several minutes, trying to decide. I'd been dying to try a slice of custard pie since meeting Buford Smith, so I

Sarah Webster and Minister Wilburt Miller, Memphis, TN

grabbed one of those for myself and then an assortment for our new friends.

"Lord have mercy!" I heard someone say when I finally slid my tray forward. The custard was awfully eggy, and the soft, soggy crust spoke volumes about volume baking. I can't say the pies had any of that homespun richness of our Mississippi Mammy pies, but I looked around the room and people were enjoying their pie with relish. Even Sarah. They were eating for comfort, and what tasted better than custard pie after church with the family?

Uh-huh.

That's right.

Amen.

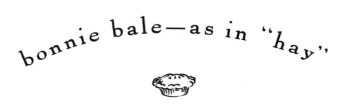

At Graceland, the kitchen was our favorite room in the house. All the appliances were avocado-green. On the counter sat a microwave as big as a '57 Chevy.

Bonnie Bale would have called it the perfect pie-baking kitchen.

bonnie bale—as in "hay"

> *"I have always depended on the kindness of strangers."*
> —BLANCHE DUBOIS
> TENNESSEE WILLIAMS, *A STREETCAR NAMED DESIRE*

We met Bonnie Bale the next day, on our drive to Lexington, Kentucky, where we hoped a horse trainer at the Kentucky Horse Park could point us toward some state chess pie or the famous Derby Pie™ we'd heard so much about.

In a town called Horse Cave, we stopped at a thrift shop and bought a stack of old pie tins from the 1940s for only $1 a piece. The owner of the store wondered if we were opening a pie shop. So we told her about our trip. She didn't have any suggestions on where to go for pie, but she gave us a Kentucky cookbook instead.

We pulled over to look for more pie paraphernalia at the Pumping Station Antiques Shop, about 20 miles or so north on the Jackson Highway.

The owner sat in a rocking chair, talking to a neighbor on the telephone. While we poked around, I saw her peel back the curtain and crane her neck to assess our license plate.

"You two ladies aren't from around here, are you?" she said after hanging up the phone.

"I'm Bonnie Bale," she said, extending her hand. "That's B-a-l-e, as in a bale of hay.

"What brings you to this sleepy part of Kentucky?" she asked.

"We're looking for pie," said Kris.

"Paaaaahhhhhhhhhhhhhh?" Bonnie said, raising her plucked eyebrows two inches and her voice two octaves. "I'm the BEST paaaahhhhhhhhhhh baker in Kentucky. I'm famous in these parts for my butterscotch pie and—get this—(she leaned forward in her chair and whispered) I make it in a *mi-cro-wave!*"

She articulated every syllable of *mi-cro-wave*, the way people must have pronounced it when microwaves were still a novelty, back when Elvis bought his. Pie? In a microwave? We were skeptical and it showed.

"You don't believe me, do you?" she said, pushing herself out of her chair. "Do you have time to come my house so I can prove it? It won't take long . . . I can make it in less than twenty minutes—start to finish."

Bonnie put the CLOSED sign on the door and sent us down the road to get a carton of milk while she went and readied her kitchen for an audience. We met back at her home, which was set slightly back from the Jackson Highway, on a hill, in the hamlet of Canmer. Her house was filled with Early American furniture and her kitchen was Brady Bunch Kitsch.

She had already lined up on her kitchen island all the ingredients she would need: eggs, milk, margarine, brown sugar, salt, and cornstarch. And, of course, a store-bought pie shell she had been keeping in the freezer for just such an emergency.

She had also applied a fresh coat of persimmon lipstick and was raring to go.

"There's just no telling how many pies I've made in my lifetime," she said, mixing the ingredients for the filling. Kris was snapping pictures and Bonnie would often pause midsentence to flash a million-dollar smile. She always baked pies for church gatherings and other civic functions, she said, and when the nearby town of Edmonton was hit hard by a storm months back, she'd baked a slew of pies for the shelter.

"Y'all can't imagine how people like my pies around here."

With the ease of a television chef, Bonnie worked and talked simultaneously as we sat perched on kitchen stools. She talked about her recent thorny separation from her husband ("he was much younger than me") about her fiftieth high school reunion, which she had just hosted ("I was voted the *least* changed") and about her mother, who lived in a trailer in Bonnie's backyard ("we do need our privacy, you know").

She also talked about her constant battle with her weight.

She stopped to slip the filling mixture into the microwave. Pursing her lips for precision, she set the timer for eight minutes.

Then she turned to tell us about Earleen, the pastor in the next town over, who had, of late, become her best friend and confidant. The woman who had sold us the pie tin in Horse Cave had mentioned a son named Earleen who was a preacher. It had to be the same Earleen, so why hadn't the woman mentioned Bonnie's famous pies, we asked. Bonnie became as stiff as the egg whites she was whipping into meringue in her grandmother's aqua-green mixing bowl.

"Oh, women around these parts are very jealous when it comes to these kind of things," she said.

Then, with a forced smile, she switched topics. "You've got to be careful with meringue, you'll kill it if you're not absolutely gentle," she said, carefully stirring in the cornstarch.

For the fourth time, she opened the microwave door, eyed the filling like a sharpshooter, and gave it a good stir.

"You've got to keep control because otherwise it'll control you."

Once the filling was cooked, she poured it into her pie shell and layered her just-made meringue on top. She popped the pie in her oven and set a timer for fifteen minutes and ushered us into the living room where, from the comfort of her favorite velvet high-back armchair, she could tell us a little bit more about herself.

The small house was beginning to smell like a county fair.

"I was a Depression baby and my family was very, very poor," she began. "My parents were tenant farmers and they were very young when they had me. They were both sweet eaters. My mother would make nine pies a week and she'd cut them in fourths! She made her pie fillings in an iron skillet over a wood-burning stove . . ."

We talked about her high school reunion where her butterscotch pies were "a hit with the boys, let me tell you." Then, ding! The timer went off and Bonnie bounced out of her chair. We followed her into the kitchen where she yelped with joy when she saw that her meringue had turned a perfect golden brown.

"Now, ordinarily, I would let this sit and cool for a while so that the filling could harden, but since you girls are in a hurry, I'm going to cut you a piece right now." We promised we would not hold it against her as she sat us in the formal dining room.

We asked for small slices, since we were still recovering from our Piccadilly pig-out, but she cut the pie in fourths anyway. Old habits die hard. She wouldn't join us for a slice but she hovered over us to see what we thought.

"Weeeeellllllllllllll?" she asked, coyly pressing her palms together and leaning her head to one side.

Many months have passed since that first bite of butterscotch pie but I remember it well. I remember the hot, creamy puddle of honey-sweet caramel on my tongue balanced by a spiny meringue. I

"There's just no telling how many pies I've made in my lifetime."

don't remember the crust, just the filling: warm, soft, and puddingy.

We heaped on Bonnie the compliments she fully expected.

"Maybe I'll be famous someday," she said, walking us out to her deck. "I'm so glad you dropped by. This has turned out to be one fine day. Y'all have a safe trip, ya hear?"

We'd spent only an hour with Bonnie Bale but I felt I knew her. I knew how she'd behaved in high school and the wiles she relied upon to charm the boys at the dance. And, as we hoofed it toward horse country, I was sure Bonnie was sitting in her velvet chair, enjoying her slice of pie with guilty pleasure.

We still needed to find some chess or Derby Pie™ the state was known for. We drove past miles and miles of horse farms, all joined, it seemed, by one continuous white fence. Every farm had its weeping willow, and that seemed appropriate since most of the old barns in the area were painted mourning black.

The pretty young lady behind the information desk at the horse park listened intently as we explained what we were after: a horse trainer at the park who happened to also like pie. Did she have any suggestions?

"MY trainer," she said. "Every time we travel to a horse show somewhere, he always makes us stop to try different restaurants, and he always orders pie." She called him at home, and although he was busy getting twenty saddlebreds ready for a horse show in Ohio, he could take a few minutes to talk to us about pie. He lived in Richmond, about 45 miles due south.

We met Tommy Clouse inside his "office"—a horse stall festooned with dozens of first-place ribbons, with fluffed-out cat curled in the corner behind a bale of hay, a reminder of Bonnie.

American saddlebreds are known for their beauty and grace, Clouse told us. "They pick their feet up when they walk and know to keep their heads set and alert and their ears pointed forward." Clouse sat slumped in a chair, displaying none of the fine posture his horses are known for, but his warm, grinning eyes were filled with grace. He was 12 years old when he got his first horse—about the same age he discovered his love of pie. He had planned to become a doctor and was well on his way, but his unbridled passion for—and understanding of—horses led him on a different path. His second passion was dessert, pie specifically. He highly recommended the Boone Tavern Hotel in nearby Berea for their chess pie, a Southern favorite with a basic filling of sugar, butter, eggs, lemon, and a small amount of flour, that often invites sweet deviations.

"It's a pretty common-tasting pie," said Tommy, "but theirs stands out from the rest."

Just thinking of the pie made his eyes twinkle. If he hadn't been going to this horse show, he would have accompanied us to Berea, he said. Tommy wouldn't let us leave without introducing us to one of his favorite horses, a striking, albeit nervy, 3-year-old horse named Pablo. Pablo, who belonged to a local dentist, seemed perfectly aware that he had just won a blue ribbon in Knoxville, Tennessee.

Boone Tavern Hotel is affiliated with Berea College, a small, unique liberal arts-and-crafts college, which gleans 80 percent of its students from southern Appalachia and Kentucky. Students, who study anything from furniture-making to weaving, pay no tuition, but in exchange must work on the campus in one capacity or another.

Many work at the hotel, which was originally built in 1909 as a guest house for visitors to the college. Most of the hotel furnishings were handcrafted by Berea students.

Mark Williams, the chef at the hotel, was alone in the spotless kitchen when we arrived in the middle of the afternoon, between shifts. He told us, with some consternation, that the hotel's chess pie had recently gone back to its original name: Jefferson Davis pie, after the president of the Confederacy.

The previous dean of the college was a pacifist—the Dalai Lama has visited the campus on several occasions—so he had the name changed to chess pie. But, when he retired, the name was changed back to Jefferson Davis pie "because that's how locals remembered the pie best," said Mark, visibly bothered by the name himself.

We asked to try a slice of this Confederate pie. And though the dining room was closed, Mark gave us a table by the window and brought us each a slice decorated with bright orange nasturtium petals. The pie had a rich, bright, lemony taste. The crust was remarkably firm, with a posture as beautiful as Pablo's.

I enjoyed the pie, but I couldn't get past the notion of eating a pie named after a man who defended slavery. Call me crazy.

We asked to try a slice of Derby Pie™, which many consider Kentucky's state pie, and the chef was more than happy to bring out a slice of his version of the chocolate nut pie, so long as we didn't call it Derby Pie™.

The term "Derby Pie™" had been trademarked by Kern's Kitchen, the Louisville bakery that created the famous pie in 1954 in honor of the famous horse race, Mark said.

Still, restaurants continued to serve the Derby Pie™, and recipes for Derby Pie™ continued to appear in cookbooks across the country. Determined to protect their pie—and their bread and butter—the Kerns did what Americans do best: they started suing people left and right. They took on *Bon Appetit* and PBS for appropriating the name, and even Nestle (their own supplier!) for printing a Tollhouse Derby Pie™ recipe on the back of their chocolate-chip packages.

Since the pie is so popular, Kentucky restaurants have come up with alternative names for similar chocolate-nut concoctions: Race-horse pie, Winner's Circle pie, and Triple Crown pie are just a few examples of the Derby derivations. Boone Tavern's version is known as Race Day pie.

We liked Mark a lot, but all this negativity made us realize we really weren't hungry for a second piece of pie after all.

By the time we found a room at a hotel it was 9:30 P.M. We'd eaten nothing but racially insensitive pie all day and needed a square meal. Nothing was open at this hour on a Monday night in rural Kentucky. Nothing save for the Kentucky Fried Chicken where we had to beg the janitor to squeeze us in as they were closing. I had never eaten at a KFC before but Kentucky seemed like the best place to start.

I guess I was a little too effusive thanking the janitor, because as we left with our bucket of extra crispy, he proposed marriage and a new, better life for me in his native Bombay. We were four thousand miles and nineteen pies into the trip. Nothing fazed me anymore.

We set up our table in front of the television and poured our-selves a shot of Bourbon to go with our chicken. A *Brady Bunch* marathon was on Nick at Nite.

The gods were with us.

BONNIE BALE'S
BLINK-OF-AN-EYE
BUTTERSCOTCH PIE

CRUST

1 9-inch pie crust (Bonnie uses frozen)

FILLING

3 eggs

2½ cups of milk

1 cup brown sugar, firmly packed

½ cup of cornstarch, plus 1 heaping tablespoon

¼ teaspoon salt

½ stick butter or margarine

1 teaspoon vanilla

⅓ cup white sugar

Separate the eggs, being careful not to get any of the yolk into the whites. Using a whisk, beat the egg yolks in a mixing bowl. Add milk. Mix well. Stir in brown sugar, cornstarch, and salt. Mix well. Add the butter or margarine, in pieces. Cook the mixture on "high" in the microwave for about 8 minutes, pausing to stir every couple of minutes or so. Pour the cooked mixture into a ready-to-go pie crust and let it cool.

To make your meringue, make sure you use a bowl that is absolutely grease-free. Beat egg whites on a high speed with a hand-held mixer until they are very stiff. Gradually add ⅓ cup of white sugar while still beating, then add a heaping tablespoon of cornstarch and beat well. Spoon the meringue onto the pie, and bake in a pre-heated oven at 350 degrees until golden-brown, about 15 minutes.

JEFFERSON DAVIS PIE

CRUST

1 unbaked pie shell

FILLING

2 cups brown sugar
1 tablespoon sifted flour
½ teaspoon nutmeg
1 cup cream
4 eggs, lightly beaten
1 teaspoon lemon juice
½ teaspoon lemon rind, grated
¼ cup melted margarine

Sift sugar with flour and nutmeg. Add cream, mix well. Add eggs, mix well. Add lemon juice, lemon rind, and margarine. Mix well. Pour into pie shell. Bake at 375 degrees for 45 minutes. Cool and serve with whipped cream.

dutch treat

"Work and pray, live on hay
You'll get pie in the sky when you die."
—JOE HILL, "THE PREACHER AND THE SLAVE"
(AN OLD LABOR SONG)

By the time we got to Pennsylvania, about two and a half weeks into the trip, we became acutely aware of the passage of time. Not just how a hundred miles on the open road can seem like a thousand, but how time is measured.

Most of the pies we'd uncovered on this sweet treasure hunt could all be traced to the apron strings of white-haired women with calloused, rolling-pin palms. Grandmothers who took the time to bake pie because that was time well spent.

Who takes that kind of time anymore?

Over the last two weeks we'd been living on drawn-out time, the speed at which syrup slithers down a stack of hot cakes. From the long back-road stretches past lazy willows and tobacco barns, and the drip-drip-drip manner of talking in the South, to the meandering way people gave directions, this trip was as much about slowing down as it was about pie.

Slowing down long enough to talk to a stranger at a stoplight; to pick some flowers for the waitress at your local breakfast joint, to bake a pie for the new neighbor who just moved in down the road.

Today's pace isn't a pie pace.

Was that why we were finding so many cast-off mixing bowls and rolling pins in those roadside antiques shops?

In Lancaster, Pennsylvania, the contrast between old and new, fast and slow, hit us like a ton of pie weights.

We had hoped to arrive in Pennsylvania Dutch country early enough to scout out a women's quilting circle for local pie recommendations, but this time we were waylaid by a pair of twisters in Kentucky and West Virginia that had us holed up in tacky motels catching up on journaling and reading for a couple of days.

This part of Dutch country is a bundle of two-lane, unmarked roads dotted with 100-acre farms, each with its spartan oversized barns and quaint wood-frame houses with orderly vegetable patches. It was dusk, but many Amish farmers were plowing their fields with their teams of stocky horses, refusing to call it a day before the sun had.

Like that of most Americans, our exposure to the Amish culture was limited to the Harrison Ford movie *Witness*. So we read up on the Amish and Mennonite cultures in our West Virginia motel. As we drove through the small townships, we were struck by how visually accurate the movie had been. There were no cameras rolling, and yet these women riding alongside us on old-fashioned bicycles really were wearing white caps and dark peasant dresses with thick stockings, their hair parted as straight as the inner spine of a brand-new Bible.

We passed by several horse buggies with big spoked wheels, driven by stern-faced men with scraggly isosceles beards and wide black suspenders. In the backseat facing out, their boys in crisp periwinkle-blue shirts and drop-fall trousers grinned under the broad brims of their straw hats.

We did know that the Amish, also known as "the plain people," do not like to be photographed. We wanted, above all, to be respectful but we also wanted their advice on where to get good pie.

In the town of Intercourse, founded in 1754, we stopped at an educational center and asked the two young women in summer

dresses behind the counter if there was a proper way to approach the Amish and Mennonites without offending them.

The two young women looked at each other and giggled, coyly cupping their hands over their heart-shaped mouths.

"*We're* Mennonites, and you're talking to *us*," they said in unison. "We could recommend some good pie."

They were such a striking contrast to the white-capped buttoned-down women we'd seen on the road, we were confused.

"We're New Order Mennonites," explained Carol, the elder of the two. "Our guidelines aren't as strict."

Carol's mother made a wonderful shoofly pie, she said, but she wasn't too proud to go to the Bird-in-Hand Bakery in town for shoofly pie when time ran short. Carrie, her 19-year-old colleague, agreed that Bird-in-Hand made great shoofly. They called the bakery for us but it had already closed for the night, so we agreed to go to Bird-in-Hand, in the village of Bird-in-Hand, first thing in the morning. We asked if shoofly was something that was eaten only on special occasions or for the benefit of tourists, and they laughed again at our innocence.

"Oh no, we love shoofly and we eat it all the time," Carrie said. "Farmers like to eat it for breakfast before heading to the fields."

By then the last visitors had left the center, so the two young women, who weren't in a hurry to get home, sat with us in a circle on the carpet. Well past dark, we talked about what it was like, growing up Mennonite in '90s America.

They explained the vast differences in lifestyle between Old Order Mennonites and themselves. Yes, they watched television. Yes, they went to movies. Yes, they "dated," although that was something they were less comfortable talking about with strangers.

Carrie said her favorite TV show was *The Simpsons.*

"I think it's really funny, and they've had two episodes with Amish characters," said Carrie, who drives an '88 Dodge, not a horse-drawn buggy. They explained why the Amish disapproved of mirrors and rag dolls with faces sewn in. "Vanity is completely frowned upon," said Carrie, who, with her long, cornsilk-blond hair and pearled smile, would have every reason to be vain.

They admitted with visible relief that the Old World ways were disappearing in some families.

"My mother had to wear *black* shoes at her wedding," Carol said, eyes wide as pie. They told us how common it is for teenagers in their community to go through a rebellious phase. Boys often grow their hair long, drive souped-up cars, even get tattoos. Parents around here know better than to fight it, they said. Eventually, the rebels come back to the harbor that is their faith.

"What I like most about being a Mennonite is our emphasis on peace," said Carrie. "A lot of us have gotten away from that."

Indeed.

Throughout the trip, we'd often marveled at how different each state and region felt to us. The difference was sometimes as subtle as the way the air felt when we cupped our hand out the window, to the landmarks people chose when sketching us a map. Lancaster, we agreed, taking leave of Carrie and Carol, made us feel as though we had traveled through time as well as space.

We found a hotel run by an Amish family in Strasburg, a small town nearby. As late as it was, the purity of the air here, the absence of traffic, and a very bright moon called for a walk, our first on the trip so far. We followed the narrow road that led out of town, lit only by moonglow and fireflies (still following us since Oklahoma). Most of the Amish farmers were beneath handwashed cotton sheets by then, but a few of the homes were still lit by candlelight. When we would hear the clop, clop, clop of hooves, we'd jump out of the buggy lane and onto the shoulder, carefully avoiding pies of the inedible sort.

Shoofly pie is, in fact, the most popular dessert in Pennsylvania Dutch country, which says a lot, as the locals have always been big dessert-eaters. In an earlier time, the Pennsylvania Dutch ate pie up to three times a day, and pie was always served with the rest of the meal, not just for dessert. When a Pennsylvania Dutchman proposed to his wife, he gave her an elaborately carved rolling pin as an engagement gift.

Originally considered a filling breakfast pie for farmers, made with the workhorse ingredients left in the larder, shoofly pie has evolved into a fancier two-layer dessert with a gingerbread cake–like topping and a gooey molasses filling.

Some say the word shoofly comes from *choufleur,* the French word for cauliflower, because of its crumbly, creviced surface. Others, like food historian William Weaver, author of *Pennsylvania Dutch Country Cooking,* insists the pie was named after the Shoofly brand of molasses. That makes sense, since, after all, one of the main ingredients is molasses.

Carol and Carrie told us they thought the pie was so named

because Amish women were always shooing flies from the pies cooling on a windowsill.

I liked this interpretation best.

Either way, we were eager to try some shoofly for breakfast—farmer-style. On our drive to Bird-in-Hand, we stopped to take a picture of a vintage sign advertising shoofly pie, on the brick side of a country store somewhere on the old Lincoln Highway. Shopkeeper Wayne Meyers stepped out on the porch of his shop. Meyers was "English," like us (what the Amish and Mennonites call people outside their faith). He sells his own shoofly pie, which he buys from an elderly Amish woman in Paradise Township, who bakes in her basement kitchen at sunup using a recipe handed down by generations of baking women.

"I always look forward to picking up the pies at her kitchen," said Meyers, who was sorry he hadn't restocked since the weekend. "There are always a group of women baking together. They use large pizza ovens that are run by air compression."

Meyers was on his way to a produce auction in Ephrata to buy some strawberries, and invited us to come along. We hung back and watched as Old World Amish men craned their necks and stroked their beards in concentration to better hear the auctioneer's chant. Behind them, their demure wives, with five or six children in tow, waited patiently to help load up the buggies with crates of plump berries and rhubarb stalks that would most likely end up in jams or pies.

We would have liked to have gone to Paradise Township to meet his shoofly pie supplier, but Meyers didn't think that would be appropriate on such short notice and we respected that.

We met with the same reticence at the Bird-in-Hand Bakery, where the manager told us his pie baker was indeed in the kitchen but he doubted she would come out to talk to us.

"She's Old World Order Amish, you know, and they don't like to have their picture taken," he said, "but I'll ask her."

Becky, 25, who had been baking since before sunrise, invited us into her immaculate kitchen even though she was eager to get home. "I guess it's OK to have my picture taken as long as it's not going to appear in the local paper," she said, smiling. Then she insisted that her cobaker, Eva, an Old Order Mennonite, be in the picture as well. They adjusted their plain bonnets and straightened their aprons before posing by the pie rounder, each proudly holding a pie baked that morning. One was a shoofly; the other, a cherry pie with a lattice crust as delicate as the border trim on their aprons.

"Shoofly is not that difficult to make," said Becky, making up in humility, it seemed, for her brief lapse of vanity. "You mix the wet ingredients together and then you mix the dry ingredients together. Growing up Amish, you learn to make pie when you're real young."

And then the two young women looked at the time and excused themselves, as they had to go home "to do chores."

We bought a pie to go, grabbed two forks, and dug into it on our way out of town. It was jammy in texture and stuck to the roofs of our mouths, the way it must stick to a farmer's ribs.

As we drove out of town, wiping crumbs from our faces, we caught up with Becky and Amy walking briskly on the side of the road in their black, sensible shoes. They were chattering away. They were so young and yet so self-assured, inside the bakery and out.

I looked in the rearview mirror and pinched my cheeks, searching for some of their rosy spirit.

SHOOFLY PIE

Marcia Adams's Shoofly Pie, from *New Recipes from Quilt Country*, is the best I've tasted so far.

Pastry for a one-crust, 9-inch pie

FILLING

1 cup all purpose flour

⅔ cup light brown sugar, packed

1 rounded tablespoon cold butter

¼ teaspoon salt

1 egg

1 cup light molasses

¾ cup cold water

¼ cup hot water

1 tablespoon baking soda

Preheat oven to 350 degrees.

Roll out the pie pastry and line a 9-inch pie pan. Set aside.

In a food processor bowl, combine the flour, brown sugar, butter, and salt. Remove ½ cup of the mixture and set aside. Transfer the rest to a medium mixing bowl. In a small bowl, beat the egg lightly. Add the molasses and cold water, and blend but do not beat; you don't want bubbles in the batter. Set aside.

In a small bowl, mix the hot water with the baking soda and blend into the molasses mixture. Add to the flour mixture and mix well. Pour into the pie shell and top with the reserved crumbs. Bake for 35 minutes. The pie will appear quivery but will firm up as it cools. Transfer to a rack to cool completely before cutting.

connecticut

"Lux et Veritas" (Light and Truth)
—THE MOTTO FOR YALE UNIVERSITY

Never trust a man with a dead fox on his head.

With only two days left before I had to report to work in New York, Kris and I decided to squeeze in one last state. We made a beeline for Connecticut, on the advice of the biker we'd met on Route 66, at Lucille Hamons's gas station.

The bearded biker had recommended a "sweet, family bakery" in Hamden, the blue-collar town where he grew up. He'd scribbled the address on the back of a Route 66 postcard. *Best pie I ever had,* he wrote.

Only this biker forgot to mention one thing about this family bakery . . . it belonged to *his* family. They were expecting us, thought they might get some good press out of it. He should have at least mentioned it, Kris and I agreed. We might have been more forgiving if the pie had indeed been good. But I could tell it was Dumpster pie just by looking at it—not the pie note we wanted to end our journey on. Reluctantly, we turned around and headed for New York.

A stop at the Frisbie Pie Company in Bridgeport, Connecticut, would have been better. But that famous bakery closed its doors in 1958—exactly one year after the Frisbee toy, inspired by the bakery's lightweight pie tins, made its debut on beaches and lawns across America.

Students at Yale claim they were the first to discover the aerodynamics of the Frisbie pie tin in the early 1940s. But administrators from Middlebury College in Vermont credit *their* students with the discovery.

According to Middlebury lore, three undergraduates were driving through Nebraska in 1939 when they got a flat tire. As two boys fixed the flat, a third wandered off alone and, in a cornfield, he stumbled on a discarded pie tin from Frisbie's Pie Company. He picked it up and threw it in the air, and an American picnic tradition was born. In 1989, the college went so far as to erect a bronze statue of a dog jumping to catch a Frisbee, to commemorate the fiftieth anniversary of that pivotal roadside discovery.

It was Walter Frederick Morrison who took the campus game and turned it into a cool million. An inventor at heart, Morrison had flung a few pie tins and paint-can lids as a youth, and he wanted to capitalize on the nation's runaway obsession with unidentified flying objects.

He experimented with stainless steel discs to which he welded a steel ring inside the rim for stability. When that didn't work, he turned to plastic, America's new material wunderkind. Cheap, light, durable, and malleable, plastic was perfectly suited for America's new "use it, then lose it" culture driven by planned obsolescence.

Morrison called his plastic disc the Pluto Platter. A new California toy company called Wham-O, which had just hit it big with its Hula Hoop, bought the rights to Morrison's design. Once they learned about the college kids and Connecticut pie company that started the whole craze, Wham-O decided to call the disc a "Frisbee."

picture-perfect pie

"The English are not an inventive people;
they don't eat enough pie."
—THOMAS ALVA EDISON

Pies used to be part of every American holiday, so is it any wonder that George Eastman, the man who made holiday photos possible, was also a pie lover?

Eastman, who invented the first Kodak camera in 1888, even had a kitchenette attached to his darkroom so that he could whip up a pie on a whim.

"He was a regular Betty Crocker," says Kathy Connor, curator of the George Eastman House, the fifty-room colonial mansion in Rochester, New York, where Eastman and his mother lived.

Eastman loved to cook and bake. He planted fruit trees and a vegetable garden just so he could have the freshest ingredients available to him, she said. The man who toyed with gelatin emulsions in his mother's kitchen sink especially liked to tinker with recipes. Toward the end of his life, when he discovered Africa, he would often concoct dry-mix recipes for biscuits and pancakes to make his trips to the Dark Continent more enjoyable.

And while he may have called one of his most popular cameras "Brownie," Connor says it's plain that the entrepreneur was a sucker for lemon meringue pie, especially his own. It's not clear whether the recipe came from his mother or another close relative, Connor says, but, upon his death, a recipe for lemon meringue pie was found, scribbled in Eastman's own cursive script, in a box of personal correspondence.

Eastman, who liked to spice up a round of billiards by putting a case of champagne on the line, was extremely competitive when it came to pie.

That is painfully obvious in the following epistolary exchange between Eastman and a distinguished doctor in town named Edwin S. Ingress, launched after Eastman had tasted one of the doctor's pies.

April 7, 1927

My dear Ingress:

That lemon pie was absolutely top notch technically. I cannot hope to surpass it and will be satisfied if I am able to equal it. As to the recipe, however, I have got you beaten as I will show you at the first opportunity. As I did not originate it that will be no credit for me. All I am hoping for is to make the contest a draw.

With kindest regards, I am,

Yours very truly,
George Eastman

Five days later, Eastman received the following missive from the good doctor:

April 13, 1927

Dear Mr. Eastman:

In judging a lemon pie contest the decision should rest on an impartial consideration of the pie's component parts. Your crust was undoubtedly more flaky than mine. The two meringues were about on a par. In regard to the filling, I still maintain that there might be a difference of opinion.

However, I noticed that, when I asked for a second piece of your pie, I found that it had been entirely consumed, and, as I do not ever remember having had this happen so quickly to one of my pies, I feel that perhaps you are entitled to the decision.

Sincerely yours,
E. S. Ingress

GEORGE EASTMAN'S
FAVORITE LEMON MERINGUE PIE,
EXACTLY AS IT WAS WRITTEN, IN
EASTMAN'S OWN HAND

FILLING

6 eggs. Beat yolks. Beat in 1 cup granulated sugar. Stir in grated rind and juice of two lemons. Cook in double boiler 15 minutes. When cooked and cooled, stir in beaten stiff whites of three eggs.

CRUST

1 cup flour
½ cup shortening
a little salt
sprinkle in water
make paste & roll [were it that easy!]

Connor says she once tried to make Eastman's pie for a charity event, but the filling did not quite fill out a standard nine-inch pie pan. "It looked like I was being chintzy," she said, "but they just used smaller pie pans back then." Connor wasn't quite sure how to fix the problem, not being a pie baker herself.

"I would love nothing more than to spend time baking with my daughter," she said, "but who has the time?"

new york

*"If children grew up according to early indications,
we should have nothing but geniuses."*
—GOETHE (1749–1832)

Kris rummaged in the backseat for the Frank Sinatra tunes her father had given us. She found the one with "New York, New York," popped it in the player, and, to the delight of the drivers on either side of us, we rolled down the windows and let it blare as we crossed the Hudson River, going west on the Tappan Zee Bridge.

To my left, I caught a glimpse of the Manhattan skyline, 20 miles downriver. From this vantage point, the city looked small and manageable, as if in a snow globe.

This was home now.

When I called my new editor to let her know I'd finally made it to New York, I asked her if she could recommend a good local pie to end the trip on. She suggested I pay a visit to Deborah Tyler, better known as the Pie Lady of Nyack. Tyler sells fresh fruit pies at the Nyack Farmers Market on Saturdays, my editor said, and from her back porch the rest of the week.

This being a Friday, we followed the handpainted signs for "homemade pie" leading to Tyler's home, not far from the spot on the Hudson where the shad fishermen gather every spring when the forsythia bloom.

Children's laundry and vintage kitchen towels hung, drying, on a line above potted pink geraniums and purple petunias.

Tyler had just returned from a trip to a Hudson Valley orchard, where she bought bushels of apples and peaches for pie. She looked harried. For the first time on this spontaneous adventure, I felt bad we hadn't called ahead to warn her of our visit. Reality was setting in.

The single, fortysomething mother finally eased up after she'd washed and stored the fruit. She'd started her business, a true cottage industry, she said, after a divorce left her and her three children financially crippled. She'd read an article in *Yankee* magazine about a woman selling blueberry pies from home and thought: "I can do that."

She had learned to bake as a child, and honed her skills while working at a college cafeteria in England. Until then, everything she'd heard or read in cookbooks about making pie "made it sound so traumatic and mysterious," Deborah said. "The secret is more in your attitude than in your technique."

In that regard, she said, pie-baking is a lot like child-rearing.

"You are the one in charge of that dough. Until you get that straight, it doesn't work. You have to be fearless.

"Children, by the way, are great pie bakers," she added, "precisely because they have no fear."

And then Deborah said something that gave us even more hope for the future of pie. Turned out, there was a boy in the neighborhood, Darrell, who wanted to become a professional pie baker when he grew up. The 12-year-old boy dropped by Deborah's house every day after school and tackled all sorts of pies, even some with lattice crusts.

"The hardest part at first was rolling out the dough," Darrell said when we spoke. "But I kept watching Deborah, the way she rolled hers back and forth, the way she patched up the cracks and made a perfect circle.

"I needed to watch someone before I could do it myself. Now it's pretty easy. And it tastes so much better than store-bought."

Like Elva Twitchell, Darrell said baking pie gave him "a real sense of accomplishment." He paused, lowered his voice: "It makes me feel like I have a talent."

What's the best advice he would give a novice pie baker, tackling crust for her first time?

"Take your time," he said. "You just can't rush a pie."

DEBORAH TYLER'S
APPLE PLUM PIE

CRUST

1 cup unsalted butter (8 oz)

3 cups unbleached all-purpose flour

½ teaspoon salt

¼ cup cold water

FILLING

6 oz sugar

¼ cup cornstarch

3 cups thinly sliced, peeled, cooking apples (about 1 lb)

3 cups quartered Italian plums

1 oz brown sugar

2 tablespoons butter

Cut butter into flour and salt until mixture is the consistency of cornmeal. Add water, turning mixture with a fork until it comes together in a ball. Wrap in plastic wrap and chill for one hour before rolling out, or roll out right away.

Combine sugar and cornstarch and add to prepared fruit. Fill a pastry-lined 9-inch pie plate with fruit mixture; sprinkle brown sugar on top; dot with butter. Adjust top crust. Seal and flute edges. Bake at 450 degrees for 10 minutes and at 350 degrees for 45–50 minutes more.

part two

"Nobody sees a flower—really—it is so small—
we haven't time—and to see takes time,
like to have a friend takes time."

—GEORGIA O'KEEFFE "ABOUT MYSELF"

rush

When you walk, just walk. When you eat, just eat.
—BUDDHA

One of the first things I learned about New Yorkers—and it nearly cost me my life—is that they don't know how to merge.

In California, merging onto the highway means patiently letting all cars pass until it is safe to proceed. In New York, merging means muscling your way into oncoming traffic.

Survival of the fastest.

It is this same fiercely urban instinct that causes pedestrians to rush the crosswalk even as the red light commands them not to. "The light's a challenge, not a warning," a friend and native tells me.

Californians praise multivitamins. Multitasking is the New Yorker's mantra. Sell a stock, a house, a manuscript, while on the treadmill, the subway, or in the colorist's chair.

In his book *Faster,* science writer James Gleick claims our society is plagued by "hurry sickness." Symptoms include standing in front of the microwave and instinctively pressing 8-8 instead of 9-0, to save a fraction of a millisecond. (Guilty!)

Studies show that advances in technology have gifted us with more leisure time than we've ever had before. To do what?

Grab an energy bar in the cafeteria. Eat it in the elevator or at your desk.

Balance makes a "lemon meringue"–flavored energy bar.

Only in New York can you eat a piece of pie on the fly.

Old-fashioned, sit-down pie seems antithetical to New York. Pie is soft in the middle, and New York is all about keeping your edge. Pie is about taking time, and New York is all about beating time.

I'm standing in line at Gourmet Garage on the Upper West Side, when a bright orange flyer on the community billboard catches my eye:

TOO BUSY TO LIVE YOUR LIFE? I CAN HELP.
WILL RUN ERRANDS FOR YOU,
EVEN FILL OUT YOUR DIARY FOR YOU.
CALL DAVE AT (212) . . .

rhymes with "pie"

"A back road is so easy, it just rambles on and on
Take it or leave it as it rolls along
Drifts through things it cannot change and doesn't even try
Wouldn't that be something for you and I."
—KATE WOLF, "BACK ROADS"

There were two pieces of personal mail waiting for me when I arrived at my new home in New York.

The first was a letter from Harrison, Arkansas, home of Martha and Curtis Purvis.

"It was so much fun chatting with you girls in Leslie," it read. "I told Curtis that had we all been traveling north, instead of south, we would have taken you both home with us. We would have made some ice tea and swung on the gazebo up on the hill.

Here's the photo of The Sugar Shack I promised. Did you ever make it there?"

Written in purple ink and curly script, the letter was signed, "a new friend, Martha P."

Attached was a blurred photograph of a truly decadent pie display.

The second piece of mail was a "card" with the lyrics to Kate Wolf's song "Back Roads" scribbled on the back.

Actually, it was a thick piece of cardboard that had been cut out in the shape of a large fish. All the postage stamps, at least thirty of them, were beautiful, carefully chosen, uncanceled stamps from the 1940s and '50s. The postmark told me the fish and I had left San Francisco on the very same day.

The fish was not signed, nor did it have a return address.

But I knew who it was from.

I'd met Ty a year earlier in San Francisco. He was just crawling out of a long-term relationship and I was contemplating settling down. Our timing could not have been worse. A dreamer and a drifter, Ty thought he had all the time in the world to become pre-dictable. He was an oyster shucker today, but who knew where he'd be tomorrow? He liked to drive all the way to Santa Cruz to buy old stamps at a cluttered coin shop, because they made envelopes artful.

I was on the priority-mail track. There were things I wanted and I wanted them fast. We were driven by completely different engines.

Predictably, things got rocky. And when they did, and the New York job beckoned, there was no question I would make the move solo.

The plan was to not look back.

That was the plan. But he turned up. In my thoughts, in Elva

Twitchell's kitchen, and on the back roads of Kentucky. Then in my mailbox. Often.

Thanksgiving was approaching, and Ty hoped we could spend it together. A new beginning. Perhaps I should meet him in Colorado, where he grew up and where some of his dearest friends, who lived in a log house high on a hill, hosted a special "pie ritual" every year on Thanksgiving Day. They invited lots of friends, baked plenty of pies, and a "chosen" guest got to read a beautifully written ode to pie, out loud, before dessert.

"An ode to pie?" I asked.

The next day, the following Susan Bright essay from *Tirades and Evidence of Grace* came over the fax machine in the newsroom.

PIE

Ice water. Two silver knives to work through the flour and shortening, add salt. It is an old art. Do not work late into the night, with sleep nipping at your sleeves, you will fall off, wake up at 3 A.M. to a room full of smoke, two black disks in the oven, bad smell. Do not think about business, or the wave of darkness spreading through the Arts, do not think about depression looming on the horizon or the rhetoric and nonsense our leaders toss into its mouth, or the prospect of revolution in America. Zen. Concentrate on the art of pie. It is an old art. Ingredients spread through the house like a layer of snow, later people say: "O, Pie. Pie. We love pie." It is a good art. No one will say, "Make this pie with only one silver knife, or no ice, or make it with chalk instead of flour." Fill pie with ingredients at hand, cans of things, fresh fruit, cheese. Add it to a feast. Eat leftovers for breakfast the next day, the celebration begins again, pie filling the recesses of the body, exhilaration. Pie, it is an old art. If we lose it, infants will wither in their mothers' stomachs, writhe at sunken nipples, men will lose direction, U. S. Steel will manufacture rubber and the pillars of society will flop around like spangles on a half-mast flag. Pie, the planets are lined up—Saturn, Uranus, Mars, Jupiter pull earthquakes, pull poison from beneath the surface. Pie, cut through the mix gently, roll out on a layer of wood and flour, pie. Flute the edges, pour in apples and cinnamon and spices. Pie. Zen. Concentrate on the art of pie. The rites of passage pull us through the gates of depression and war. We shall make pie. Cannot resist. We shall celebrate Christmas, Thanksgiving, the Fourth of July; holidays shall find us traversing the continent in search of heritage. No one makes pie like Mother does. Pie. No one says one pie should represent all pies. Pie is like a thumbprint. Some are sour. Pie is silent, making only a light simmering noise as it bakes in the oven. It spreads scent gently into our hearts. There is ceremony as pie is lifted out of the heat. They gather. O, Pie. The clutter is swept away, space around pie is brought to sharp focus. Light pours down on pie. Concentrate. The art of pie is an old one. Try to imagine life without it. Like the unveiling of a great painting, breaking a champagne bottle over the bow of a ship going off to sea, the ceremony as a cornerstone is laid, pie. Do not roll the crust too thick, roll gently or the center will unfurl, rub extra flour on the rolling pin every fourth stroke, remember these things. Create pie often so the art is not lost. Do not forget temperature. Cold is essential, then heat. You must have an oven, cannot make pie over an open fire or in a barbecue pit. Be firm with those who insist pie can be made in a crockpot or on the

back window ledge of a Pontiac left out in August sunlight.
Respect the rules of pie.

Ty's invitation sounded tempting. But to go out West would be going back. I was going forward.

My parents weren't expecting me until Christmas and it felt right to spend the holiday East, where the glowing fall foliage spoke of cranberries and golden yams.

I'd always felt like such a fraud on this, the most *American* of holidays. Yes, my family served a token turkey with chestnut stuffing but we had none of the traditional trimmings. We started the meal with oysters on the half shell and a peppery *mignonette* sauce. Puree and haricots verts, yes, but never cranberries. *Iles flottantes* supplanted pie. No football, but the florid retelling of family stories after dinner.

Since the leaves had started to turn, I had gotten it into my head that spending Thanksgiving in the heart of New England, specifically Plymouth, might make up for so many holidays without pumpkin pie.

"Let me come with you," he said.

And I heard myself say "yes."

Because every relationship needs a road-trip test. And, if this confusion really was just homesickness I was feeling, as my well-meaning friends suggested, certainly a week on the road with Ty would let me know.

He flew in a few days later. He dropped his army duffel bag on the top stair of my attic apartment and, before taking off his coat, reached into the bag and pulled out a beautiful ceramic pie pan, jay bird–blue, which he'd wrapped in a favorite, scratchy wool sweater that no longer fit.

"I think we should make a pie together before we hit the road," he said.

I still had not made a pie since moving to New York. There had been no reason. No time. We'd never made a pie together, but I'd watched Ty make bread in San Francisco. Although the method for making bread dough is very different from that of making pie, I knew this: he had a way with dough.

"I'll make the filling," I said, not sure if I was ready to tackle my first crust. He smiled. "No pressure."

I had just bought some Macoun and Crispin apples while reporting a story on the Hudson Valley harvest. I still had blueberries in the freezer from a friend's trip to Maine. So it made sense to make the apple-blueberry pie from Mammy's Cupboard. Ty had read all about Doris Kemp's "accidental pie" in the series of newspaper articles I'd written about my cross-country journey.

We slipped a bowl in the refrigerator so that it would be cold by morning. When I woke up at dawn, Ty had already made the coffee and laid out all the ingredients. Otis the cat had perched himself on the radiator cover near the kitchen window to watch. A light snow had sugarcoated the fire escape.

Ty wore his Lucky Brand fleece and I asked him if lucky pajamas was the secret to a good pie crust.

"A good crust has nothing to do with luck," he said, sifting the flour over a yellow bowl. "It's all about feeling."

He used his bare hands to cut the shortening into the flour and massaged the two together with his ploughman's fingers until the mixture looked torn between sawdust and cornmeal. He poked a hole in the middle of the flour mound with his thumb, and to the hole he added water, one icy teaspoon at a time.

What scared me the most about going forward with Ty was his lack of direction or ambition. I had known I wanted to write since I was 12 years old. At 30, Ty was still aimless. But not with dough. With dough, he was rooted. Confident and in control. In his hands, at that very moment, nothing could go wrong. Babies could feel safe.

When he'd added enough water, Ty gathered the flour into his palms, and patted it into a rough ball. He plopped it on the flour-dusted counter.

"Perfect," he said, caressing the ball, smooth and slightly wet, though not slick. With the heel of his hand, he flattened it into a disk, then gently cloaked it in plastic wrap and placed it in the refrigerator to chill before rolling it out.

Respect the rules of pie.

"How did you know how much water to add?" I asked.

"You have to watch your dough, feel it, read it with all your senses," Ty said.

"It's hard to explain," he went on. "But you know it when it feels right.

"You just know."

pilgrimage pie

"It is hard in this day in which the American tempo is so speeded up,
to sit back and be satisfied with what you have. It requires
education and culture to appreciate a quiet place,
but any fool can appreciate noise."

—SINCLAIR LEWIS, ADDRESSING A VERMONT
ROTARY CLUB ON SEPTEMBER 23, 1929

Solo road trips are great for kneading thoughts. But a copilot offers another set of eyes. Same windshield, different landscape.

I saw gypsy flowers and funky mailboxes. Why so many tanning salons?

Kris spied roadkill and Dairy Queens (Oooh! Oooh! Can we stop? Please?).

Ty saw clouds, old trucks, and muscle cars.

"Check out the grille on that 1937 Willy's," or, "Did you hear the long-stroke engine on that '69 'cuda?"

I hadn't known the full extent of Ty's fascination with taillights, fins, and granny gears until we pulled onto the Taconic Parkway that gray fall morning, our bellies full with breakfast pie.

We were very pleased with our first joint-venture pie. Reluctantly, we left half of the pie on the kitchen table for the neighbor who would be feeding Otis in our absence.

Thanksgiving was three days away, and the plan was to slowly make our way to Plymouth, Massachusetts, to see, among other things, the rock where the pilgrims first set a buckled shoe onto the New World. And, of course, we hoped to experience a pretty traditional Thanksgiving meal in the part of the country where it was conceived.

Since we had some extra time, we decided to meander through Vermont first and get a feel for the Ben and Jerry state and for spending time together again.

Ty could identify every year and every make of every car that zoomed past slow-poke Betty. He could even list the cars his elementary-school teachers drove in Boulder.

When we crossed into Vermont, the glorious fall foliage was long gone, leaving only silver branches reaching skyward like giant whisks.

A colleague had mentioned some family friends, Don and Deb, who lived in Londonderry and made genuine Vermont maple syrup under the small Hell's Peak Farm label. Maybe they'd show us their sugarhouse, she said. She handed me their address, and with it came a gentle warning about how austere and intensely private Vermonters can be.

Driving through Vermont's rolling hills was like watching a silent movie. So quiet, yet so much drama. We drove across covered bridges with lattice woodwork sides, past proud barns that were sweater-green. Every porch, it seemed, was graced with pumpkins or bulbous hunter-green squash known as Hubbards. Road signs warned of wandering moose.

Ty wondered if we should call ahead to let Don and Deb know we were planning on dropping by, but spontaneity had worked so well for Kris and me on the pie trip, I suggested we didn't.

Not to worry, I said. We'd use pie as our calling card.

Hell's Peak Farm, on top of a hill at the end of Pitchfork Road, is nothing more than a gambrel house with cedar shingles, surrounded by sugar maples. The actual sugarhouse is down the hillside a ways, tucked in a thicket of trees.

Deb was washing dishes when we arrived. She wiped her hands on her apron as I mentioned our mutual acquaintance and, sensing a need for serious ice-breaking, I immediately brought up pie.

"I always make Hubbard squash pie this time of year," Deb said. "Made one last night. Don ate the last piece this morning, otherwise I'd offer you some."

Deb was shy but far from private. She was glad to show us around the farm and explain how the art of sugaring works. She threw on a thick cardigan sweater she took from a wooden peg, and then we followed her to the "sugarbush," or the stand of maple trees, closest to the house.

"Don's family has been sugaring for generations," she said, walking right up to a tree, and leaned into its silver-sage trunk. She pointed to where the tree had been tapped to extract the slightly sweet crystalline sap that flows through a sugar maple's veins.

Don and Deb tap six hundred trees a year to eke out about one hundred gallons of medium-amber syrup, which they sell in markets in and around Londonderry.

"The best yielders tend to be older trees," said Deb. How much sap a tree will surrender often can be predicted from the shape and fullness of its crown.

Deb led us down the hill to the wooden sugarhouse, which wouldn't come to steamy life until about four months later. It's in the sugarhouse that the sap is evaporated in large pans and boiled down. "Some people use oil for heat," she said, "but firewood makes the syrup richer in taste and in color."

Deb pointed to the funnel on the sugarhouse roof. When the sap boils, she said, it sends a fragrant billowing steam through the vents.

"When the air stops smelling sweet, you know the sugaring season's over."

Vermonters use maple syrup to sweeten just about everything, Deb said.

She added it to her baked beans, and most children dripped it onto their breakfast cereal. In fact, Deb said her children were incredulous the first time they saw someone sprinkle sugar on their cereal on a train.

Some bakers used syrup for their pie fillings, Deb said, but as often as she made pie, "we're better off selling the syrup." She did, however, use fresh cream from the dairy down the road for her fillings, whenever possible. And, like Duarte's in Pescadero, she used cold milk in her dough instead of water.

"My grandmother used to rub the top crust of her pies with milk to make them golden brown," she said.

A truck pulled up on Pitchfork Road. "There's Don," she said, and we climbed back up the hill to greet him. "Don isn't much of a talker," she warned. "He doesn't like to put himself out in the open."

Don said he'd answer any questions about sugaring so long as he could work on his truck at the same time. For the next twenty minutes, he spoke to us from the floorboard of his Dodge Ram, where he was, allegedly, installing a fuse. The truck door was ajar and his long legs hung out the side. And though we never had eye contact, he talked at length about the days when his family used a horse and sled to collect the sap buckets from tree to tree.

"The younger kids tapped and the older kids boiled," he said. He talked of the time the sugarhouse almost burned down when he got distracted and let the sap boil down to a sticky nothing.

"Hell's Peak Farm has had four sugarhouses in all," he said. "The original sugar shack dated back to the Civil War."

Don explained how Vermont Fancy is the queen of maple syrups. Drawn from the first sap of the season, which usually starts in March, it's considered much more delicate than the more robust syrups made with sap drawn later in spring. Sap drawn after the first budding tends to be bitter, he said.

Ty said he'd like to return to Hell's Peak Farm one day and help tap. We heard a grunt from the floorboard. Ty took that as a yes.

Over dinner that night at an inn in Dorset, Ty talked excitedly about spending six weeks in Vermont the following year.

Clearly, I thought, the drifter in him was alive and well and ready to jump the next train. Part of me was annoyed. Another part wanted to quit my job and learn to tap too.

Morning rose crisp, cold, and blue. We ate fat stacks of banana pancakes in amber syrup. At an antiques barn in town, I found a textured brown bowl with a pockmarked glaze. Ty emerged with a 1940 Ford Coupe Hot Wheels car that cost only 50 cents and put a million-dollar smile on his face.

"Aren't you a little old for these?" I asked, examining the tiny car.

Ty said nothing. I took the wheel for the next couple hundred miles and Ty played deejay, spinning everything from Ben Harper to Louis Armstrong.

"Did I ever tell you about the first road trip I took with Dennis?" he finally said.

I settled into the driver's seat sensing that Betty was about to become a confessional, as so often happens on long drives when the light and music and moment are right.

Dennis was Ty's adoptive father. Ty never knew his real dad, only remembered the sound of his motorcycle. He was only six when Dennis took him on a long drive from Colorado to Kansas to pick up a truck.

On the drive home, Ty was feeling cranky and Dennis stopped at a toy store to buy him two Hot Wheels.

"One was a Lincoln Continental," said Ty. "The other was a Ford Maverick."

Their first night home, Ty stuck his shiny new cars, which he'd clutched the whole drive home, under his mattress for safekeeping.

When he woke up, the cars had vanished.

"I never figured out what happened to them," said Ty, staring dead ahead. "When I go back home to visit, I still check the closets and look under beds hoping I'll find them."

Around 10 P.M., after heading north all day, we pulled off Route 91 in Wells River for a late-night snack at the the P & H truck stop. The full-service truck stop is one of the few that still offer showers, sleeping rooms, and a full-service restaurant decorated with Peterbilt wallpaper.

Understandably, it's a popular pit stop among long-haul truckers pulling rigs across New England and Canada. The twenty-four-hour café is also a favorite among local hunters and ramblers, like us, just looking for pie.

From our stools at the counter, we watched as truckers in thick red plaid shirts wandered in, slightly bowlegged. Some left their lumber trucks idling in the yard while they ducked in for coffee or a quick bowl of chowder. Those who planned to stay awhile took off their mesh caps, patted down their hair. Many of the truckers seemed to know one another by sight or name. Some truckers like to take their wives along on long drives, and at one corner table we saw one such couple saying grace over a bowl of cole slaw.

Nearly every trucker stepped up to the pie display to see what slice of home was on tap that day. The P & H usually offers ten pies daily. For the benefit of the Canadian truckers, they are listed in French on the menu, as well as in English.

There were several pies to choose from but maple cream pie was the obvious choice. They cut the pies in fourths at the P & H, so we asked to split a slice of the thick, caramel-custard pie.

"You're lucky," said Linda, our waitress, working the overnight shift. "We usually run out of that one pretty early.

"Truckers do love their pie. I can't tell you how many of them eat their pie before their eggs."

Nelson Baker, who owns the P & H, introduced himself. I'd watched him work the room at this late hour, sliding into booths to chat with regulars. In a prior life, Baker had been a criminal defense lawyer in Boston. He used to come to Vermont on weekends to unwind. One weekend, when he was going through a rough personal time, he picked up a realtor's brochure and saw that the truck stop was for sale. He stopped in on his way home that Sunday and made an offer.

Since chucking his ties and cuff links, he's become an expert on the trucking life, which, he admits, he tends to romanticize. "Truckers are the last American cowboys," says Baker, who is also fighting to preserve America's last few independent truck stops.

"They're all being swallowed up by the big chains," he said. "The independents are a vanishing breed."

Baker heads a national association of truck-stop operators, which took its message of preservation to Congress last year.

To drive their point home, they brought a fleet of truck-stop pies to Capitol Hill.

The Wednesday morning before Thanksgiving found us on Route 44, in Massachusetts, headed for the coast. We passed a turkey farm where people were lining under handpainted signs that said "A-M" and "N-Z," to pick up their fresh turkeys for the big day.

"I wonder where we'll be eating turkey tomorrow," I said to Ty. He squeezed my hand.

In Plymouth we saw a sign for a sandwich shop named Paulie's, and had to stop for lunch. Paulie's was where we'd had our first lunch date in San Francisco.

"Kismet," said Ty.

A cheery freckled woman in her 50s was sitting alone by the window, eating a sandwich and reading the *Patriot Ledger*. Occasionally, she'd look out the window and smile at all the tourists filing past on their way to Plimoth (sic) Plantation.

"This is one of the busiest weeks of the year in Plymouth," she said, sensing we were watching her. "What brings you here?"

I was about to explain about my Thanksgiving yearnings, when Ty jumped in:

"Pie," he said. "We're looking for good local pie. Any ideas?"

She chuckled. "My husband is the pie lover in the family," said the woman, who introduced herself as Ann Roach but sure looked like an Annie to me. "He makes a terrific strawberry rhubarb.

"Still, if you asked Rod, he'd tell you his best friend, Richie Brown, makes the best pumpkin chiffon pie in the world.

"Richie's a dentist in Cambridge," she went on. "He runs marathons, plays the mandolin, and bakes. He's a real Renaissance man.

"In fact," she said, "we're going to be eating some of his pie tomorrow."

In recent years, Thanksgiving was always at Rod's cousin's house, in Orleans, the crease in the elbow-shaped Cape. "Richie has a house in Chatham, nearby. He always brings the pie—and his mandolin, of course.

"Rod and Richie used to be in a bluegrass band called Stoney Lonesome," Ann said. "They always play some old fiddle tunes before and after turkey."

It sounded magical. And, oddly, deeply familiar.

Ann stretched her arms, then got up to leave.

"Well, it was nice chatting with you two," she said. "Good luck with your research."

I started to panic. Something deep inside me wanted to taste this Richie Brown pie, to sit next to Annie at the Thanksgiving table and hear myself say, "Will someone pass the cranberries, please." Somehow I knew the cranberries at Annie's table would not be the scarlet slinky stuff out of a can.

"What a coincidence," I heard myself say. "We'll be in Orleans tomorrow, too."

Ty kicked me under the table.

"Well, er, uh, maybe you can drop by and say hello and meet Richie," she stammered. "We'll be on Monument Road."

It wasn't exactly an invitation, but it was more than Don's grunt. It certainly was enough to warrant buying a bottle of wine for our hosts—just in case.

We wandered in an antiques shop to look for mixing bowls, but when we realized the store sold only big-ticket items, like rich mahogany armoires, we turned on our heels and headed for the door.

"Can I help you find something?" said a tall woman with a crisp British accent.

"Thanks, but we were looking for mixing bowls and rolling pins.

You know, pie stuff," said Ty as we opened the door, unleashing a clanging of little bells.

"What about pie birds?"

I closed the door again.

"What's a pie bird?"

She curled her finger and ushered us toward her office.

"I don't sell them here, but I collect them," she said, opening a catalog to show us.

Pie birds, also known as pie funnels, are small, open-mouthed ceramic figurines that double as steam vents in a pie, she said.

"Just like the vents on a sugarhouse roof," said Ty, who'd never heard of a pie bird either.

Since Victorian times, bakers in England have placed pie birds in the center of covered fruit and meat pies to prevent oven drippings and soggy bottom crusts, said the woman, who introduced herself as Jackie.

"My grandmother back in England used them all the time." Jackie had come to New England from Norfolk to work as a nanny when she was only 20. She fell in love with an American and stayed.

Traditionally, pie birds were always fashioned in the shape of a blackbird, she said, but eventually molds were designed in all shapes and characters.

"There's even one of Princess Diana," she said.

Jackie started collecting them twenty years ago, "long before they were all the rage on eBay." She owns about eight hundred figurines, which she finds at the same places I find my mixing bowls: church sales and flea markets.

"I just love the hunt," she said, eyes shining. "Usually, the people selling them have no clue what they are used for.

"It's a shame, really, because an apple pie isn't complete without a blackbird poking out of it," she sighed. "But then, nobody really bakes pies from scratch anymore, it seems."

Jackie belongs to an international group of pie-bird collectors. She said the "hot" pie bird of the moment, the one all connoisseurs coveted, was the rare Donald Duck funnel—worth a cool $1,500.

I took Jackie's card and promised to keep an eye out for Donald and other pie birds in my foraging. In exchange, could she recommend a place to stay for the night? She could.

Her friend Richard owned a B&B down the street, she said, right upstairs from his tea-and-curiosity shop. "It's across from the Mayflower Society Museum and just steps away from Plymouth Rock."

Richard, dressed like a pilgrim, was the biggest curiosity in his dark, cluttered shop which sold soaps, tea, pewter, and candles.

"How do you two know Jackie?" he asked. We explained how we'd bonded over parallel pie quests, and his face brightened.

"My great aunt in Portsmouth, New Hampshire, used to make the most delicious strawberry rhubarb pie," he said, stepping out from behind the counter.

"She grew the strawberries and rhubarb in her backyard and she'd shoo us all out of the kitchen when she baked," he recalled. "We'd wait in the garden and, when she was done, she'd rest the pie on the sill to cool.

"It was a regular Norman Rockwell painting."

His B&B, the Captain's Inn, had only one room, he said, "but it's an entire apartment and it was built in 1725."

It was available, so long as we promised to be out by noon, since he and his wife, Yoko, planned to serve their Thanksgiving supper there.

"You're free to come back for the meal," he said, "but we just need the space to cook in."

"Thank you," I said, "but we have plans on the Cape."

·   ·   ·

Our room had two fireplaces, creaky pine floors, and a window that looked out on Old North Street, one of the oldest streets in America. In the morning, we awoke to the musical sound of recorders, a "Pilgrim's Progress" procession headed straight for the Rock. We followed suit.

Like most first-time visitors, we were surprised by how small the Rock was in stature. Small and lumpy as misshapen dough. In the 1800s, it was common for visitors wanting a relic of the Rock to simply chisel away at it. In fact, de Tocqueville wrote about relics of the rock he encountered throughout his travels:

"Here is a stone which the feet of a few poor fugitives pressed for an instant, and this stone becomes famous . . . a fragment is prized as a relic," he wrote. "Does not this sufficiently show how all human power and greatness are entirely in the soul?"

Perhaps, but in the end, Americans got so greedy the Rock had to be enclosed by protective iron gates, like a lion at the zoo.

"Don't you feel kind of sorry for the Rock," I heard a woman say to her husband as we walked away. And I had to agree.

When we returned to our room, Richard had slipped our bill beneath the door. It read: "One night at the inn."

We headed south, toward the Cape, under a battering rain. At Ty's urging, we stopped at a phone booth on the side of the road to call Ann and Rod Roach (they were listed) to see if it was really OK for us to drop by and meet the illustrious Richie Brown—and to get the exact address on Monument Road.

There was no answer. We got the listing for a Richie Brown in Cambridge and tried that number, but got an answering machine. I was secretly pleased, because no answer was better than being turned down. I was determined to break bread with the bluegrass players.

I hung up the phone and noticed a soft kangaroo mouse, color of gravy, nestled against a rock, trying to find shelter from the rain.

When we got to Orleans, it was bigger than it appeared on the map. Monument Road was no narrow country lane. It was about three miles long, and houses were scattered on either side of the road from beginning to end.

Not only did we not have an exact address, but we didn't even know the name of Rod's cousins hosting the holiday dinner. We'd just have to try each house, one door at a time.

"Is this where the Roaches are having their Thanksgiving dinner?" I asked at the first house. That didn't sound right, and at the next house, I massaged my technique. But they had not heard of Ann Roach or of the famous Richie Brown, either. Neither had the next house or the house after that.

We'd covered about one third of the south side of Monument Road, when a gentleman who'd been watching us through his kitchen window for a while stepped out onto the side porch and signaled us over.

"Are you lost?" he asked, ushering us into the kitchen where the whole family was busy with last-minute preparations and barely noticed our intrusion. Wickedly handsome in a Hubbard-squash-green cashmere sweater, Steve Peno looked as though he'd just stepped out of a Ralph Lauren catalogue. As though everything in his visibly lush, terry-cloth life had come easy.

He knew just about everybody on this stretch of Monument Road, or so he thought, but he did not know their cousins or dentist friends who baked. If we had so much as a name, a phone number, an address, he'd take us there personally. Steve was a genuinely nice guy, and beneath all that WASP-y wool was a definite adventurous streak.

We pressed on, knocking on a least a dozen more doors. The rain had finally let up but too late for Ty, who was wearing a brown suede jacket that made him look a bit like that wet kangaroo mouse.

I sat on a curb, crushed and guilty for ruining Ty's Thanksgiving.

"Let's go back to Plymouth and find a nice restaurant for dinner," Ty said, pulling me to my feet. "Or we can go back to the inn and take Richard up on his offer."

"You're right," I said. "This was a crazy idea."

As we drove out of Orleans, we passed a sign for Chatham and that got me thinking. Didn't Richie Brown have a summer house in Chatham?

"If he's in charge of pie," I said, "shouldn't he be in Chatham baking just about now?"

Ty pulled over at the next phone booth and handed me a quarter.

Doc Brown was listed on the Cape and, while I dialed, I crossed the fingers on my free hand. Richie Brown picked up himself.

"Do you mind holding for one minute," he said, "I've got to pull a pie out of the oven."

I gave Ty the thumbs-up.

"How does it look?" I said when Richie returned to the phone.

"Not too bad," he said. "Who *is* this?"

I didn't want to scare him off with our convoluted story, so I stretched the truth a little, told him we were new friends of Ann Roach and she'd asked us to drop by so we could taste his pie, but we'd left the exact address at the hotel. Could he tell us where everyone was convening on Monument Road, and, er, the names of our hosts?

"I don't know the address," he said, "my car just goes there automatically once a year on Thanksgiving. It's a Cape-style house, I think, with gray shutters. Jim and Ellie's last name is Spainhour."

That was all we needed. This time, when we returned to Steve's house, we had something to work with. The Penos were just sitting down to eat in their formal dining room when we rapped on the kitchen window. Steve greeted us with a carving knife in one hand, a dishtowel in the other, as though we were old friends. "We have a name," Ty said. Steve grinned.

He put down the knife and paged through the small Orleans White Pages. I could hear an elderly relative ask: "Is it those wanderers from New York again?"

"What do you know," Steve said, dialing the number for us, "they're just a few houses away."

"Hey, neighbor," he said to Jim. "Happy Thanksgiving. Some of your dinner guests seem to be lost, but I'm sending them your way."

Steve followed us out to the car. "If it doesn't work out over there, you can always come back here for some food."

"Now we have two backup plans," Ty said.

A confounded Jim Spainhour was waiting on the lawn when we pulled up the drive. He had a nice broad face with a smile to match.

We were the first to arrive, which was good, because we had lots of explaining to do. But all we really had to say was that we were driving across New England researching good pies and that Ann had told us about Richie's pumpkin chiffon, and they were satisfied. Of course, they didn't know I had every hope of being invited for supper, too.

Jim lit a fire and opened some wine. He showed us some of the furniture he made by hand, including a beautiful Windsor chair that would have looked right at home at the Captain's Inn. By the time Ann and Rod arrived, we were looking pretty cozy in the living room, Boo and Clio, their two Labradors, at our feet. Ann nearly dropped her pan of braised leeks when she saw us on the couch. When Richie arrived with his pie and his wife, Margaret, we told the story all over again.

"I've got to hand it to you two for your stick-to-it-iveness," Richie said.

It didn't take long for Rod and Richie to bring out their instruments. Rod played a 1931 Gibson RB-6 Mastertone banjo. Richie's beautifully inlaid mandolin was also a Gibson, made in 1925.

They played classic fiddle tunes like "Soldier's Joy," "Gray Eagle," and, of course, "Turkey in the Straw."

They took a break, and Rod regaled us with tales of his wild years as a young banjo player in Bristol, Vermont, more than thirty years ago. Desperate to preserve a dying musical form, he and his friends would go into the woods to round up old fiddle players and bring them to bluegrass festivals, he said.

"We'd yank them right out of their cabins."

He told us about Fletch McIntyre, the fabled rambling fiddle player who knew nine hundred fiddle tunes. Fletch managed to get himself thrown in jail every year right after the first frost, just so he could have a warm bed and a roof over his head through those unforgiving Vermont winters.

"To thank the sheriff, Fletch would fashion orchestra figures out of tin cans," said Rod.

"Yeah, those old fiddle players are disappearing pretty fast."

Inevitably, talk of preserving traditions led us back to pie, specifically the one Richie Brown had placed on Ellie's sideboard.

The pie is an adaptation of Craig Claiborne's sour-cream pumpkin pie from the *New York Times Cookbook*, Richie said. It was his first wife's mother, Onnie, who first made the pie for him more than thirty years ago. He had to wait years before he could make it himself, he said, "because Onnie liked to think of herself as the only cook at the table."

When he finally was free to make it on his own, he tinkered with different crusts and settled on the buttery short crust from the *Vegetarian Epicure Cookbook*.

"They're never pretty and they're never uniform," he said, "but I'll admit, my pies are good." Lately he'd been experimenting with adding lemon to the crust.

"I don't know how you do it, Richie," Rod said, "but your pies get better and better every year."

Richie turned to me and Ty. "You'll have to tell me what you think."

An awkward silence filled the room and, though I don't blush easily, I felt my cheeks burn crimson. As cozy as we all were, and as much as the house was filling with irresistible smells, the fact was, no one had invited us to stay yet.

Ellie stepped out of the kitchen, where she'd been making the gravy, just in time. "Jim," she said, "will you get two more chairs for the dining room?"

Then she looked directly at me. "You *are* staying for dinner, aren't you?"

Ty ran to the car to get the wine and then we took our places in the dining room, around the cherrywood table, which Jim had also made.

Rod caught me eyeing the fresh cranberries. "I discovered a wild bog while taking a walk on the Cape the other day," he said. "I stuffed as many in my pockets as I possibly could for today."

Ellie set her famous yeast rolls on the table and, at that moment, all was right with the world.

We raised a glass to family and friends—the old and the very new.

HELL'S PEAK FARM
HUBBARD-SQUASH PIE

CRUST FOR ONE 9-INCH PIE SHELL

1 cup flour

⅔ stick of butter

3 tablespoons milk

FILLING

2 cups cooked squash (steamed or baked), mashed with a fork

¾ cup of sugar; use a little less if using refined maple sugar

1 teaspoon ground cinnamon

½ teaspoon salt

½ teaspoon ground ginger

½ teaspoon nutmeg

3 eggs

⅔ cup evaporated milk or ⅔ cup fresh cream

½ cup whole milk

Put the flour and butter in the food processor. Mix, then slowly add cold milk. Pulse. When it clumps together, take it out of the processor and roll it out.

Mix all filling ingredients together in a bowl. When thoroughly mixed, pour into a 9-inch pie shell and bake at 350 degrees for 50–55 minutes.

the pie siren

They took all the trees
and put them in a tree museum
And they charged all the people
a dollar and a half just to see 'em
Don't it always seem to go,
that you don't know what you got
Till it's gone
They paved paradise
And put up a parking lot

—JONI MITCHELL, "BIG YELLOW TAXI"

I came home from New England to a stack of unread newspapers piled at my front door. I scanned them briefly and was about to toss an obituary section in the recycling bin, when a headline caught my eye: SAXOPHONIST FRED FORD DIES AT 69.

Fred Ford . . . Why did I know that name? I read on:

"Saxophonist Fred Ford, a versatile jazz and rhythm and blues musician who recorded with B. B. King and Jerry Lee Lewis is dead after a battle with cancer. . . . A mainstay of the Memphis music scene . . . Ford was known for his baritone sax skills."

Of course. Ford was the Beale Street musician who'd recommended the Greater Harvest Church for gospel and Piccadilly's for pie.

Though he was a minor character in our pie adventure, news of his death distressed me, disproportionately so. I'd been thinking, you see, about how Elva Twitchell in Utah was getting on in years, as was her sister Beulah. Gloria and Ruby, both in nursing homes. So many veteran pie bakers who would soon be leaving us. And taking their rolling pins with them.

My favorite yoga teacher, Liz, walks us through meditation after each class. Focus on the inner light, she says. Surrender. Have no agenda. But no matter how hard I try to turn my mind to blank, a laundry list of "shoulds" and "whats" and "whys" struts before my eyes: I'm thinking of the mole on my arm that needs to be checked out; the names of the children I may or may not have.

But in the weeks that followed our Thanksgiving journey, I kept seeing the same singular image floating past my mind's eye during meditation: an infinite number of winged pies parading past me in assembly-line fashion, and then, one by one, floating upward and disappearing into the ether.

Ohm.

Then, my mother underwent emergency surgery for a cancerous tumor in her belly. Doctors warned us that the high-risk surgery would take eight hours, but if the cancer was too far gone, they would sew her up after two. My father and I spent the first two hours staring silently at the clock. And when two hours became three, then four, and the surgery continued well into the night, we bawled like children. When my mother finally came to, she reached for my father's hand to look at his watch.

I'd only been back from Los Angeles a week when Betty bit the dust. Not in the Ozarks, or the Nevada desert, as my parents had feared before I drove east, but in Peekskill, of all places. A young woman had ignored a stop sign and barreled straight into me. We were both fine, but Betty's front was pleated like a tart pan.

The collision was a logical culmination of my first year in New York, a crash course from start to finish. I was in the ambulance when it hit me. The epiphany, I mean, that I'd only scratched the surface of pie in those three weeks on the road, and that I needed to finish what I'd started.

My knees were scraped from hitting the dash but paramedics worried I'd also hit my head, because I kept asking about the piemobile.

"She can't die now," I said. "She's got miles and miles to go on the road to pie."

I called Kris in San Francisco the next day.

"How would you like to go back out on the road this summer and pick up where we left off?"

Silence. Then, "Can we bring our roller blades this time?"

Kris was in a funk herself. The advertising world was gnawing away at her now more than ever. In the year since the pie trip, she'd dived into photography as a hobby. She'd found a niche, taking artful black-and-white nudes of her pregnant friends. And they were all pregnant. I thought it was a ferociously brave and creative way to face her biological clock head-on. She wanted to quit the ad biz and pursue photography full-time, but found it hard to walk away from the money she made producing ads, no matter how stressful.

A soul-searching summer suspended in time was just what she needed.

I told her I wanted to stay out on the road longer this time, linger awhile. Rushing was antithetical to pie. I wanted to take this trip a little deeper. Besides, I was beginning to see the possibility of a book in this strange quest.

"Aren't you worried we'll run out of things to talk about?"

"Unlikely," I said. "Very unlikely."

Kris had a prior freelance job commitment for the end of the summer, so I'd have to find another pie traveler for part of the trip. Ty had turned out to be a great co-pie-lot. But, as he so rightly pointed out, "This is a chick trip."

I was glad he said it so I didn't have to. Besides, I was still unsure about us. He'd taken a gamble and moved to New York. I wavered. What if he wasn't the one? What if there was something shinier around the corner?

What if I took a leap of faith and fell?

What if I made a pie and the crust was tough as plaster?

Best to keep on driving.

I put out the call to my women friends to see who could join me on the road to pie. Teri was the first to call back. We'd met working at a newspaper in San Diego. We'd spent the year we turned 30 backpacking through India, Africa, and Europe together. Not only could she kill large pests with one swift blow of her Teva sandal, but she could read a map upside-down and roll with the punches and my ever-changing moods. Teri was also enrolled in film school at UCLA. Would it be all right if she brought along her video camera?

I felt it was my duty to remind Teri that she was getting married later that summer. Did she really want to drive around America eating pie three weeks before she had to squeeze into a wedding dress?

Bless her. She did.

My new New York City friend Nicole, a pastry chef, also answered the call. Food critics raved about her desserts, but Nicole was burnt out on the grueling hours. "I want a life," she said. "I WANT A LIFE."

Martha Stewart had offered her a job as pastry consultant on her television show, but Nicole fantasized about finding a small, honest bakery where she could Zen out and bake bread for a while. She was at the top of her game and wanted to sit out the season.

"Is there something wrong with me?" she said. I was the wrong person to ask, of course. I was finally working as a journalist in New York and all I really wanted to do was flee.

Four restless women in their 30s, all going through major life shifts. Four driven women in need of one long drive.

As with the first trip, pie-stop suggestions from friends, colleagues, readers of my newspaper column, poured in. I drew pie dots on the states I planned to hit, following a northwestern route from Michigan to Montana, straight down to New Mexico, then Texas and Louisiana. I'd feel my way slowly, through Alabama and the Carolinas and call it a trip in Washington, D.C.

I connected the dots and tried not to read too much into it when the outline looked just like a bat in flight.

my two betties

Fact: One of Jimmy Stewart's favorite co-stars was a horse named Pie. Together, they rode through seventeen westerns.

One cannot underestimate the bond between car and driver on an extended road trip. It's a relationship that requires lots of give and take.

You get me up this climb, and I promise I will check your oil at the next filling station—or at least within the next 1,000 miles.

Betty and I had that kind of bond. The teal-green 1988 sedan was my first serious car. I had bought it used, but it had power windows and locks and seat warmers—features that made me feel decidedly grown up and not a moment too soon, at 34.

On the pie trip, Betty cleared fifteen states without a hiccough. She did lose her antenna at a car wash near Berea, Kentucky, but that was entirely my fault for forgetting to retract it in my haste to pounce on a salty snack from the mini-mart. Through twisters and tread-melting heat, she'd kept her cool. Somehow, she always made room for one more mixing bowl, and always made it to the next filling station even when we were on fumes.

To filch my favorite Katharine Hepburn line from *The Philadelphia Story*, "My, she was *yar*."

So you can understand why I was so upset after the Peekskill crash. My New York mechanic, Tim, took one look at Betty and bit his lip: "Sorry," he said, "but Betty's gone on her last pie ride."

A friend at the paper sent me the following e-mail when she heard the news:

"I'm sorry about Betty, m'dear. She had a good run, served you well, and got to see a lot of fun places, listen in on some good talk. She had a better life than most and, now, she can rest in peace."

Ty surprised me by baking a Funeral Pie—a simple raisin pie that Mennonites and Amish traditionally bring to funeral services—the day a charity came to haul Betty away. (Just because you're in mourning doesn't mean you can't get a tax break.)

Replacing the piemobile proved a lot harder than lining up a new pie crew. Sure, buying a new car would have been easy. But it seemed inappropriate to drive across America seeking something old and handcrafted in a generic new Camry. No, the new piemobile would need a certain patina. Patina and personality.

Betty had been so loyal, it made sense to replace her with one of her own. Only this time, I'd look for a station wagon—more room for mixing bowls and vagabond musicians. A month before my late-June departure, I still hadn't found an old Volvo wagon and I was getting nervous. So nervous, I came this close to buying the 1951 Plymouth Cranbrook on the used-car lot in Croton-on-Hudson where I'd moved that spring, to a small cottage in the woods.

The car was mixing-bowl green with custard-cream whitewalls: pure automotive eye candy. On the test drive through Croton, the Cranbrook, which only gets nine miles to the gallon, cruised slow as molasses. The perfect speed for the kind of trip I was taking.

Just in time, gas prices shot up to $2 a gallon and the *Pennysaver* listed a 1990 navy-blue Volvo 240 station wagon in Bedford. Same as Betty, only bigger, newer, and bluer. I was immediately smitten with her retro chrome luggage rack and classy red pinstripe.

The salesman introduced himself as Ernest. Good sign, I thought. Then he slapped his card in my hand. "Ernest Wolf."

And what a wolf he turned out to be, pretending another couple on the lot was ready to buy the car and refusing to go down one penny on the price.

Driving her home, I decided to call her Betty Blue instead of Betty Two. To make it official, I decided to get some "IBRK4PIE" vanity plates, too.

My cynical New York colleagues worried this could be subject to misinterpretation—so, to make things perfectly clear, I attached a wooden rolling pin to her front grille and one to the rear handle.

There was *no* mistaking what this car was all about.

I picked Kris up at JFK airport on a humid day in June. "Meet Betty Blue," I said as she tossed her roller blades in the back.

We were still inside the terminal, stopped at a light, when the driver of a Holiday Inn shuttle bus honked for our attention.

"What's up with the rolling pin?" he shouted across two lanes.

"We're driving across America looking for pie," Kris shouted back.

"My mama makes the best blueberry pie you ever had," he said.

"That so?" said Kris. "Where does she live?"

The light turned green. Kris dug into her purse for a pen.

"Baton Rouge, Louisiana," the driver said before pulling away. He stuck his head out the window: "Her name's Madear. Madear Johnson. Euclid Avenue.

"Tell her her baby boy sent you . . ."

Kris jotted it all down in the palm of her hand.

It had been more than a year, but she hadn't lost her touch.

FUNERAL PIE

Adapted from the *Pennsylvania Dutch Cook Book—*
Fine Old Recipes, Culinary Arts Press, 1936

1 cup of raisins
2 cups of water
1½ cups of sugar
4 tablespoons flour
1 egg, well-beaten
juice of 1 lemon
2 tablespoons grated lemon rind
¼ teaspoon of salt

Wash raisins and soak in cold water for three hours. Drain. Combine
2 cups of water, raisins, sugar, and flour. Mix well. Add the salt,
lemon juice and rind, and the egg and mix thoroughly. Cook the
mixture over hot water for 15 minutes, stirring occasionally. Set
aside and let cool. Pour mixture into a 9-inch pastry-lined pan.
Cover with narrow strips of dough, criss-crossed, or lattice-style.
Bake at 450 degrees for 10 minutes. Reduce heat to 350 degrees and
bake another 30 minutes.

part three

"What is a man but all his connections?"

—ROBERT FROST

"The everyday kindness of the backroads more than makes up for the acts of greed in the headlines."

—CHARLES KURALT
ON THE ROAD WITH CHARLES KURALT

oh-my-oh, ohio

"Slump? I ain't in no slump. I just ain't hitting."
— YOGI BERRA

We'd barely left the cottage when we came across a helmet in the middle of Furnace Dock Road.

A fist with eyes poked straight out one end of the khaki dome, and we realized this was a turtle. I swerved, and Kris jumped out of the car to carry it to safety.

A guy in a sportscar zoomed up behind us and started honking, flashing his lights, even though it was obvious we were on a rescue mission.

He was in a hurry. And he was wearing hospital scrubs.

We crossed the Hudson River, east to west, on the Bear Mountain Bridge. A giant American flag hung from one of the towers. I reminded Kris that Jack Kerouac had also begun his journey by crossing this very bridge, though in the opposite direction. Purely coincidental.

Since we'd already covered Pennsylvania on the first trip, we would zip through the Keystone State, then cut through Ohio to get to Michigan for some cherry pie.

I had no firm plans for Ohio, figured it would take me a day or two on the road anyway before I got my bearings. Other than my friend Jerry, who writes about food and travel at one of the nation's largest newspapers, I had never met anyone from Ohio.

I had lunch with Jerry at Picholine, near Lincoln Center, shortly before my departure, and asked him where he would go for pie in his home state.

Jerry, who grew up in Wooster, remembered picking tiny, tart purple elderberries for pie when he was a boy—but not fondly.

"It was a real pain in the ass. You'd have to pick about a million berries to make just one pie."

He could muster plenty of state pride for the Cleveland Indians, who were having a great season, but Ohio pie left him dry.

I'd read of a place called Henry's Sohio in West Jefferson. A flotilla of county- and state-fair blue ribbons was tacked to the pie display. They'd have good pie, *really* good pie, but that place was famous and I was hoping to find something fresh and original, particularly this early in the journey.

"We'll figure it out when we get there," I told Kris.

We lumbered onto US 6 and, judging from the map, we'd be staying on it for 700 miles or so, clear on to upper Ohio where we'd head north and let US 6 continue on without us to Indiana. There was something reassuring about knowing we'd follow the same two-lane road for such a long time.

About 200 miles into it, Kris had an epiphany.

"I think US 6 is probably the longest relationship I've ever had."

Like most relationships, US 6 has its ups and downs. At its best, it hugs the Susquehanna River and is lined with poppy-colored day lilies and quaint houses that face each other off across the thin highway like square dancers. At its worst, US 6 morphs into a tawdry four-laner, barreling through the grainy coal-mining northeastern part of Pennsylvania.

Talk of relationships led Kris to ask where things stood with Ty.

He'd been great on the road to pie, I told her, but I wasn't sure how we'd fare together on the road to life. He was the patient, sensitive soul I'd been seeking, and the best listener I could hope for, I said, but he had no set goals or ambitions. No five-year plan.

"Can I have children with a guy who thinks 401(k) is a breakfast cereal?" I said.

"Sounds like you want your filling and your crust, too," she said.

We stopped in Wellsboro for the night. We didn't want to kill ourselves the first day out and we'd spotted a cool, retro diner that would make for a fun breakfast stop. In keeping with our vow to exercise on this trip, we rose early and power-walked through the Wellsboro Cemetery. At least we tried, but we kept stopping to marvel at tilted tombstones from the mid-nineteenth century. Women's names were so dramatic back then: Isadora, Harriet, Matilda. So full of duty, purpose, and self-denial.

Harry was the name of the widowed dairy farmer we sat next to at the Wellsboro diner counter. He alternated between breakfasts at the 1939 diner and the McDonald's in town "because the coffee at McDonald's is a few cents cheaper and that adds up over time."

At the diner, the broad-backed waitresses all knew Harry by name, even knew how to get his goat by threatening to bring him tuna casserole. Still, to save only 30 cents or so a week, this lonely old man ate at McDonald's—where he was virtually anonymous—three times a week.

In Meadville, about 30 miles from the Ohio border we stopped in an antiques barn to look for a mixing bowl for good pie karma.

The owner, a crotchety old cricket, pointed to the rolling pin on my car and said: "You know what we call that in my business? A woman's best weapon!"

As we poked around the cavernous shop, the owner went on and on about Sharon Stone being Meadville's most famous resident. Personally, I thought Gideon Sundback, the guy who invented the zipper, had made more of an impact, but I let him blather on. I fell in love with a 1920s wicker table with great legs (OK, maybe not Sharon Stone–great, but whimsical great). A totally impractical purchase, but, as Kris pointed out, when they were passing out the practicality gene, I was out shopping for handwashables.

She started to talk me out of it, but knew better. And, to her credit, when the table slid back and forth on the luggage rack through the windswept plains of South Dakota, she kept her "I told you so"s to herself.

Oddly enough, from the moment we left Meadville, Betty Blue's glove compartment door started popping open at the slightest bump in the road.

Was she giving us a sign?

The state sign for Ohio was smaller than any I'd seen thus far. No motto. No sunset. No big-mouthed bass jumping out of Lake Erie. Just: OHIO. But then, who could top the Pennsylvania sign across the highway: AMERICA STARTS HERE.

Fiddling with the radio dial, we stumbled on a voice as smooth as Tootsie Price's chocolate silk pie in Pine Bluff, Arkansas. It belonged to Fitz, the host of the Fitz's Hour of Blues, on the local public radio affiliate.

The music was great and it got me thinking. Wasn't disc jockey Alan Freed, the guy who first coined the term "rock 'n' roll," from Cleveland? In the absence of anything more logical, my source for Ohio pie, then, would have to be affiliated with rock 'n' roll in some way. We'd head for the Rock 'n' Roll Hall of Fame Museum in Cleveland and take it from there.

We found a parking spot smack in front of the Rock 'n' Roll shrine and inches away from Lake Erie. Unfortunately, the Hall of Fame had just closed for the night. We were back at square one.

What about Fitz? Kris said.

I dialed up the station and Fitz answered the phone himself. "I'm a food writer from New York just passing through Cleveland and I was wondering if you had any suggestions where to go for pie around here."

"Excuse me?" he sneered. "Did you say *pie?*"

"Yes, pie. As in apple pie," I said, to distinguish it from the numerical pi.

"I don't eat pie," he growled. "Why are you asking me? Why don't you go ask a cop?"

"If I were looking for doughnuts, I might have asked a cop," I said. In as few words as possible, I tried to explain the treasure-hunt nature of my journey, the whole Alan Freed rock 'n' roll angle I was trying to weave into my story, which I hoped to turn into a book.

"What do *I* have to do with Alan Freed?" he barked. Then he hung up.

Was Fitz's behavior a harbinger of how this trip would go? Kris turned up the radio to see what Fitz would say, or play, next. And here is, roughly, what his Cleveland listeners heard late that warm Friday night in June:

"I've been in this business for 27 years and I've never, I mean never, gotten a call like the one that just came in. This lady from New York just called the station and said she was driving around America looking for pie. She's got a rolling pin on her car . . . Well, I don't know about you folks out there, but when I think of pie I don't think about apple or pumpkin. You know what I mean? She says she's thinking of writing a book about her journey. All I can say is: Good luck, sistah! This is going to be one helluva book!"

We laughed so hard, every walleye in Lake Erie must have

headed straight for Canadian waters. As we hightailed it out of Cleveland, Fitz continued to entertain us with his playlist. "Where Can I Get Some Cherry Pie?" was followed by a 1962 Bo Diddly tune called "Can't Judge a Book by Its Cover."

At least Fitz had found his sense of humor.

As late as it was, laughter had juiced us up, so we drove straight on to Sandusky to find a room for the night. We found some over-priced chain hotel where the nightshift hotel clerk was drunker (and smellier) than a skunk. I stared at the twinkly stucco ceiling for a long time, unable to sleep.

Instead of counting sheep, I calculated how many cups of coffee Harry could buy at the Wellsboro Diner with the money I'd spent on my wicker table.

cat in the tree leads to great pie

"Commonplaces never become tiresome. It is we who become tired when we cease to be curious and appreciative."
—NORMAN ROCKWELL
"COMMONPLACE," *THE AMERICAN MAGAZINE*

I learned to speak English when I was five, from my neighbor Marietta Smith and from watching reruns of *Leave It to Beaver* and *The Andy Griffith Show.*

Which is why, growing up, I felt secure in the notion that in small-town America cats never stayed stuck in trees long.

A stop in tiny Munith, Michigan, shattered that myth for good.

Our plan for mitten-shaped Michigan was to hit the National Cherry Festival in Traverse City, then head farther north to rugged Charlevoix.

On the way, I wanted to make a quick pit stop in Armada, just north of Detroit, in the thumb part of the state. A fellow food writer at the *Detroit News* had told me about Wendy Achatz, a young woman who baked luscious fruit pies in her creaky old home with her husband, Dave.

That sounded promising, so we drove through Detroit, Betty Blue feeling self-conscious, a "foreigner" among a sea of big American cars. Kris called the bakery for directions as we got closer and got a chirpy machine telling her the bakery was closed on Saturdays. Closed on Saturdays?!?

This threw us for a complete loop. Ohio had left a bad taste in my mouth and we needed to find some pie fast.

I pulled over in a Dairy Queen parking lot to plot the next move while Kris did some Pilates stretches on Betty Blue's hood. I remembered having a conversation once, with San Francisco chef Douglas Keane, a Michigan native, about an artisan bakery in Munith, near Ann Arbor, where his family owned a campground. He used to get pies there as a boy, and although he hadn't been to the bakery in years, he assured me that it was still open and worth any detour.

If central and lower Michigan were the palm of the mitten, then Munith would be where the life line and love line intersect, off of US 106, a short-lived two-laner that cuts right through the lush Waterloo Recreation Area.

Once in Munith, we needed only follow our noses and let the familiar scent of sour dough lead us to the Mill Pond Bakery at the end of the main street through town. The bakery looked plucked from a Marcel Pagnol novel. In one corner, an old bank vault next to the Blodgett Ovens serves as a reminder of the building's prior incarnation as the town bank. John, the owner, bought the bakery as a quality-of-life move. He forms the bread by hand, using flour from local mills. He waters down his bread with a garden hose.

People thought he was crazy to open a "yuppie" bakery in conservative Munith in the heart of Wonder Bread country.

Fortunately, enough restaurants opened up in Ann Arbor to keep the bakery busy and afloat. The bakery is considered so "alternative" that all the local youths want to work there in the summer as a rite of passage.

John had stayed up all night baking for a pack of seven hundred cross-country cyclists who had stopped in for some healthy carbo-loading that morning. He was exhausted when we dropped by seeking pie.

John said he did in fact make pies in the early years. "They weren't real big sellers back then because of the 'health food' craze," he said. Then, when the country went "gourmet," pies were dismissed as too pedestrian. But John was sensing a "back-to-basics movement" in America, he said, and he'd been talking to his wife about bringing pies back.

"Maybe your coming to Munith is a sign that we need to start making pies," he said. Maybe it was.

John had taped a quote from Calvin Coolidge on the wall, and I jotted it down in my journal while Kris bought some loaves for us for the road.

> Press on: Nothing can take the place of persistence.
> Talent will not; nothing is more common than unsuccessful men
>   with talent.
> Genius will not; unrewarded genius is almost a proverb.

Education will not; the world is full of educated derelicts.
Persistence and determination alone are omnipotent.
                                                    —*Calvin Coolidge*

Inspired by this humble little bakery, we went for a brisk walk along the road that connects Munith to the township of Waterloo. For a good hour, we walked along fields of chirping crickets and darting jackrabbits getting in their last kicks of the day.

We were on our way back to the car we'd left parked in grass behind the bakery when we noticed an older woman talking to a walnut tree in her backyard.

"You come on down now, kitty," she said. "You come on down here to Mama."

"Where's the fire department when you need it," I said, crossing the lawn to help. "Oh, they won't come out for a silly old cat," she said, laughing, "*even* in Munith."

She puckered her face and glared at a smug bruiser cat sitting in a patch of rhubarb also known as "pie plant." "See that tom? He's the one who chased my cat up the tree," she said. "That tom is nothing but trouble."

She was wearing loose cotton shorts and a matching top, and her dark hair was in tight Bette Davis curls. She was well into her 60s but there was something positively girlish about her and the way her exposed bony knees faced the world.

We took turns coaxing the cat who gingerly made his way down the trunk, like a skier on his first non-bunny slope. She picked him up, held him against her chest. "I'm Juanita," she said. "You two ladies getting your exercise?" she asked, as though we'd just met the week before at a church. We told her about pie.

"Well, isn't that too much?" she said. "I was just fixing to cut some rhubarb to make some pie. My feller is visiting for the weekend and so I thought I'd make a pie tomorrow morning."

"Feller" is a word you don't hear too often outside of America's pieways.

"Your *feller?*" I asked, to see what the word felt like.

Juanita said she'd been married once but now she preferred her independence. "I only date on the weekends. During the week I'm too busy, washing my car, working in my garden, puttering about."

I liked this woman enough already that I hoped she would offer to let us watch her make pie. And, I hoped, she'd do it fast, because mosquitoes were eating us alive. She must have read my mind, because she said, "Where are you ladies going to be in the morning?"

And so a plan was hatched that we would return first thing Sunday to bake pie with Juanita.

Juanita, the walk, the fact that my gut was back—all had conspired to put us in a great mood. The drive toward quaint Chelsea, where Juanita told us we could find a room for the night, could not have been prettier. The fireflies were out in full force and, again, the great DJ in the sky seemed to be keeping an eye out for us, because Gershwin's "Summertime" came on the radio.

Juanita was in her garden cutting giant stalks of rhubarb when we arrived. She seemed genuinely excited to see us. She'd carefully picked out her baking outfit and I particularly liked her fetching leopard-print apartment slippers. Such a coquette.

She had probably been up since dawn because, to my dismay, she'd already made her dough, rolled it out, and lined two pie pans. Most of the ingredients for two distinct pies, one rhubarb custard, one raspberry, were all laid out on her kitchen counter in perfect *mise en place.* Maybe the thought of making dough in front of two strangers made her nervous.

Juanita and her rhubarb

I realized that her kitchen window looked right out on Waterloo Road where Kris and I had enjoyed our walk the night before, and I envied her that serene view to wash dishes by.

"I love that window," she said, catching my gaze. "I've only used my dishwasher twice in eight years."

Her feller, Mike, stayed in the living room to watch sports on television and we sat at the kitchen table and watched Juanita work.

"Pie and coffee, it's a friendship thing, don't you think? If I go to somebody's house for dinner, I bring a pie. I often make a lemon pie for a lonely gentleman I know who lives in a nursing home. Last week, I made a pie for my neighbor who broke her arm in two places in a car accident. And the week before that, I made a coconut cream pie for my chiropractor's wife. Oh, and I paid the gentleman who cleaned my eaves in pie—and cookies—that I left on his porch. I just made a berry pie for the neighbor who helped me out when my well went dry."

She poured us more coffee.

"My late mother-in-law taught me to make pie," she said, chopping the fresh red rhubarb into inch-long segments.

"Not your mother?" I asked.

"My own mother gave me away when I was five," she said, not wasting any time to get personal. "My parents had divorced and my mother didn't want me, so I was sent to live with my aunt."

Juanita stopped chopping and smiled at us. "That's OK. I was strong, so I could take it.

"My aunt was strict and not very nice to me, but I never went wanting for clothes or material goods. I tell you though, I would have done anything to be the girl next door I used to give my clothes to. She didn't have much but she had *love*."

Juanita left her aunt's house at 17 to look for her mother in West Virginia, with the help of an uncle who thought they should finally meet again. "When we found her, I asked my mother if she wanted me, if I could stay awhile to finish high school.

"And she said, 'I want you, and I'll keep you forever.' "

I asked Juanita if she'd ever asked her mother why she'd sent her away in the first place and she shook her head no. "We never quite could talk about it." She dabbed her eyes with a kitchen towel. "I'm sorry," she said.

Don't be, we said. Pie, we'd found, often acted as a wooden spoon, stirring up the soul. Maybe it was the rhubarb, I said.

In ancient China, rhubarb was once cultivated and revered for its cathartic, purgative qualities.

"Every now and then all the sadness in my life just wells up on me," she said, "but I move on. I've learned to put my sadness on a shelf. It doesn't help to dwell on it or blame others for how you live your life."

She talked of how she met her husband, a dairy farmer, at a

Masonic Temple dance when she was barely 20. What she loved most about him, she said, was his extended family who treated her as though she were born into theirs.

"My mother-in-law, Opal, had hard, farmwife hands and she taught me how to do everything on the farm," she said. Every summer, Juanita followed her husband to the state fair in Detroit where his Black Angus cattle always snagged the blue ribbons. Eventually, she got to be such a good baker she worked up the courage to enter her pies and cookies at the fair competitions. She's garnered an impressive collection of blue ribbons herself.

"Baking was like an escape valve for me," said Juanita. Her husband was a drinker, it turned out. "He carried that burden to his grave and I stood by him," she said.

"You have to give more than you take in this life," she went on. "You'll be rewarded in ways that you don't always realize."

After her husband's death, she took care of her mother-in-law and when she died, Opal left Juanita almost everything.

Now, Juanita said, she's always looking for "any old excuse" to bake.

I asked her about the no-nonsense mixing bowl she held in the nook of her hip. "I've grown quite attached to it," she said. "I can't make pie without it.

"All bakers have their favorite little something they like in their kitchens. Opal had a favorite bowl she used to make her fudge in. She sold it at an auction. If I'd even looked at it cross-eyed she would have given it to me, but she didn't know how much I wanted it."

"I sure wish now I'd said something. It would mean a lot to me to have Opal's bowl," she said.

Ordinarily, Juanita would layer a meringue onto her rhubarb pie when it was almost baked, but she decided she'd leave this pie uncovered to save time.

While we waited for the pie to bake, she got to work on the second, raspberry pie made with berries picked by her friends near Chelsea. Talk went from hair color to men. Juanita had just dyed her hair a shade or two too dark and, although she'd washed it three times since, could not lighten it up. Mike didn't seem to mind, she said. Juanita and Mike met nine years earlier and, she said, she was finally truly happy.

"He's a quiet sort and he lets me rattle on and on. When I was little, my aunt wouldn't let me talk much, so I guess I'm making up for lost time," she said. She was glad that they lived apart, because it's romantic to miss someone. "We send each other cards and letters when we get in a mood."

She called Mike in to join us when it was time to lay the lattice top crust on the raspberry pie. Mike had seen it done on television and picked it up "just like that," Juanita said.

One by one, he layered the thick bands of dough across the top, delicately lifting one to slide another beneath it. Juanita stood right by his elbow, watching and praising his every move.

The oven buzzer went off, indicating that the first pie was ready, and Juanita started looking for her glasses, which were pushed back in her curls.

She was nervous. She wanted this pie to be perfect. Technically, we should have waited for the quivering rhubarb custard pie to cool, but we needed to get back on the road so we could catch the cherry-pie eating contest in Traverse City, so she sliced it anyway.

The crust made with lard, just as Opal said, was among the flakiest I've ever had. I can still taste and feel the hot, sweet custard burning the roof of my mouth. Like Juanita's story, the filling was bittersweet.

She gave us the recipe and then made us peek at the raspberry pie in the oven before walking us to the car. This "feller" was a keeper: the lattice work was stunning.

Juanita took a minute to figure out my license plate and when she did, she clasped her hands together. "Thank you for coming," she said. "Let me know if you find another rhubarb custard pie on the road, all right? Safe trip."

And as we drove off, past the yucca plants and four-o'clocks lining her drive, Juanita waved slowly. Her cat was rubbing up against her leg and I realized we'd forgotten to ask its name.

What was it that made strangers want to open their hearts to us, Kris asked as we headed north to Traverse City.

"Maybe it's just like Juanita said," I replied. "Everyone needs to be listened to once in a while."

JUANITA'S RHUBARB CUSTARD PIE

CRUST

1 unbaked pie shell

FILLING

3 cups fresh rhubarb stalks, cut in cubes the size of your thumb
(preferably from a part of the garden where the toms don't go)
1½ cups sugar
2 tablespoons cornstarch
3 eggs (use 2 yolks and 1 whole egg and save 2 egg whites for meringue
topping—optional)
1 cup milk
½ teaspoon nutmeg

Line pie plate with pastry. Fill with rhubarb. In a favorite bowl, mix together sugar, cornstarch, eggs, and milk. Pour mixture over the rhubarb and sprinkle the whole with nutmeg. Bake at 375 degrees for

1 hour or until set. If you plan to add a meringue topping, remove the pie after 45 minutes, layer the meringue on top, and slide the pie in the broiler for another 15 minutes or until the meringue is golden brown.

the cherry states

"Years ago, manhood was an opportunity for achievement and now it's just a problem to be overcome. Guys who once might have painted the Sistine Chapel ceiling are now just trying to be Mr. O.K. All-Rite, the man who can bake a cherry pie, cry, be passionate in a skillful way, and yet also lift them bales and tote that barge."

—GARRISON KEILLOR,

THE BOOK OF GUYS

Turning 8 is a rite of passage for children growing up in and around Traverse City, Michigan. That's the pivotal age after which kids entering the pie-eating contest at the National Cherry Festival are no longer allowed to use their hands.

From ages 5 to 8, children keep their balled-up fists behind their backs until moderator Nancy Grin, known throughout Michigan as "The Pie Lady," tells them it's all right to use their hands—about a minute after the starting bell, or midway through the event.

That's when tiny arms, thin and malleable as a cherry stem, fly to the forefront and the shoving begins.

· · ·

"Please remember to chew and swallow. CHEW AND SWALLOW!" shouted Grin through a bullhorn. "It's more important to chew than it is to win *any* contest."

Clearly, she was also addressing the frenzied parents who were crouched directly across from their children, screaming "Faster, *faster.*"

Grin, who has been moderating the pie-eating contest for 11 years, said critics of the event—which used to involve a whole pie rather than just one slice—claimed it encouraged gluttony. (And what exactly about American culture, from corporate raiding to jumbo-sized soft drinks

Pie-eating contest,
Traverse, MI

and baseball players' pie-high salaries, doesn't?). So Grin kept reminding the audience that "seriously, folks, this is not something you want to practice at home."

"I've only had kids throw up on me three times," said Grin, who was decked out in festival-mandated maraschino red. As an extra precaution against gagging, young assistants stand behind the contestants, pulling back wayward pig- and ponytails.

That wasn't good enough for Kristy, a mom who snuck into the festival tent to hold her daughter Nicki's thick braids herself. Nicki captured first place in the 6-year-olds division. The tomboy blonde shot her arms straight up in the air when she was announced the clear winner after only one minute and forty-five seconds of scarfing that would put any truffling pig to shame.

Towheaded Cody, who later that morning took first place in the 9-year-olds division, told me he'd figured out the winning strategy:

"The more you wear, the less you have to eat," he said, before plunging his head in the designated water trough.

The pie-eating contest was a highlight of the weeklong Cherry Festival, which was celebrating its seventy-fourth anniversary when we breezed into town. The festival drew five hundred thousand visitors annually and started out as a simple ritual for cherry farmers calling on the agriculture and weather gods to protect their delicate crops each May.

The first "Blessing of the Blossoms" was held in 1925—about the time when local cherries started being produced in commercial quantities. Michigan now produces three quarters of the nation's annual sour-cherry crop.

At the festival, we learned that cherry juice can help relieve arthritis pain and that grinding the hulls of the seeds of cherry pits can help strip paint from heavy metals (but could it strip Cody's earlobes clean?).

With that in mind, I sure hoped someone came around to collect the hundreds of stray pits that were strewn about the long plastic tarp used for the cherry-pit spitting contest. The winner, a local guy with a pickle-barrel chest, had remarkable form. He would thrust his hips forward and his chest back, like a mating peacock, then pucker up and fire his pit. With a spitting distance of 48 feet, he left his competition in the dust and sideline observers freshly showered.

Each year during the festival, the elected Cherry Queen goes to the White House to offer an extra-large cherry pie to the president. I'm not sure if he was pulling my leg, but a spokesman for the event told me that after the Monica Lewinsky debacle, festival organizers decided they'd abstain from delivering a cherry pie to the White House that year.

At a brew pub in town, we met some locals who volunteered as festival "ambassadors" each year. When they heard about our trip, they graciously invited us to their home for barbecued pork chops the next day. We had plans to go to Charlevoix, farther north, for more pie research, but we'd be back in plenty of time for dinner and sure could use a home-cooked meal. Naturally, we offered to pick up a pie for dessert.

"Please," they said . . . "Anything but cherry."

I was having dinner with my friends Larry and Dorothea Smith one night before my departure, when Larry announced that his grandmother, Mary Baumbach, was known in her day as "the best cherry-pie baker in the Wolverine State, hands down."

Now, I had been on this pie kick long enough to know that conversations about pie invite hyperbole. But Larry, a former *New York Times* editor and the editor of *Parade* magazine, *had* to be objective . . . didn't he?

"There's only two kinds of pie, my grandpa Rollie used to say: warm or cold," Larry said.

His grandparents were long deceased, but the two aunts who raised him as their son, Grace and Bessie, were still living in the Charlevoix area. They were both feisty, in their 80s, and *loved* to have visitors, he said. In fact, he'd just talked to Bessie that morning. She and Grace had gone to the Charlevoix cemetery. Bessie described the outing as "the half-dead visiting the short-dead and the long-dead."

I liked her turn of phrase, so I put a star next to Charlevoix on the map.

The widowed Bessie, the elder of the two, lived alone in an apartment in Elk Rapids. Her sister Grace, also widowed, lived on a dairy farm she still ran with her son, in Charlevoix proper. We'd arranged to pick Bessie up on our way to Grace's farmhouse where it might be more pleasant to chat.

About five miles before arriving at Bessie's, we pulled over near a cherry orchard to tidy up the car. After only four days out, she was crawling with cookie crumbs and sunflower seeds, and already smelled like a boys' gym locker.

Bessie was waiting patiently for us in her living room, her handbag at her feet. And two cherry pies made with local Montmorency cherries on the counter. I was delighted and surprised she'd bothered to bake at all. While I would have never admitted this to Larry, I had never had a slice of cherry pie. Not once, not ever. And I couldn't be happier that my first would be baked by the hands of a woman named Bessie in the heart of cherry country.

On the twenty-minute drive to Charlevoix, Kris sat in the back with one of the pies next to her on the seat, and Bessie sat up front, holding a cherry pie on her lap. I thought of my mother and her traveling floating-islands, and prayed that the glove-compartment door would behave just this once.

As we drove, Bessie explained how the old art of cherry picking had evolved over the years from simple, honest hand-picking to high-tech gadgetry.

Charlevoix sits on a scenic stretch of US 31 that hugs the shore between Traverse City and Petoskey. Once a lumbering community, it's now known mostly for its beaches and lakes.

"Tourism, T-shirts, and fudge, that's what Charlevoix is all about these days," harrumphed Bessie as we pulled into the dirt drive of her sister's farmhouse, a sturdy white house wrapped by a tidy, tended garden with a red milking barn out back. Grace, who has lived in that house since 1929, came out on the porch to greet us, and I noticed they were wearing the same exact blouse. We all sat around the table in the kitchen window, facing the barn. The kitchen was almost surgical it was so clean, spare, and white. The two warm cherry pies on the counter was as brightening as red lipstick on a geisha.

Unlike Juanita, Grace and Bessie were reserved and shy, at first. We spent a few minutes just staring at each other around the table, commenting on the glorious weather. Kris cleared her throat.

"So do you sisters always dress alike?" she asked to break the ice. As it turned out, they often went shopping for clothes together in Midland, about 200 miles away, and they had picked these blouses up on their last shopping expedition.

"So you are road trippers, too," I said.

We learned that both had taught in one-room schoolhouses. Both had been married and left widowed with one son. Kris and I had noticed that many of the women in Michigan had a certain masculine quality about them—broad shoulders, deep voices, and an undeniable strength. Grace and Bessie were no exception.

"There's a saying around here that goes 'all my sons are daughters,' " said Grace, who, at 82, still helped out with the milking and calving.

I asked them about Larry's claims regarding their mother's pie, and they shook their heads and smiled.

There had never been any official proclamation from the governor or anything like that, they said. But it was common knowledge among local folk how good Mary Baumbach's pies were. Everyone wanted to come help out during thrashing season because a hard day's labor was always rewarded with a slice of Mary's cherry pie.

Their mother knew a thing or two about hard labor. She made her pies in a cast-iron skillet. She churned her own butter, did laundry by knuckle and washboard, and quilted, too. She still found time to cook three square meals a day for her husband and nine children, and on this Bessie and Grace agreed: those hearty meals in childhood were the reason for their longevity.

Was it intimidating to tackle pie when their mother's was so good, I asked. The sisters guffawed. As much as they admired their mother's baking skills, baking was not what either one of them wanted to be remembered for. These were educated women slightly ahead of our time, let alone theirs.

"I think it's puttery," Grace said about cooking in general. "Fools work, wise men eat."

Bessie glanced over at her sister quizzically. "I must be a fool then," she said, pointing to her two pies.

Sisters always seem to look at each other with a distinct set of eyes that alternate between judgment and admiration. Kris and I were witnessing "marvel," as though the two had never talked among themselves about the topics we broached that afternoon, or at least not in a long while.

No surprise, Kris and I had spent the first three days of this leg of our trip talking about relationships and why so many of our women friends were still single in their late 30s. In their day, an unmarried woman in her mid-30s was cause for alarm and pity, they said. But, as Bessie pointed out, women today really don't *need* to get married, or at least not for the same reasons women used to seek out a husband. The trouble with being so financially independent, we told them, is that it makes women too demanding.

"It's easier to find a man that can provide than it is to find one that can communicate," Kris said.

"You can never be too picky when it comes to that," Bessie said. "Isn't that right, Grace?"

"That's right, Bessie. You two girls just keep on doing what you're doing."

We hardly knew these women, yet at this very moment, their blessing meant the world to us.

We asked them how their parents, who married in 1900, had met, and neither one knew the answer.

"There are so many questions I wish I'd asked them when they were still alive," said Bessie. "I wish I'd asked my grandmother what toys she played with, who her friends were, what her house was like growing up. It just never occurred to me to ask."

One thing they did know for sure was that their mother made her pie crust with suet, the hard fat deposited around the kidneys and loins of cattle and sheep. Grace and Bessie used regular shortening to bake their own occasional pies. Like most Michigan homemakers, they used tapioca as a thickener for the cherry filling.

Before tasting the pie, Grace wanted to take us on a tour of the barn. We asked her to show us how to milk a cow, just so we could say we've done it. We snapped pictures of one another, each with a teat in hand, and among the stack of Polaroids from the trip I keep on my desk, my favorite is the one of Kris tugging on a teat, with an ear-to-ear grin, and Grace standing right next to her, her mouth open wide.

Bessie, who had a little trouble walking these days, had stayed back in the house and she was cutting into and serving the pie when we returned to the kitchen, still laughing.

Hers was a no-nonsense crust, as sensible as her Rockport shoes. Along the edges, rather than crimping, Bessie had drawn distinct slits, thin as the stripes in her seersucker shorts. She'd also cut in the middle of the top crust random steam valve slits that looked like a sandpiper's footprints on wet sand.

In her book *The Pie and Pastry Bible* Rose Levy Beranbaum says cherry filling (her favorite) should taste "like a cardinal singing." It's a sound I've gotten to know well since moving to my cottage in the Hudson Valley, where a pair of brazen orange-plumed cardinals serenades me most mornings.

Bessie's pie sounded more like a church bell. The taste was clear, but it had serious cherry depth. No glaze, no goo. Just cherry. Ruby-slipper red. Bessie had scooped vanilla ice cream on top and it was melting fast, slithering into a puddle of scarlet juice.

Grace was impressed, and so were we.

I confessed that this was my first cherry pie.

"Oh my," they both said simultaneously. I think Bessie was relieved I had nothing to compare it to.

We left feeling sated on so many levels. Bessie gave us a tour of Charlevoix—the old schoolhouse, the cemetery where "the half-dead go and visit the short-dead and the long-dead." When she slipped inside her apartment, we gave her a warm hug and thanked her again for her pies. Silently, we thanked both her and her sister for paving the way for independent women.

Then we thanked Betty Blue for keeping her glove compartment shut.

BESSIE'S ADAPTATION OF
HER MOTHER MARY'S
"BEST CHERRY PIE IN MICHIGAN"

CRUST

1 full cup (heaping) shortening

¾ cup of cold water

2 cups of flour

pinch of salt

FILLING

1 quart pitted sour cherries (Montmorency)

3 tablespoons tapioca (or flour or cornstarch)

1⅓ cups of sugar

Take the juice from the pitted cherries and mix it with the tapioca and sugar, then mix together with cherries in a bowl. Place the cherry mixture in an unbaked pie shell and bake for 30 minutes at 400 degrees and another 30 minutes at 350 degrees.

Serve with vanilla ice cream and eat in good company by a window that looks out on a bright red barn . . .

P.S. Cooking the cherries before baking the pie makes them lose their redness.

We stopped at one of the roadside fruit stands to buy fresh cherries to snack on and an apple pie for the barbecue. Our hosts turned out to be true ambassadors indeed, treating us to a fancy meal and late-night conversation under the stars on a private dock in the bay.

"I don't know too many people who would have taken in strangers for dinner," I said. "Certainly New Yorkers are far too jaded for that."

"I'm not familiar with that expression," said one of the gentlemen. "What does 'being jaded' mean exactly?"

"Being jaded means having seen so many cherries you can't see the beauty of just one," I said.

cherries redux

"Kindred Spirits aren't so scarce as I used to think."
—LUCY MAUD MONTGOMERY, *ANNE OF GREEN GABLES*

We left Traverse City the following morning, on the Fourth of July—a big day for pie-eating in America. Our plan was to take a car ferry to Wisconsin and then drive north to Door County, the windswept finger of land wedged between Green Bay and Lake Michigan's western shore, also famous for its sour cherries. Our dinner hosts had suggested we follow the Lake Michigan shoreline to get to the Ludington ferry dock and stop for a catnap near the Sleeping Bear Dunes. An isolated beach at the foot of Esch Road would impress even two jaded women like us. They were right.

A delicious swim put us behind schedule and we really had to rush to make the ferry. It would surprise none of my friends to know that we were the last car to board.

The ferry ride was four hours long, which meant we'd arrive in Wisconsin around 10 P.M.—too late to catch a fireworks display. We were disappointed, but no feat of pyrotechnics could rival the sunset that night. Even the bingo players came out on the deck to take it in. A tall man with a gaunt face took pictures of the sky. I offered to take one of him. He did the same for me and then small talk led to pie talk.

R., in his early 40s, had made his first pie in home-economics class in the seventh grade and hadn't stopped since. In fact, he had recently thrown a party for which he'd baked a panoply of pies, with lattice crusts and fancy crimps. He told me about a place in Randolph, Wisconsin, near his brother's house, where he was living temporarily that sold pie for $1.25 a slice on Thursdays! He handed me his card and asked us to give him a call if we were anywhere near that area.

It was starting to get cold out on the deck, so Kris and I retreated inside the cabin to write in our respective journals and study our maps. A professorial-looking gentleman leaned over and asked:

"Are you really looking for *pi*?"

We were not on the same oven rack.

Although many have described my quest as *irrational*, I told him, we were *not* looking for the irrational number by which the diameter of a circle must be multiplied to obtain the circumference.

A social worker, he was more interested, it seemed, in the spiritual virtue of pi than its mathematical significance.

"Many people believe that the answers to life's bigger questions lie in the numerical pi," he said. "Perhaps it's also true for the kind you bake."

I smiled. He didn't know how right he was.

In Two Rivers, not far from the landing, we found the quintessential shoreline motel complete with a view of the bay and a large freezer near the ice machine for traveling fishermen to drop off their catch. The owner of the motel lived right next door, and we paid for the room in his kitchen, which smelled of buttered popcorn. His under-shirt was stretched so taut across his belly, it looked like an apple pie or a short-sheeted bed.

"Pie?" he said, when he saw me write my license-plate number on the motel registration card.

"Do you like rhubarb? That's my favorite." He leaned back in his chair, put his hands behind his head, revealing heavily forested armpits. I'm not sure, but I think he gave me some sort of "pie" dis-count, he said. When I pushed open the door to our room with my yoga mat, we gasped at how positively kitsch it was: vinyl wall pan-eling, a faux anchor above each bed, and an orange rug as shaggy as the owner.

Among the people we met on this trip, some stand out more than others, like characters in a pop-up storybook. In Mishicot, Wiscon-sin, our first stop the next morning, a thirtysomething woman named Lisa was a merry marker on the road to pie.

It was the "math guy" on the ferry, as Kris called him, who sug-gested we stop in charming Mishicot for lunch on our way to Door

County. The drive there was stunning. Barns in this part of the country are a soft, soldier blue, with minarets that pierce the sky.

On Main Street, we ducked into a store with vintage kitchenware in the shop window. It was a gallery and an antiques store, and Lisa was one of the artists who displayed her work there and occasionally worked the register.

Lisa was pleasingly plump, and I mention it only because her plumpness seemed inextricably tied to her personality, just as fuzz is to a peach. She had a distinct 1940s air about her, right down to the way she painted her lips.

A powder-blue bowl with an art-deco pattern in the back of the store caught my eye almost immediately. At $45, it was beyond the $35 cap I'd set for myself on bowl purchases. But I couldn't stop looking at it. Finally, I set it on the counter but told Lisa I hadn't made up my mind. If I was going to bend my rules, I had to at least put up a bit of a fight.

"It's so pretty," Lisa cooed. "But I understand having to limit yourself. I have a collection myself. I collect rolling pins."

Why, I asked, not wanting to let on quite yet that we were kindred collectors.

"I just love pie," she said, putting a hand on her heart.

Go on, I said.

"Pie is the last holdout of the Great American comfort foods," she said. "It's America's dessert darling.

"You eat pie when you're happy, don't you? That's because pie means somebody loves you," she said. "And all pie bakers are angels."

Maybe we should make room for Lisa in the car, I thought.

"Crust has a huge emotional content in my family," she said. For years, she and her mother were in a tiff over a difference of opinion on how to prevent a soggy bottom crust. I wanted to know more, but Lisa didn't want to go there. She was more interested in our trip. Where were we headed?

"Oh no! You're headed straight for 'Magazine Food' country," she said. "You know . . . *Ladies' Home Journal*, circa 1952. Everything is that same awful bland color and every recipe begins with cream-of-chicken soup."

Lisa's husband was a minister, and they'd just spent a few years living on the Plains, on the border between South Dakota and Minnesota. She was glad to be back in Wisconsin. Since she seemed to have a good grasp on the Midwest, we asked her to explain all the lawn gnomes and trolls we started seeing the moment we got off the ferry.

She rolled her eyes. We'd hit a nerve.

Turned out, she'd served on a regional arts board in Minnesota whose role it was to decide how to allocate public-art funds. A proposal came in to plant a 30-foot-tall troll in the middle of a small rural town. The entire committee thought it was grand, she said, "but I told them I'd rather burn at the stake than use public money to erect a 30-foot troll."

She put her hand on her hip so that she looked like a teapot: "I always was the turd in the punchbowl," she said.

I bought the bowl, of course.

We continued straight north on US 42 until we crossed into Door County. With its New England–style architecture and harbor towns, it felt quite different from the Wisconsin we'd left behind, as though we really had pushed through a door to get there.

People on the ferry had recommended Berry Best, an orchard and specialty-food market in Gill's Rock. The place was owned by the Teskies, an extended Door County fishing family with deep roots in Door. The Teskies' shop was known for its smoked chubs and its two-pound cherry pie.

At the Fourth of July parade, the Teskies and their seven children made pies on their float, tossing flour into the crowd.

The shop was already closed for the day when we pulled into the drive. Neil Teskie walked out to the car to tell us we were out of luck. Could we come back tomorrow? We explained that we weren't your typical tourists and that all we really wanted was to talk to the baker of the famous cherry pies.

"That's my wife, Fran, but she's had a long day and I doubt she'll want to talk to you," he said bluntly. "Fran usually goes for a run on the shore and then dives into Lake Michigan after a day of baking. I'm not sure if she's back yet."

Fran stepped out on the porch with a towel around her head, looking way too young and fit for a mother of seven kids, many of them full grown.

Fran warmed up pretty quick. She said she learned baking from her Belgian grandmother, an immigrant from Antwerp, who used to get up at 5 A.M. on Saturdays and bake until noon. Her grandparents were part of the flock of Belgians who moved to the Chicago area during World War I and joined the janitors' unions. For years, it was the same group of Belgians who banked the fires through the bone-chilling Chicago winter nights. "My grandmother would let me roll out the dough with her. It was fun, sort of like playing with Play-Doh."

When Fran and her husband became farmers, it made sense to the young newlyweds to turn the childhood memory into a bankable hobby. With the variety of fruit from their own orchards, she experimented a lot. Now she taught a pie class in the summers, to young couples hoping to recoup what they missed out on as children, she said.

Making pie was like learning a language or learning to ski, she said. "It's best to learn young before the fear settles in." I thought of young Darrell back in New York.

Talk turned to fishing—Neil's area of expertise. We found out his tug was called *Betty*, just like the piemobile.

He had spent the day trimming down his fishing nets, a laborious task he used to dread. But only a few days earlier, something had happened to Neil. He'd had an epiphany.

"After 30 years of wondering if there was a right way to do it, I figured it out and it was like the sky just opened up before me," he said.

"Must be what it's like to finally figure out what pie dough is supposed to feel like in your hands," I said, looking at Fran. She nodded. And she wrapped her arm around her husband because she knew what a good feeling that could be.

They opened up the shop to give us for the road a cherry pie, which, we told her, we'd eagerly try once we'd had dinner.

"You *are* going to a fish boil tonight, aren't you?" Neil asked as we climbed back in the car.

Sure, if you tell us what it is, we said, slightly embarrassed by our Wisconsin ignorance. We'd seen the signs for "Fish Boils" all over the county but they'd left us clueless.

"It's a pretty dramatic fish-eating ritual unique to Door County," Neil said. He glanced at his watch. "If you hurry, you can still catch the boil at the Square Rigger, in Jacksonport. If you're not there by 8 P.M., you'll miss it."

What kind of restaurant—other than Alain Ducasse in New York—has only one seating per night?

"This isn't just for tourists, is it?" we asked.

"Nope. This is where Fran and I go whenever we are craving a good piece of boiled fish. And I *know* their fish is fresh, because I'm their main supplier."

It was already 7:30 P.M. and we had a good 30 miles or so to go, so I let Kris, aka leadfoot, take the wheel and I secured the pie on my lap. When we arrived at ten minutes past eight, the waitress ushered us straight to the outdoor deck where the other guests were already gathered, all eyes directed toward a huge kettle suspended over an oak-wood fire about 50 feet away, near the edge of Lake Michigan.

The restaurant's "master boilers" had lit the fire beneath the 22-gallon kettle about ninety minutes earlier. Once the water started to bubble, the two boilers tossed the baby red potatoes. Thirty minutes later, they added the peeled, sweet boiler onions. About twenty minutes after that, right when we got there, they'd dropped in the thick whitefish steaks, which must stay in the water exactly thirteen minutes to be cooked just right. All of the ingredients were dropped into the kettle in stainless steel baskets, easily removed once the kettle has boiled over.

The "boil over," we learned, was what made the event so dramatic. Right before the fish was done to a turn, the boilers doused kerosene onto the flames to make the preparation boil over—intentionally. This helped remove the scum and oil that came to the water's surface, and put out the fire in the process. But not before sending giant, roaring flames into the sky.

Despite the furious boiling method of cooking and the absence of any herbs or seasonings other than salt (15 pounds!), the fish was remarkably firm, flaky, and flavorful—(hmmm, all the traits of a perfect pie crust).

And, like pie, our waitress said, "there isn't a holiday or special event or church social that doesn't include a fish boil."

The table next to ours was celebrating a family reunion. Since we had Fran's pie in the car, I asked them to help us eat it, not knowing that cherry pie also came with dinner at the restaurant. Everyone ate two slices that night. Fran's pie tasted more dense, more deep than the restaurant pie.

It was good, but I still liked Bessie's best. I'd gone 36 years without tasting cherry pie and now I'd had three slices in 48 hours.

•   •   •

We found a roadside motel in Algoma. The innkeeper had a funny accent I could not place. When she heard about our quest, she said "hmmmm" and then signed us in. The next morning, she came to find us as we loaded up the car. "You are going to try some Belgian pie, aren't you?" she asked.

The pies are a regional specialty in the heavily Belgian communities of Kewaunee and Brown counties just south of Door, she said. I had no idea so many Belgians were clustered in Wisconsin, so many, they even had their own pie.

I do love that about America: the fact that it's so vast, you could actually stumble on an entire subculture you didn't know existed, like finding a pair of never-worn shoes in the back of your closet. The woman wrote down the name of a polka musician who lived in Rosiere who could help us find good Belgian pie.

Since it looked like we might be having pie for breakfast, Kris suggested we go for a quick roller-blade. We found a fairly smooth stretch of paved road bordered by fields of tall grass and barns with gleaming silver silos. Kris took off ahead of me like a fish-boil fire. I sputtered behind, trying to remember if there was ever any mention of pie in the *Adventures of Tintin*.

Most of the older houses in Belgian Wisconsin were fashioned from "three little pigs" brick and had outdoor kitchens with large bake-off ovens.

We drove through a one–stop sign town called Duvall, closely named after a specialty Belgian beer I happened to be extremely fond of. A Duvel, or Belgian Chimay, sounded divine after roller-blading but it was early yet, and we were still on pie duty. So, when we stopped at a bar and grill, it really was in the hope of tracking down that polka musician.

Nancy the bartender was playing *cuyoo*, a Belgian card game, with two of her customers right on the bar top. "We've been playing *cuyoo* every Thursday for more than twenty years," said Joe, the eldest in the troika wearing a bolo tie and a bad toupee. Seeing Budweisers on the bar, I asked why no one was drinking Belgian beer. They look puzzled.

"Budweiser's our local beer. It's our biggest seller," said Nancy.

I didn't feel so bad for not knowing what a Belgian pie was.

Did *they* know what Belgian pie was?

"Oh sure," said Nancy, her eyes never leaving the cards. "Prune pie is as traditional Belgian as chicken *booyah.*" Then, never tearing themselves away from the cards, the three argued over whether rice, raisin, or prune is the most traditional filling for Belgian pie.

Clearly, I needed an expert. The polka man could be that, they said, only he was away. Nancy scratched her head with the corner of a playing card. A woman at the bar said she'd just come from a funeral at the church across the street. "A lot of the locals and long-timers are there," she said. "You should be able to find someone in the bunch who can help you."

I had never been to a funeral, let alone crashed one, I told her.

"Don't worry," she said. "We're not so uppity here in Wisconsin."

Kris was happy to play reporter on this trip, but she drew the line at funerals. So, while she tried to learn the rules for *cuyoo*, I slinked over to the church parking lot and stood there among whispering mourners until somebody noticed me.

"Can we help you with something?" a woman with a kind face asked.

"Uh. Uh. I'm really sorry to barge in like this, and I'm truly sorry about your loss, but I'm trying to find someone local who knows a thing or two about Belgian pie," I said sheepishly.

"Oh. Too bad, you just missed some good Belgian pie in there," said a cousin of the deceased. "Is there any left?" asked another. "What about Emily Guilette? Has she gone home?"

There were echoes of agreement that Emily Guilette was definitely the person I needed to see. "My cousin and I can take you to her house," said the woman with the kind face, Roxanne. "It's in Brussels. You can follow us there."

"I can't believe you got a pie tip at a funeral," said Kris as she settled up at the bar. I wasn't proud of it, I told her. But I got the distinct feeling that the distraction was welcome. Roxanne, our age, was clearly fond of Emily and welcomed any opportunity to visit with the old woman.

Emily, 91, was milling about in her kitchen when we knocked on the back door of her red brick house. She did not seem sad, and my guess was that, at her age, the best strategy was not to dwell on the losses. Her physique and nervous energy reminded me a lot of Granny Clampett—without the shotgun.

"So you're interested in Belgian pie," she said as she cleared some room on her kitchen table. "Too bad you came today instead of next week. I'm getting ready to make sixty of those pies for the Belgian Days Festival."

Belgian pies are small and so difficult to make, bakers rarely make fewer than three or four dozen at a time, she said.

The pie consists of a flat circle of raised sweet dough that is layered with a filling of sweet cooked rice, pureed prunes, or raisins. The pie is always topped with a sweetened cottage-cheese mixture. What makes it truly unique is that the sweet fluffy dough is made with *mashed potatoes.*

"There's no cutting corners with Belgian pie," Emily said. Who sells frozen Belgian-pie crusts?

Pie recipes floating around this part of Wisconsin "have not changed since the first Belgian grandmothers landed here in the mid-1850s," Emily said.

In those days, Belgian women would gather to make Belgian pies for the Kermiss—the annual harvest celebration. "For Belgian women, making pie was always a good excuse to get together among friends," she said.

Some say Belgian pies help new brides break the ice with their mothers-in-law. Emily, for example, learned to make the pies from her husband's mother who worried that her son might not get his Belgian pies with the regularity to which he was accustomed.

Though only 17 at the time, "I learned fast," Emily says, "in part because I had 'the baking hand.'

"I've made thousands of pies, thousands," she said. "People tell me mine's the best Belgian pie around. I've never heard anyone say different."

Then Emily practically jumped out of her chair. She remembered having stuck a raisin Belgian pie in her freezer the last time she made a batch, for a friend who had threatened to visit unannounced.

She was so tickled that we would get to taste some of her pie after all, she popped it in the toaster oven. Even without the cottage-cheese topping, the pie was delicious. But it tasted more like danish to me than pie. Not that there's anything wrong with that.

Emily told us we really couldn't find Belgian pie anywhere outside this tight-knit Belgian community, so I was glad our Algoma innkeeper had been such a busybody.

"So you drove here from New York," Emily said, when she grew bored of talking about pie. "I've been to New York once. I just had to go and touch the Statue of Liberty with my own hands."

She disappeared into her bedroom and returned with lips that had been touched up. "I do love my lipstick," she said. "I put some on every morning, first thing, to take on the day."

Her current favorite was a "mood" lipstick, which looked green in the tube but changed color on her lips depending on her disposition.

I know Kris well enough to know that this was right up her alley.

Emily must have read our minds, because she leaned over and whispered in Kris's ear:

"They sell it at Wal-Mart."

. . .

As we approached Ripon, I realized we weren't too far from the home of R., the tall, gaunt pie fanatic we'd met on the ferry. We called to say hello and that we probably wouldn't have time for the café in Randolph. His family was having a party in honor of his brother's fiftieth birthday. "Come on over," he said. "We don't have a pie though. My sister made a cake."

So we found our way in this very rural section of southern Wisconsin to the old farmhouse where R.'s brother lived. Off a dirt road, the house sat near a creek and a patch of sunflowers. R's nieces and nephews were playing with sparklers and let us join in and get our yayas out.

His father, Art, a dead ringer for Jason Robards, was kind of an old coot. He didn't say much until the very end of the evening, when we were all gathered in the kitchen saying our good-byes.

Art sat alone at the kitchen table, taking it all in: his three sons and his daughter and his grandchildren all together, in one room. And then, I heard him say to no one in particular:

"All this happened because of me."

We found a motel in Ripon, the town that birthed the Republican party, or as my niece Natalie, 8, calls it, the Pelican Party.

In the morning, we filled up on gas before leaving town. The attendant was talking to a man with a shotgun in his hand. "Hey," he said, pointing to Betty Blue's grille.

"Did you know you hit a rolling pin?"

Astute, those pelicans. Very astute.

EMILY'S BELGIAN PRUNE PIE

THE POTATO CRUST

2 eggs (1 whole plus 1 yolk)

⅓ cup melted butter

¼ cup of sugar

¼ teaspoon of salt

½ cup of mashed potatoes

¼ can of condensed milk

1½ cups of flour (varies)

FILLING

1½ pounds of prunes, pitted

1 pint of applesauce (takes the tartness out of the prunes)

1 cup sugar, more if you like sweeter taste

a pinch of salt

CHEESE TOPPING

1 24-ounce tub of small-curd cottage cheese

4 egg yolks

½ cup of sugar

¼ cup of butter (4 tablespoons)

Boil the prunes in water until they are done (about 1 hour). Puree them in a blender or food processor, add applesauce, sugar, and salt. Set aside.

Put cheese through a food mill. Add the yolks, sugar, and melted butter. "Beat the hell out of it," says Emily, and then spread it over the face of your pie.

Mix crust ingredients and then let the dough rise until it doubles in size.

Prick the bottom with a fork. Put your prune filling in. Then add the cheese topping in a circle of a smaller circumference, about ¼- to ½-inch thick. Bake at 350 degrees for about 20 minutes. Can be eaten warm or cold.

iowa

> *"SHOELESS" JOE JACKSON: "Is this heaven?"*
> *RAY KINSELLA: "No, this is Iowa . . ."*
> —FIELD OF DREAMS, SCREENPLAY BY
> W. P. KINSELLA AND PHIL ALDEN ROBINSON

Long after I'd moved to New York, I kept my expired California car-insurance card in my wallet. On the back of the card was scribbled a phone number, next to "Aunt Anne. Bernard, Iowa. Baked eight pies every Sunday for her eight children." Someone had drawn a big star next to her name.

I had no idea who this Aunt Anne was or who had given me her name, but even before I knew I'd go back out on the road to pie, something told me to keep it in my wallet.

I was glad I had, when we approached the Hawkeye State with no firm plans on where to find pie, other than a tentative lead on a natural hog farmer in Thornton.

As the crow flies, Bernard is only 20 miles southwest of

Dubuque, which we had to drive through anyway since we were coming from Wisconsin.

Driving across Dubuque, Kris and I shared a moment of silence in honor of her late grandpa Felix "Tubby" Leonard, a dapper clothier who for many years had managed the lingerie floor at the Zuckies department store. Tubby always sent Kris lingerie draped in tissue on her birthday. It was always elegant and aptly chosen. Still, I had a hard time imagining my French grandfather sending me teddies air-mail.

My Breton grandfather was an iodized fisherman who never left the house without his sailor's cap and *bleus de marin*, or navy blues. He spent the years between retirement and death sitting on an old stone wall in his village of Sainte Marine, watching the tides and the younger generation of fishermen slip out to sea.

On US 151, we passed the home of the New Melleray Abbey, a Trappist monastery founded in 1849, where thirty-five monks still live today supporting themselves by building wooden caskets entirely by hand from cutting down the trees to sewing the muslin lining.

Ironically, the monks shun caskets for personal use, preferring to be wrapped in robes in death.

With a population of 120, Bernard, only slightly bigger than a base-ball field, was the smallest hamlet we'd visited so far. We stopped at Pearl's, the lone café in town, to ask a woman standing in the door-way if she knew who this "Aunt Anne" might be and where she lived. She stepped away from the shadows and pointed to the end of the road—and the end of Bernard, for that matter.

Anne's white clapboard house sat directly across a sprawling corn-field with stalks pushing six feet tall. All the window shades were drawn, which could have explained why there was no answer on the telephone when I'd tried to call from Ripon.

I knocked anyway, and was surprised to hear a "come on in."

Anne was sitting right in the middle of a very long white couch, almost in the dark. She apologized for the darkness.

"I can' t let my African violets get too much sun," she said.

Anne seemed to be expecting us, or at least expecting something, the way she sat so tall and regal in the exact middle of her stretch couch, beneath framed photographs of her eight children when they were still toddlers.

Anne cleared up the mystery. I'd met her niece at a dinner party in San Francisco more than a year ago, when the subject of pies had come up. I immediately asked about the eight pies she used to bake on Sundays. She laughed.

"I only baked three at a time," she said, "*never* eight."

Anne said she used to wake very early on Sundays to get to first mass and then come home and make her pies while the children went to a later mass.

"Kids are so fidgety in church," she said. "I liked to be there alone."

Anne, who had lived in this very house for forty-five years and in Bernard all of her life, still bakes a pie now and again for a special occasion, but since all the kids moved out, there hasn't been much incentive, she said. She learned to make pies from her mother, who baked up a storm, especially during thrashing season. Anne remembered gathering berries with her siblings for her mother's pies.

"I was always so busy looking out for snakes, my bucket was rarely very full," she said. Anne still uses lard for her crust, mainly because "I never got good with that Crisco."

It was abundantly clear by the look on her face that Anne didn't want to dwell on the subject of pies.

India. Now there was something she wanted to talk about.

"My children bought me a trip to India as a present after my husband died," she said. "I was 70 years old, but I'd always wanted to go there."

Kris and I had a hard time imagining this flower petal of a woman maneuvering through India's crowded, dusty streets. I had spent a few months in India myself and knew firsthand how the sights, smells, and sounds of India assault the visitor at every turn. I also knew how India can change you. We talked about the saris, color of saffron and mint, and the cows that amble through towns smugly asserting their sacredness. She remembered the women who wandered the streets carrying carved birdcages. Each cage carried a live sparrow, and locals paid hard-earned rupees for the privilege of setting a caged bird free.

"India was the highlight of my life," said Anne. "I have a little bit of an adventurous streak, you see. I still put my hair in pin curls."

Kris asked Anne if she ever went to Dubuque to shop and if, perhaps, she had known her grandpa Tubby, and Anne's face brightened. "I used to shop at Zuckies all the time. Your grandfather had a way with the ladies, didn't he?"

Kris blushed.

We asked Anne for a favorite pie recipe and she offered up her friend Pat Larkin's lemon meringue recipe from the St. Patrick's parish cookbook.

The introduction read as follows:

You are right in suspecting that the parish had a very Irish origin, however, the pastor for the first 15 years was French. Many of the pioneer names remain in the parish, and the grandsons and daughters of the pioneers enrich the bloodstream of the parish mingled with a sturdy influx of Germans and other nationalities. Intermarriages have mixed much of the blood of these five peoples, making us typically American and melting us into the mainstream of the 20th century, holding onto, we hope, the good from the old and the new.

The recipes in this book may not have been laboratory tested, but their merit has been established by church or civic groups and the most critical group of all: husbands and families . . .

Anne walked us to the door and I commented on the height of the corn across the street. She told us the crop alternated from hay to corn year to year.

"I like it when its hay, best," she said. "With the corn, the heat just seems to close in on you."

On our way out of town, we drove the two miles along a narrow road to see the beautiful limestone church where Anne had spent so many Sundays in her own private world. The sun was a giant Sweet-Tart dropping into a cornfield. A white sheet on which someone had spray-painted "Congratulations Dan and Vera" hung from a tractor in a field where cows grazed. One cow had wandered away from the group, staking her independence in a patch of clover.

We headed northwest toward tiny Thornton, up near the Minnesota border in search of hog farmer Paul Willis. I had tasted one of his Willis's Niman-Ranch pork chops in a restaurant in New York, and it was hands-down the juiciest, sweetest pork chop I'd ever tasted. The chef said that was because Willis's hogs are allowed to roam free and are fed mostly organic foods. It stood to reason then that this farmer, who raised his pigs the old-fashioned way, would know a thing or two about old-fashioned pie.

Thornton was a one-stoplight town anchored by a gas station, a quaint corner church, and a seedy bar and grill. In a town so small (only slightly bigger than Bernard), how hard would it be to find a hog farm?

We stopped at the gas station first, where the woman at the mini-mart register said: "Make a right, then a left through town, and then, when you see a dirt road on your way out of town on your left, go *straight off.*"

Huh? We stopped at the bar and grill and tried again. This time Kris did the asking and she came out shaking her head. "What the heck does *straight off* mean?"

We drove back through town and saw an elderly couple meticulously applying the black magnetic letters for the holy message of the week at the corner church. We'd chuckled at so many of these church ditties, but had never seen one being applied. We really were on a different pace.

The gentleman, a retired schoolteacher, told us that he and his wife had recently donated the church sign to the community and, consequently, got to select its first message.

They picked: "Jesus Calls Today, Come Follow Me—to the Park for a Picnic 7/9."

The sign had cost them a pretty penny but, he said, "if we can get just one new person to come to the church because of it, it'll be worth it."

We wondered if he could maybe buy a sign for Paul Willis's hog farm next, because we were having a hard time getting there. He laughed and gave us directions. And Kris and I high-fived each other when we finally stumbled on a Willis mailbox.

We turned into a long dirt drive that bordered an open muddy field with lots of pigs lolling in a pool of mud slush to stay cool. It didn't seem like a very big operation. The outbuildings were nothing fancy, to be sure, nor was the farmhouse framed by vines and wildflowers. We knocked, no one answered.

We wandered over to the farmhouse directly across the road, to ask a guy on a tractor where Paul Willis could be found.

"Try the Dream House," he said.

"The Dream House?" Kris and I looked at each other, puzzled.

"See that dirt road on the other side of the main road?" he said. "Just take that *straight off*, then make a left on the second paved road. The Dream House is the last house on your left."

Just as its name suggested, the Dream House was a pale yellow two-story house, with a side garden and a yawning back porch. It was the house of small-town novels. Several cars were parked on the dirt drive, so we figured Paul Willis was in our midst. But all the blinds and curtains were drawn, just like at Anne's, and no one answered our knocking or our bellows.

We were pulling out of the drive when we heard a woman's voice coming from the back porch:

"Do you two girls need some help . . . or do you just need some coffee?"

We backed up. The woman was tall and strong but with a soft, pudding face. "I'm Phyllis Willis . . . Come on inside."

Her husband Paul was sitting at the kitchen table, next to his sister Anne. Oscar, their father, was also there. They all looked up at us, waiting to hear what we'd come to sell.

Everyone looked a little groggy, as we'd just roused them all from their afternoon nap.

When we assured them we were doing research for a book, not witnessing Jehovah or selling vacuum cleaners door-to-door, they relaxed.

Before launching into pie, though, I was dying to know about the Dream House.

Phyllis leaned back in her chair and smiled. "We'd always wanted a vacation home, a place where we could get away from all the stresses of the farm and of daily living," she said. "But this was the house we fell in love with—less than a mile away from home." Since Phyllis didn't like to be away from her chickens and garden for too long, it made sense, they reckoned, to buy a vacation home in the neighborhood.

"What makes it a vacation or dream house is its spirit, not its location," said Phyllis.

Unlike their real house, *this* house didn't come replete with overflowing junk or project drawers. There were no piles of bills or paperwork that needed to be filed. Stress stayed on the porch, next to muddy shoes. The entire second floor was occupied by full-size beds—just like the dwarves' house in *Snow White*.

Napping was not only allowed, but encouraged.

"In fact, if you girls need a nap . . ." said Phyllis. It sounded tempting, but we did need to get back on the pie track.

We explained the loose rules of the pie trip and how it was that a fine pork chop had landed us here. Paul told us that his father had been among the first farmers in Iowa to shy away from the "factory" approach to raising livestock. Paul followed suit, taking it one step further. He manages thirty-five small hog farms in the area, where hogs are treated as humanely as possible.

"The whole point is to raise the hogs without any sort of trauma or pain," said Paul. "Even on their way to the slaughterhouse, we forbid the use of shockers to prod them."

We asked if they knew of a place around here that treated pie crust as lovingly as Paul treated his pigs. Paul, who'd just grabbed a piece of raspberry pie that morning at the farmer's market, said the best place for pie was a bakery-café that just opened in Sheffield, in a former Methodist church.

He offered to drive us there, since he had to take Oscar back to the retirement home in time for supper. Anne and Paul were torn up about recently moving their father to the home, but it needed to be done.

Anne was visiting from California, with her son, Casey. She'd come specifically to clear out Oscar's farmhouse—an emotional task, to be sure.

We had to fly, because the café closed early on Saturdays, Paul said. So, Kris, Oscar, Paul, Anne, and I all piled into Paul's truck. Phyllis stayed behind, alone—I suspect, to finish that languid nap.

Driving past cornfields "high as an elephant's eye," Paul told us the stalks had been growing about a foot a day in the last week. "You

Our Daily Bread

really have to watch those corn corners," he said, referring to the intersections where corn was high enough to obscure oncoming cars.

Sure enough, Sue Collins was locking up her bakery-café, Our Daily Bread, when we pulled up.

She let us inside for a quick peek. The pews had been replaced by flea-market tables draped in red-and-white checkered cloth. Still, the cathedral ceiling and the arched windows were unmistakably holy. Sadly, the pies had all been sold for the weekend, said Sue.

But she dug through her recipe box and pulled out a yellowed, grease-stained index card. "Here, you can have my mother's recipe for rhubarb pie," she said. "It's popular, and I know it by heart."

Paul and Anne took turns hugging Oscar in the parking lot at the retirement home. Paul slipped behind the steering wheel and was silent for a while.

"How would you two like to see some native Iowa prairie?" he said, perking himself right up.

When early explorers like Lewis and Clark crossed Iowa, they walked knee-deep in an endless sea of tall prairie grass. More than 85 percent of the state was covered in prairie, rich with hundreds of deep-rooted plant systems.

For years, roaming herds of buffalo and elk kept the prairie low and thriving by grazing smartly and selectively. But the Homestead Act, combined with the invention of the plow by John Deere in 1837, changed the prairie and Iowa forever. By the 1860s, most of Iowa prairie had been tilled for farming. Today, less than 1 percent of Iowa's original prairie land remains pure and unplowed. And a patch of that surviving prairie belongs to Paul's good friend Daryl.

It may be Daryl's land, but these 40 acres have become Paul's raison d'être. Although slightly blasé about the hog-farming revolution he helped stir, Paul became solemn as soon as we stepped onto the prairie—a privilege not granted to many, we gathered.

Paul and Daryl have been meticulously collecting seeds from the prairie as part of a statewide effort to restore prairie lands. Paul could identify every species of flower and weed on the hilly, vital terrain, from the purple coneflowers, on their last July bloom, to the thirteen types of milkweed, a favorite snack of monarch caterpillars.

I asked Paul about the tall, sunflower-like plant I had never seen before. "Oh, that's a compass plant," he said. The plant oriented its leaves to a north-south direction, away from the sun's heat, he went on. Early settlers often relied upon its guiding foliage on foggy days, when the sun and land forms could not be relied upon for direction. Every flower and plant on this land seemed to have sprouted with a purpose, and seemed to know exactly what that purpose was.

How lucky for them.

On the way back to Thornton, we stopped in a Sheffield watering

Paul Willis and his hogs

hole where Paul was sure we'd find Daryl, to thank him in person for sharing his prairie with us. I offered to buy a round of drinks, but Daryl refused. I insisted, and, eventually, we arm-wrestled for the honor. I lost. We toasted the prairie.

Daryl told us that the sheriff had been out to his house that day, because Daryl's pet ducks had been mysteriously vanishing, one by one, from his backyard. We'd noticed signs for duck races in the area, and he suspected there might be a connection.

When we returned to the Dream House, Phyllis had made the executive decision that we were staying for dinner: pork burgers and fresh vegetables from her garden, bouncy baby lettuces and deep-green Swiss chard. This was by far the healthiest meal we'd had on this trip. And to wash it all down? A tall glass of cold whole milk— something else I lived without, growing up French.

By the time dinner was over, it was past 9 P.M., and although Kris and I were game to hit the road for Minnesota, the Willises convinced us to stay the night. Anne and Casey had Oscar's big house all to themselves.

On our way to Oscar's funky farmhouse, Anne issued a warning. Her father, she said, had an obsession with contraptions, mainly metal. Indeed, in every room, metal rods, cables, and pulley systems hung from the ceiling and jutted out from walls, in a decor I could only describe as Rube Goldberg meets Chitty Chitty Bang Bang. Even the couch sat on a raised metal frame. Above the kitchen sink, an unwieldy contraption dispensed plastic wrap. In his bedroom, Oscar had even developed a pulley system to hang-dry his boxer shorts.

We slept in a set of twins in Anne's old room—happily contraption-free. As late as it was, it was still hot as a casserole, so we left the windows wide open. In the middle of the night, a racing wind blew the curtain sheers over my face. I dreamt of coneflower petals.

We all woke up early, took long showers, and drank good coffee. On one of the Sunday-morning news shows, ironically, the topic at hand was biogenetically engineered corn. Anne groaned and changed the channel.

Paul poked his head in the kitchen door, inviting us all to the "real" house for a Sunday-morning breakfast. This family was so easy to be around, it was hard to leave. Besides, I really wanted to see how the real house compared to the Dream House. One look, and it all made sense. Paul and Phyllis Willis were pack rats.

Daryl showed up, as did a friend of Phyllis's who brought a pineapple and carved it real fancy. We grilled up pork sausages and ate them with farm-fresh eggs. Life was good.

But the road to pie beckoned. Paul offered to tighten the ropes holding down the wicker table on Betty Blue's roof, and the rear rolling pin. Anne gave us the gift of an "itch stick" for mosquito bites and some portable plug-in contraption to boil water on the road. Like daughter like father, I said. She rolled her eyes.

Phyllis came out of the house with a stack of old *Kitchen-Klatter* magazines she'd been saving since the '70s.

"Now I know why I've been hanging on to them all these years," she said, tossing them in the car. We drove off—"straight off"— toward Minnesota.

On I-35, we passed the turnoff for the town of Britt, where, I'd read, hobos have been gathering for their annual convention since the 1930s. I thought of Norman Rockwell's famous illustration of a hobo running down the street with a stolen pie still steaming in his hands.

"Hey, we didn't have a single piece of pie in this state," Kris said.

I hadn't even noticed.

PAT LARKIN'S LEMON MERINGUE PIE FROM THE ST. PATRICK'S PARISH COOKBOOK

CRUST
1 9-inch pie crust, prebaked

FILLING
1½ cups sugar
¼ cup cornstarch
dash of salt
1½ cups hot water

3 slightly beaten egg yolks
2 tablespoons milk
juice of 3 lemons
2 tablespoons butter

MERINGUE
2 egg whites
½ teaspoon of cream of tartar
½ teaspoon of salt
6 tablespoons of sugar

Mix 1½ cups of sugar, cornstarch, and salt. Gradually blend in water and bring to a boil, stirring constantly. Cook until clear. Remove from heat, add egg yolks and milk to hot mixture. Bring to a boil again, stirring constantly. Add lemon juice, reduce heat, and cook and stir for about 4 more minutes. Add butter, stir. Remove from heat and let cool for 10 minutes. Pour into a cooked pastry shell. (Use your favorite pie shell recipe and blind-bake it).

Beat 2 egg whites slightly. Add ½ teaspoon of cream of tartar and ½ teaspoon of salt. Continue beating until soft peaks form. Still beating, gradually add 6 tablespoons of sugar, one at a time. When egg whites form stiff peaks, spread meringue over the pie filling so that it touches the crust all around. Bake at 350 degrees until meringue turns golden brown—about 15–20 minutes.

SUE COLLINS'S MOM'S RECIPE FOR RHUBARB PIE FROM OUR DAILY BREAD IN SHEFFIELD, IOWA

CRUST

1½ cups of flour

½ teaspoon of sugar

½ teaspoon baking powder

¾ teaspoon of salt

½ cup of lard

4½ tablespoons of cold water

FILLING

4 cups fresh-cut rhubarb

4 tablespoons of flour

1¾ cups of sugar

2 beaten eggs

Mix one cup of the flour with the other dry ingredients, then add lard. Add water and remaining flour.

Mix filling ingredients well, pour into an unbaked pie shell and bake at 350 degrees for an hour.

PUMPKIN-APPLE PIE PLUCKED
FROM THE DECEMBER 1965 ISSUE
OF *KITCHEN-KLATTER* MAGAZINE

CRUST

Cider pastry for 1 single-crust pie

CIDER PASTRY

(MAKES TWO BOTTOM PIE CRUSTS)

2 cups flour

½ teaspoon salt

1 cup shortening

¼ cup cider

FILLING

4 large tart apples

2 tablespoons apple cider

¼ cup sugar

1 cup mashed pumpkin (canned or fresh)

¼ teaspoon salt

¼ cup light cream

1 egg, beaten

⅓ cup brown sugar

1 teaspoon cinnamon

½ teaspoon nutmeg

½ teaspoon ginger

¼ teaspoon cloves

Mix flour and salt. Cut in shortening. Mix lightly with cider to make pastry. Roll out and fit into 2 pie pans.

Peel and slice apples; combine in a saucepan with cider, sugar, and salt. Cook 10 minutes at medium heat, or until just tender. Allow to cool. Line a 9-inch pie pan with half of the cider pastry. Let chill for at least an hour. Pour cooked apples into the pie shell. In a separate bowl, combine pumpkin, salt, cream, and egg. Add sugar and spices. Stir to blend well, then pour over apples. Bake pie at 425 degrees for about 45 minutes. Serve at room temperature.

braham (as in "graham cracker"), minnesota

"If I were asked to what the singular prosperity and growing strength of that people ought mainly to be attributed, I should reply to the superiority of their women."
—ALEXIS DE TOCQUEVILLE, *DEMOCRACY IN AMERICA*

The obvious destination in Minnesota would have been Betty's in Duluth, practically world-famous for its pies. But I'd heard of a little town called Braham in east-central Minnesota, which hosts an annual Pie Day and boasts a giant mural of a deep-dish pie in the center of town.

I was curious about this small town's love affair with pie.

We could have bypassed Minneapolis altogether, but since we were so close and had both been weaned on the *Mary Tyler Moore*

Show, we thought we should at least try to find the famous intersection where Mary Richards tossed her wool hat in the air, maybe even fling our baseball caps in solidarity.

City centers can be so stark and depressing on Sundays, and Minneapolis was no exception. We drove around in circles, recalling favorite episodes, and wondering why it was that Mary never stood up to Mr. Grant when she was in his office, or how Rhoda could fit all of that furniture in her tiny studio apartment. We finally gave up and headed for Braham.

Garrison Keillor kept us entertained on the drive north. We particularly enjoyed a sketch on the myriad uses for duct tape, having just borrowed some from Paul Willis that morning to strap that darn glove-compartment door shut.

Braham (pop. 1,300) is so small, we had no trouble finding the mural painted on the side of the Tusen Tack store right where Main Avenue hits Route 60.

We parked across the street from the mural, and leaned against

Betty Blue to admire it from a distance. It was a big pie, all right. Berry, judging from the purple-red drippings. Ribbons of steam billowed from the tawny top crust, its edges coarsely crimped. The mural was bordered with heavy ceramic coffee cups, giving it a real diner feel. The painting was so absorbing and comforting, we barely noticed the elderly woman slowly pedaling past us on her squeaky three-speed bike. I caught her cherry-red tennis shoes in the corner of my eye.

"Excuse me, do you know anything about this mural?" I shouted after her. She made a big circle in the empty street and rode back toward us. I don't know if she was tickled by out-of-towners ogling her hometown mural or if she was just plain happy to be alive and exercising at the end of a glorious summer day, but she was beaming.

She introduced herself as Jerrie Aune, and she wore her Scandinavian ancestry in her high cheekbones, her thin-lipped smile, and the slight tilt of the head.

"Well, you *do* know you're in the 'homemade pie' capital of Minnesota, *don't* you?"

"Braham? Really?"

She laughed demurely.

"It's *Bra*-ham, like the *gra*-ham cracker," she said. "Braaaaaaam."

I had been mispronouncing Braham since we first saw it on the map, giving it a mystical twist—as in Brahman.

"For more than fifty years," she said, "people driving from Minneapolis to Duluth have been taking the shortcut through Braham and stopping for pie at the Park Café."

Of course, I pointed out, it's not much of a shortcut if you stopped and ate a slice of pie at the café.

"No, I guess not," she agreed.

She popped the kickstand on her bike and faced the mural as we did, her hands on her hips.

Her father opened the café in 1946. It had changed hands several times since, but the "hands" have always made the pies from scratch to keep the café's reputation intact.

The Park Café was already closed for the night, she said, "but if you want to come to my house, I have all sorts of information about the town and the Pie Day festival."

So we climbed back in the car and, at 10 miles per hour, followed Jerrie across Route 107 (called Pie Tin Alley as it goes through Braham) past the old railroad tracks and to her quiet, tree-lined neighborhood. Her husband, Herman, was reading the Sunday paper in the living room, and he didn't seem the least bit surprised that his wife could go out for her evening exercise and come back with two strangers. Jerrie poured us each a tall glass of cranberry juice and set out a tray of pecan-turtle cookies she kept in her freezer for surprise guests.

No sooner had we finished explaining our quest to the Aunes than Jerrie grabbed the phone and asked her friend Phyllis Londgren to come over.

"Phyllis is our own Barbara Walters," she explained. "She knows *everything* about Braham."

"But I have to warn you . . . she's *very* intense." I could hear Herman snicker from his recliner. "That Phyllis. She's something all right."

Herman had the most amazing way of looking at his wife. Miss Sweden could have walked into the living room in a bikini and stilettos, and Herman would barely notice. The two had met their senior year at Braham High School where Herman had gone on to become the music teacher and bandleader.

Herman knew what about Jerrie had caught his eye back in high school, but he wanted to know what had made us stop her on her bike.

"Those snappy red tennis shoes," I said. "If she hadn't been wearing them, we might have photographed the mural and forged on to South Dakota."

Herman crinkled his nose. "I really like those a lot, too," he said.

Then Herman excused himself to go find something he thought I might be interested in. He returned ten minutes (and three pecan turtles later) with the September 1956 issue of *Ideals* magazine, which contained the following Harriet Beecher Stowe excerpt on pie:

> *The pie is an English institution which planted on American soil forthwith ran rampant and burst forth into an untold variety of genera and species. Not merely the old traditional mince pie, but a thousand strictly American seedlings from that main stock, evinced the power of American housewives to adapt old institutions to new uses. Pumpkin pies, cranberry pies, huckleberry, cherry, green currant, peach, pear and plum, custard, apple, Marlborough pudding—pies with top crusts and pies without, pies adorned with all sorts of fanciful flutings and architectural strips laid across and around and otherwise varied, attested the boundless fertility of the feminine mind, when once let loose in a given direction.*
>
> *Fancy the heat and vigor of the great pan formation, when Aunt Lois and Aunt Keziah and my mother and grandmother all in ecstasies of creative inspiration, ran, bustled and hurried, mixing, rolling, tasting, consulting, alternately setting us children to work when anything could be made of us and then chasing us all out of the kitchen when our misinformed childhood ventured to take too many liberties with sacred mysteries. Then out we would all fly at the kitchen door, like sparks from a blacksmith's window.*

The doorbell rang and Phyllis Londgren blew in like a twister. Her arms were loaded down with history books, folders, pictures, and even official Braham pie tins—as though she had been preparing for this moment for years.

Careful to pronounce Braham correctly, I asked Phyllis how the town had earned the title of pie capital of the state, particularly when lutefisk eaters across Minnesota speak so highly of Betty's Pies, off of old Highway 61, in Duluth.

The mere mention of Betty's made Phyllis bristle.

"Betty's may have good pies, but *Braham* is the pie capital," she said, and, in one long uninterrupted breath that would have put Harry Houdini to shame, recounted the story.

It all started when state officials launched a "Celebrate Minnesota" campaign to promote tourism across the state. They encouraged smaller communities to "brighten themselves up a little," put their best foot forward, even host an annual celebration of some sort. Since Braham had long been known for its Park Café pies, Phyllis suggested at a civic meeting that the town host an annual Pie Day. The first festival was held on July 20, 1990. All the church ladies of Braham made pies by the dozen. There was a pie-eating contest for the kids. "It was all very garden-variety," Phyllis said.

About a year later, then-governor Rudy Perpich stopped into the Park Café unannounced, with his wife, after visiting a local rodeo. Perpich had made a campaign stop at the café once, and he'd remembered the pies.

Phyllis heard that the governor was in the house, as it were, and she raced over to the Park Café. "I grabbed a pot of coffee and refilled his cup and then I sat down right next to him in the booth," she said.

"And that's when I told him, 'Governor, you should name Braham the Homemade Pie Capital of Minnesota!' "

Phyllis pounded her fist on the table so hard that both Herman and the pecan turtles jumped. Phyllis popped one in her mouth.

"Jerrie, you're a regular Perle Mesta!" she said.

Because no one ever says no to Phyllis, the governor's official proclamation arrived in the mail within days and was immediately hung in the main dining room of the Park Café. Bolstered by its official status, the town's annual Pie Day just grew and grew until it finally required a committee to make preparations year-round.

A group of women named the Peach Ladies—all in their 70s and 80s—are called in to peel and slice buckets of peaches for the event. Entertainers are flown in from Sweden, and competitive pie bakers travel from as far as Maine to participate in the various contests.

"It's gotten totally out of control," said Phyllis, beaming. Of course, with expansion have come problems.

A few years ago, the committee approved a "cow pie" contest, in which festivalgoers had to guess in which section of an open pasture a Holstein would leave, ahem, a *cow* pie.

"The Swansons would bring in a couple of their heifers, and then you'd have to wait all day for those cows to crap," Phyllis said, rolling her eyes. The event was shelved after three years. Herman snickered.

Pie Day has even had its first political scandal.

To celebrate and cement its new identity as the "pie capital," the people of Braham decided to put out a cookbook of prize-winning pie recipes in 1993. They solicited pie recipes from all over the state to compete in a number of categories. The clear winner in the custard-and-cream pie category was the creamy peach pie "family" recipe submitted by a certain state senator. None of the judges noticed that the creamy peach pie, made with Jell-O, ice cream, and instant-pudding mix, was, in fact, absolutely peachless. The local press had a field day. What's more, the governor's "family" recipe had, in fact, come from the back of a General Foods package. The scandal erupted the same week said governor had been slapped with a paternity suit.

Phyllis insisted we meet with the pie committee at the Park Café early in the morning before leaving town. She would make sure Gary, the high school media center director, would be there. Gary was in charge of the pie-baking contest, she said, and "he's a *very* eligible bachelor." She winked at each of us.

Phyllis snapped a picture of us in front of our license plate. Then she handed me a soft-cover book the size of *Webster's Dictionary*, on the history of Braham—a little something she threw together for Braham's centennial.

Our heads were spinning when we got in the car. As much as we loved Phyllis, we thought of calling up Garrison Keillor and suggesting another use for duct tape.

There were still about thirty minutes of daylight left, so, as soon as we got to the dreary Cambridge Imperial Motel about 12 miles away, we put on our roller blades and headed toward the local high school, where we bladed in circles in the newly paved parking lot to work off our day's intake of calories: pork sausage and pecan turtles.

I stayed up far too late reading about the history of Braham, with characters straight out of Lake Wobegon.

My favorite was J. Wallace Rock, an undertaker and fireman who also served as city clerk for thirty-four years. Rock always did his books in the mortuary or the fire hall. I learned that the "pooper-scooper" was invented in Braham, and that Braham was also the birthplace of the first handheld egg beater.

I stayed up so late reading that I managed to sleep right through the alarm. The committee was waiting for us at the café, tapping pencils, at a U-shaped table when we came screeching in, without our morning coffee, "like sparks from a blacksmith's window."

We were surprised at how serious everyone was about Pie Day, especially Gary the Bachelor, a real stickler about the entry rules for the contest. The event was only a couple of weeks away, and, clearly, nerves were a tad frayed.

What's more, the committee was on pins and needles, waiting to hear if their request to have a highway sign posted on Route 107 promoting Braham as Minnesota's pie capital had been approved.

No one was more serious than pie baker Lola Nebel. Though not on the committee herself, Lola had gotten a call from Phyllis late the night before, urging her to attend our breakfast meeting.

Lola had been the first-prize winner at the very first pie-baking contest at the first Pie Day in 1990. She had since gone on to win several state-fair sweepstakes and had even recently been a finalist in the Pillsbury bake-off held in San Francisco.

"I guess I've always been kind of competitive," she said, her hands resting on her stack of winning recipes.

Marilyn McGriff, a local historian and librarian, was much more low-key, even though she is the one who is ultimately responsible for getting five hundred pies baked for Pie Day each year.

"Basically, we've got it down to a science now," said Marilyn. "As long as you're breathing, you can volunteer to help make pies for Pie Day."

The pies are prepared over a three-day period, with volunteers working three shifts a day, mixing the dough, then pressing the crust in tins, then filling the shells and layering them with a top crust. The pies are baked off in the high school cafeteria—about eighty at a time. Most of the pies are fruit: rhubarb, raspberry, cranberry, and apple, and many combinations thereof, she said, because the local health inspector, rightly, had "issues" with cream pies being sold on the sidewalk unrefrigerated.

Pies are so integral to the identity of Braham that when Marilyn visits local schools on Community Day, she always brings a just-baked pie to illustrate the meaning of community.

"I tell the children that every community needs a good foundation and infrastructure—*that's* the crust," she said. "The filling is made up of churches, businesses, banks, and schools—all the things that make a community work.

"The fluted or crimped edges are more decorative than essential," she went on. "They are the trees on Main Avenue, the gazebo in Freedom Park. They are what makes a community a much more pleasant place to live."

The banana cream pie at the Park Café is what makes Braham such a nice place to live, a customer at the counter chimed in. "We never go without it," said owner Ellie Grell.

Kris and I ordered a slice of fresh rhubarb with a Dutch-crumb topping instead. It looked healthier, and maybe we needed some tartness to transition back to the real world.

When I returned to New York, there were two pieces of mail with a Braham postmark waiting for me. One was Lola Nobel's recipe for Rosy Raspberry Pear pie, which follows. The other was a copy of the July 22 issue of the *Star,* Braham's local newspaper, with the words "See Page 4" scribbled on the front page.

I turned to Page 4 and saw this screaming headline:

"Pie Book Author to Include Braham in U.S. Pie Book."

Beneath the headline was a very large picture of Kris and me, standing next to Betty Blue, in the Aunes' driveway. Jerrie and Herman are standing close together, on their lawn, off to the side. Oddly enough, the setting sun is hitting the IBRK4PIE license plate in such a way that is glows.

"Your license plate looks like a halo," Phyllis Londgren had scribbled on a Post-it note affixed to the article, which was, I'm guessing, written by her, although it had no byline.

The article related our visit—blow-by-blow—and ended with this paragraph:

By the time they left Braham, around noon, they had a vast amount of information regarding the role pie plays in east cen-

tral Minnesota. There are many in Braham who are looking forward to the book. The author had not arrived at a title yet, but Braham hopes to be one of the first communities to know when the book is available as well as its title . . .

You betcha, Phyllis.

LOLA NEBEL'S
ROSY RASPBERRY PEAR PIE

CRUST

1 15 oz. package Pillsbury Refrigerated Pie Crust, softened as directed on package

FILLING

3 firm ripe pears, peeled and cut into ½ inch slices

1 tablespoon lemon juice

½ teaspoon almond extract

¾ cup sugar

3 tablespoons all-purpose or unbleached flour

1 cup fresh or frozen whole raspberries without syrup, partially thawed

1 tablespoon butter or margarine, melted

1 tablespoon sugar

Heat the oven to 400 degrees. Prepare pie crusts as directed on the package for one-crust filled pie using 9-inch pie pan. Reserve second crust for cutouts.

In a large bowl, combine pears, lemon juice, and almond extract; toss to coat. Add ¾ cup sugar and flour; mix well. Spoon about half of pear mixture into crust-lined pan. Top with raspberries. Spoon remaining pear mixture over raspberries. With 2½-inch floured round cookie cutter, cut 9 rounds from second pie crust. Brush each with melted butter. Place 8 rounds, butter side up, in a circle on the outer edge of fruit, overlapping as necessary. Place one round in center. Sprinkle rounds with 1 tablespoon sugar.

Bake at 400 degrees for 40–50 minutes, or until the crust is golden brown and the filling is bubbly. If necessary, cover the edge of crust with strips of foil after 15–20 minutes of baking to prevent excessive browning. Cool 3 hours, or until completely cooled. If desired, serve with vanilla ice cream.

political pie

Bachelor Pie: it's what cowboys ate on the wagon trail . . . basically a quick biscuit dough filled with whatever filling was handy or available, such as prairie oysters (bull testicles) sliced thin and fried in bacon grease.

My rough plan for the camel-skin plains of South Dakota was to get invited to one of those weeknight church socials. I hear they are big in the Mount Rushmore state. And they almost *always* serve pie.

Shortly before leaving New York, I met a fashion photographer named Sean who was from Aberdeen, South Dakota, a hog's breath away from the North Dakota border.

Sean was feeling homesick. Pining for the one diner in Aberdeen that served good pie. I told him that maybe I'd check it out when I got to South Dakota.

In the following week, I received a barrage of e-mails from Sean. He had telephoned all of his relatives in and around Aberdeen to tell them we might be coming through. Even Mel, a friend of the family who lives in Eureka and still roasts fresh pumpkins for his pie, had been put on pie alert.

Sean had made it so easy.

Perhaps—on the heels of sugar-coated Braham and in a state known for its harshness—*too* easy.

So when Betty Blue crossed over into South Dakota from Minnesota, I told Kris we were bagging Aberdeen and heading south, instead of north, straight for the Badlands.

"Huh?"

I pointed to my gut.

She switched lanes.

. . .

It was almost dark, and our plan was to drive as far west as we could manage that night so that we could make it to the Badlands, clear across the plains, by the following afternoon.

Route 14 was dark as a bat cave, for long stretches at a time. We drove through De Smet, where Laura Ingalls Wilder and her family homesteaded.

I took in a deep breath and got a faint whiff of those thick Wilder books I used to borrow from the Santa Monica public library.

It was my father who taught me to smell books. Every September, when my sister and I would get our new batch of textbooks, my father, his own schooling halted by war, would crack them open and sniff.

"This," he would say, "is the smell of knowledge."

In Huron, I smelled trouble. Lots of hotels, not a vacancy sign in sight. "Sorry, ladies. Truckers keep us booked solid 365 nights a year," said hotel clerk after hotel clerk. "You won't find anything until Pierre."

Pierre was a long, dark, and lonely hour away.

Kris handed me the keys. "We'd have found pie and gone to bed already if we'd stuck with the plan and gone to Aberdeen."

She passed out as soon as she buckled in. What kept me awake was a gas gauge close to bone dry.

I was never so happy to see a blinking neon vacancy sign, right at the entrance of Pierre.

Mike, the owner, was remarkably perky at this late hour—about 2 A.M.

"We have a really nice pool," he said as I signed the credit card slip. He was curious about the license plate and rolling pins. I gave him the abridged version of the quest, and then we retired to our rooms and collapsed ourselves.

In the morning, we got up early enough to swim laps and work off some crankiness. At lap forty, I stopped to catch my breath and felt a light tap on my swim cap. I looked up, and there was Mike, chipper as ever.

"I've been thinking about your pie adventure," he said. "Did you know that pie is a political force in South Dakota?"

I shook my head from side to side, to clear water from my ears.

"There was a big scandal a couple of years back. Something about voters being bribed with pie during elections."

OK. This was good. Worth getting out of the water for. He handed me a towel. His details were sketchy, but he suggested that we walk on over to the Capitol building and talk to the governor. "He'll fill you in."

"We're just going to waltz right into the governor's office?" Kris said, as we crossed the Capitol building's beautiful gardens thirty minutes later, our hair still wet.

"Apparently so," I said. The black domed Capitol building was exquisite and so clean, we could have rolled out a pie dough right there on the rotunda's shiny marble floor.

"We're here to talk to the governor about pie," I said to a man who looked fairly official standing in a doorway.

The man whisked us into his office. His name was Larry Long and he was the deputy attorney general. He said it was actually his boss, Mark Barnett, the attorney general, who was behind *l'affaire* pie. Barnett, who just happened to be eyeing the governor's seat, was not in the office that day, but Long would happily fill us in.

It all started when Attorney General Barnett decided to clamp down on an age-old law barring enticements on Election Day. The law had been on the books since 1891, but it had resurfaced in 1994 with reports that Democrats had been serving lunch to voters on local Indian reservations on Election Day.

Barnett, a Republican, drafted a letter describing the law's intent and sent it, as a gentle reminder, to all political parties and election officials in every town and South Dakota municipality.

It just so happens that for more than eighty years, the little old ladies of Wasta (pop. 70) had been baking pies from scratch, to serve and sell on Election Day. Since Wasta, a former cattle turn, is made up largely of ranchers, the Election Day pie social provided just the right incentive for farmers to hang up their overalls for the day and come to town. For many, it was the only socializing they did all year. Sure, it was a bribe. A bribe to get farmers to come out and vote, though for whom, it did not matter.

So you can imagine how upset the people of Wasta were when they found out that their sweet tradition, which had also helped them raise money for their church and community center, was now illegal.

Wasta's indignation and outrage made the local newspapers. And, on Election Day that year, only 49 percent of the 109 eligible voters turned out in Wasta, down almost 20 percent from the last nonpresidential election in 1994.

Commentator Charles Osgood read a little ditty about the scandal on the air.

No fool, Barnett fired off a poem of his own to prove that he wasn't antipie:

There was a town called Wasta
where they fed the voters pie.
The people came from miles around
To vote and nibble, eye to eye

It was fine tradition
These hot apple pies from Mom
Until the prosecutors
dropped a legal bomb
The law, you see, is very clear . . .
No pie, no steak, not even beer!
The Legislature's spoken,
The tradition must be broken.
Said one hungry rancher:
"Who will make this nightmare right?
We hardly get a turnout
If there isn't food in sight."
"I can't help you with your problem,"
Said the General on his horse . . .
"If it's pie that is the trouble
I will buy you some, of course!
"Come ye to the Capitol
To see the Christmas trees . . .
A week before the Lord is born,
Is when we plan to please
"Have your pie and eat it too . . .
On the 19th of December
We'll bring the food and hope you have
A Christmas to remember!"

And so, a bus came to Wasta on the 19th of December to whisk
its residents to Pierre for pie. Only twenty-eight Wasta residents for-
gave the attorney general enough to attend. They ate deer salami on
the bus ride to the capitol and brought Barnett a cow-pie clock to
show there were no hard feelings.

We were heading for Wasta.

· · ·

After days of gazing at endless silos, in South Dakota our gaze rose to the dramatic sky, which seemed higher than it had been until now.

We stopped to take pictures of a wild horse on a ridge and it started to canter along the ridgeline, mane flying, the moment we approached. It was easy to see why Kevin Costner had come to the dramatic Dakotas to film his epic *Dances with Wolves*. We stopped in Philip for gas and strawberry popsicles, which tasted divine in this heat, even if they made our tongues vixen-red.

In the middle of nowhere we stumbled on a small pioneer museum where we learned that cowboys used to call the chuck wagon "the pie box," because pie could always be counted on after a day of cattle rustling *and* it was the warmest spot on the cattle spread.

In Badlands National Park, we took a quick walk through the moonscape. I felt like Frank Lloyd Wright who, upon seeing the Dakota Badlands for the first time, said: "I was totally unprepared for the revelation called the Dakota Badlands . . . What I saw gave me an indescribable sense of mysterious elsewhere—a distant architecture, ethereal . . . an endless supernatural world more spiritual than earth but created out of it."

Nothing could yank us further from this spiritual beauty than the garish signs for Wall Drug.

It would have been un-American, I guess, not to stop at the famous drugstore. Besides, we'd been brainwashed by the hundreds of arrogant road signs advertising the store since we crossed into South Dakota from Wisconsin. For endless miles of crew-cut prairie on either side of the highway (quite different from the prairie Paul the Hog Farmer had shown us in Iowa), the only splashes of color were painted Wall Drug signs: WALL DRUG OR BUST, ONLY 5 CENTS COFFEE, WALL DRUG.

Ted and Dorothy Hustead moved to Wall from Canover, South Dakota, in 1931, hoping to make a living in this impoverished town of 326. Their family thought they were crazy. Not only was the drugstore in the center of nowhere, but the Depression and drought had made the residents, mostly ranchers, dirt poor.

The Husteads, who lived with their young son in a room behind the Main Street shop, took in only $360 the first month. They gave themselves five years to make a go of it. Six months shy of their do-or-die deadline, business was still slow as diner ketchup.

One particularly hot afternoon in July, Dorothy went home for a nap. The rumbling of the jalopies on Highway 16 kept her awake. What could they do to persuade these drivers to pull off the highway and visit the drugstore, she asked herself, staring up at the ceiling. And then she got an idea: what if they put out on the highway a sign advertising free ice water—something any driver would go out of his way for on a scorching day.

Her husband was skeptical at first, but he and their 9-year-old son planted a wooden sign on the highway that read: GET A SODA/GET ROOT BEER/TURN NEXT CORNER/JUST AS NEAR/TO HIGHWAY 16 AND 14/FREE ICE WATER/WALL DRUG."

It wasn't Wordsworth, Ted Hustead quipped years later, but it worked. By the time they returned to the drugstore, it was crowded with customers. They came for the water, yes, but many left with a piece of toffee candy, or an ice cream cone. The following summer, the Husteads added more signs and the store got so busy they put behind the counter salesgirls in candy cane–striped A-line dresses. Within a few years, the place with the free ice water had evolved into what many call "The Mother of All Tourist Attractions."

Since they'd worked so well for him, Ted Hustead became obsessed with the painted-wood road signs, planting them in every state in the union. The signs have since come down because of Lady

Bird Johnson's Highway Beautification Act, which was passed by a pressured Congress in 1965. Fortunately, Hustead got himself appointed to the South Dakota Transportation Commission to protect the signs in his state. In time, Hustead was spending about $300,000 annually on road signs. Some cropped up on London buses, near the Taj Mahal, and in the train stations of Kenya. Many of the signs still visible in Germany, Korea, and Vietnam were placed there by homesick GIs from South Dakota.

On a good day in summer, about twenty thousand visitors visit the 75,000-square-foot Wall Drug, which stretches across several city blocks and takes in $10 million in sales a year. For the busy summer months, the Husteads hire a fleet of eager workers, from senior citizens to European exchange students, to handle the crowds.

In the fudge shop (kitty corner from the Travelers Chapel and the Apothecary Shoppe) we met a young woman named Luciana who was visiting for the summer from Slovakia. Her English was limited; still, she managed to convey that she had already gained two kilos in the two weeks.

We told Luciana we could relate. We explained all about our road trip, and she was envious of how much of the country we were seeing—since she was confined to the drugstore for the summer. She'd learned about Rocky Road and marshmallows but she was curious about the "pie."

We told her she'd have to have a slice of pie before heading home, because as fond as Americans are of fudge, pie is the quintessential American dessert. Luciana thanked us for the tip.

We couldn't wait to get out of this crazy crowded place, and we were about to make a clean break when we noticed a sign for homemade pie, pointing to the cafeteria.

We bought one slice for us for later, and one for Luciana. She was sweeping the shop when we returned. She happily accepted our slice

of pie, which she gobbled right in front of us. With every bite, she nodded approvingly, heaping us and the wedge of America in her hand with compliments.

Feeling righteous about our good deed, we headed toward Wasta, about 20 miles away, in pitch darkness. Fortunately, the town motel with the pink neon sign had a room for us. Esther, the motel owner, was really friendly and chortled when she laughed, like a chipmunk. She'd always dreamed of owning a vintage motel. After putting in forty years in the office of a trucking company in Minneapolis, she heard this one in Wasta was for sale and she started a new grand-plains life for herself.

We poured ourselves some bourbon in plastic cups and sat in the tomato-red vintage chairs outside our motel-room door, going over our day. I brought out our slice of Wall Drug pie to eat in the moon-light. It was truly a perfect moment. Then we took a bite of the pie. It was foul. Chemical-tasting. This pie was about as far removed from an apple tree or a flour-dusted rolling pin as Luciana was from home.

Poor Luciana! To think she would go back to Central Europe thinking that she'd tasted the quintessential American dessert!

"I feel like I've contributed to the delinquency of a minor," I told Kris.

We managed to fall asleep anyway, like Dorothy Hustead, to the rumble of trucks on I-90.

In the morning, we told Esther we were looking for some of the pie-baking ladies of Wasta. Esther suggested we talk to Lloyd and Margee, first. The couple was renovating a turn-of-the-century buttercup-yellow hotel around the corner. "They know everyone in Wasta."

Lloyd and Margee, who had moved to Wasta a couple of years earlier from Los Angeles, were in spackling mode when we knocked on the door. Esther had called ahead, so they were expecting us and invited us into their living room for a chat.

Both had gone to school in the Rapid City area, then went their separate ways and, coincidentally, ended up out west, she as a sheep farmer in Utah, he as a computer consultant just outside of Los Angeles. They reconnected at a high school reunion in 1988. Both were going through a divorce at the time, and so they made a date for five days later. They'd been together ever since.

"There's a unique trust and friendship that develops when you've known someone since you were a child," said Margee. "There is much to be said about where you come from. The thing about Lloyd is that he knows the little things about growing up in

South Dakota. He knows that you always bring a pumpkin pie and a lemon meringue pie to a funeral. That's a South Dakota thing."

What they also both knew was that they were not cut out for life in Los Angeles and both wanted to go home, to their prairie roots. They found this old hotel that needed some care. Margee would like to turn it into some sort of artists' retreat or a cozy hideaway for family reunions. They seemed happy in their new surroundings.

"It's not Wasta per se that makes the experience, it's the people," said Lloyd. "Here, they don't know about plastics, or the Bloods and the Crips. But they know about the stars and the price of hogs and when it's time to cut the corn. They know how to treat people, that's what they know."

Since their arrival, Lloyd and Margee have plunged themselves into local politics. In addition to trying to get their hotel, which was built around 1906, listed as a historical monument, Margee was trying to get the community center a sorely needed face-lift. Barnett's pie party aside, she said, the pie scandal created deep fractures in the community.

She suggested we talk to Ruth Bruce, a longtime Wasta resident who had been making pies for Election Day since the 1940s. Ruth and her husband, Charles, had recently moved to an assisted-living facility in Rapid City, due to his failing health.

We thanked Lloyd and Margee, told them we might be back some day, maybe to rent a room for the summer to work on a book, and then we headed for Rapid City.

Ruth came to Wasta to teach in the new schoolhouse in 1941. Six months later, she met Charles, who delivered gas to farmers for Standard Oil. He'd asked permission from the town doctor to take her out on a date. They'd been married fifty-five years. With her husband as sick as he was, shy Ruth seemed like a doe caught in the headlights.

She made it clear she didn't want to make waves about what happened in Wasta. Didn't want to stir up any more trouble.

"I just think those folks in the capital misunderstood what the pie was all about," Ruth said. "It was all social, not political. The bachelor ranchers would buy whole pies to take home, and we'd make a little extra money for the church."

"Sometimes politics gets in the way of common sense," she said, "don't you agree?"

We asked Ruth if there was one pie that was particularly popular in Wasta, and Ruth didn't skip a beat: "Mildred Snook's Sour Cream Raisin pie," she said. "I once saw a woman on the elections board eat three pieces in one sitting."

Mildred lived on a cattle-and-wheat ranch with her husband. "She was a real hardworking ranch lady. They didn't have children but they were active in the community and she was a member of the Rebecca Lodge," Ruth said, still visibly impressed by Mildred's flair, so many years after her death.

Ruth had been making Mildred's pie for years.

"I got the recipe from Mildred herself. There are some people in Wasta who won't share their recipes. There was one lady in particular who would tell only part of the recipe but keep a part of it to herself, so that it never came out right."

Ruth dug through her recipe file and brought out a yellowed sheet of paper with Mildred's recipe.

"The meringue's tricky," she said, looking it over. "You better hope nothing comes to distract you or it will burn."

Charles, who'd barely said a word, except to agree that Mildred's pie was best, shuffled with his walker into the bedroom, in search of something to show us, too. He returned flashing his Black Hills Ordnance Unit Badge.

Ruth said she learned to make pies just by watching her mother. Eventually, without any fanfare or ceremony, the roles were switched in the kitchen and Ruth's mother started watching her. The roles of this sweet couple had also been reversed, it seemed.

Kris wanted to take a portrait of Ruth and Charles on the couch, below an old, framed aerial photograph of Wasta taken in the middle of last century. Charles reached over and put his arm around Ruth's shoulder, sneaky-like, as though he were 14 again, stealing a grab at the picture show. Ruth put her hand on his thigh.

We left the retirement home and smiled at the dinner menu posted in the lobby. Dessert was pumpkin pie.

MILDRED SNOOK'S SOUR CREAM RAISIN PIE

CRUST:

1 9-inch baked pie crust

FILLING

1 cup raisins

¼ cup water

1 cup sugar

1 cup sour cream

2 egg yolks, lightly beaten

2 tablespoons flour or cornstarch as a thickener

1 teaspoon vanilla

MERINGUE

2 egg whites

½ teaspoon of cream of tartar

½ teaspoon of salt

6 tablespoons of sugar

Put raisins in a pot and cover with ¼ cup of water. Simmer gently until tender, about 20 minutes. Add remaining filling ingredients and simmer, stirring often, until thick. Cool slightly and pour into pie shell.

Beat egg whites slightly. Add cream of tartar and salt. Continue beating until soft peaks form. Still beating, gradually add sugar, one tablespoon at a time. When egg whites form stiff peaks, spread meringue over the pie filling so that it touches the crust all around. Bake at 350 degrees until meringue turns golden brown—about 15–20 minutes.

more political pie

"Maybe seeing the (Dakota) Plains is like seeing an icon:
what seems stern and almost empty is merely open,
a door into some simple and holy state."
—KATHLEEN NORRIS, *DAKOTA: A SPIRITUAL GEOGRAPHY*

When the plan to carve the likenesses of four presidents into the craggy granite rock of Mount Rushmore was first announced in the mid-1920s, there were protests. Early-day environmentalists argued that the natural beauty of the rock had been designed by a higher authority and should not be defaced—or re-faced, as it were.

Had the project been completed today, no doubt protesters would have thrown a pie in sculptor Gutzon Borglum's face.

Pie throwing is the latest nonviolent form of protest in vogue among antiestablishment groups seeking spotlights on their cause.

In the last few years, victims of "pie smooshing" have included San Francisco mayor Willie Brown, Bill Gates, and fur-loving fashion designer Michael Kors.

The most notorious pie thrower is Noel Godin, of Belgium, who also goes by Georges Le Gloupier. It was Godin who masterminded the pie-pelting of Gates in Brussels in 1998. For that highly publicized ambush, more than thirty activists—all members of Godin's International Patisserie Brigade—hid pies under their coats and in camera bags.

Godin told the *New York Times* that he'd targeted the Microsoft mogul for the simple reason that "he chooses to function in the service of the capitalist status quo without really using his intelligence or his imagination."

Not that a pie in the face is very original.

Buster Keaton elevated pie throwing to an art form in the 1940s. Keaton developed all sorts of slinging styles ranging from "the catcher's pie throw" to the "Roman discus pie throw."

The first time he flung a pie was in the 1939 movie *Hollywood Cavalcade*. Alice Faye was his target, and Keaton practiced by throwing a wooden plate at a wall on which he'd drawn, with chalk, a circle the approximate size of Faye's head. Keaton even drove nails into the plate to make it as heavy as the real custard pie he would actually toss. He learned the hard way that a double-bottom crust was essential to prevent the pie from crumbling midflight.

If he was pieing a blonde, Keaton liked to use a chocolate, strawberry, or blackberry filling for contrast. For brunettes, lighter lemon meringue was the flavor of choice.

Most of the young, radical pie throwers these days use vegan or organic pies made with a tofu custard. As much as I support many of their causes, I cannot endorse any pie made with tofu.

That, I'm afraid, is as serious an offense as a capitalist lack of imagination.

montana,

the mother lode

"Every blade of grass has its angel that
bends over it and whispers, 'Grow, grow.' "
—THE TALMUD

I've always admired doctors who can engage in small talk in the examination room. My doctor in San Francisco was unusually chatty and during my last physical, before I drove to my new life in New York, he talked at length about huckleberry pie.

"You can't drive across America and not go to Montana for huckleberry pie," he said. His in-laws were from Montana and "ever since I tasted huckleberry pie there . . . say AAAAHHHHH . . . *no* pie has compared."

Unfortunately, I wasn't taking a northern route on that trip. But when I set out for the second trek, I put Montana at the top of my list.

I'd only been to Montana once, briefly, for the wedding of my friends Doug and Susann. They were living in Los Angeles at the time, but the ceremony was held high on a wind-kissed ridge near Livingston, where their log home would soon be built.

I didn't try any huckleberry pie that weekend, but I did get a dizzying dose of that stretched blue canvas that passes for sky there and knew I wanted more.

Kris and I entered the state from the bottom southeast corner on a hot morning in late July. Route 212 showed us nothing but flat river valley for a long time. We passed a slew of small, two-bit towns with abandoned homesteads and the occasional gas station. Betty Blue's windows were open, and the air outside felt hollow and quiet, like the ripping silence of a hawk circling its prey. We stopped in Broadus to get some gas. I pumped and Kris went to forage for some snacks in the mini-mart.

"Nice license plate."

I turned and saw a lanky man sitting—his back against the gas-station brick wall, one knee bent—in the shadow of his Harley. He had helmet hair, wore dark shades, and was eating Oreos.

"Yours isn't so bad either," I said, noticing the "My Honi" plate on his '98 Road King.

Tom worked in a plant that made aerosol cans, in Wisconsin. A high-pressure job, he said, in more ways than one. His favorite escape was a long, winding ride on his bike, alone or with his bike club, the Fairbault chapter of HOG (Harley Owners Group). I asked if they were anything like the Hell's Angels.

"Naaa. We're much more family-oriented," he said. "The highlight of most rides is stopping for ice cream at a Dairy Queen . . . Unless we're in Duluth, then we stop at Betty's, of course, for pie."

Phyllis Londgren's ears were ringing for sure.

Tom said he used to have a drinking problem and since he turned in the bottle, he'd developed a craving for sweets that just wouldn't quit.

"I know it sounds weird, but now I get my kicks out of sugar. I've got this thing for chocolate silk and peanut butter pies."

He was heading toward Billings, though his route was a little fuzzy. Tom had sketched out a detailed itinerary for his two-week solo ride, but had left his map on the kitchen table at home.

"Accidentally?" I asked. He shrugged.

Today he was going to visit the historic site of the battle of Little

Big Horn but tomorrow was a question mark. He liked not knowing where he'd be from one day to the next. Not knowing the next can would roll off that assembly line as sure as the odometer would click over at the next mile and every one after that.

Tom seemed lonely, but he also seemed to know he still had a few demons left to conquer before he could let anybody else ride on that bike with him.

We left the gas station at the same time. It was understood that Betty Blue would fall in behind Honi. For the next 150 miles or so, we followed his one-note silhouette on the highway. He leaned far back on his banana seat, the scenery yielding like an open book before him. He rode like someone who knew exactly where he was going.

We passed rivers with funny names like Pumpkin, Rosebud, and Tongue, and then we honked and waved good-bye to Tom as he turned off to the site where Custer met his doom.

We had planned to spend the night at Doug and Susann's newly completed home, Sky Ranch, west of Livingston. Our plan was to track down Dave, the bear trapper and pie baker in Choteau, but I also hoped to find a horseman or maybe even a horse whisperer, to tell me where to go for huckleberry pie in cowboy country.

I didn't think there was a native American tribe that considered pie a traditional food, but thought I should at least inquire, while in Montana, just to make sure I wasn't missing anything. Near where US 212 T-bones into I-90, I saw a sign for Crow Agency and, figuring it was some sort of agency representing the Crow Indians, I took the exit. Crow Agency, in fact, was the name of a town, not a bureaucracy. I ducked into a corner market to inquire about pie but was greeted with such steely stares, I turned right around and walked across the street to the post office. I approached a woman with soft, doe skin, and posed my pie question.

She took a full minute to absorb my request. "We eat Juneberry pie," she said tentatively. "You need to talk to Alma Snell out on the reservation. She's in Yellowtail. She's the expert on Juneberry pie and all traditional foods and herbs."

I called information for Alma Snell's number and was surprised that she was listed. Her voice on the line was like a bird on a branch. She just happened to be preparing a traditional Crow feast for a lecture she was giving at Montana State University the next day. She was getting ready to make a Juneberry pie, in fact. "But you better hurry if you want to watch because I'm going to make it very soon."

"She's making a pie? Now?" said Kris. She'd been looking forward to a nice relaxing glass of wine and a meal on Doug and Susann's deck after so many days of dining on soy nuts. It was an hour's drive to the Crow Reservation on US 313, a desolate stretch of highway at the foot of the Big Horn mountains.

We got held up by road work. A long stretch of US 313 was being tarred, and we had to wait ten minutes in the broiling sun for the pilot truck to come get us. Two Crow men pulled alongside us in their pickup. "Are you two going for a swim?" they asked. That was usually the reason white folk went to the reservation. "No, we're going to visit Alma Snell," I said, "for advice on Juneberry pie."

"That's my grandmother," said the younger of the two. "She makes good pie." And they drove off. Since it was one of the hottest days on record—105 degrees, according to radio reports—I stupidly left the air-conditioning on while we idled and, sure enough, Betty Blue overheated.

The young, cheerful Crow woman, who stood in the middle of the freshly paved road holding a STOP sign without breaking a sweat, chirped into her walkie-talkie: "I have two white girls here who are having car trouble. Can you send someone?" We were back on the road within a few minutes, but we'd lost so much time, I feared Alma would be finished with her pie.

Alma's house was nestled in the crook of a hill, in a part of the reservation that is called Windblowing Place. It was a modern, modular home with a cozy living room and large, updated kitchen. Alma was standing at the stove when we knocked on the door. "Come on in," she said. "Door's open."

Strangers drop in on Alma Snell all the time. They come from as far away as Australia, Africa, and Germany, to the tune of two or three a day. "I don't always know how they find me," she said. "But they come."

She grew up during the 1920s and '30s, as part of the second generation of Crows to be born into reservation life. It was her grandmother, Pretty Shield medicine woman, who taught Alma about all things Crow. Pretty Shield was a deeply spiritual woman who led her life by nature's rules and forces. If an otter touched you while you were swimming, for example, that meant grave illness or death, and a cleansing was in order. Alma, too, spent her days digging for roots, communing with birds, and conversing with creeks. She had devoted her golden years to passing on these customs and traditions. That's why the people came.

"I'm trying to stay as authentic as I can," she said, pointing to the ingredients lining the kitchen counters. She'd even rendered some buffalo bone marrow to use as butter. We'd taken so long, she'd already made her dough and was letting it chill in the refrigerator. She was stirring the Juneberries in a large soup pot on the stove. When she finally looked up from her pot, showed us her round-moon face, Kris and I both tripped on our breath at her radiance.

Alma was once known as Lady that Searches for Rocks with Holes in Them, but, to her delight, Pretty Shield changed her name, when Alma was only eight, to "Well-Known Woman," a name she clearly has lived up to.

The Juneberry, a native of the Northern Great Plains, also answers to many names, including saskatoon or Rocky Mountain blueberry.

Alma explained that her great ancestors didn't eat pie, in the tra-

*"We all need one another to get along
and survive in the universe."*

ditional sense, but they did eat pie filling. After a day spent hunting
and foraging in the aspens, they would gather around the fire to eat
and tell stories.

First, they'd pass the smoke pipe around, she said. And then
they'd pass around the cooked Juneberries, which they'd eat with a
round piece of push bread made with turnip or cattail flour.

Eventually, the push bread evolved into pie crust.

She lay her disk of dough on the counter and, with a smallish
rolling pin, began to stroke it with slow, gentle, deliberate movements. She raised the pin after each stroke, and, after two strokes,
she'd lift the disk and give it a quarter spin. Gentle. Always gentle.

She lay the crust in her pie pan as though it were a shroud, and
filled the shell with the purple berries, one spoonful at a time.

Then, in the same way she had turned her dough, Alma turned the conversation onto something else, something bigger than berries and pie.

She told us about the birds that come into her yard each morning, which she quietly observes from her window.

"Some of the birds have red spots and some of them have yellow spots," she said, speaking slowly. "Some have white spots. I watch them, these birds with different colored spots, gather in the morning and talk together. I watch them communicate. And, after a while, they stop talking and each group goes its separate way."

Then she stopped and looked at us both with those pools of wisdom that passed for her eyes.

"Nature is trying to tell us something, don't you think?"

She moved in closer and her words began to take flight.

"The white people, like you, they are the people of the sky," she said, raising her hands into the air. "They are the stars in the universe, they are the light and are always reaching for the light. The red people, the Indians, like me, they are the people of the earth. They draw from the earth for their medicine. If a red person has a belly-ache, she lays down, presses her body against the earth."

She pressed her hand against my belly.

"The yellow people, Asians, they are quiet and powerful, like the wind in the air. They are like a whisper. They make things *bend*. The black people are fiery and magnificent like the jewels and minerals that live beneath the earth. They entertain us with their fire and their beauty.

"We all need one another to get along and to survive in the universe," she said, shrugging her broad shoulders slightly.

Bill, her husband, walked into the kitchen. With his shock of white hair set against deep eyes of coal, he looked like a winter white rabbit. He smiled. How many times had he watched strangers get drunk on his wife's words?

Instead of a recipe, Alma gave us a copy of her autobiography, *Grandmother's Grandchild, My Crow Indian Life*. She signed mine thus:

"May the great spirit lead you in paths of love wherever you may go."

It was 11 P.M. by the time we got to Billings, and we still had an hour's drive to get to Doug and Susann's Sky Ranch. We offered to take a hotel in Billings, but they insisted we drive up anyway; the buffalo steaks were ready to toss on the grill.

"Betty's feeling a little sluggish in this mountain air, but we'll get there as fast as we can."

"Who's Betty?" asked Susann. "Should we put another steak on for her?"

We laughed and set her straight.

We ate our steaks and salad at midnight on their deck, and it was 3 A.M. before I finally hit the pillow in a loft with windows to the stars.

While helping Susann feed their infant twins the next morning, I mentioned that I had a tip on a bear trapper in Choteau who baked pie, but I also hoped to find a true horseman to point me toward some good Montana pie.

One of their neighbors on the pass just happened to be a horse whisperer (though he dislikes that term). "I'm not sure how Bill Devine feels about pie," Susann said, "but he's amazing with colts."

In Montana lore, horse charmers, men who could cajole wild horses into submission, were once considered charlatans. Skeptics believed the root of the asafetida herb—not personal magnetism—was the horse charmer's secret weapon. Charmers allegedly rubbed the dried root powder all over their clothes to render horses docile as dormice.

It took about five minutes around Bill to find out that he smelled of clean cotton and soft leather, *not* asafetida, and there was nothing crooked about him, except the way he walked—with a tilt—from a riding accident that left him partially paralyzed.

A shy sort, Bill was happy to talk to me about pie, so long as we could talk while he worked. He was busy "breaking" three colts for a local rancher. Only three days earlier the horses, about three years old, were running wild on the range. "Breaking" is an ill-fitting term to describe the method Bill used to get the horses to respond to him. Everything about his manner was gentle, soft, and subtle, like Alma with her dough.

"Horses aren't mean by nature," he explained as he stood in the center of the pen. "Horses have always seen us as predators, and they've survived all these years by being hypervigilant." He had tied a rope around the colt and, as he spoke, he moved around the ring, trying to get the scared and confused horse to face him from every angle. The horse's inclination was to turn away, show Bill his hindquarters, but Bill kept asking for the face.

"That's 'a give,' " he'd say every time the horse would turn a quarter step in his direction. "If you get angry with a horse, you've lost its trust. Then you become part of the problem."

Devine knows about losing trust. After returning from Vietnam, he said, he felt the nation had turned its hindquarters on him. He formed a veterans' group where other men could gather in confidence and talk about how the war and the country had played tricks on them. It was about that time that he decided to get back into riding horses. He'd heard about the horseman Ray Hunt who had a uniquely humane and caring way of training horses. After studying Hunt's technique, he started breaking colts professionally himself.

One day in 1986, a wily horse he was breaking on Crazy Mountain got spooked and bucked him. Bill landed on the corral floor with a broken neck. It was months before he could move, let alone walk again. For a long time, Bill wore a metal contraption that circled his head and was held up by four rods bolted to his skull. One morning, he was at a local coffee shop when Rachella, a petite red-headed woman, approached him on the line and asked him about his "halo." They've been together ever since.

Although doctors told him he could never mount a horse again, Bill has found an ingenious way to get back in the saddle. He shimmies himself up against the inside railing of the ring and has trained his beloved palomino, Sweetheart, to press herself against his legs, so that all he has to do is fall back into the seat.

And if Bill can do that, anyone can make a crust.

I asked Bill if there was any connection between making pie and breaking horses. "Only that when Rachella makes me a pie, my ears twitch," Bill said, and his belly shook with laughter.

Actually, there are a lot of similarities, I realized as we drove across the vast Montana prairie to meet Dave, the bear trapper. The goal, Bill says, is to be "so present" with your horse, that eventually there is no separation between the two of you. "What happens then," says Bill, "transcends the physical senses and evolves into a higher, spiritual union with the horse."

I remembered what Ty had said that November morning I watched him make pie in his Lucky Brand pajamas in my apartment in New York.

"You have to watch your dough, feel it, read it with all your senses," he'd said. "You have to become one with your dough."

Our talk with Dave lasted well into the night. Like Bill, Dave had turned to animals at his most vulnerable and reaped the benefits of this union on a daily basis. The matchmaker in me couldn't help thinking there was a Rachella out there for Dave, too. And I hoped she would spot his halo soon.

On Sunday morning, we headed north, toward Glacier National Park, to find some huckleberry pie. Dave had mentioned a town called Hungry Horse, near the West Glacier entrance, where we were sure to find huckleberry pie at a restaurant called the Huckleberry Patch.

The drive up was stunning. Purple and yellow wildflowers rustled to either side of us and the sky was so generous, I felt I could never repay it.

As we approached Glacier National Park, we started noticing roadside shacks selling buffalo and venison jerky and fresh huckleberries. We went straight to the Huckleberry Patch and Gift Shop. Oh, they had pie all right: served à la mode with a crass scoop of commercialism. It's one of the things I hate most about this country, this knee-jerk tendency to take something precious and market the hell out of it so that it loses all its preciousness in the process. The Huckleberry Patch sold *everything* huckleberry from T-shirts to key chains to baseball caps and coffee mugs. This was *not* the huckleberry experience we were hoping for, so we turned on our heels and walked directly across the street, where a flimsy wooden shack on the side of the road advertised fresh huckleberries—just picked.

Henry David Thoreau once said that only the grizzly and the hunter ever get to truly taste a huckleberry, because a huckleberry loses its intensity of flavor the moment it leaves the woods. Clearly, Thoreau had never met Marc, an aging French hippie and huckleberry-picker in hot pants.

Marc, who wore a long gray beard, a black beret, and itsy-bitsy denim shorts, had spent years working in restaurants in Los Angeles before moving to Montana for a change of pace.

We asked him if there was any particular art to picking huckleberries, which were going for $10 a pound.

"The only secret," he said, "is that once you find a patch, you cannot tell a soul." Marc said that, shortly after moving to West Glacier, he'd been lucky enough to stumble on a glorious 50-yard patch at about 4,500 feet elevation. Every summer he held his breath when he returned and "so far," he said, knocking on the wooden beam of his shack, "no one else has discovered it."

Not even the bears? Marc, who wore a lion's-head necklace, said the bears were the least of his concern. Much more worrisome were the greedy pickers who came from nearby Idaho and Wyoming armed with tennis racket–like contraptions to beat the hucks out of the bush.

Being French, Marc did not make pie with his huckleberries. He prefered to soak them in lemon juice, sugar, and brandy. Nor did he feel qualified to send us anywhere local for pie.

"Je ne mange pas de pie [I do not eat pie]," he said, shrugging his shoulders, as though it should be obvious to me and . . . didn't I feel a bit like a traitor?

"But I do know that a lot of the locals like the Spruce Park Diner in nearby Coram and I've heard them mention how good the pie is there. *Bonne chance!"*

We had to double back to find the Spruce Park Diner, which was tucked behind an Esso gas station. The proximity to the gas pumps made me a little skeptical about finding homemade pie there. We ordered some huckleberry lemonade and then wandered over to the pie case to examine the goods: huckleberry peach, huckleberry marionberry, huckleberry raspberry, and for hard-core huck lovers—straight huckleberry. Most had lattice crusts, only four strips across, giving them that oafishly rustic look.

After much deliberation, we decided to split a slice of huckleberry peach, and I could not think of a happier combination. The firm, just-ripe peach slices stood up in texture and flavor to the wild-and-woolly huckleberries. And the sure, flaked crust was bold and buttery without being bossy. We clinked our lemonade glasses. "Here's to a Frenchman pointing us to one of the best pies in America," Kris said.

The café belonged to Mary Lou Covey and Laura Hansen, two women in their 40s, who'd been friends for twenty-five years, ever since Laura drove to Montana from Illinois in a '66 Dodge van seeking a new life. "A lot of men in suits tried to talk us out of going into business together," said Laura, a former mail carrier. "They said we'd ruin our friendship and lose a lot of money."

But ten years later, their business and their friendship were as solid as ever. She credited the pies, which had the locals talking from the get-go.

And, one local in particular, had a large audience.

George Ostrom, a local radio personality and a member of a seniors' hiking club called the Over the Hill Gang, discovered the pies at Spruce Park one afternoon after a long hike in Glacier. After that, the elderly hikers made it a habit of stopping in for pie after their weekly hikes. George would always wax lyrical about the slice he'd had—and later dreamed about—the next day on the radio.

"Pie has talking powers," said Laura. "It speaks to people in the middle of the night.

"People tell me they wake up in the middle of the night in their campgrounds thinking about pie."

One gentleman came in every single day for a slice of pie and he accused Laura of being a "temptress." Another regular was convinced that the secret to Laura's flaky crust was bear fat. (Laura thought that particularly funny, because she uses the very tame crust recipe that is the back of the Crisco can).

The divorced mother of two said she hadn't gotten any marriage proposals—yet—but a handsome Italian man was so taken by her huckleberry pies that he asked her to come to Italy and bake for him. She was considering it. If only we could roll back the tape and give Luciana a taste of Laura's pie instead of the disastrous Wall Drugs apple, I told Kris.

Bringing so much joy to people on a daily basis made it hard for Laura to imagine doing anything else for a living. Two years ago, when she was diagnosed with multiple sclerosis, she worried she might have to, particularly since the pain from the disease had, curiously, lodged itself in her hands. Oddly enough, she said, the pain went away whenever she was making pies.

"There are mornings when I wake up in so much pain, I think, there's no way I'll be able to use my fingers today. Then I'll get my hands on a rolling pin and the pain will disappear."

When people tell her they could never roll out a pie crust, she says "hooey." "I've made a thousand pies in the last three months, in this tiny hallway of a kitchen," she said. "I just made fifteen this morning.

"You try it. Be FEARLESS. It won't be such a mystery after you've done it a couple of times."

She admitted she was lucky to have a Polish grandmother who baked and got her "over the fear of the rolling pin at a very young age." Although they made apricot klatchkes, *not* pie, Laura had her own mini–rolling pin and got used to having her fingers in dough, and flour on her cheeks.

Laura took photographs as a hobby and she was considering

entering a National Geographic photo competition calling for photos of subjects that were uniquely American.

"I've been thinking about this for a while now," she said. "And I really want to photograph a slice of huckleberry pie."

We bought one whole huckleberry peach pie for Doug and Susann, who, once again, were waiting up for us. At least this time, we were armed with pie—possibly the best on the entire trip.

We got to the bottom of Elk Ridge road, a winding dirt-and-gravel stretch that climbed straight up almost one vertical mile to their ranch, around 11 P.M. Two big brown bears appeared in our headlights about 100 feet ahead of us. We both screamed.

"Are the doors locked?" Kris asked.

We did, after all, have a huckleberry pie in the car.

For reasons I can't explain, I developed a completely irrational fear of bears when I hit thirty. When my parents used to take us camping in Yosemite, bears ran rampant through the campgrounds at night. They'd poke their big heads inside the old aluminum trash cans that are no longer allowed under the bear management program, and, inevitably, their heads would get stuck and they'd stand on their hind legs and shake their heads until the can popped loose and went rattling down the road. We'd peel back the tent flap and watch, more excited than afraid. Now, the idea of being this close to a bear made me limp with fear.

We stayed in stare-down mode for a good ten minutes.

"Just be fearless," I said, repeating Laura's mantra for crust, as I drove toward the bears. They lumbered out of our way.

Inside, by a crackling fire, Doug poured us a much-needed bourbon, and we dug into the unharmed pie. We told them about how good Montana, the Treasure State, had been to us.

Then, not too loud, because the twins were asleep, Doug broke out into a jazzy rendition of "If I knew you were coming I'd have baked you a PIE."

"Well, it sure seems like you've got a pie angel pointing you on your path," Susann told me after she'd walked me to the room with the stars.

An angel. A reliable gut.

And lots of fancy footwork—courtesy, I'm sure, of Mr. Poulet's rabbits.

LAURA HANSEN'S RUSTIC HUCKLEBERRY PEACH PIE

use a deep, 9-inch pie pan

CRUST

1 9-inch double-crust:

(Laura uses the recipe on the back of the Crisco can)

FILLING

3 cups of huckleberries (fresh or frozen)

2 cups of peaches, sliced and peeled (fresh or frozen)

1 cup sugar

3 tablespoons of tapioca

Pick your huckleberries clean of stems and leaves. If you plan on freezing them, do not wash them as they will release too much juice when they cook.

In your favorite mixing bowl, gently toss huckleberries, peaches, and sugar together. Add tapioca, mix well but gently. Score bottom crust with a fork.

Pour fruit mixture in your deep-dish pie tin lined with your favorite crust recipe.

Cut the remaining dough into four wide bands, interlay them on top of the pie to create a weave effect. Sprinkle top with 1 tablespoon of sugar.

Bake at 350 degrees for 75 to 90 minutes. Top crust should be golden brown.

Eat with your best friend.

roadkill

"Words are holy. Treat them with respect, there's power there."
— PRETTY SHIELD MEDICINE WOMAN

In my fifteen years as a journalist, I've interviewed hundreds of people, from child molesters to government spies to truffle hunters and high-ranking politicians.

But Pat Dahl—beauty queen turned naturalist—will always stand out from the pack.

Pat Dahl lived for roadkill.

From the basement of the Museum of Natural History in San Diego's Balboa Park, Dahl ran the "stuffed-animal lending library," a place where teachers in search of wildlife teaching tools could borrow a stuffed fox, hawk, or raccoon for their classroom.

A flattened-out badger on the side of the road wasn't merely roadkill to Dahl. It had the potential of becoming one inner-city child's pivotal first encounter with wildlife.

So, whenever she drove around her rural Poway neighborhood,

she'd be on the lookout for dead animals on the road. A leggy doe-eyed blonde right out of Raymond Chandler's imagination, Dahl would slam on the brakes for a fur flat that wasn't too mangled. Using a shovel, she'd scoop up it into the necropsy bags she always kept in her trunk, then give the animal a mortician's makeover.

Pat Dahl would have had a field day on this trip, though we probably wouldn't have made it far.

Like pie—yes, there is a connection—roadkill changes from state to state.

The brittle roads of Texas are paved with dead armadillos. There is nothing quite so peaceful as a dead armadillo, flat on its armored back, tender yellow legs sticking straight up, candles in a birthday cake. Near Roswell, New Mexico, we saw lots of dead cows—more on these later. Michigan was riddled with rigor-mortis raccoons. Once, we came upon an entire family of them—a mother and her five pups in tow—still in a row, dead on the road. The Montana River Valley gave us more dead rabbits than *Watership Down*.

One piece of New York roadkill really threw us for a loop. We had just stopped to rescue the turtle parked in the middle of the road and were feeling righteous, when we saw a bloody red mess splayed across the yellow line just ahead. I winced and looked away and let Kris ID the poor critter.

"Eeeewwwww! Pepperoni pie."

I systematically recoiled at roadkill. Kris whipped her head around to get a better look. "Visualization helps me process," she said after I caught her staring.

"Visualization makes me gag."

As the trip progressed, Kris became more and more obsessed with roadkill. The attraction was philosophical, not grisly.

"I just don't understand," she'd say each time we passed a bloodied fur flat, countless times a day. "Why do they cross the road? They see cars coming. Why do they cross anyway? Why?"

This rhetorical line of questioning would go on for about ten minutes. At first, I thought it was sweet, how Kris failed to recognize the distinction between the peanut-sized brain of a roving raccoon and that of, say, a thirtysomething college-educated woman. But after a few weeks, it became as annoying as her tirades about the "ego-driven, shallow, soulless" world of advertising from which she couldn't tear herself away.

Of course, *she* had to listen to my endless questions about Ty.

"He's such a good listener, he's so communicative, so supportive . . . but why couldn't he have a job with benefits? A five-year plan? A matching pair of socks?"

Everything came to a head on our way to pick up Teri in New Mexico. In the late afternoon, when we came upon a freshly killed doe. She lay on her side, and her graceful legs were stacked, front and back, one on top of the other, hooves touching. Five chicken hawks were lining up for happy hour.

This one really set Kris off.

"WHY DID SHE CROSS? IT'S SO DANGEROUS! WHY DO THEY KEEP GOING BACK?!?!? WHY?"

"Maybe all these animals are wondering the exact same thing about you," I said. "Why do *you* keep going back—to advertising?"

Kris was silent for a good 10 miles.

"No," she finally said, staring dead ahead. "They're too busy wondering why you're always searching for something better around the next bend."

She switched on the radio, and it was my turn to say nothing.

a slice of heaven

humble pie: 1. a popular 17th-century English dish for servants in which deer innards (heart, liver, kidney) were mixed with apples, sugar, and currants. While the rich dined on succulent venison, the servants ate "humble" pie. 2. to eat humble pie is to take back one's words or deeds.

I'm not a bumper sticker kind of gal. Never have liked those narrow strips of vehicular vanity and have always found a voting booth a more effective place to make a political statement than a car bumper.

Though essential, the "IBRK4PIE" vanity plate was embarrassing enough. Now, Betty Blue also sports a bright purple bumper sticker in her rear window that reads: "Pie Town, New Mexico, *A Little Slice of Heaven.*"

I smile every time I see it.

They call New Mexico the "Land of Enchantment," and, having been bewitched by tiny Pie Town (pop. 70 or so), I see why. "Town" is a generous term for the funky cluster of run-down houses and trailers, two churches, seven sleeping dogs, and post office that make up Pie Town, located along a tumbleweed, rolling-pin stretch of US 60.

You'd think a place named Pie Town would be famous. But I never heard of it until the tip of my finger landed on it while skating across the map of New Mexico. Was this a joke? Had someone rigged my atlas? There it was, in legitimate type, and in sprawling Catron County, quite possibly "pie Mecca" at 8,000 feet above sea level. Nestled between the Gallo (rooster) and Gallina (hen) Mountains, it appeared within spitting distance of the Continental Divide, although hard to tell on which side.

I drew a fat pie dot on Pie Town with a straight line above it, so that it looked like an exclamation point.

In the early 1920s, Pie Town was known simply as "Norman's Place"—after Clyde Norman who had filed a 40-acre gold-and-silver mining claim there. But the mining venture turned out to be a bust, and Clyde went broke. Since US 60 was a coast-to-coast road, and America was discovering road tripping, Clyde opened up a gas station. For extra flourish and cash, he started selling fresh-baked pies and doughnuts he bought from a small baker in Datil, a few miles east. When the baker found out he was selling *her* pies for profit, she nearly clocked him with her rolling pin and told him to bake his own. And so he did, using dried fruit for filling, as well as pinto beans—the only sustainable crop in this parched part of the country. Turned out, Clyde had a real knack for pie. His pies were so delicious, everyone started calling the pit stop on US 60 "Pie Town." Eventually, the gas station became a pie shop and, together, they became a town and a natural place for homesteaders to end up.

The history of Pie Town had been relatively easy to pin down, but it was much harder to find anything current about the place, and I was a little worried about what we might find, or not find, there.

Teri, who was going to be relieving Kris through Texas and Louisiana, was curious about Pie Town, so she flew into Albuquerque a couple of days early. Kris and Teri would "overlap" in New Mexico and Texas, at which point Kris would fly back home and Teri and I would carry on to Louisiana together.

I took it for granted that Kris and Teri would get along, although, looking back, it was probably foolish to introduce two of my girlfriends this way, confining them to a station wagon for three days in a 100-plus-degree heat. Things had been a little tense since our road-kill spat, and I, for one, was grateful for the infusion of new energy.

Teri's camera was rolling the moment we pulled up outside baggage claim—late, of course. She panned from the rolling pin and license plate straight to the tarp and table on the luggage rack.

"Oh, my God! What on earth is that?"

We stopped for gas near the airport, and the guy waiting for the pump across the island noticed my "IBRK4PIE" license plate and the bug-covered rolling pin on my grille. "Going to Pie Town?" he asked. He was a reporter for the Associated Press, based in Albuquerque, and had once, years before, written a feature article on Pie Town.

"There isn't much left in Pie Town," he went on to say. "Not much at all."

"But there is *pie*, right?" I asked.

The man winced. "There *used* to be a café in town, but I think that shut down years ago."

Teri refused to believe such a thing.

"Oh, come on. If you can't find pie in Pie Town, just where are you going to find it?"

We pulled onto I-25 toward Socorro, after which the more intimate two-lane new US 60 would carry us through Catron County, the largest county in New Mexico and one where the elk population easily outnumbers humans.

"I promise not to read all the road signs aloud, like my mother used to do," Teri announced, and then she demonstrated by reading every billboard in sight: "Tom's Taxidermy . . . The Owl Bar . . . Brownbilt's Western Wear . . ."

In Socorro, we stopped for lunch at a *taqueria* where, predictably, there was *no* pie but where we enjoyed some spicy, soft chicken tacos with fresh tomato-and-chipotle salsa.

Teri looked at her watch, and in her lovable, uniquely dramatic style said:

"I've been on this trip for two hours now and I haven't had a slice of *pie* yet. What kind of *pie* trip is this?"

Was this the same person who had made me promise she would not gain an ounce on this trip, scheduled three weeks before her wedding?

Truth be told, the gold shantung-silk wedding dress—with its empire waist—was relatively forgiving. Teri was more concerned about maintaining a tortilla-flat tummy for the clingy, garnet, beaded number she planned to wear at her twentieth high school reunion in New York, where she was headed directly after her stint on America's pieways.

When we returned to the car, she pulled the skimpy number out of her suitcase and held it out in front of her to show us. Two cowboys walking by whistled. Kris and I hadn't seen a steamed or fresh vegetable in weeks. We traded a knowing glance and said nothing.

Once we hit the open range on US 60, Teri hung out of the passenger seat and gasped in amazement at everything she saw. Even mole hills. For the past two years, she'd been commuting from her job in Santa Ana to the UCLA campus in West Los Angeles along the dreaded I-5 corridor. Scenic it's not. Comparatively, I guess even New Mexico roadkill had its cachet.

"Who lives out here? I would love to live right in that house," she said, pointing to a bone-bare adobe dwelling complete with rusty, red, crinkled Ford pickup out back. Teri's unbridled appreciation for everything from vultures to barbed wire made me realize how road-jaded I'd become. Those long stretches through South Dakota had numbed me, and I was grateful for the wake-up call. I love the mountain roads but the bareback desert did have a haunting beauty I could learn to appreciate.

As we drove west in the hot afternoon, Teri regaled us with stories from the outside world. Kris and I hadn't read a serious newspaper since we'd left New York, and, although it was liberating, we did feel out of touch. Was it true that Meg Ryan and Dennis Quaid had called it quits?

Teri had worked quite late on a story the night before, trying to track down the mystery man from Microsoft who had given a $20,000 tip to a limousine driver for driving him from Disneyland, in Anaheim, California, to Seattle in one straight shot.

"I bet the guy would have thrown in an extra ten grand if the chauffeur had stopped in Pescadero for some olallieberry pie," I said.

"God, that was good pie," Kris agreed. We seemed to be back on track.

We stopped to stretch our legs in tiny Magdalena, not far from the Navajo Indian Reservation, and about 60 miles east of Pie Town. An eclectic used-book store caught Teri's eye. A power outage had forced her to pack in the dark, and she'd left the book she meant to read at home. We knew she would have no time to read on this peripatetic journey, but we pulled over nonetheless.

The book selection was decidedly unfrontier-like: Simone de Beauvoir's *Second Sex*, Ayn Rand, and Oscar Wilde. The owner was a recent transplant from Algoma, Wisconsin, where, he said, "I never really fit in."

I thought of Lisa, our Wisconsin rolling-pin collector who always felt like "the turd in the punchbowl."

He was an avid appreciator of pie, but diabetes had forced him to edit pie from his life completely. This was particularly hard for him, since he'd been raised on a dairy farm, where he had churned his own butter for pie crust. A graphic artist by training, he said his absolute favorite illustration was J. C. Leyendecker's portrait of a mother holding an unbaked pie out in front of her, using a paring knife to trim the overlapping edges of dough.

"The dough is just coming down in curls, like an apple peel, and there's a little boy standing by her side, watching the crust come tumbling down," he said. "I always thought that little boy was me."

Life seemed pretty unfair at that moment, I thought.

To avoid temptation, he had never gone to Pie Town. But he thought there was a café in town that still served pie. He wasn't sure.

I was getting nervous that Pie Town would turn out to be a complete bust. But it was hard not to be hopeful here in the heart of Catron County, with piñon and juniper trees rising from the brush, in the shadow of mountains the color of eggplant. The juniper made us think of gin, which made us long for a gin-and-tonic.

We passed through tiny Datil, "date" in Spanish, so named by the first Spanish settlers who mistook the dark seedpods of the native yucca plant for dates. Talk of Spanish settlers led right into a graphic discussion about Antonio Banderas (Kris had just had a vivid dream about him) and what his wife, Melanie Griffith, had done to her lips to make them stick out like a grouper's. This was clearly a bonding moment for Kris and Teri, and one so riveting that I actually missed the sign for Pie Town.

In fact, we almost missed Pie Town altogether. Easy to do.

The only evidence of a "town" on the highway are the adobe Pie Town post office, with its apricot window frames and hand-painted sign, and a phantom gas station. The residences are all clustered together, east of the highway, along the original Route 60, which branches off from its replacement in a spit of gravel and dust.

The town was perfectly still, save for a light breeze that made the sage brush shiver. I slowed down to a crawl and wanted to roll down my window and shout: "Anybody home?"

Then I noticed a woman pedaling jauntily on a rusty bike toward the residential part of town. She had long brown hair and wore a sage-green summer dress splashed with a field of daisies. I thought of the bicycle scene in *Butch Cassidy and the Sundance Kid.*

"Excuse me, do you know where a person could find some pie in this town?" I cried out through the open window, dust filling the car.

The woman turned around and caught a glimpse of Betty Blue's license plate. She pedaled toward us, then stopped and straddled the bike inches away from my door.

"Aloha!" she said, leaning into the car and flirting with Teri's camera—rolling, of course, and pointed right at her. "Welcome to paradise. Welcome to the Pacific side of the Divide."

Well, that answered one of my questions about Pie Town. This woman looked so deliriously happy, I thought at first that she'd dipped into some peyote. But, by the end of our afternoon in Pie Town, it was clear that Nita, a Southern California transplant, was simply high on small-town life in high ranch country.

"I make pies for the café over there," she said, pointing to the Pie-O-Neer Café, right across the highway, which all three of us had somehow missed. "I'll take you there. Follow me!"

She pedaled across the highway to the Pie-O-Neer, where she propped her bike across the porch and burst through the café screen door like a kid with a great report card. "Kathy, we've got some visitors looking for pie. You gotta check out their license plate!" The three of us hung back on the wide-open porch, under a string of red chile pepper lights, to read the sign by the door.

> *Due to the stragetic* [sic] *location of our town, folks have always found it a pleasant place to stop, rest and—refresh. The first merchant in town had such a demand for some home-made pies and they were of such quality that they became justly famous . . . Local folks as well as travelers began to refer to the community as "Pie Town."*

Kathy, the owner, stepped out of the kitchen, wiping her hands on her apron. She had been cooking pinto beans for the next day's blue-plate special, green chile burgers, and was flushed.

Before I had a chance to tell them about my quest, Nita had already slapped on the counter two large pieces of pie with three forks. One was an apricot cream pie made with sweet, fleshy apricots from a neighbor's tree and a basic cream filling Kathy's grandmother, Rosie, liked to use as a pie base. The glazed apricots formed a circle slightly smaller than the actual pie shell, revealing a yellow-white custardy cream filling so that it looked like a large egg fried sunny side up. The oatmeal date pie made no bones about being a cookie parading as a pie. They were both delicious.

While we dug our forks into our two pies at the counter, the two women shared a little Pie Town and personal history. Clyde's pies may have given the town its name, they said, but it was Russell Lee who put Pie Town on the map in the 1940s. Lee was a photographer for the Farm Security Administration, who had been sent out west to document social problems as a way to bolster support for federal assistance programs.

Drawn by its name, he landed in Pie Town, where he found two hundred homesteading families. Each had been given a second chance—320 acres to plant and build a home on.

"Pie Town was a real boomtown back then," said Nita, "nothing like it is now."

Nita was born in Hawaii but raised in Malibu, and moved here more than twenty years ago, when her husband got a job fighting fires for the Bureau of Land Management. She had vowed to herself that she would raise her children in a town that was "at least 100 miles away from a McDonald's" and fell in love with Pie Town the moment she set her sandaled foot here.

"It's on the same latitude as Malibu, but it's worlds away," she said. Her children have names like Prairie and Autumn, and they also work in the café when they aren't going to school—a 22-mile bus ride. They are beautiful in an earthy, golden, wheat-stalk kind of way. They radiate health, which is a very good thing since there is no doctor in Pie Town, only one who passes through Quemado, 20 miles west on US 60, once a month.

Nita told us her Malibu mother can't understand why her daughter has chosen such a tumbleweed life for herself. Her husband didn't like the isolation either. "He lives out in the valley now," she said.

Kathy has lived in Pie Town for only four years. She was enjoying a successful career in advertising, in Dallas, when she and her then-husband, Thomas Hripko, a radio producer and songwriter, came to Pie Town on a road trip vacation in 1995, intrigued, like us, by the name. When they arrived, the café had closed down and so there was no pie to be had. (The owner of the long-running café had broken both legs in a car accident and never fully recovered.)

The letdown moved the songwriter to write the following ballad, which I pop into my tape player most mornings these days when I sit down to write:

Wild west is on its last ride
Sun is sinking fast in the frontier sky

Town of sixty people gives you no good reason to stay
No city lights, no shopping malls, all the young kids moved away.
Navajo Motor Lodge is closed down
And there's no more pie in Pie Town

Boys took jobs working with the highway crew
To help put in a freeway bypass town and wreck the view
Girls are changing sheets and scrubbing toilets as motel maids
At the brand new Best Western down by the Interstate.

Town of sixty people gives you no good reason to stay
No city lights, no shopping malls, all the young kids moved away.
Navajo Motor Lodge is closed down
And there's no more pie in Pie Town
No more pie in Pie Town

A year later, Kathy and her husband decided to remedy the situation by buying the café themselves. Kathy's mother, a gifted pie baker, came out from California to help run the place and teach her daughter how to roll out a dough. "I was a complete novice," says Kathy. "It had never even occurred to me to make a pie."

At first, they made all their pies with lard, but since they cater to so many health-conscious hikers and cyclists in the area, they quickly switched to a butter-flavored shortening crust. The business was just starting to take off when Kathy's mother had to return to sea level because of her emphysema. That's when Kathy tapped Nita to help with the pies. They meshed instantly.

"Hey, Kathy, show them our 'special' pie," Nita said, grinning.

Kathy returned moments later with a fossilized piece of peach pie à la mode on a glass plate. She held it upside down but the pie didn't budge.

"We found this in the café one day after it had been sitting for a week on a shelf," said Nita. "It's part of our café art." (Nita presses dried flowers under glass when she isn't making pie.)

Most afternoons, after baking, the two women sit on the porch with Sadie, Kathy's missile-shaped mutt with one black eye, and a shaggy cat, and watch the world go by on US 60.

"We peel apples, dream up pie recipes, watch for rainbows and lightning, and try to solve the world's problems," said Kathy. "On really dark nights, we sit out here and watch for star shadows. It's like living in a postcard."

The women liked to talk about the interesting people who dropped by the café, "everyone on their way to somewhere else."

They all came for a slice of pie and for some reassurance that you could still find pie in Pie Town. And they all left crumbs of their far-flung lives behind. "It's a lot of pressure," said Kathy. "We want every pie to be perfect because some people have made a very long journey to have pie here."

Having experienced Pie Town without pie, Kathy explained, she made sure everyone who passed through got a slice.

"We're closed on Sundays, but I'll always open the door if all you want is a slice of pie," she said. A tattered, dog-eared spiral-bound notebook was filled with comments from such visitors—Divide hikers, European road trippers, elk hunters, snowbirds, and other back-road travelers trying to make sense of America.

"Good conversation, beautiful women, and great-tasting pie," wrote one visitor. "Don't tell my mother, but your pie is better!" wrote another.

Kathy practically lives at the café, which doubles as mercantile, community center, and yoga studio. She and her husband have separated, and he remained in Dallas. "We've stayed very close friends, and we're both happy that the other is finally doing exactly what fulfills them," she said.

"I used to make a six-figure salary and take business calls from my swimming pool," Kathy said. "I got a real dose of humble pie when I moved here. A real big dose."

She said she'd blossomed since she shed her fast-paced lifestyle and moved to the high desert. Her cheeks had a creamy apricot glow that you wouldn't find at any counter at Bendel's.

"There's something very gratifying about being out here in the middle of nowhere making pie," she said. "You can have a personal problem weighing on your mind, and you can go in and make a pie, and by the time it's done, you don't even know what was bugging you because you've just finished a labor of love.

"And when you bring people a slice and they tell you it reminds them of home, what could be more gratifying than that?"

The banana cream pie was the only whole pie left in the display case, so Kathy brought it out onto the porch for Kris to take a picture of it in the desert light. We turned our backs for a minute, to watch a house rumble across a highway on a trailer bed. "Someone's going out west to start a new life," Kathy said. And that moment of distraction was all it took for the long-haired cat to dive whiskers-first into the pie's cream topping. Sadie followed suit. In a previous life, Kathy might have reacted. But here, in Pie Town, her laughter ricocheted off the canyon walls.

It isn't all rosy, of course. July brings monsoon rains, you can't order moo shu chicken in the middle of the night, and everybody knows everybody else's business, thoughts, even. And, added Nita, it can be hell cashing checks when your address is Pie Town, USA. "No one believes you when you tell them where you live!"

A thin stream of locals trickled through the café while we visited. A wickedly handsome rancher named Ace tipped his baseball cap and smiled at our quest. "My favorite's coconut cream," he said before climbing back in his truck. Kris was ready to climb in after him. "Every woman in town is in love with him," Kathy said, "but he's a Mormon."

Mary, a rancher, who came to help with the pies occasionally when she wasn't branding cattle, dropped by to visit awhile as did Pop McKee. McKee had lived in this part of the world since 1937, when his father, Roy, drove his family here by tractor from west Texas, after dust and sandstorms pitted their farmland. With his sea-foam beard so long it almost touched his chest, and the two-inch raised vein shaped like an anvil on his right temple, he looked like a character the Joads might have encountered on their journey west.

It was Pop who had brought the apricots from his garden for the pie we'd just tasted. Pop invited us to drop by his house before leaving town. Nita and Kathy encouraged us to take him up on this offer because Pop rarely invited anyone to his home, and, said Nita, "it's something to see."

Kathy gave me her two recipes and the purple bumper sticker, which I ceremoniously applied to Betty Blue's backside while the girls gathered around and belted out a chorus of "Bye, Bye, Miss American Pie." We all hugged, promising to stay in touch.

Pop's front yard was straight out of *Alice in Wonderland*. A bare tree was strewn with cobalt-blue bottles hanging from its branches. Old pie tins were tied to the tall wooden fence, flapping in the wind.

"They got old," Pop said, "so we gave them a new life."

He took us inside the house to show us all the furniture he'd made by hand. As he pointed to each object, I noticed how large his hands were. One hand, fingers outstretched, could easily fill a nine-inch pie pan.

He was particularly proud of his collection of Vicks Vapo-Rub bottles that lined an entire shelf in his kitchen, which reeked of Spicy Taco Mix, and of a rolling pin he'd carved displayed above the kitchen window.

Pop announced that he wanted to give me a present. He disappeared in his shed and came back with a single four-pointed deer antler that had been blasted white by sun and age. If you held it a certain way, point tips up, it actually looked like a cupped hand with fingers outstretched, a hand only slightly bigger than Pop's.

"Where's the other one, Pop?" Teri asked. "You can't have just one antler!"

It was an odd gift, to be sure. I wondered how de Tocqueville reacted when the chief of the Saulter Indian tribe on Lake Superior plucked one of two sacred feathers he wore on his head—as proof that he'd killed a Sioux—and handed it to the Frenchman.

I'm not an advocate of hunting, and if you'd told me a year ago that I'd some day grace my living room with a deer antler, I would have laughed.

But perspectives change out on the open road. Things aren't always what they seem. Sometimes the seedpod from a yucca plant looks like a date.

Sometimes the middle of nowhere feels like the center of the universe.

Sometimes a deer antler is a perfect place to rest a stereo speaker.

KATHY'S APRICOT CREAM PIE FROM THE PIE-O-NEER CAFE

PIE-O-NEER PIE CRUST
(Makes 5 bottom crusts; the gals at the Pie-O-Neer like to make dough in advance because, they say, it's much easier to work with once it's been frozen!)

5 cups flour

2 cups shortening (Kathy and Nita use butter-flavored Crisco)

2 teaspoons salt

½ teaspoon baking powder

1 egg

1 teaspoon vinegar

1 cup cold water (roughly)

In large bowl, sift together flour, baking powder, and salt. Cut in shortening until mixture resembles peas. Break egg into a liquid-measuring cup. Add vinegar to egg, then add cold water to make 1 cup. Beat slightly with fork.

Add liquid mixture to dry ingredients, stirring lightly with fork until just moistened. Lightly form into 5 equal balls. On floured surface, lightly shape balls into patties. Place patties into plastic freezer bags and freeze. When ready to use, thaw at room temperature, but do not allow patties to become warm. Roll out on floured surface.

Note: Dough may be chilled and used immediately; however, Nita and Kathy find it easier to work with after freezing.

"BASE" CREAM FILLING (FROM GRANDMA ROSIE)

(enough for 1 pie)

3 tablespoons flour

3 tablespoons cornstarch

1 cup sugar

3 egg yolks

2¼ cups milk (whole milk is better than reduced-fat)

1 teaspoon vanilla

APRICOT TOPPING

(enough for 1 pie)

2 cups ripe apricots

1 cup sugar

About 2 tablespoons cornstarch, plus a little cold water

1 tablespoon butter

Mix together flour, cornstarch, and sugar. Stir in milk and egg yolks. Bring to boil while stirring constantly. Add vanilla. Continue to cook and stir until mixture thickens. Let cool and pour into a pre-baked pie shell.*

Bake for about 20–25 minutes, or until pale golden brown. Remove weights and lining before filling.

Cut apricots into halves or quarters, and lay them on top of the cream filling, working from the middle out, so as to form a circle of fruit about three inches smaller than the actual pie. The idea is to let the creamy yellow filling smile through.

For the glaze, stir sugar and 1 cup water in a saucepan. Mix a little cornstarch (about 2 tablespoons) w/cold water in a cup, then stir the cornstarch mixture into the sugar water and cook, stirring often, at medium heat. Add 1 tablespoon of butter and keep stirring until glaze thickens a little. Remove from heat and let glaze cool slightly before pouring over fresh fruit.

big hair, big pie, big lie . . . texas

" 'We are what we eat,' the proverb says. But that is only half true. In some sense, we remain hungry even when stated, because food is an emotional trigger to things long forgotten, trapped in memory . . ."
—EDNA O'BRIEN, GOURMET MAGAZINE

---

*When "blind baking" an unfilled crust, you should preheat your oven to 425 degrees at least 20 minutes before baking. Prick the bottom of the crust with the tines of a fork to prevent the bottom crust from blistering while it bakes. Line your empty pie shell with foil or parchment paper and fill it with dried beans or pie weights or uncooked rice.

What makes Kris and me such good friends and road-trip partners is that we both have dual personalities. We are both adventurous, some might even say reckless. On the other hand, we are both self-professed nesters seeking creature comforts. Very independent women who wouldn't mind leaving a little bit of that independence on the side of the road somewhere. Constant seekers who would like to be found someday.

Where Kris and I go different ways is that her "seeking" knows no bounds. Kris believes in extraterrestrials, UFOs, and all things crystal.

And on our way to Texas, she really wanted to stop in Roswell, New Mexico—just to look. "I'm sure we'll find good pie there," she said.

I was pretty sure we wouldn't. "Pie is down-to-earth," I said. "Nothing otherworldly about it."

But since I didn't want to be "the turd in the punchbowl," and since I was still feeling bad about our roadkill row, and since Roswell would not take us too far astray from our next stop, I obliged.

Teri, short for Tarantino, was game. "Great visuals," she said.

We stocked up on bottled water in Socorro and took US 380 right across the Rio Grande, the backbone of New Mexico, and past the White Sands Missile Range, the main missile testing site of the United States Army. We drove within only about 20 miles north of Trinity Site, where the first atomic bomb was exploded in July 1945. It was about 150 degrees outside, but we all got the chills.

As we approached Roswell, Kris briefed us on the mysterious "crash" of 1947: the shallow trench, the scattered debris, the mutilated cattle.

So, you can imagine my surprise and Kris's relative delight when for the first and only time of the trip, we started seeing cow roadkill strewn about US 380.

Of course, this was a main thoroughfare for truckers between Texas, New Mexico, and Arizona, and cattle ranches abound. Still, it was creepy.

As in most American cities, the gateway into Roswell is one big strip mall anchored by a chain of car dealerships. Only here, the Roswell Honda dealership had a green balloon, shaped like a two-stories-tall alien, tethered to its sales office. Green aliens were in every shop window, even the bridal shop in town had a four-foot-tall green alien doll modeling a lacy white dress in the window.

We stopped at the International UFO Museum hoping someone could tell us where to go for pie in this town. Wendy, a white-haired lady behind the welcome counter, was more interested in talking about the crash.

"In those days, if you'd said you believed in something like that, they would have put you in the booby hatch," she said directly to Kris, sensing a sisterhood.

Wendy called over the owner of the museum, Walter Haut, to come talk to us about pie. A strapping guy with the biggest ears I've ever seen, Haut was the public relations officer on the base at the time of the crash. He claims he actually wrote the press release for Colonel Blanchard about the flying saucer—only to have it rescinded a day later.

Haut's memory of the incident is a little fuzzy, as have been his facts in interviews over the years.

In fact, Haut was much more interested in talking about what it was like participating in the Bikini A-bomb tests, something that clearly left some scars. For years after that, he said, some of the other men who'd participated in the bomb-testing would get together and bake pies, for relaxation.

"We were pretty competitive about it, too," Haut said. "Mine were the best." And although I'm sure he made a fine pie, I wasn't sure if I believed his story and I certainly wasn't moved to add his recipe to my collection.

·   ·   ·

At a supermarket on the way out of town, we bought some ice water and fresh fruit for the road, and as we were climbing back into our oven of a car, an elderly Latina woman with saddlesoap skin motioned us over to the supermarket bench where she was sitting. *"Tamales?"* she whispered. *"Seis dolares para doce."*

Fifty-cent undercover tamales sounded divine, so we followed her to her parked van where her husband reached into a box and pulled out a sack with a dozen still warm mini-tamales. No aliens on the wrapper, just grease.

As searing as the temperatures were outside, the spicy tamales tasted great, and the chile peppers were just the kick we needed to orbit us out of the weird Roswell vibe.

We'd been back on the road for about an hour or so, when Betty Blue's temperature gauge shot right up toward the dreaded scarlet zone. I pulled over, turned off the engine, and grabbed the manual.

"DO NOT TURN OFF THE ENGINE," it said in block letters.

Our throats parched and our breath on fire, we stumbled out of the car and popped open the hood. Kris was wearing a short skirt, and to keep her legs from sticking to the leather seats, she had put down some paper towels, which she forgot to remove before getting out of the car.

Our Tarantino was zooming in on those vertical stress lines between my eyes and the temperature gauge on the dash.

"We need a man. We need a maaaannnnn," Kris wailed into the camera. Somewhere, Gloria Steinem's ears were ringing.

Just then, a man rode up in a white pickup truck.

Rodney had zipped past us on his way to his job repairing truck engines, when he spotted us and turned around to help. He wore a black felt hat and a circus-red, heavy cotton jumpsuit, the pant legs tucked into knee-high black cowboy boots with Western stitching.

"You ladies need some help," he said, tipping his brim as he sauntered up to the car.

I thought for sure Kris would faint from karmic and cosmic overload. "We asked and you came," she told the shy Rodney, who was trying to size up our little group.

It didn't take Rodney long to figure out what the problem was, mechanically: some gauge thingie had stopped working and was preventing water from getting into some doohickey. The liquid in the tank had gotten really hot, and, when he unscrewed the cap, lime-green hot goop shot up like a geyser and dribbled all over the tank.

"Ooooh," I said. "It's extraterrestrial green."

"Is that what you gals are here for?" Rodney said, extracting his disappointed face from under the hood.

No, I said, our mission was pie. Rodney was relieved. From under the hood, he reminisced about his mama's pecan pie. His mother had survived cancer then died suddenly of a massive heart attack, he said.

"But she did make some good apple pie." Rodney wasn't exactly Brad Pitt–handsome, but there's something about a cowboy on a rescue mission talking about his mama that gets to a gal. We had to refrain from a group hug.

"You should be fine from here on out, ladies. Just be sure you get your radiator flushed before wintertime."

"Whatever you say, Rodney." And then, with another tug of his brim, he walked away with a slightly bow-legged swagger.

"We should have offered him a tamale," Teri said, reaching for another. Kris patted Betty Blue's dash. "It's our own fault for neglecting Betty," Kris said. Indeed, since Teri arrived, we'd fallen out of our habit of patting Betty's dash each morning for good luck.

Our plan for Texas was to go to a small town called Ponder, where, I'd heard, there was an authentic steakhouse called Ranchman's Café, known for its T-bones and titanic pies.

Since we were going to be in the Dallas area, big-hair country, Teri suggested we hit one of those beauty salons and get our hair teased.

She loved the idea of talking to some Texas hairstylist about pie while she teased my hair. "Great visuals," she reminded us.

"I don't want a helmet head," I told the girls.

This led to a philosophical discussion about Texans and their obsession with all things armor: helmet hair, belt buckles big as hubcaps, mighty American stretch-metal cars. Even the nine-banded armadillo, the Lone Star State's favorite critter, is anything but furry and cuddly. And what about those longhorn cattle?

Pies at the Ranchman's Café, Ponder, TX

Road trips can lead to cheap psychobabble, and we were about to dismiss Texas as a cold and unfeeling state, when we drove past the Texas state sign and smiled. DRIVE FRIENDLY, THE TEXAS WAY, it said.

We decided that meant socializing with some of these truckers in ten-gallon hats. We filled up on gas and fell behind an older trucker with a supershiny rig without those stupid mud flaps bearing a torpedo-breasted bimbo. He was kind of shy, but we did get him to talk to us about the cotton fields we were passing and the dreaded boll weevil wreaking havoc on the fibers. On the subject of pie, he had some firm convictions. No Texas pie was as good as the cherry cream pie they dish out at the TA truck stop in Sweetwater.

"Did you say 'cherry cream,' good buddy?"

"Ten-four, cherry cream. Ten-four."

They were plum out of the cherry cream pie when we pulled into the TA truck stop close to midnight, having eaten nothing but tamales all day. The waitress with a bushy horsetail and prairie-cut bangs served us up a slice of lemon meringue pie and a slice of peach pie à la mode. I saw it as a bad sign when the back crust on both slices somehow divorced itself from the rest of the pie and fell back on the plate like a windblown picket fence.

The meringue atop the lemon pie was hard and perky, as unnatural and uninviting as breast implants. The peach pie was gelatinous and soupy, and the vanilla ice cream matched the artificial yellow of the Formica counter.

A couple snuggling in the booth behind us asked Teri why she was filming a piece of pie—and an ugly one at that. We got to talking, slid right into the booth with them.

Ken and Deborah had dated ten years earlier and had only very recently reconnected—after a fluke encounter. Ken was a long-haul trucker and he invited Deborah to ride in his rig with him for a few days, to get reacquainted. She had called in sick at work and here they were, on their way to California, eating a late-night burger snack at a Texas truck stop.

They were coming from Dallas where they'd already eaten soul food for dinner at Sweet Georgia Brown's. They'd ordered a piece of sweet-potato pie to go, and, on I-20, she had spoon-fed him the pie for miles, as he drove, positively giddy.

"You have not lived, honey, unless you have had your baby by your side, in your rig, feeding you sweet-potato pie," he said. As it was happening, he'd tortured his fellow truckers by smacking his sweet-potato lips into the CB radio.

Just thinking about the moment made him slide out of the booth and onto one knee. "Deborah, will you marry me?" he said. "I guess so," she said with a casual shrug. And then she moved right on to her mama's extraordinary pie crust.

"What made it so good?" I asked.

The ample-breasted Deborah extended her arms out in front of her like a sleepwalker, and began to undulate.

"It's all in the motion," she said with a knowing smile. "It's all in the motion."

"That's right, honey," said Ken, who was back in his seat and glancing at her sideways. "Uh-huh."

She shot him a disapproving look.

"My mama makes her pies with love," she said. "Pie is all in the love and it's all in the motion."

"Do you think Ken's proposal was for real?" Kris asked back in the car. Teri and I groaned, because we weren't very hopeful.

We found a room in a Motel 6 across the highway, which made me homesick for our kitschy midwestern motels. Teri ducked outside to call Jeff, her fiancé, and she came back grumbling something about a prewedding-jitters spat.

"You didn't tell him we'd been rescued by a cowboy riding a white pickup, did you?" we asked.

"Oy. Men!" Teri said behind her Zsa Zsa Gabor leopard-print night mask.

The next morning, we had breakfast at the Ramada Inn across the street, because that sounded a lot more festive than the stale doughnuts and instant coffee on the card table in our lobby.

We ordered breakfast burritos, which were delicious, and then, I'm not sure how it happened, but one moment the glass globe of the hurricane lamp was in the middle of the table and the next it was pressed against my ear, delivering a symphony of the ocean, and yes, even the call of whales. Kris pressed it against her ear and heard the same thing. Woo, woo, woo, she cooed, sounding more like an owl than a whale.

The young couple at the next table over giggled at our antics, so we struck up a conversation. They were newlyweds and enjoying breakfast with the groom's mother, Judy, a friendly woman with dramatic Frida Kahlo eyebrows.

Since Judy's accent was undeniably Texan, we asked her if she knew of any good pie in Sweetwater or the Dallas area. Judy said they were from Seminole and in town for their annual family reunion— three days of storytelling, domino playing, and cooking up old family recipes in their hotel kitchenettes.

"My mom's chocolate pie is the best in the world," she said. "You really ought to talk to her. She's in the next room playing cards with her sisters."

We settled our bill, returned the hurricane globe to its cradle, and followed Judy into the club room, where her mother, Dorothy Lou, was at the card table with her sisters Ansa Lee, Mary Jo, and Clara May.

Dorothy Lou did not consider her pies one of her most memorable accomplishments, so she pooh-poohed the notion of talking about them in any serious fashion. She said she would gladly share her recipe, but even though she'd been making it for more than fifty years, she couldn't, for the life of her, remember it off the top of her head.

Judy seemed disappointed that her mother wasn't as excited about her pie as she was. The other sisters chimed in with stories about the pies their mother used to make on the dairy farm where they grew up, and about farm living in general.

"Remember when we used to milk the cows, and the rats would

come out from hiding behind the cottonseed bins, and we'd squirt them with fresh milk?" said Ansa Lee, laughing. "We'd wear those silly bonnets so that the cows wouldn't hurt us with their tails." Ansa Lee's husband had passed on recently, and this was her first family reunion without him. Judy seemed happy to see her auntie laughing so heartily.

They all admitted that although—and possibly because—their mother had been a talented pie baker, none of them had learned how to make a pie before they married, and then they learned in a hurry, to keep their husbands happy.

I heard a long sigh of relief and realized it was coming from the soon-to-be-wed Teri.

Dorothy Lou and her husband, Whitt, had met in Fort Worth in 1943, while they both worked at Consolidated AirCraft, assembling B-17s. Dorothy Lou was one of the six million American women who joined the workforce at the urging of Rosie the Riveter, the fictional character created by the U.S. government to coax women to the assembly line.

"Only Dorothy Lou was prettier than that Rosie ever was," Whitt said, finally finding reason to pipe up.

We stepped outside, by the pool, to take some pictures of the four sisters. "Say 'PIE,' " Kris said. And they did.

As we gathered our belongings, Judy pulled me aside to tell me she'd send along the chocolate pie recipe.

"This whole pie thing is kind of bittersweet for me," she said. "On the one hand, I can't think of pie without thinking of my mom's chocolate pie. But then, I know she's not going to be around forever and nobody makes it quite like she does. None of her sisters can. I know, because I've tried theirs.

"So where," she pleaded, "will I get my chocolate pie when my mother is gone?"

The sisters in Sweetwater, TX

We both knew the question ran deeper than that.

And there it was, the meaning of pie in America, delivered poolside at the Ramada Inn off the interstate in Sweetwater, Texas.

With plans to get to Ponder in time for dinner, the idea of a side trip to Dallas for a big-hair tease grew dimmer. I was crushed.

We headed east, through Shackelford and Pinto Palo counties, on a rail-thin back road, parched and plain as a stale Rye Krisp. We passed a number of small Texas towns, abandoned and fig-dry.

We passed mousy-brown fields peppered with pumping oil rigs, which frantically pecked the bedrock, like giant, gluttonous prehistoric chickens.

When a New York photographer recommended the steakhouse

with good pie in Ponder, I was immediately drawn by the name which, I thought, captured the spirit of this meditative road trip.

He'd described it as the kind of place where "you have to call ahead and order your baked potato." Perfect.

I looked Ponder up on a map. I was doubly thrilled to see that, in fact, it was dead on the path of the Chisolm Trail.

As the three of us drove across the Panhandle Plains, I thought of the thousands of *vaqueros*, cowboys, who led hordes of longhorn steer from south Texas to railheads in Kansas.

When the rail system extended down south into Texas, the cowboys were no longer needed to rustle cattle. Since cowboyhood had already assumed mythic proportions by then, the rodeo was created to keep the myth of the cowboy alive.

Ponder, named for a rich and influential local banker, was famous for its rodeo, which the whole town pitched in to build in 1930. Population dwindled for a long time after the rodeo moved to Denton, but there's been a resurgence lately, with city folk willing to brave the daily commute to Dallas and Fort Worth in exchange for certain amenities, like wide-open spaces and pie every day at the Ranchman's Café.

The café was opened in 1948 by Grace "Pete" Jackson, a pistol of a woman who learned early on that her success would depend on her knowing how every rancher in town liked his steak. Eventually, the oil men in Dallas found their way to the café and now, most weekends, fancy cars sidle up right next to the pickups in the parking lot for T-bones and meringue pies ten-gallon high.

On weekends, a local fiddler plays bluegrass music with his young shy son, who follows close behind, strumming a washboard with a wooden spoon. "Don't let anyone fool you," the fiddler said. "This may be a steakhouse, but people come for the pie. People worship Evelyn around here.

"I've seen people go straight into that kitchen and slip her a $20 bill to thank her for her pies," he said. "I've seen people come straight from the Dallas airport for a piece of pie. I'm telling you, I've seen it all."

So you can see why Dave Ross, the current owner, was worried when Evelyn underwent sextuple-bypass surgery and was out of commission for several long weeks right before our visit. Since Evelyn kept all the recipes in her head, Ross had to scramble to find alternative recipes on the Internet, then make them himself.

"We're really glad to have her back," Ross said. Evelyn had already gone home for the day, after baking about thirty pies, so we decided to relax, enjoy a steak dinner, and return to meet Evelyn after taking Kris to the airport the following morning.

I was already worrying about what the pie trip would be like without my Beaumont, my Dr. Watson, my Ethel. My Thelma.

Kris was sad not to carry the pie journey to the bitter end, but I knew she was ready to get home and sleep in her own bed, and, more important, to eat sushi and bountiful green salads again. And, although she'd never admit it, I think she missed her cool, fast car, too.

We went into the kitchen to select our T-bones, which were stacked on a round, three-legged butcher block. Next to the block was a large plastic bucket filled with ribbons of trimmed fat, which Ross uses to make lye soap. As we ate our steaks and football-size Idaho potatoes, I watched customers file past Evelyn's pies and stare as though they were in a museum. Some pretended to be looking for the bathroom, clear on the other side of the room, so they could get a closer look.

The rustic pies were something to see. Most of the crusts, slightly charred, were shorter than their tins, so their edges curled up, like burning paper. Meringues, toasted-marshmallow brown, were unevenly distributed, the way snow clumps on a fir tree. The primitively beautiful pies looked as though they'd been made on the wagon trail. Real cowboy pies.

After dinner, Ross brought us a twelve-slice sampler plate of Evelyn's pies and cobblers. The pie lineup included mini-slices of buttermilk, pecan, chocolate, and lemon meringue (made with limes in summer). For Kris, it was the pie equivalent of the grand finale at a Fourth of July fireworks display.

That night, Kris handed over the mosquito itch stick she'd hung on to since Ohio, and gave Teri the yellow highlighter pen to chart our course.

Evelyn had already made four chocolate pies and was moving on to a batch of lemon meringue, by the time we arrived the next morning at 9 A.M. She'd also made a batch of thirty crusts.

"No time to waste," she said. "Sunday nights are always busy." Standing in front of an old industrial range, stirring the lemon filling in a tall banged-up metal pot with a long wooden spoon, she was a little wobbly on her feet. And in spirit.

Some of the pie recipes she'd refined over the years but never written down had slipped her mind in the hospital. She hoped it was temporary.

Evelyn never thought she'd become a minor celebrity. "When I was a young girl, I just worked the farm with my brothers and father, and never took the time to wonder what I'd do when I grew up," she said. "I'm just a country girl.

"I don't feel like an artist, but if pie pleases so many people, then it must be an art. Right?"

We nodded.

"I feel at home when I make pie," she said. "I feel good about myself. I didn't have much of an education, but this is something I can do well."

It was Pete, the former owner, who showed Evelyn how to make pies and swore her to secrecy about the crust.

Evelyn took a long, slow drag of iced tea.

"One of these days, y'all are going to look up and you're going to be looking for fresh pies, and you're going to realize there's nobody cookin' them no more."

As we left, a customer who'd overheard us talking pie to Evelyn followed us out into the hot July morning. "If you're looking for pies," she said, "you really should check out the pies at Catfish Haven, near the Oklahoma border. The baker is a neat ol' lady with a beehive."

My friends Doug and Jeanette were expecting us for dinner in Houston, in the opposite direction.

Teri put the key in the ignition. "So, I take it, we're heading toward Oklahoma?"

The first thing you see when you walk into Catfish Haven is a huge center table laden with whole pies, each covered in plastic "to prevent the calories from jumping out," according to a staffer. The next thing you see is D'Ann Davis, the beehive lady, manning the fryers with the dexterity of a foosball champion.

Her beehive shot straight up like a thumb. Only on the sides, which were cut shorter, did strands escape, sticking out like catfish whiskers.

Teri, who still hadn't decided how she'd wear her hair on her wedding day, was transfixed.

(Interestingly, the beehive was created by a non-Texan—Margaret Vinci Heldt of Chicago. Heldt had been the 1954 National Cosmetology Association's hairstyling champion. She owned a posh salon on Michigan Avenue, when the editors of *Modern Beauty Shop* magazine challenged her to come up with a 'do to outdo all 'dos. Inspired by a Moroccan fez hat she'd seen, and armed with gobs of hairspray, she developed the famous high-swirling, round-topped hairstyle. She stuck a pin in the 'do, and an editor exclaimed: "It looks like a beehive!")

．　．　．

When D'Ann finally stepped away from the fryers to come talk to us, her face was wet with sweat, and her dark eye-makeup running so that she looked like a Raggedy Ann doll. She was all smiles talking about pie.

"Why do so few people make pie from scratch?" I asked.

"Cuz it's work, girl," she said, tamping her moist cheeks with a paper napkin.

D'Ann insisted that each and every crust at her restaurant be rolled out by hand. Since they sold three to four hundred pies a week, she and her staff made the crusts in assembly-line fashion in the early part of the week, then froze them. They filled and baked them off as they needed them. Although she had trained most of her staff to make the pies, she said "people can always tell which ones are mine," because of her distinct crimping technique.

While Evelyn's pies were rough-and-tumble, D'Ann's pies were kind of prissy.

"Pies reflect your personality," she said. "If you make a pie, it should be like you."

I asked D'Ann to describe her personality in three words.

"Let's see," she said, staring at the ceiling. "Happy. Satisfied. Contented."

That seemed to describe a lot of the pie bakers we'd met so far.

My eyes kept going back to D'Ann's hive, and I asked her how long it took her to maintain the style day after day.

"I've been wearing my hair like this since high school," she said. "I just say 'get up,' and it jumps up by itself. It's just like my pie recipes," she added. "If something works and pleases people, why mess with it?"

Any advice for people willing to give it a whirl, I asked, meaning the pie, not the 'do.

"Don't get in a hurry," she said, "and don't take shortcuts. Patience makes good pie."

Teri and I bought a slice of cream-cheese pecan, D'Ann's most popular pie. We shared it in the car after a barbecued beef sandwich at Clark's Outpost in Tioga, Gene Autry country.

It was good, but so rich and cloying I was glad hypoglycemic Kris was safe on a plane home.

DOROTHY LOU'S CHOCOLATE PIE

CRUST

1 9-inch prebaked pie crust

FILLING

1½ cups whole milk

½ cup PET evaporated milk

1 tablespoon butter

1½ cups sugar

3½ tablespoons flour

3 tablespoons cocoa

pinch of salt

3 eggs yolks, beaten

1 teaspoon vanilla

In a heavy-bottomed saucepan, heat whole milk, evaporated milk, and butter together. Do not boil. In a bowl, mix sugar, flour, cocoa, salt, and beaten egg yolks. Mix well and add to hot milk-and-butter mixture. Cook over low heat until thick. Add vanilla, stir, and pour into a prebaked pie crust.

MERINGUE

3 egg whites

3 tablespoons water

1 heaping tablespoon cornstarch mixed with sugar, so they combine to
   make ½ cup

Beat egg whites and water together until stiff. Gradually add the
mixture of cornstarch and sugar, beating constantly, until egg whites
form stiff peaks.

Layer meringue onto hot filling, being careful to completely
cover the pie. Bake in a preheated 400-degree oven until meringue
turns golden-brown—about 15 minutes.

le pays Cajun

> *"I went to the woods because I wished to live deliberately, to front*
> *only the essential facts of life, and see if I could not learn what it had*
> *to teach, and not, when I came to die, discover that I had not lived."*
> —HENRY DAVID THOREAU, *WALDEN*

Mixing bowls aside, I've gathered an odd assortment of mementos
on the pie trip, and the most peculiar one sits on top of my blueberry
iMac computer.

It's an alligator bone. An osteoderm, to be precise—one of the
many bones tucked beneath a gator's handbag skin that give an alligator's back its rough-and-bumpy character. The porous bone looks

like a smooth piece of bleached coral, only it's got a ridge down the middle, like the nose on a face.

When people ask, I say I had to wrestle a few alligators to get the best pie recipes in Louisiana. But the "button," as osteoderms are called, was a gift from Greg Guirard—crawfish fisherman, environmentalist, poet, swamp photographer, and distinguished crawfish pie baker in Catahoula, Louisiana, the heart of Cajun country.

After leaving the creature comforts of our friends Doug and Jeanette's lovely house in Houston, we took the interstate to the border of Louisiana, at which point we slipped on to US 14 to *le pays Cajun*. Teri was so excited to be back in Louisiana, her adopted home state, she squealed for 12 miles past the state line, right past all the "vasectomy reversal" billboards.

Teri grew up in Levittown, New York—America's postwar paradigmatic suburb—and later studied philosophy at Binghamton. So it made perfect sense that her first job out of college would be as a general-assignment newspaper reporter at the *Daily Star* in Hammond, Louisiana.

Her friends and family thought it was odd, but Teri knew she'd landed in the right place when, shortly after she took the job, the paper slapped pictures of a jazz funeral procession for an alligator, known as "Ole Hardhide," on the front page. Ole Hardhide had been the town mascot in neighboring Ponchatoula, which also boasts a giant red strawberry on the police department's roof. Ole Hardhide lived in a cage in the center of town. Apparently, he'd been dead for days before anyone noticed.

Teri tells great stories about the transition from Long Island to Louisiana. Most of them involve big bugs. Our plan was to pass through Hammond on our way to New Orleans, not necessarily for pie, but to visit Teri's dear old friend Claude, a former photographer at the *Daily Star*. It was Claude who taught Teri how to eat catfish, and other basic Southern survival skills.

But first, I wanted to see what kind of pie we would find in Cajun country.

US 14 is a lean road lined with corrugated tin barns, sugar-cane fields, and murky ponds where white egrets stand knee-deep and still on dipstick legs.

We stopped in historic Abbeville, because Doug, our friend in Houston, remembered a killer crawfish pie at a place called Madame Ouida's. Heretofore, I'd really tried to limit my research to sweet pies, but in Louisiana, where rules are meant to be broken, I was willing to bend. Besides, Doug had spent the morning installing a coat hanger as a makeshift antenna for us. Betty Blue's antenna had mysteriously disappeared somewhere between New Mexico and Houston. Near Roswell, no doubt.

From the phone of a corner music store in downtown Abbeville, I called Madame Ouida, who had already closed up shop for the day and had zero interest in letting us drop by to talk about the art of making pie.

"I don't give out my crust to anybody," she snipped.

This was a sign, I told Teri, that I needed to stick to my sweet plan. "If you're looking for dessert pie, you might try the place across the street," said the shopkeeper who'd listened in.

Bollino's Coffeehouse and Café with its loft space, vermilion walls, exposed brick, and oversized cubist-style paintings felt more Amsterdam than stodgy Abbeville. Its pastry case was a veritable pie fun house: turtle pie, grasshopper pie, brandy pecan. All made in-house by the young and bubbly Libby Bollino, who was busy mixing the filling for key lime pie when we walked in.

Libby told us she and her husband, James, had met tending bar in New Orleans, and had moved back to Libby's hometown to start their own business and a family. She said the town was adjusting to the notion of a coffeehouse. Some people still didn't know, for example, that you can't just sit at a table all day without consuming. She smiled.

"But the pies are selling. *Everybody* loves pie."

I asked Libby why that was.

"Look how pretty pie is," she said, pointing to a dark pecan pie with plump, scalloped edges.

"There's something organic, sort of artistic about pie," she said, "and yet unlike most works of art, it's practical, because you know someone's going to eat it."

She stood, hands on her hips, staring at her pies in the display case.

"Or maybe it's the *round* shape that people like. There's something very mystical about a perfect circle. Plus, pie appeals to all the senses: it has a salty crust with a sweet filling and gushiness all around."

Libby said her mother was *not* a pie baker and, in fact, the only pies she remembered from childhood were the chocolate ice-box pies from Piccadilly's Cafeteria. (Remember Sarah Webster in Memphis and her pillbox hat?)

Libby learned to make pie the hard way: practicing—and failing.

The weekend before they opened the coffeehouse, she spent two days making four pies—er, four pies she could sell, that is.

"I won't tell you how many I *actually* made."

"Pie-baking isn't hard, but it does take patience," she said, leaning against the pastry case. "And everyone wishes they had more patience. Don't they?"

Even here, in the Deep South, customers didn't believe her when she told them she made the pies from scratch. "People are really impressed. They don't react that way to a cobbler. A cobbler is about as impressive as a casserole."

Libby was an English major and didn't imagine, when she was staying up nights crafting term papers in college, that she'd return to Abbeville one day and bake pies for a living. But life, like a road trip, takes odd and unexpected twists—if you let it. William Faulkner had always been Libby's favorite author, and I asked her if she saw any parallels between Faulkner and pie. Whip-smart Libby didn't skip a beat.

"Faulkner is all about the triumph of the human spirit," she said. "When he accepted his Nobel Prize for Literature, Faulkner gave this great speech in which he talked about how important it is to write about man not merely *enduring*, but *prevailing*.

"Making pie is *prevailing*," she said. "It's saying, I'm not going to make a simple cobbler, I'm going to make a *pie*." She waved her fist and dish rag in the air. I thought she might break out into a verse of "The Internationale."

I really liked Libby. If I lived in Abbeville, I'd want to hang out at the café with her and make pies and talk books all day. She and James had a baby boy, and they took turns baking pies and caring for him. It sounded like a rich life. One that gave her time to, occasionally, sit down and read.

Libby remembered reading something, in fact, about a parish in Cajun country where the entire community sat down and ate pie on Good Friday, but she wasn't sure where exactly it was.

That was enough to go on, we told her. We'd find it.

We wanted to buy a whole pie to take to Claude in Hammond, but Libby said all the pies were already spoken for, so we bought a slice of each of her pies and put them in the cooler in the car.

We went to a bookstore in Lafayette and sat in the regional-cooking aisle until we found the parish in question: Catahoula. It was getting dark and so late, we decided to stay near Lafayette overnight. We stumbled onto Breaux Bridge, a small, historic town along the Bayou Teche, famous for its two-hundred-year-old footbridge and known as the Crawfish Capital of the World. (Who decides these things, anyway?)

We drove past an old, overcrowded cemetery, its raised tombstones buckling in the moonlight, and Teri, who was driving, pulled over and jumped out of the car. "We *have* to walk in a cemetery in the dark while we're in Louisiana," she said. "It's a tradition."

This being swamp country, all of the tombstones were raised, like osteoderms, something I'd never seen before. An invisible stray cat followed us with a strident cry, as we meandered through the maze of tombstones. Only when we finished our tour did the cat jump out onto our path to reveal itself—in true Faulknerian fashion—as pitch-black. I jumped about three feet in the air. We decided to keep walking through this quaint downtown and get a closer look at the bridge, where colorful crawfish had been painted on the overhead structures. (The bridge was built in 1950, and Ana Belle Dupuis Hoffman Krewitz, a local resident, was the first person to drive across it in her Model-A Ford. Talk about a leap of faith.)

We turned off on a dead-still side street, drawn by a beautiful, vintage Acadian home with a sweeping front porch that reminded me of Buford's in Russellville, Arkansas. A sign said "bed and breakfast," but all the lights were out. A note on the door said: "Call this number if you want a room." So we did. "I'll be right over," said a cheery voice, before we had a chance to inquire about the rate. Mary Lynn must live right around the corner because she pulled into the gravel drive within minutes. Mary Lynn was a big woman. She had to be, to make room for a heart as big as a house: When I explained we were on a no-frills, no-lace budget, she shrugged.

"Just leave what you can in the guest book when you check out in the morning." Her only requirement was that we join her at Café des Amis down the street, for an authentic Cajun breakfast.

A school administrator who had renovated this old boarding-house as a hobby, she gave us a tour of the place, formerly the Old

City Hotel, where "drummers," traveling salesmen like Willy Loman, had been laying their weary heads since the 1850s. The front part of the house was an original Creole cottage that had been built in 1812, with four-inch hand-hewn beams.

We were the only guests, as the renovation wasn't quite complete, so Mary Lynn let us pick our room. We picked the one with twin poster beds. It opened onto a side porch looking out on the River Teche. After Mary Lynn left us with the key to the place, we retrieved the car near the cemetery, slid Libby's pies in the refrigerator, and then skidded across the hardwood floors, giddy as cats on 'nip.

In the morning, we washed our hair and nursed coffee in a rocking chairs on the porch. It was a nice change from the concrete motel parking lots I had been waking up to for weeks. As promised, we met Mary Lynn at Café des Amis where we enjoyed some eggs topped with crawfish étouffée and sweet chicory coffee. We asked Mary Lynn if she knew anything about this annual Pie Day event in Catahoula. Her eyes grew as wide as the biscuits on Teri's plate.

"Why, Tootie Guirard started that tradition," she said. "Her son Greg is a good friend of mine. He can tell you all about Catahoula's Pie Day."

She got on the phone and talked to him, then gave us directions for Catahoula. Easy as pie.

We thanked Mary Lynn for her hospitality, retrieved our pies from her refrigerator, slipped a check in the guest book, and headed toward the *coeur* of Cajun country, St. Martinville, where thousands of French settlers turned up in 1755, after being forced out of Nova Scotia by the British.

The *grand deplacement*, as the exile was called, was the backdrop for Henry Wadsworth Longfellow's epic love poem "Gabriel and Evangeline." Legends of Evangeline can be found everywhere in St. Martinville, where the young woman came in search of Gabriel, only to find the rascal had married someone else. St. Martinville is also where French (Let-Them-Eat-Cake!) aristocrats fled during the French Revolution, which is how the town got its nickname of "Petit Paris."

Once in Catahoula, we had trouble finding Greg Guirard's house and weaved in and out of dirt roads, bordered by reeds and leafy sugar cane, just like the cat at the cemetery.

We pulled over to ask a local in overalls and a straw hat.

"Greg's house isn't really in Catahoula," said the man. "Technically, it's not really *anywhere*."

That was helpful. The truth was that the "house" was on Bayou Mercier Road, a dirt snake of a road that led to the levee and had only recently been given a name—at the local fire department's insistence.

We drove up and down Bayou Mercier Road until we finally spotted a thin opening in the woods that was, indeed, a drive, and took it to the end, where a cottage with green shutters sprouted from the earth amid sweeping cypress trees. Several dogs and even more cats emerged from the chirping, natural woodwork to greet us. Two of the dogs had the signature pale-blue eyes of the Catahoula leopard dog, a breed of warrior dogs brought here by the Spaniards. The dogs eventually mated with the red wolf. No doubt, these were a rich gumbo of breeds. Greg Guirard, a handsome, proud man in his late 50s at least, pushed open the creaky screen door and waved hello. I noticed the crawfish-red workboots planted upside down on a fence post on either side of him on the front porch.

We sat on an outside bench, with the crickets and grasshoppers and frogs attempting to drown out Greg, whose voice was as soft as the lowlands.

There was no small talk because Greg had no time or patience for it. His parents, Tootie and Mr. Jim, as they were known, came from two of Cajun country's most prominent families, the Martins and the Guirards. His parents had camped at this cottage on their honeymoon in the late 1930s, and they liked it so much they eventually moved there, to the surprise of the rich folk in town. His mother, Tootie, now in a nursing home, took Good Friday very, *very* seriously, Greg said.

She believed that you had to really, truly fast on Good Friday— no water, no coffee, no brushing of teeth. But while the church thought the fasting should last until sundown, and the Cajuns thought noon was quite sufficient, Tootie firmly believed that fasting until 10 A.M. was penance enough.

"She's always had her personal theology," said Greg with a smile. "When we were little, she'd wake us up at 6 A.M. on Good Friday with scary stories of two-headed calves or the like, just to get us out of bed to make sure we would get at least four hours of suffering in before breaking fast at 10," Greg said, shaking his head at his mother's antics.

Once that clock struck 10, Tootie was ready to party and to eat until she could eat no more.

The early French settlers had always broken their fast with a "sweet-dough pie"—a simple custard pie—and over the years the tradition evolved into breaking fast with any old pie. For many years, Cajun families would make their pies on Thursday and spend Good Friday traveling from neighbor to neighbor's house delivering and trading pies. One year, more than forty years ago, Tootie decided to put an end to all this traveling and host the annual Pie Day exchange at her cottage in the woods, also known as "the camp."

"The only rule for attending was that you had to bring a pie that was made entirely by hand," Greg said. One year, five Cajun brothers, roving musicians, were camping in the woods near the house. Greg invited them to Pie Day but warned them about the hand-scratch pie rule. "Well, wouldn't you know it, they managed to whip one up on their campfire. And it was pretty good, too."

Tootie always made arrangements for the local priests to come bless the pies before breaking fast and, usually, the priests were happy to oblige.

One particular priest, however, objected to Tootie's celebration, which he deemed sacrilegious on the day Jesus died for our sins.

This priest was so determined to squelch Tootie's annual party that, one year, he organized a competing Catholic ritual to coincide with the festivities. In the seven miles of road that separated St. Martinville from Catahoula, there were twelve old oak trees, each bearing one of the stations of the cross. The priest invited non-pie-eating Catholics to join him on a flatbed truck for a prayer procession stopping at each station of the cross. Not only did the 10 A.M. procession conflict with Tootie's "break fast" party—it blocked the roads for anyone who was trying to get to her house in the woods. "Fortunately," said Greg, "this priest did not stay long in the parish."

Even though his mother was now in a nursing home, Greg said it was vital to keep the Pie Day tradition alive. People continued to flock to the house from all over the country because they knew "it's the one day of the year they are sure to see old friends and family," he said. "Cajuns really like to get together and celebrate life."

Greg said it was especially crucial to keep these cultural traditions alive when so much of the Atchafalaya Basin was disappearing. Drying up. Twisted bayous were now filled with sediment and overrun by trees. Flooding had buried the basin in silt. The catfish and the crawfish fishermen were having to find new ways to feed their offspring. "This may be the last generation of fishermen in the basin," said Greg who had personally planted thousands of cypress trees to replace those razed by loggers. "A lot of them are forced to sell their skiffs."

He devoted his precious free time to photographing the vanishing swamp in all its eery splendor and interviewing the people who'd made it their home for generations, living off of trapping and fishing and even bootleging, years back. He supplemented his income by talking about the grace of the swamp to passengers aboard the *Delta Queen* steamboat.

His pictures of the vermilion-red swamps and bayous at sunset were almost otherworldly. Greg said it was the burning of the sugar-cane in the fall that turned the sky acid-red. The oaks cloaked in mantilla moss and muscadine vines worked their own magic.

As a parting gift, Greg gave us each an osteoderm, which he used to make jewelry, and sent us down the road to Lillian Blanchard's to see if she would give us Tootie's blackberry pie recipe, which he did not have.

On the short drive to Lillian's house, I stopped to answer nature's call in a sugarcane field, and Teri could not stop laughing when I parted two cane stalks to wave hello and sunk two feet in the mud. I had to ride to Lillian's with my muddied feet hanging out the window, and when I got there, I made a beeline for the garden hose, hoping to rinse off before she saw us.

Lillian caught me, of course, hose in hand. She spoke Cajun French with a heavy Canadian accent, so I couldn't understand much of what she was saying. But I knew she wasn't upset. She talked a bit about Tootie and the pleasures of Pie Day, and then she told us how her mother and aunt had married two men who were brothers.

I thought that was sweet until Lillian said they were also cousins.

Since that wasn't allowed, the parish made each couple pay $10 for the right to marry.

"I guess they thought it was worth it," she said, laughing.

Lillian gave us Tootie's blackberry pie recipe, and we found our way back to the rickety wooden bridge that led to the raised levee, which would take us to Lafayette. We drove "straight off" it, singing "Drove my Betty to the levee but the levee was dry" clear through to the interstate.

On Greg Guirard's advice, after returning to New York, I called Pat Rickels, an English professor and folklorist in Lafayette. Pat hadn't missed a single Pie Day in Catahoula for forty years.

Pat was as warm and friendly on the phone as everyone in Louisiana had been in person. "So, you met Greg," she said, "the Henry Thoreau of the bayou." She was sorry to be the one to tell me that Tootie had passed away since our visit.

"Greg was on the *Delta Queen* when it happened," she said, "and they had to pluck him from the steamboat by helicopter."

I knew this was a great loss for Greg, in the midst of so much loss already.

"Don't worry," said Pat, "in typical Cajun fashion, the funeral was a blast. Tootie would have loved it."

One of Pat's clearest memories of Tootie, she said, was watching her feed *la cuit* to her grandchildren. "First, she'd boil some cane syrup down until it was brown and thick. She'd dip a silver butter knife into the syrup and then dip the knife into a bowl of chopped pecans. Usually, she'd have a grandchild on each knee when she was doing this," said Pat, "and each would take turns licking the sweet crunch right off the blade."

At the funeral, the priest recounted many of Tootie's favorite confessional stories. Like the one about the very loud woman whose sins could be heard by everyone waiting their turn outside the confessional. Tired of asking her to keep her voice down, the priest suggested she jot down her sins on a piece of paper. At her next confession, she slid her list through the small window. "What's this?" he said. "Eggs, milk, butter . . . ?"

"Oh, darn!" the loud woman exclaimed. "I left my sins at the A&P!"

Pat said Tootie was "always aglow" on Pie Day.

"For some reason, it never rains on that day, and all the new babies born that year are there, spread out on a quilt under a tree."

Pat worried about the future of Pie Day, she said, because in recent years, busy people have started bringing "fifty-fifty" pies to the event.

"Fifty-fifty pies?" I asked.

"Yes," she groaned. "Homemade fillings with store-bought crusts—fifty-fifty. It just isn't right. Tootie wouldn't like it one bit."

She paused. "Ah, Tootie . . . She would always watch the clock on Pie Day. And as soon as the priest had blessed the pies, she'd say: 'Let's eat!'

"And then," Pat sighed, "we would all fall into pie."

LIBBY BOLLINO'S RECIPE FOR TURTLE PIE

1½ 14-ounce bags of caramels

½ cup evaporated milk

1½ sticks of butter

3 ounces unsweetened chocolate

1 cup flour

1½ cups sugar

3 eggs, whole, lightly beaten

¾ cup chopped pecans

1 teaspoon vanilla

1 cup chocolate chips

½ cup pecan halves

Combine the caramels with evaporated milk in a pot and cook at low heat until the caramel melts.

For the brownie layer, melt together the butter and unsweetened chocolate either in a microwave or in a pot on the stove. When chocolate is melted, stir in the flour, sugar, eggs, chopped pecans, vanilla.

Generously grease and flour a 10- or 11-inch pie tin and pour almost half of the brownie mixture into it. Top with a little more than half the caramel mixture, then layer with the rest of the brownie mixture. Spread to cover the caramel entirely. If a little "peeks" out, don't worry. Keep the remaining caramel warm on the lowest possible setting on your stove or reheat when ready to use.

Bake at 350 degrees for 30 minutes. Remove the pie from the oven and let it rest about 5 minutes. Spread remaining caramel over pie and sprinkle with chocolate chips. Arrange pecan halves around edge of pie, then swirl chocolate chips decoratively with a toothpick or a small sharp knife. Refrigerate for at least 1 hour before serving. This pie keeps and travels well. Kids and adults love it.

In the store, we use a sharp knife dipped in very hot water to cut turtle pie. (Use ¾ recipe for 8- or 9-inch pie tins.)

TOOTIE GUIRARD'S GOOD FRIDAY BLACKBERRY PIE

2 quarts blackberries

3 cups sugar

1 crust, plus more dough for the lattice

1 tablespoon flour

2 tablespoons butter

Cover blackberries with sugar and let stand awhile in a bowl. Cook blackberries at low heat until cooked—about 20–30 minutes. Line pie tin with your favorite crust recipe. Sprinkle flour on bottom crust. Pour cooked blackberries into pie shell and dot with butter. Cover top with strips of dough, criss-cross. Bake at 350 degrees for 25–30 minutes. Wait until 10 A.M. before digging in!

let the good times roll

*"He was a preacher . . . and never charged nothing
for his preaching, and it was worth it, too."*

—MARK TWAIN, *THE ADVENTURERS OF HUCKLEBERRY FINN*

Even though we knew Claude was expecting us in Hammond, I did not want to drive past Baton Rouge without at least trying to track down Madear Johnson. Madear was the mother of the shuttle bus driver who'd praised his mother's blueberry pie at JFK airport.

We drove up and down Euclid Avenue and never found the house number Kris had scribbled in her palm. We gave up and pressed on.

Claude had just brought home a floppy black puppy from the local shelter when we arrived. He had not named her yet, so Teri suggested the obvious: Pie.

"I kind of like that," said Claude. "Paaaahhhhhhh it is."

Did Claude really want to commit to a name that would have people scratching their heads?

"Oh, that doesn't bother me," said Claude. "I used to have a cat named Sofa."

We celebrated the naming by eating Libby's slightly weathered pies. Everyone loved the turtle pie best. The edges had softened in travel, but that sweet caramel filling hit a home run—especially with Claude. Claude's best friend Rodney, also an old friend of Teri's, dropped by to take us out for catfish dinner. Rodney was a handsome

man who could charm the skin off an alligator. Teri had warned me about his legendary womanizing. But the only woman he was talking about that night at dinner was his mama. Mama Millsap and her apple pie.

"She doesn't use a top crust," he said with a certain pride. "And she adds whipping cream to the filling to take the edge off the apples."

He licked his lips.

"Nothing can ever top your mama's pie," he said. *"Nothing."*

I had very high pie hopes for New Orleans.

After all, "let the good times roll" refers to a rolling pin, does it not?

We stopped at Café du Monde to get beignets and our bearings. Claude and Rodney said a man named Omar peddled his small sweet-potato pies and pecan pies in the streets of the French Quarter and, with some confectioners' sugar still on our lips, Teri and I set out to find him on foot.

It was dangerously hot. Adultery weather.

On Dumaine Street, one block from the St. Louis Cathedral, we paused in front of a witchcraft shop, and something—supernatural, I'm sure—pulled us inside. A young man named Chesley, with hair dyed violet and cut à la James Dean, sat in a cloud of burning frank-incense behind a counter cluttered with potions. Behind him, shelves were lined with old apothecary jars of herbs and roots and powders. His eyes lit up when we mentioned pie.

"I love pie," he said, lowering his voice on the word *love*. Chesley was from Moscow, Texas, originally. Population 200. His fondest memories, he told us, were of picking blackberries along rutted dirt roads so that his French grandmother, Marcelle, could make her famous blackberry pie. More important, he'd recently made a "love pie" for his girlfriend on her birthday. For the filling, he used rose petals, hibiscus, and raspberry jam.

"No one had ever baked a pie for her before," he said. "It must have worked because we ate the whole thing, and she *still* loves me."

Chesley is a true fellow believer in the power of pie. He reached for the *Victorian Grimoire*, the famous book of spells, and read pie passages aloud to us. The Grimoire suggested that baking pie is a wonderful way to manifest your desires. "Concentrate very hard on what you desire while you're making the pie, and then while you're eating it, and your desire will come true."

What if your desire is to learn how to make a flaky, tender crust? I asked. Is there a spell for that?

Chesley rubbed his pointed chin. "I don't have a spell, but I could certainly come up with an herb potion that might do the trick.

"Kava kava would work to relax you before you went into the kitchen," he said. "And valerian and galangal root would both help for courage."

And while we were on the subject of magic potions, I asked Chesley if he had any quick-potion fixes for my unresolved love life. He handed me a tiny red pouch with a black drawstring, filled with a mysterious batch of herbs sure to make me irresistible. I was seeking clarity, not another man, but heck, it was only $3, so I bought it. Even though Teri was getting married in three weeks, she bought one, too. (On her wedding invitation, Teri was described as someone who didn't know "if marriage was a word or a sentence.")

We asked Chesley, who was in his late 20s, why wicca and other forms of "natural" witchcraft were so popular among men and women his age. "I think people of my generation have really lost touch with their spirituality," he said. "They're searching for something, anything, to bring meaning into their lives."

A young man with a goatee came in for a tarot card reading—so we said good-bye. "Good-bye, ladies of pastry," Chesley said. "Good luck on your rolling-pin chronicles."

We'd barely rounded the corner onto Chartres Street, when two city police officers on foot patrol stopped us in our tracks.

"Hey, ladies," said one of the officers. "You looking for a date?"

"Wow. Those pouches are amazing," I whispered to Teri. Then I realized the officers were jokingly offering up a town drunk they were arresting—not for the first time. They were waiting for a patrol unit to come take their handcuffed charge away, killing time teasing tourists. The drunk knew the drill. He was laughing right along with them.

Since these officers worked the street, I thought they might know Omar. They did, but they said Omar was very elusive.

"You just never know where you're going to see him next," the burlier of the two said. "I haven't seen him in a week."

"But you know who else makes really good pie?" one officer began to say. "Carl Dennis." I swear to God, just then, Carl Dennis himself crossed the street. He was also in uniform, though he was a security guard at a museum—not a cop.

"Did I hear someone mention pie?" Carl said, smiling. Turned out, he, too, sold sweet-potato pies and pecan pies in the French Quarter, on his breaks before and after work. "My father's the baker," said Carl. "He's a preacher and he makes them from scratch several times a week."

Naturally, we invited ourselves over to watch later that day.

Minister Edgar had been baking for more than fifty years, and he seemed delighted to be finally baking for an audience. He was wearing a bright white guayabera shirt and had all of his ingredients laid out on the island in the middle of his sunny kitchen. His plan was to make sixteen pies—eight sweet-potato and eight pecan—for Carl to sell in the Quarter the following day, at $2 a pop. Edgar went to school to learn how to cook after a stint in the army, courtesy of the GI Bill, and before becoming a merchant marine, he spent time cooking in a local hospital.

He confessed to having led a wanton life while at sea, but, he said, he'd been walking on very firm ground since he'd come home for good. He credited his wife, Archie Ernestine, for setting him straight.

"Women always take men to church," he said. "Men take women every place else."

Minister Edgar said he was "a preacher, not a teacher," but when making dough, he became both.

In a large stainless-steel mixing bowl, he mixed together flour and shortening, a dash of salt and a bit of sugar. He did not measure any of his ingredients, and bristled when I asked about that. For the next fifteen minutes or so, he held the bowl firmly down with one hand. With the other, he used a fork to mix its contents, working it in tight, concentric circles. How would he know, exactly, when to stop mixing?

"How can I explain in words something you've got to see with your eyes?" he said. "I just can't explain."

I was riveted by his wiry forearms and his hands, especially the one holding on to the bowl for dear life. The thumb was long and thin and capped by the smoothest of nails, as pointed as a papal hat.

The dough resembled gritty cornmeal as he added ice-cold water, one drop at a time. "See how it's holding together?" he said. "*Now* it's ready."

He scooped the dough out from the bowl and onto a circular work board, and pressed all his weight onto the dough mass, working it with his knuckles like a knotted muscle. He pinched a piece of the dough mass, and tossed it from one palm to the other like a hackie sack. He'd then flop it on the board to flatten it out with his old rolling pin with loose red handles.

"I've had this rolling pin as long as I've lived in this house—and that's more than 40 years," he said.

It was easy to see why the handles hadn't come off despite years of wear and tear: he didn't use them. The pies were so small, and the pin so long, he griped the pin about four inches in from the handles. He rolled twice back and forth, added a speck of flour, turned the disk, rolled again, twice, back and forth. He picked up the disk of flour and dropped it into an aluminum pan about 5 inches across. Since the dough was a hair short, its edges fluted straight up. He tamed the petals of dough by crimping the edges down with the tines of a fork ("no fancy tools necessary"), and then, with a knife, he trimmed the excess edges so that they curled into a small pile, like wood shavings on a carpenter's floor.

As he worked, he threw in the occasional preacher's pearl of wisdom.

"The trick to a long and happy marriage," he told Teri, who'd brought up her impending wedding, "is respect."

"Let me ask you this. Do you say 'thank you'?" He pointed a floured finger at her. "People don't say 'thank you' anymore out of foolish pride," he said. "But a 'thank you' goes a long, long way. It's all about respect."

The minister continued to roll out his small discs of dough. "Ahem. Uh-huh. Amen."

As I stood there, leaning against the kitchen wall, I thought this was a church I could come to every Sunday.

There was a knock at the back door. Two grade-school girls came looking for "icebergs"—popsicles without the stick the minister made and sold to the kids in the neighborhood for 50 cents a pop. Popsicle sales helped pay for the pie ingredients, Carl explained.

When the pie pans were lined, the minister worked on the fillings. He added melted butter to about two pounds of cooked, peeled, and quartered sweet potatoes. Then he scooped up two generous scoops of sugar from the sugar bucket under the island, tossed some cinnamon into the mix, gave it one good stir, and, pleased with the deep, burnt-orange color of the mixture, poured it straight from the bowl into each pie shell.

"See? How could I learn to make pies? Not only does he not measure anything, he doesn't *taste* anything, either," wailed Carl.

For the pecan pie, Minister Edgar mixed Karo syrup "black or white, it doesn't make much difference," melted butter, sugar, and a handful of flour, which he stirred with a whisk. He dropped a handful of pecans (from a neighbor's tree down the street) into the bottom of each pie, and then poured the sweet filling right on top.

"This gets me every time," said Carl. "Watch how the pecans start at the bottom but then float right to the top."

"It's one of those life mysteries," said Minister Edgar. "It's kind of nice that people don't know *everything* in life."

While the pies baked, filling the house with a warm spicy incense, Archie Ernestine, who had stayed in the living room, finally wandered into the kitchen. Was it the smell that brought her in, I asked.

"No," the minister said. "My wife told me many, many years ago that she likes her sweets walkin' and talkin.' "

Archie Ernestine had also done her part for this country. In the early 1950s, when only 20 percent of the black population was registered to vote in the South, the NAACP launched a massive get-out-the-vote campaign. Archie Ernestine set up a folding card-table on a dock on the river to help rural blacks register to vote. Many of them did not know their own age, and Archie Ernestine helped them figure it out. She was arrested for helping to sign up about a hundred blacks, she said with surprisingly little rancor. "Those were different times."

The minister, clearly, did not want to go there. Didn't want to talk about those times. Not when pies were in the oven.

He swung open the oven door and practically stuck his head inside. He liked what he saw.

"These pies are ready!" he declared. Usually, the minister went to the trouble of naming each pie as he pulled them out of the oven, Carl said, "as if they were hurricanes." The minister did it merely to keep track of them, but on this day, the pies remained nameless, if not faceless. Teri and I bought two of each and dug into the sweet potato right then and there, in the minister's kitchen. The filling was so steaming hot, it burned the roof of my mouth without even touching it.

"They say American as apple pie," said the minister. "But this here sweet potato pie is *Negro* pie."

I couldn't think of a better pie for Teri, who was flying out the next morning, to end her trip on. I was tempted to ask for the recipe, but I knew what the minister would say.

"Some mysteries are better left unknown."

Archie Ernestine shoved an old crinkled envelope in my hand, as we were leaving. "I wrote it long ago," she said. "Take it."

Teri drove us back to our hotel in the French Quarter. It was still light out, but the heat was starting to slink away. I smoothed out the paper in my hand, an old bill-payment envelope from Whirlpool, and read out loud:

Minister Edgar Crawford and "helpers"

To open the door, facing your own future for the first time,
Is quite a frightening thing to your heart, soul, and mind.
When you open the door to your future, you get a chill.
You must pray for strength, placing all things in God's will.
From this day forward, you are beginning on your own.
It is a great step, yet mind-boggling to face all the responsibilities
now that you are grown.
Forge ahead with great determination, do what you must,
It's your salvation.
Don't look back, be firm in things you do.
Remember, every successful person has passed this way too.

"Did she really write that?" Teri asked.

"Teri," I said, "some mysteries are better left unknown."

The day had been as rich as roux, and we couldn't think of a better way to end it than listening to some scratchy live jazz at Preservation Hall.

"Tuba Fats" was in the house that night. The celebrated street musician had lugged his tuba around the world, but this was where he was born to play. After the set, I reached into my purse to leave a tip for the musicians in the designated basket. Instead of my wallet, I grabbed one of Minister Edgar's small pecan pies. I tentatively handed the still-warm pie wrapped in plastic to Tuba. His eyes bulged.

"That's a Carl Dennis pie," he said, extending his open palm.

And I do believe that was the best barter ever made in Ole Louisian'.

MAMA MILLSAP'S OPEN-FACED APPLE PIE

CRUST

1 9-inch pie crust

FILLING

1½ cups granulated sugar

⅓ cup flour

1 pint tart apples, sliced very thin

¼ teaspoon nutmeg

1 cup heavy whipping cream

Mix the sugar and flour together well. Sprinkle some of this dry mixture on the bottom of the crust. Add sliced apples, sprinkle rest of dry mixture over the apples, then add the nutmeg.

Pour cream over the mixture. Toss gently by hand. Bake in oven set at 400 degrees for 15 minutes. Reduce heat to 350 degrees and bake 45 minutes longer.

the nicole states
(most of them, anyway)

"The very essence of apple pie nowadays is its frozenness . . .
Instead of saying 'as American as apple pie' it would
obviously be more accurate to say: 'as cold as apple pie.'
Who wants our national warmth, charm and
loveability likened to frigid pastry?"

—RUSSELL BAKER, *NEW YORK TIMES*

Nicole had barely buckled her seat belt when she announced that she had a hankering for junk food.

"Bring on the hydrogenated oils," she said.

What is it about the open road that makes a grown woman pine for purple jawbreakers and Tennessee-style barbecued corn chips—stuff we wouldn't dream of buying at home?

"Eating junk food is the whole reason for a road trip," says Nicole.

And the gas stations know it, don't they? The way they cram those goodies right next to the cash register prompting impulse purchases of Bazooka bubble gum, Red Vines licorice, and Slim Jim beef sticks.

In the Rocky Mountain states, gas station counters are lined with jars of buffalo jerky flavored with everything from cherry to jalapeno. In Wisconsin, cheese products in all shapes, and even on a stick, taunt the traveler. And in Alabama, pickled pig lips are the road tripper's snack of choice.

"I've never had them," said the cashier at one Amoco station, of the ballerina-pink hog smackers floating in a murky liquid that looked like formaldehyde. "But we go through two of those tubs a week."

"They go down great with Budweiser," a lanky trucker chimed in as he grabbed a couple pairs to go.

Nicole and Teri had crossed paths in the middle of the night in New Orleans. There was no official passing of the highlighter pen as there had been with Kris and Teri in Ponder, and I was sorry about that.

I took Nicole to Café du Monde for breakfast, and spread the Southeastern states map on the table. Nicole's face went blank.

"I can't read maps," she said.

"HA HA," I said, removing the highlighter pen cap with my teeth.

"No, really, I couldn't read a map if my life depended on it."

How could a woman who knew how to temper chocolate and make beignets as light as baby puffer fish not know east from west, or that the little red arrow meant an exit off the interstate?

"I'll drive, you navigate," she said.

It was probably for the best, since I had done very little advance work for this, last leg of the trip, and would be doing some reporting in the car.

I knew I wanted to find good pie near the White House and, of course, Golden Peach pie in Georgia. But no pie came immediately to mind when I thought of Alabama. We'd play the Yellowhammer State by ear.

Shortly after leaving New Orleans, at a gas station near the Mississippi-Alabama border, Nicole went inside a gas station to use the ladies' room and emerged with a fried peach pie, pleased as Punch. The greasy pie was a belly bomb of the highest order.

"I was hoping to keep my junk food and my pie intake separate," said Nicole. I demonstrated the concept of "Dumpster pie" and we carried on to US 43, which cut straight through Alabama from south to north.

Of all the roads I've taken across America, the stretch of US 43 between Mobile and Demopolis has got to be the creepiest. For miles on end, we passed mysterious industrial complexes, which offered no clue as to what went on inside.

Weird genetic research, we decided.

In fact, our stint in Alabama was creepy from start to finish. It is not a state I wish to malign, so I will spare you the details. Suffice to say that we did not get a good pie vibe. And, if we didn't bail soon, I was worried Nicole might jump ship.

Things improved markedly the moment we left Tuscaloosa and headed for Georgia on Route 78, a lush, wily road that meandered through the Alabama Pine Belt and continued almost straight on through to Atlanta.

Rusted-out dishwashers and disemboweled refrigerators lined the road for a good 20 miles.

"A different kind of roadkill, I guess," said Nicole. We dubbed Alabama the Multitasking State after spotting a gas station peddling chicken wings, and a bait shop that offered cheddar biscuits and tanning beds. Our favorite was the hair sea-lon with inflatable pool toys in the window. "Get a trim while you swim?" asked Nicole.

We crossed the Sweet Georgia sign just as the bruised peach of a sun was pressing into the horizon.

WELCOME, WE'RE GLAD GEORGIA'S ON YOUR MIND.

Late July is prime peach season. The plan was to head to Fort Valley, right in Peach County, to get our hands on some fresh peach pie. But an acquaintance who grew up in Atlanta told me I couldn't leave Georgia without stopping in the capital for some of that white-bean pie, so popular in the black West End neighborhood.

We drove through a bleak, industrial section of town where we watched black Muslim families setting up picnic tables on loading docks in factory parking lots. Sunday picnic amid abandoned cars and brimming trash containers. We talked of the parks and trees we'd taken for granted as children.

My Atlanta friend had told us we could find white-bean pie anywhere in the neighborhood, so we stopped at the first restaurant we saw.

Three black men in colorful African djellabas, who were standing on the sidewalk, said they owned the place, which was vegan, but they'd never heard of white-bean pie.

Perhaps we'd have better luck at Chanterelle across the way, they suggested. Chanterelle was a soul-food postchurch mecca. Men in suits the color of Buicks, and women shoehorned into tight, frilly dresses gathered around the display case examining the goods.

"White-bean pie? Never heard of it," said the chef. "We serve red-velvet cake here." He pointed to a ruby-red frosted cake. Dessert as bridesmaid dress. "Maybe the Jamaican place down the street could help you out."

Taste of Tropical, anchoring a nondescript strip mall, was, unfortunately, closed. I peered through the glass anyway, and noticed a gentleman in a floral shirt sitting on a ladder, changing the licorice-red magnetic letters on the menu board. I rapped on the door, and he scissored his hands in the universal gesture that means "we're closed." But I wasn't about to leave Atlanta without a taste of this mystery pie.

"Do you sell white-bean pie?" I mouthed. His frown melted into a smile, and he stepped down from his ladder.

"How do you know about white-bean pie?" he asked, opening the door. "White-bean pie is a down-home specialty." Joscelyn Crumbery's voice was hilly, and I wished we could pipe him through Betty's radio for those long flat stretches of the road like that dreadful US 43 in Alabama. Shortly after he'd opened this restaurant, Joscelyn said, an elderly Jamaican offered to make the traditional pies for a fair price. Joscelyn tried one of the old man's pies, and they brought him straight to the shade of a coconut tree. A deal was struck.

"They have been flying out the door ever since, mon," he said, slapping his knee. We asked Joscelyn if we could meet the baker, maybe even add the recipe to our collection.

"Sorry, mon," he said. "It's Sunday and that's a sacred day for his family." He pulled a small, individual white-bean pie out of the freezer for us to take on the road. We popped it in the still-broken glove compartment. "It'll thaw by the time we get to Fort Valley," I said.

Nicole hadn't said much all morning. In fact, Nicole could go for hours, it seemed, without so much as a peep. It was where she was in her life, and that was fine with me. I'd absorbed so much in the last few weeks, my thoughts were swirling.

Then, out of the blue, Nicole said: "I don't think I would have ever ended up in an all-black neighborhood on the outskirts of Atlanta, if we hadn't been looking for pie." And, although our first couple of days together on the road had been trying, I was glad she was beginning to see the point.

It took a while to escape the urban sprawl that was Atlanta, but when we entered peach country, everything changed. Even Betty Blue ran better.

Stately pecan trees replaced steely office buildings. They were draped in Spanish moss, *abuelas* going to mass in their mantillas. Spanish moss, also called horsehair, is a relative of the pineapple. It isn't really a moss at all, but an epiphyte with no root system, which lives off moisture in the atmosphere. I wondered why it hadn't started growing in Betty Blue's interior.

We stopped at a McDonald's for a soda, and the woman ahead of us in line was demanding one of their new lemon pies. McDonald's had launched a new pie flavor, and I wasn't informed? McDonald's pie, incidentally, is the only pie in America that comes with a warning label—HOT.

The counter girl kindly explained that they'd run plumb out of the new pies. "As I told you yesterday, lady," the cashier said, "the new shipment won't arrive until tomorrow."

In Perry, we got a room in the stodgy but classic 1920s Perry Hotel. We took a dip in the tiny pool, then dined in the gussied-up coffee shop.

I begged our waitress for something—anything—green.

Nicole may have been craving Pixie Stix, but I wanted vegetables. Sure, you can find a salad in Middle America, but you will have to excavate through a mountain of packaged, cardboard croutons and a heaping cup of creamy ranch dressing before you come across anything green or fibrous that's ever hit dirt.

Vegetables are either tucked in a casserole or deep fried—rarely served in the raw.

At a catfish restaurant in Alabama, the young waitress took a timid step back when I told her I would kill for a side of vegetables, reinforcing all her stereotypes about aggressive New Yorkers. And no, I kindly told her, those itsy bitsy chopped scallions in my hushpuppies didn't count.

"We don't have vegetables, except for turnip greens," she said. She returned swinging a sand pail of turnip greens drenched in a butter bath.

Our waitress in Perry suggested we try the "congealed shower salad," a house—and Georgia—specialty.

When she set the oval dish in the middle of the table, Nicole and I stared at the jiggly pink scoop for a long time, afraid to touch it. The texture resembled grainy watermelon flesh, and it was topped with a dollop of Miracle Whip.

Nicole braved it first. She tasted pineapple, grape, and cherries, before she identified it as canned fruit cocktail that had been Robo-couped. What made it a "salad" was the single Iceberg lettuce leaf on which it sat, triumphant.

"Look," said Nicole, "you got something green."

There was pie on the menu. After our chicken-fried steak, we ordered apple and pecan, since peach was conspicuously absent. This was Nicole's first fresh pie slice of the trip and I could read the disappointment in her eyes the moment they arrrived. The crusts were yielding, spongy, anemic. The fillings listless.

"The person who made these doesn't love pie," said Nicole after two bites. The restaurant manager came around like a cat in heat, asking about the pies.

"They're absolutely sinful," I said. I winked at Nicole. No harm. No foul.

Our bellies anchored, we retired to our room to plan the next day's itinerary. I remembered the white-bean pie still in the glove compartment and snuck out in my jammies to get it. It was at the perfect melting point. The gingerbread topping still crunched, and the crust had not lost its spine despite the heat and long drive. The Navajo-white filling was creamy, like a pudding.

"Now *this* is pie, mon," said Nicole.

When the writer M. F. K. Fisher was asked by Richard Sax to describe her most memorable meal, this is what she said:

I was about eight, with my father and my little sister, driving in our Model T from the desert foothills of southern California . . . [Irish Mary had given us] a big peach pie for the trip down past Los Angeles to our little town of Whittier, and beside it in the wooden lug-box, she put a pint Mason jar of thick cream, with three old chipped soup plates and three spoons and a knife . . . once down into the winding mountain roads, live oaks cooled the air, and we stopped at a camp where there were some tables, and ate the whole peach pie, still warm from Irish Mary's oven . . . We poured cream from the jar onto the pieces Father cut for us, and thick sweet juices ran into delicious puddles.

"That's the peach pie experience I'm looking for," I told Nicole over breakfast the next morning, before we doubled back to Fort Valley.

Fort Valley was initially named Fox Valley, but, as the story goes, when the name was submitted to the Post Office in 1825, the illegible cat scratch was misread as "Fort," and the name stuck. Fort Valley used to be a cotton center primarily, but that changed after 1875, when Samuel H. Rumph introduced a new peach variety: the Elberta. Rumph named the clear-seeded peach with yellow flesh and a crimson blush on its cheek after his wife, Clara Elberta Moore.

He'd been experimenting with many peach varieties, but the Elberta was his favorite. It was so firm that when Rumph sent a test shipment to New York, he didn't even pack them in ice. They arrived intact.

The Elberta became the workhorse peach of the area. Back then, and even as recently as 1970, there were thirty peach-packing facilities within 30 miles of Fort Valley. Only six are left. On our way into town, we followed signs toward one of them, advertising free tours.

There were several pans of gooey peach cobbler in the plant restaurant, but not a slice of pie in sight. Maybe one of the assembly-line workers could suggest a place in town for peach pie.

"I'm Bertha Mae and I separate the good from the bad," said a black woman with curlers in her hair, whom we approached in the "sorting" line. Peaches rolled by Bertha Mae at the rate of two hundred thousand per hour, and her job was to spy the ones with flaws and send them barreling down a separate chute.

She'd been with the company for thirty years, had worked "just about every line," but she liked sorting best. She still took pride in her job and even wore dangling peach earrings.

Bertha Mae told us she was more of a cobbler person herself, and she was about to give me the name of a dear friend in town who made a wicked peach pie, when her supervisor ordered her back to work.

Thirty years with a company won't buy you five minutes of chitchat. I apologized on her behalf, but he was intransigent.

I wanted to jump on the sorting machine and hold up a UNION sign but stuck my tongue out at his turned back instead. Bertha Mae laughed behind her hands.

On Main Street, signs like SKIPPER'S PEACH SHOE REPAIR and BRENDA'S PEACH PIANO had me convinced that everything peach was within reach. But neither café had peach pie on the menu.

MaryAnne, a chatty woman behind the pharmacy counter at the local drugstore could help us, but only if we wanted pecan pie, not peach.

Her husband was a pecan broker, she said, and she'd spent years tweaking her pecan pie recipe.

"You want to know my secret?" she said. "I use brown sugar instead of Karo syrup. My husband goes nuts over it.

"Men just love pie," she added. "Steak'll get 'em in a heartbeat, but pie will finish the job."

Georgia, Texas, and Alabama all produce pecans, MaryAnne said, but Georgia's are superior since they get more rain, which makes them more oily and more flavorful.

"Texas pecans tend to run very dry," she said with condescension, "which is why they usually end up in box candies, like Whitman's Samplers."

We agreed Georgia's pecan trees looked particularly regal.

"Don't be fooled," she said. "It doesn't take but a puff of wind to knock one down."

For all things peach, she suggested we talk to Matt Mullis. The young Matt was the man in charge of cooking the gargantuan peach cobbler for the annual peach festival. The cobbler fed three thousand.

Matt, a contractor, was remodeling an antebellum mansion, soon to be the city administrations office. He was taking measurements in the mayor's new digs when we turned up.

He said he'd recently taken over the cobbler responsibility to honor his late mother, famous in the area for her pies, which were as delicious as they were pretty.

The cobbler, which must be stirred with yard rakes, was baked in a pan that was 6 feet wide by 11 feet long and 1 foot deep. It required 90 pounds of sugar and 75 gallons of Georgia peaches.

"Fresh peaches, of course. I won't eat a canned-peach pie or cobbler. When you live here, you can taste the difference."

That is, if you can ever find a slice.

"Maybe we'll have better luck in Savannah," Nicole said, as we left peach country, peach-deprived.

Cemeteries have always given me the willies. So I considered it a real breakthrough that I traipsed through so many of them on this trip. From the power walk in the Wellsboro Cemetery with Kris, to our stroll through the Breaux Bridge Cemetery with Teri, I was learning to appreciate their stillness and grace. So, when Nicole made a request to visit Savannah's Bonaventure Cemetery, the literal midnight garden of good and evil in John Berendt's runaway best-seller, I obliged.

One of the secretaries flat-out sneered when we walked into the musty office, suspecting we were like the millions of tourists who've descended on Savannah since the book's success. I assured her we were not *Midnight* groupies. Intrigued, she sniffed the air like a pointer.

"I just was wondering if you could tell us where to go for good pie in Savannah," I said. "Unless you make a good pie yourself."

She was visibly thrown.

"I . . . I . . . I have a wonderful recipe for sweet-potato pie," she said. Then she stiffened. "But what makes you think I would give it to you? No way. I ain't telling. I ain't telling you about my crust, and I ain't telling you about my filling neither. No sirree. Uh-uh."

Nicole, who isn't big on confrontation, was already backing out the door. I, on the other hand, would not leave until I'd found a soft side to this woman. I asked her which of the tombs in the cemetery was her favorite.

"Everyone makes such a big deal about the little girl on the cover of the book," she said, shaking her head. "But my favorite tomb is the one of Gracie.

"She was a beautiful little girl, and she done died too young."

Gracie Watson was the only child of W. J. Watson, who owned the Pulaski Hotel in town. She was born in 1883 and died of pneumonia six years later. Her parents commissioned a white marble sculpture from a local artist. His sculpture had her in a frilly dress and high-buttoned shoes, sitting on a tree stump, with a wildflower in her hand.

For some reason, visitors have never been able to keep their hands off of Gracie, the secretary said. For years, they stroked her sculpted hair and her legs, so that much of the statue's fine detail had been worn away. A few years ago, a protective fence was finally erected around the tomb.

We told her we'd go take a look at Gracie. The woman smiled. She wouldn't give us her sweet-potato pie recipe, but she'd loosened up enough to suggest we try The Lady and Sons, right downtown. We strolled through the cemetery for a good hour and, as promised, we stopped to pay our respects to the little girl.

Paula Deen, the lady behind The Lady and Sons restaurant, was sitting in one of her restaurant booths, reading glasses pinching her nose, going over the books when we turned up.

"Pie?" she said, removing her glasses. "Haven't you heard? Pie is on the endangered species list.

" 'As American as apple pie'? Huh! Pie's becoming obsolete."

Deen, considered by many to be the doyenne of Georgia cooking, admitted she was just as guilty as the next turncoat, having substituted cobbler for pie at her restaurant. "It just isn't cost- or time-efficient to make pie at a restaurant that serves between four and six hundred people a day.

"It's *first-rate* cobbler, mind you, but it's not pie. And there is a difference." I was glad we were on the same page.

Deen told us she learned to make fried-apple pies and dried-fruit pies from her grandmother. "I was lucky. I had twenty years of watching my grandmother cook, right by her side. Newer generations aren't that lucky. Not a day goes by that I don't tell one of my customers: 'talk to your grandmother!'

"It's so important that children don't let recipes die with their elders."

But that was exactly what was happening with pie, she said. "It used to be that people in the South showed their love and affection with pie.

"When someone moved into the neighborhood, or had a bad day, you'd bake them a pie."

"My big fear," she said, "is that new generations have been weaned on so much processed food that they actually *like* the taste of a frozen-crust pie," she said. "They think that's what they are *supposed* to taste like."

She was right, of course. I thought of my niece, of all the Dumpster pies we'd tasted on this trip, and of the woman near Atlanta, pining for McDonald's new lemon pie.

"I'll tell you, I'd run a country mile for a slice of good homemade coconut cream."

Our visit with Paula had left us deflated. Nicole hadn't really known what to expect on this trip. Truth is, Nicole had never really thought much about pie in her rarefied world of haute pastry.

But I could see it dawning on her that pie was a lot like a neglected spouse. It can be taken for granted for only so long, before it disappears.

I repeated Evelyn's words of caution that she spoke back in Ponder:

"One of these days, you're going to look up and be looking for fresh pies, and you're going to realize there's nobody cookin' them no more."

I think Nicole was starting to share some of Paula Deen's guilt.

"Maybe we should start some sort of national pie movement," she said. "Get people baking pie again."

I needed no convincing. "Yeah. Like when Gandhi tried to get his countrymen to sew their own dhotis," I said.

Dreaming up ways such a movement could work kept us entertained all the way to historic Georgetown, South Carolina, our next stop.

In the lobby of our motel, I looked down and saw that Lafayette had once stood at that very spot—although probably not fumbling for his American Express card.

The liberty-loving marquis's bust was all over historic George-town, which, we learned at the Rice Museum, was once surrounded by rice plantations. The museum ladies with their jasmine-white hair were delighted to help us find pie. They huddled and all agreed there was only one place to go: "the Kudzu Bakery, of course."

"It's not like any bakery you've ever seen," they said.

As we headed out the door, one of the elderly ladies followed us out. "I'm originally from New Jersey," she said. "So, I feel it's my duty to warn you about something."

We leaned in closer.

"OKRA," she whispered. "It's slimy. It's awful. It's everywhere."

Customers spilled out of the Kudzu Bakery screen door with children in tow and white cardboard boxes in each hand. A perfect combination of rustic and modern, homey and hip, the bakery was packed. Behind the curved glass of the display case, classic Southern desserts preened like majorettes: red-velvet cakes with fresh cream-cheese frosting; lemon cakes brushed with a honey syrup and covered with almond-cookie crumbs. And pies. Glorious-looking pies.

Nicole and I spotted the peach pie at the exact same time, and a girlish smile spread across Nicole's face.

"We're not sharing, right?" she said. We each got our own slice and carried it to the pineboard bar that jutted out of a brick wall lined with shelves of elderberry-and-kudzu jelly, pear butter, and fig preserves in the back of the bakery.

The pie had been baked in a quiche pan, so it had a regal, tall collar of a crust. The peach slices were roughly cut, churlish, and tawny. We took one bite and sighed. We weren't on the side of a Southern

California road, there was no cream, and our daddies were miles and miles away, but this was bliss.

I ranked the Kudzu Bakery pie right up there with the apple-blueberry from Mammy's Cupboard and the huckleberry-peach at the Spruce Park Café in Montana. We sought out the owner to tell him so. Joey was at his second shop next door, where he sold kitchen equipment and plenty of pie pans, rolling pins, and mixing bowls in muted retro colors. We were surprised a place as small as Georgetown could support such a fancy baking retail shop.

"People in town liked the pies at the bakery so much, a lot of them got inspired to make their own," said Joey.

We told him about our visit with Paula Deen, whose bleak pie forecast seemed to contradict Georgetown's pie spirit. Was there hope for pie in America?

"You bet there is."

Joey said the bakery sold twenty pies a day—four hundred the day before Thanksgiving. "We start making them three days before the holiday," he said. "We set up bunk beds in the loft above the bakery, so that the help can catch some shut-eye between shifts." Joey refused to use a pie press, so the staff could make only thirty-four pie crusts at one time.

"I'm a nonsymmetrical kind of guy," he explained, which was why each of his pies looked so beautifully flawed, so unconditionally loved.

We got to talking about the power of pie. I told him about Dave the Montana bear trapper who baked his way out of his depression.

Joey understood full well the power of pie-baking to transform and transcend. A therapist friend of his had once asked him to hire a young woman he knew who was going through a difficult time. She was married with two small children and "struggling with her identity," he said.

"She really had a hard time with the dough at first, but, eventu-

the nicole states (most of them, anyway) · 327

ally, she got it, and when she did, she became a much more confident person after that."

So confident, that the woman, Susan, had recently returned to Columbia, where she and her husband planned to open a bakery of their own. We told Joey we'd stop by on our way to North Carolina to visit with her.

"Tell her we all miss her," he said.

He gave us his card, and I noticed the pun, "simply *divine*," under the Kudzu Bakery name and smiled.

Legend has it that in the South, mothers keep a close eye on their sleeping babies to protect them from the mighty kudzu vine, a choker of a broad-leafed weed that can grow at the rate of a foot per day and smother anything in its path. Leave your car in the drive when you go on vacation, and, chances are, it'll be locked in kudzu when you return. Oddly enough, the nonnative plant was brought here by the Japanese as a symbolic ornamental gift for the 1876 Centennial Exposition in Philadelphia.

On our way to Columbia, we fell behind a burnished-red flatbed truck loaded down with two enormous coils of thick wire that looked like giant eyes staring us down.

We lost it when we stopped for gas at a BP in Paxville that advertised great gas prices and "butt meat and liver pudding" to boot.

Under a warm summer rain, we found our way to the bakery in West Columbia, where Susan was working temporarily. She came out wiping her hands on her apron, and, over coffee, she told us how baking had changed her life.

"I was a gifted and talented underachiever who had dropped out of school in tenth grade," she said. She'd married and had children young, she said, and one day she looked up and realized she didn't know who she was.

"I know making pie isn't rocket science," she said, "but there's something about it that is really gratifying.

"Once I conquered my fear of dough, I felt like I had conquered my 20s," she said. "Mastering crust opened the door for more achievement."

On our way to North Carolina, I wanted to stop in historic Pendleton, which, according to my handy AAA guidebook, was known for its craftspeople, namely potters. We stopped at the first potter's studio we found near Pendleton. A woman who had taken up pottery in her golden years let us watch her work in her backyard shed. I spotted a rolling pin on the table behind her and asked about it. "Oh," she laughed. "I use it to roll out my clay, but that doesn't mean I can make a pie."

For pie, she suggested we head to a bakery in downtown Pendleton, near Mechanic Street. That was perfect, since Betty Blue needed another oil change. "All the pies are handmade from recipes that come from the owner's grandmother," she said, visibly impressed.

I felt good leaving Betty Blue in the care of the elderly man who ran the garage. If he treated her as well as his perfectly pressed uniform, she'd be fine.

We walked along a shady path of dogwoods down the road to the bakery, on the first floor of an old, turn-of-the-century home. A crape myrtle tree in the side yard was afire with fuchsia blossoms. Vintage school desks were lined up on the wide front porch. With its rocking chairs, crocheted lace runners, and old photographs, the front parlor reminded me of a movie set. The woman behind the register seemed to be in character. She was dour and wore her hair in a granny bun though she appeared to be only in her late 40s. We asked about her orchard pie and when she told us it was house-made we each ordered a slice.

"We only sell the pies whole!" she snapped.

As she slid the whole pie into a box, we asked her about Grandma's special crust. Was it lard or butter? She mumbled something about the crust being made off-premise. So, we asked about Grandma's special filling. Well, that came delivered, too, she said under her breath.

"Oh, so the pies are *not* made here," I said, just to be clear. "Some are, but some are just assembled here," she said, never looking up at us. We took our whole pie on the porch and each ate a slice, sitting in the old wooden school chairs. The pie wasn't half bad, and the fruit in the filling—we guessed pear, blueberry, cranberry, and apple— stayed whole and flavorful. But there was a distinct cheapness to it. It had no integrity. This was one recipe I did not want.

The husband came out on the porch to chat and maybe make up for his wife's rudeness. When he found out we were researching pie in America, he was eager to tell us about the recent Pillsbury bake-off pie "scandal." Apparently, the most recent winner of the national competition had, er, uh, "lifted" her winning recipe from their bakery, he said, hoping to rouse some anger.

We shrugged our shoulders.

"What goes around, comes around," I said to Nicole as we headed back to the garage.

The mechanic was pinching my blackened air filter between his thumb and forefinger and showing it to a regular customer of his, when we returned.

"I've never seen one this bad," he said. "We had to order one from Clemson. It should be here in about an hour."

We handed him the leftovers of our orchard pie and decided to walk off the "bad karma" slices while we waited for Betty. This last pie had really gotten to Nicole, had wounded her and her craft. There was only one way out of her funk.

"Let's buy some crap," she said, spotting a corner market.

We walked out loaded down with hot tamale candies, bubble gum, and corn chips for the drive to Pittsboro, North Carolina, where my friends Wayne and Sally would take us in for the night.

Near the state line, in a town called Gaffney, we passed a water tower with a giant peach painted on it. It looked like a large woman's blushing behind.

An old pie safe is the first thing you see when you walk into Wayne and Sally's house, set back in the woods, off a gravel road. It's a funky, comfortable house. A house that says happy people live in it. Lots of cats and a scruffy, low-to-the-ground dog, too. It's quite a step up from the shack they lived in for many years after they were first married, which still sits on the property.

This was a pit stop, not a pie stop, but Sally wanted us to meet their pie-loving friend Laura before we left town, just the same. Laura had been baking in New Orleans and had recently come back to Pittsboro and taken a job as Wayne's Gal Friday for a change of pace, Sally said. I suspected heart trouble. Laura had no place to live, and Sally and Wayne offered up their love shack. Laura had only been there a few nights when a thick black snake slithered down from the rafters. When Laura realized the snake was merely curious, she learned to live with her roommate over the next few weeks.

Just when you've got yourself convinced you're a pretty tough cookie, someone like Laura comes along to make you feel as flimsy as a Georgia pecan tree. We met Laura for lunch the following day at the K & W cafeteria in Chapel Hill. I expected a woman who looked like she could wrestle snakes. I was way off.

She was 30 but could pass for 17. She wore her long brown hair in coiled side-braids, cinnamon buns. She wore shorts with platform shoes, and her legs were no quitters. Lolita and Princess Lea wrapped into one; all eyes were upon her in the long cafeteria line that slithered right out the door.

"A long wait means you have plenty of time to check out the goods," she said, craning her long, thin neck to inspect the Jell-O salads which, this day, ranged from indigo blue to antifreeze green. "I just love this place . . . It's like Christmas every day here."

The stacked pie display was even more impressive than Piccadilly's. As I stared at the vast assortment, it dawned on me that in my time on the road, I'd actually tasted most, if not all, of the varieties of pie on display.

And while Laura kept talking to Nicole and Sally about the glories of the K & W, I savored my own delicious, private moment of victory.

"It's not the best pie you'll ever have," I heard Laura say, "but it's good enough pie. And good enough pie is better than no pie at all, isn't it?"

Something to think about.

Laura recalled the time she made a lattice-crust apple pie for a beau. She was so nervous, she forgot to put sugar in the filling. "He ate the whole pie anyway."

"Sounds like he was a keeper," I said.

"If only love were as easy as pie," she sighed.

The K & W pies were just like Laura said: good enough. Not bad, but not memorable. Certainly not as memorable as the peach pie at the Kudzu Bakery or Minister Edgar's sweet-potato pie in New Orleans, I said.

When Laura learned we'd been to New Orleans, she dropped her jaw.

"You did go to Dick and Jenny's for their lemon meringue pie, right?"

I shook my head.

"Dick and Jenny's lemon meringue is the best pie you'll ever have," she said. "The first time I tried it, I was with my best friend," said Laura. "We normally share everything, but she wouldn't give me a bite of this pie. She made all sorts of sounds when she was eating it and so, finally, I got my own slice and I figured out what all the fuss was.

"This pie is so good that you could have just broken up with your boyfriend and about halfway through your slice, you'd forget his name. Forget he even existed.

"You've got to turn around and go back," she said. "You've just got to."

And when I started this trip, I just might have gone back to eat lemon meringue pie and forget.

But not now. I was headed home.

Laura and Sally climbed into Laura's pool-bottom blue pickup truck. Behind the wheel, Laura kissed her fingertips, then reached up and tapped the hood of her car to wish us good luck.

"Happy trails," she said.

virginia is for
lovers . . . of pie

*"Everyone on the trail dreams of something, usually sweet and gooey,
and my sustaining vision had been an outsized slab of pie. It had
occupied my thoughts for days, and when the waitress came to take
our order I asked her, with beseeching eyes and a hand on her forearm,
to bring me the largest piece she could slice without losing her job."*

—BILL BRYSON, *A WALK IN THE WOODS*

In Virginia, I could have headed to Charlottesville, the home of
Thomas Jefferson, to find some pie with historical meaning, some
crust with a solid constitution.

But I headed for the Shenandoah National Park instead. I had
just read Bill Bryson's *A Walk in the Woods,* chronicling his adventures hiking the Appalachian Trail and remembered Bryson saying
the "AT" was at its most beautiful as it meandered through the park
in Virginia.

As a fellow pie seeker, Bryson could surely be trusted.

We drove toward Shenandoah by way of Staunton, the oldest
town west of the Blue Ridge Mountains. Staunton was allegedly
named after a woman, and she must have been a head-turner,
because as we came up on a hill that gave us an overview of the
steepled downtown, we gasped at how beautiful it was.

Nicole had been quiet all morning. Mulling something over, I could tell.

She'd been thinking, she said, that she should start a collection, too. But she wasn't sure what to hunt for.

"It'll happen organically," I said. One day, she'd see something in a junky old shop that would make her heart flutter. And she'd know if it was something she could spend a lifetime discovering.

Given our current restraints, it had to be something manageable, I told her. Grand pianos were out. "How about old cake stands?"

Boring, she said.

We parked in downtown Staunton, for leg-stretching and coffee, right in front of an antiques shop that was having a white-elephant sale.

On the sidewalk stood an old library newspaper rack—something every journalist should have.

"Maybe I could use it to hang towels?" I said. In the nick of time, a young couple interrupted.

They'd spotted Betty Blue's license plate, and, as pie lovers, they had to stop and ask. They, too, were going out for coffee, to go over final details for their upcoming wedding.

She owned a vintage clothing shop in town, and, yes, she said, she would be wearing a vintage wedding dress. "It came from an Indiana bride, circa 1952, complete with shoes and handbag." The dress had been on display in her shop window for weeks for the whole town to see, even the groom.

She would have gladly gone on talking about the wedding, but he was intent on getting to the bottom of this pie-themed car. Turned out, the groom, a contractor, had a thing for pie. Not just eating it, but hearing women say it.

Specifically, women from the South. Women who say "paaaaahhhhhh" instead of "pie."

It sounded a little kinky to me. But the fiancée found it charming.

"The lady at the bank has a really strong Southern accent, and she says it for me as soon as I get to her window," he said. "A few of the waitresses in town say it for me, too."

It would be irresponsible to write an entire book on pie and not address, at least in passing, this strange attraction men have to pie, particularly in the wake of the movie *American Pie,* in which, I hear, hormones and pie go hand in hand.

I'm no Freud. But, my guess is, it has something to do with pie's dual nature; the fact that pie is both sensuous and maternal. Sweet yet sensible.

Pie just may be the Madonna-whore of the dessert world.

We were getting close to home and I had it in my head that I needed to find some last great bowls and maybe even a pie safe, like the one I'd seen at Wayne and Sally's.

We stepped inside an antiques shop and I immediately saw four pie safes I wanted. Setting my sights on something smaller, I found two butter-yellow mixing bowls, nesting.

"I have a pie story," said the shopkeeper, who'd spotted Betty's license plate and was following me around his shop. "Want to hear it?"

He used to milk cows as a boy, he said, and he'd always have to watch the milking-barn floor for those nasty rat-tail maggots, just to make sure they didn't find their way into the milk.

"Fascinating," I said, wondering where this was going and where Nicole had disappeared.

He hadn't thought about those maggots in about fifty-odd years, until recently, when his wife decided, out of the clear blue sky,

to make a mulberry pie. He was delighted, until he bit into a mulberry stem.

"It reminded me so much of those rat-tail maggots, I spit it out
and gagged. I couldn't take another bite," he said. "Told the wife to
throw that pie right out."

Nicole appeared just in time. Wearing an ear-to-ear grin.

"Cookie jars," she said.

Loaded down with two more bowls and a cookie jar in the shape of
a pig with a chef's toque lid, we pressed on toward Shenandoah
National Park. My plan was to find some hikers on the Appalachian
Trail who, like Bryson, had lusted after—and found—good pie on
the AT.

We parked at a pull-out on Skyline Drive and hiked in a ways to
join the trail. In no time at all we felt worlds away from the road.

At the first shelter, we came upon a mother and daughter who'd
just pitched camp and were enjoying a healthy dinner of corn bread
stuffing mix and herbal tea. It was their first day on a four-day backpacking trip. A butterfly kept landing on the mother's head, and her
daughter kept trying to wave it away. It was a nice moment. I found
myself really missing my mother, though we spoke nearly every day
I was on the road. The chemo seemed to be working. But she was
tired. So very tired.

They had no pie recommendations, they said, because, frankly,
said the daughter, "no one makes better pie than my grandmother's
blackberry."

We continued hiking on the trail for almost an hour and never
saw another soul. I was starting to get nervous. About bears, not pie.

We were, about an hour's hike from Skyline Drive when I swore I
heard a grunt. Nicole, or a chipmunk, no doubt. But I got it into my

head this was a grizzly who sensed I'd been around huckleberries. I kicked into high gear, started power-walking back to the car.

Nicole tried to distract me by describing some of more fabulous desserts she'd created over the years. "Did I ever tell you about the caramel-roasted figs with hazelnut phyllo, and a crème fraîche risotto I made for a Share Our Strength dinner?"

"Nice try," I said, "but I don't think it's such a good idea to be talking about sweets with a B-E-A-R in our midst."

"I'm thinking of making an old American classic called a 'fool,' " shouted Nicole, who by now was 40 paces behind. "Have you heard of it?"

Our hunt for pie-hungry hikers had been a bust, so, on the advice of a park ranger, we headed to the Big Meadows Lodge where Clara, the hostess, raved about the restaurant's cobbler.

I explained to Clara about our "issues" with cobbler.

"What about our blackberry *ice cream* pie?" she asked.

That would do.

We sat on the restaurant deck looking out at the Blue Ridge Mountains and although the pie wasn't great (more texture than flavor), the view was definitely worth hiking for days and even braving bears for.

I was about to ask Nicole if this dessert "fool" really existed, when I heard a *rat tat tat* against the windowpane behind my Adirondack chair. I turned to see an elderly couple, both in rocking chairs, inside the restaurant lounge, ogling my pie.

"How dare you eat that right in front of us!" I could faintly hear the woman say through the glass. That was a dare if I ever heard one, so I gathered my plate and went inside to offer her a bite.

Jim and Edna, both in their mid-70s, said they were waiting for a table and didn't want to spoil their appetite. "We're just having fun with you, because we both love pie," said Edna.

I asked Edna if she made pie herself, and Jim jumped in:

"Of course she does. That's why I'm *marrying* her." I'd heard right. Edna and Jim had met only four months earlier and were planning to marry in the fall. I asked them how they met, and ushered Nicole over so she could hear, too.

Edna had gone to a furniture store in Charlottesville, where she lived, to buy a new mattress. It had been a while since the long-divorced Edna had had to buy a mattress, and so she was nervous. She found a mattress that seemed just firm enough for her back. She asked Jim, the manager of the store, if he wouldn't mind lying down next to her to make sure it didn't "dip" in the middle.

He obliged. And by the time they stood upright again, Jim and Edna were fast friends. She had learned that he was recently widowed and quite lonely. He'd taken a second job, working at McDonald's in the evenings, to kill time. She'd been divorced for twenty years and had also recently lost her longtime companion.

He asked for her phone number and when he called her the very next day, she invited him over for dinner.

"She made me a strawberry-rhubarb pie that was out of this world," Jim said, pressing her hand in his. "I was hooked."

Edna and Jim had just gone apple-picking at a nearby orchard the day before to make some apple pies over the weekend. On a lark, she'd suggested they drive up to the lodge for a romantic Friday-night dinner.

The two couldn't keep their hands off each other.

This wasn't the first time on my journey that a pie made from scratch had led to nuptials, I told Nicole as we drove back down into the valley, toward Washington, D.C. Nicole contrasted Edna and Jim's story with a recent episode of *Sex and the City*, in which Miranda's elderly cleaning woman tries to convince the hot-shot lawyer that she must own—and learn to use—a rolling pin, to lasso a husband. Aren't rolling pins a sign of rolling back? Miranda asks Carrie. Carrie wouldn't know: she uses her oven for storage.

What a difference a couple of generations makes.

When Kerouac took to the highways, pie made from scratch was ubiquitous. Wherever he looked, apple pie was there. I, on the other hand, had to dig, and drive, sometimes hundreds of miles, to find a pie that was made by the person who served it. But while old-fashioned pie has largely disappeared from the American landscape, the mythology of pie lives stronger than ever. That's because pie is a symbol of something bigger than Mom and her way with desserts.

Look into the face of a pie, and you'll see many of the traits Americans pride themselves on. Resilience and determination. Stick-to-it-iveness. They are all there. You'll see the first pioneers who built supper around nothing more than lard, flour, and prairie oysters. People like Deborah Tyler who sold porch pies to pay the bills. Dave the bear trapper who baked his way out of a dark cave. Laura, in Montana, who worked through searing pain in her fingers by rolling out dough.

Pie speaks to our nation's competitive streak: an already famous George Eastman who wanted his lemon meringue to be the best; two colleges arguing over whose students first flung a pie tin in the air for fun. Generations of women vying for blue, red, and white ribbons at county and state fairs. Women like Louise Piler, of Rolfe, Iowa, who, as a young farm girl, watched her father show cattle and hogs, and now boasts her own flotilla of coveted blue ribbons from the Iowa State Fair.

It took years, and lots of collapsed meringue pies, before Louise tasted victory, she says. One day, a deflated Louise and her husband were driving home from the fair in Des Moines, and Louise announced she was hanging up her rolling pin for good.

"My pies just aren't ever going to be pretty enough," she said.

Her husband stopped the car. "Honey, you just swallow your pride and try again," he told her. Not long after that, she won "sweepstakes"—the prize for the most blue ribbons won at one fair. She headed straight for the nursing home to show her ailing father, 86, the bright purple satin (sweepstakes) ribbon.

"I walked in his room and he said: Did you win?" That was the sweetest victory of all, she said. Louise said baking was a salve from her job as a cardiac-intensive-care nurse. Which just goes to show that working women can make pies, too.

You don't have to be unsophisticated or unadventurous to enjoy making pie. Aunt Anne in tiny Bernard always made three pies by noon Sunday, and still made time for things like India in her life. Pie speaks of patriotism, yes, but more important, it speaks of a slower time, when things weren't so complicated. When there was always someone home to greet a child after school. When prairies didn't need to be saved. When firemen had time to help coax a cat down a tree.

Juanita, in Munith, managed to live on that kind of time. She baked, nearly every day, to show her friends and neighbors how much she cared.

"It's a way of paying respect," she said. Exactly the kind of respect Minister Edgar talked about while baking pecan pies on that sweltering day in New Orleans.

"Respect the art of pie," wrote Susan Bright. I wonder what she'd think of the diner in Iowa City I read about in the paper that tosses pie in a blender and calls it "a pie shake." No time to bake pie. No time to sit down and eat it properly with a cold glass of milk.

Today's pace isn't a pie pace.

We work so hard, we think, to make life easy, but easy never comes. Not with families and friends so spread out and splintered. People move, clear cross-country, for more money, a better job. Pretty soon, the only time they see their families is on the holiday. Everyone around the table stares at a pie, hoping the pie can fill the void for all that has been lost.

That's a world of pressure to put on a pie—and its baker. No wonder no one bakes anymore.

Easy as pie?

Not so easy when there's no one around to show you how easy it can be. Paula Deen, in Savannah, Georgia, was right. Based on the countless cheap-thrill pies we tossed in the Dumpster, a surprising number of Americans have never tried a genuine slice of home-sprung pie.

The quintessential American pie, be it apple or sweet potato or Mary Baumbach's cherry, sits in the cupboard of our collective consciousness. We know, intuitively, what a plump, juicy berry pie in a golden flaky crust should taste like, but we've learned to settle for less; for those "fifty-fifty" pies banned from Tootie Guirard's annual Pie Day in Catahoula. I haven't resolved in my heart whether Laura was right when she said that "a good enough pie is better than no pie at all." I remember so fondly Susan's banana cream pie made from a dry mix in Gold Hill, Colorado. But I also remember the delicious discovery of Doris Kemp's apple-blueberry pie. You can tell when a pie has been made by hand and heart. Like Ty said, "you just know." In many ways, pie in America has met the same fate as the handwritten letter, supplanted by e-mail. E-mail isn't just quicker. It expects less of the sender. Words weigh less, it seems, when they travel at the speed of light. I think of the rush I get on those rare occasions when I open my mailbox and find a handwritten letter. In our crazy, whipstitch lives, it seems inconceivable that anyone could take pause, pull up a chair, and sit down with their thoughts . . .

As Edna did, just a few days after our brief encounter in the shadow of the Blue Ridge Mountains:

Dear Pascale,

I thought I would write to you to tell you what happened to Jim and me on Monday, Aug. 7. We had decided to go to the court house to get our marriage license so we could start making plans for the wedding.

Got to the courthouse and clerk was filing forms, etc., when a judge from Richmond popped his head in the doorway asking, "Anyone want to get married?"

I looked at Jim and said "Why not?" He said, "No," and I said, "We could get it all done here and now."

He: "You want to do it?"

"Sure," I said, motioning to the judge.

He came over and said: "Come on out, I'll do it in the court-yard," and then he led us outside, toward a garbage can.

"Not here," I said. So he led us over to the front of the court-house on Market Street to the stairs between two cannons, a statue, and two piles of cannon balls, where he conducted the ceremony. People stopped to watch from the street and many people observed from the windows of the courthouse.

Jim had given me his wedding ring on Friday, which I had on my right hand. I took it off and he placed it on my ring finger. We kissed, and then the judge led us to a park bench where he filled out the certificate. We drove to JC Penney's at the mall where he purchased me a one-carat diamond ring. It is gorgeous.

Oh, I took Jim to The Nook in the mall and bought our lunch of vegetable soup and toasted cheese sandwich. Today is his last

*day working at McDonald's. Jim is a former Baptist minister. He
is the most gentle, caring, compassionate man I've ever known. I
know we will enjoy our union together for many years.*

Good luck to you on your pie "booklet."

Most sincerely, with love,

Edna Francis Cox

Bless her. She'd included her recipe for strawberry-rhubarb pie with
a woven lattice crust.

EDNA FRANCIS COX'S STRAWBERRY-RHUBARB "IT'S-NEVER-TOO-LATE-TO-FALL-IN-LOVE" PIE

CRUST

2 cups flour

½ teaspoon baking powder

1 teaspoon salt

⅔ cup shortening or lard (Edna uses lard)

6 tablespoons ice water

¼ cup milk

FILLING

¼ cup Town Crier Flour

2 tablespoons cornstarch

1½ cups sugar

⅛ teaspoon salt

1½ *cups diced rhubarb*

2 *cups strawberries (cut in half)*

1 *tablespoon butter*

1 *egg white or a little water*

Sift 2 cups flour, measure, and sift again with baking powder and 1 teaspoon salt. Cut shortening into the flour mixture. Add just enough water to hold pastry together. Roll out on a board that has been brushed with flour. Roll out enough dough to fill a 9-inch pie pan. Cut the remainder of the dough into 1⅛ inch-wide strips or bands, for lattice crust.

Brush the pastry with milk.

In a bowl, mix ¼ cup flour, cornstarch, sugar, and ⅛ teaspoon salt, for the filling. Sprinkle ¼ of this mixture into the bottom of the pastry-lined pie pan. Mix remainder with the rhubarb and strawberries. Toss well. Pour into pie pan. Dot with butter.

Moisten the rim of the bottom crust with cold water and lay half the strips across the face of the pie. At the outer edge of the pie, take the first cross strip and weave it through every other bottom strip. Use this as your guide strip. Fold every other bottom strip halfway back over the guide strip. Place the next strip down near the guide strip over the strips that are NOT folded back. Unfold the others over the new strip. Keep alternating folding strips back as you weave across to the edge of the pan. Using sharp scissors, trim the strips so that they hang over the edge about ½ inch. Moisten the dough under each strip with egg white or water and tuck the overhang under the border of the bottom crust. Press firmly to make it stick. Crimp edges. Bake at 450 degrees for 10 minutes. Reduce temperature to 350 degrees and bake 50 minutes. Let cool before serving.

capital pie

*"I confess that in America I saw more than America; I saw the image
of democracy itself, with its inclinations, its character, its prejudices,
and its passions, in order to learn what we have to fear
or hope from its progress."*

—ALEXIS DE TOCQUEVILLE

It was so early when we arrived in Washington, D.C., on Sunday
morning that we scored the prime parking spot closest to the White
House.

Two security officers promptly stepped out of their booth to take
a look, and who could blame them? We looked just like the Clam-
petts driving up to the gates of Bel Air. The tarp covering the wicker
table I'd been hauling since Meadville, Ohio, was shredded, like
Ellie Mae's denim cutoffs.

Betty hadn't seen the inside of a car wash since New Mexico, and
her wooden rolling pins, still hanging on for dear life, front and back,
were carpeted with bugs. We'd lost Doug's wire-hanger antenna
somewhere in Catahoula, but the duct tape was still there, flapping
in the wind.

And, after about 19,500 miles, I wasn't feeling exactly daisy-
fresh myself. I had hoped there might be some activity at the White
House, a press conference on the lawn, or some visiting dignitary
photo op, so that we might wrangle a pie recommendation from
someone official.

But three months away from the interminable November 2000 election, not a creature was stirring on Pennsylvania Avenue. So I stepped up to the grim-faced security officer at the Southeast Gate and asked him point-blank: if he could go anywhere in D.C. for a piece of presidential pie, where would he go?

You'd think that a guy with a name like Tyrus Ezekiel would have a sense of humor. He sat stone-faced.

I'm sure Tyrus went through hours of training to learn how to spot nut jobs in the crowd long before they try and scale the fence or start wildly firing shots. We didn't exactly fit the "wacko" profile, and that threw him. He looked us up and down, then down and up, and up and down again. Then he scanned the parking lot for a tour bus.

Then Tyrus must have remembered a warm pumpkin pie from his youth, because he finally cracked a smile.

"Why don't you ladies try the Old Ebbitt Grill just around the corner," he said. "They make good pie and they use berries from local farms."

When de Tocqueville arrived in Washington—which happened to be his final stop as well—he wrote that he was struck by the "openness" of the White House. Indeed, he and Beaumont apparently waltzed right into Andrew Jackson's salon on "visiting day," and the president even offered them a glass of madeira.

No doubt the adventurous de Tocqueville and Beaumont would have also ended up at Old Ebbitt Grill, had it been open at the time. But the famous bar did not open until 1856. Since then, a long line of presidents, including McKinley, Grant, Andrew Johnson, Cleveland, Theodore Roosevelt, and Harding, have all tossed back a few at the Ebbitt's bar. The Ebbitt has moved several times before setting down roots in its present location at 15th & H streets, kitty corner from the Office of the Treasury. Weeknights, the long galley bar swarms with journalists, political insiders, government staffers, interns, and, of course, lawyers. Lots of lawyers.

But on this Sunday morning it was fairly quiet, which gave us lots of time and room to admire the warped wood floors and the mounted stuffed-bear head, a war trophy gift courtesy of Teddy Roosevelt himself.

Blackberry was the pie of the day, and I was delighted to end the trip on a dark-berry pie, since I'd started my journey with an olallieberry pie in Pescadero, California.

Full circle I'd gone.

The pie arrived on a fancy china plate, which had been decorated with a spiderweb design of blackberry coulis as tangled as the pie itinerary. It came with a side scoop of French vanilla ice cream.

Only three bites of the filling, dark, cool, and musty like morning woods, and I was five again, in the backseat of my uncle's car. We were on our way to meet my great-grandmother for the first time, in a rural, forgotten pocket of Brittany. Her one-room thatch-roof house, which had no plumbing or electricity, sat at the very end of a narrow dirt road bordered by blackberry bushes with brambles so thick and overgrown they scratched the car as we passed, treating me to my first set of goose bumps.

My great-grandmother sat on a wooden bench inside her deep stone fireplace, making coarse buckwheat crêpes for us in a cast-iron skillet. She'd picked the wild blackberries for the filling herself, and had the arm scrapes to prove it. She filled each crêpe with the cooked, sweetened blackberries, then she folded the crêpe in a half circle, and once over again, so that the large circle became a triangle.

She offered me the first crêpe. My father had to give me a push, because this primitive woman with hair on her chin and no working toilet scared me.

They all watched as I took my first bite. I was too young to know I was tasting heritage. But I knew that the deliciousness of the moment went beyond the sweet, purple juice dripping down my chin.

"Too bad about the crust," said Nicole, yanking me out of my reverie.

It had gone completely soft. Had lost all spine or will.

Nicole was quick to jump to the baker's defense. Clearly, she said, the pie had been baked on Friday, then kept refrigerated—a capital offense. The perfectly sweetened filling was remarkably good, each berry independent, and had we eaten it out of the oven, we'd be singing a different tune.

"The kitchen had all the right intentions," she said.

Isn't that so often the case in politics, I thought.

On the way back to the car, I asked Nicole to snap my picture in front of the White House. And, although there are few things that irk me more than sidewalk cell-phone usage, I dialed up my parents to tell them which particular stretch of sidewalk I was calling from.

It was early in California, and my father was in the kitchen, making coffee for my mother who was still sleeping.

"*Papa, devines ou je suis* [Guess where I am]. *Devant la Maison Blanche* [In front of the White House]."

"Wait one second," he said, resting the receiver on the kitchen counter. I heard his worn leather slippers shuffle across the linoleum as he went to get my mother. They like to be side by side for significant moments. And ordinary ones.

"How exciting," I heard my mother say, as she made her way into the kitchen. "Does that mean she's done? Can she stop driving now?"

crumbs . . .

*"A man travels the world over in search of
what he needs and returns home to find it."*
—GEORGE MOORE, "THE BROOK KERITH"

Shortly after Ty moved to New York, we flirted, briefly, with the notion of buying a small house. We couldn't really afford it, and our relationship wasn't the least bit solid enough. Still, it soothed us somehow to wander through empty homes and imagine a future life together, as settled as sifted flour.

Happily, we'd found a realtor, Elena, who was willing to indulge this flight of fancy. Elena was twice my age (though she'd never admit it) and in frail health. At this stage in her life, she was more keen on making connections than commissions.

We looked forward to our Sundays with the eccentric Elena, who still carried herself like the stage actress she'd once been. Sensible was not in her wardrobe. Bangles and boots and rich fabrics that flowed, were.

Elena refused to let us drive, preferring instead to chauffeur us around the Hudson River Valley in her rusted, cornflower-blue Volvo station wagon, puttering at 20 miles an hour. She liked taking "scenic" detours just to point out a striking hydrangea bush or a pretty curve on a bay window.

We had other things in common, Elena and I. For years, we'd lived right around the corner from each other in Santa Monica—

without knowing it. We liked barn-wood floors and we both collected old mixing bowls.

One day, Elena invited me to her home in Tarrytown, where she lived with her husband, Jesse, to show me her collection. Most were the expensive yellow-ware bowls that are beyond my reach. She'd found them at tag sales, long before they were trendy.

"What is it about bowls?" I asked Elena. We were sitting on her living room floor, surrounded by six of her favorites.

"It's because they're *ionic*," she said, clutching a buttercup-yellow bowl as wide as the green bowl my mother used for her floating-island dessert. "It means we're *nesters*. Round receptacles are maternal, they are like cocoons."

Pies are cocoons, too, I thought.

"So, when are you and Ty going to have a baby? You're not getting any younger, you know." With every wrinkle on her face, Elena felt she'd earned the right to speak her mind.

So, when she learned a few months later that Ty and I were taking a break from the relationship, she let it be known that she did not approve.

Flaws? Some of the prettiest bowls in my collection have flaws, she said.

We didn't see Elena for many months after that.

I went back out on the road to pie, and Ty took a long journey of his own. And when we finally came back together and decided to marry, that these two islands were tired of floating, Elena was one of the first people we wished to tell.

Elena had gotten very sick in the interim. An illness so grave she couldn't bring herself to name it. "This *thing* I have," she'd say, rolling her navy-blue eyes. She spent most days confined to the upstairs bedroom of their old carriage house on Sunset Way, down the hill from where Mark Twain once lived.

Ty and I brought her French tulips, color of plums, for her nightstand. As an engagement present, she gave us the wide, wheat-yellow carved bowl I'd once admired in her bony hands. And I noticed the bowl was indeed imperfect. Beautifully so.

Inside the bowl Elena had dropped a brief note: "Dear Pascale and Ty: *Remember to triumph over the bumps. The joys will outnumber them.*"

My wish is that some day soon, the bowl will grace the mantel or sill of a funky old house Elena will have found for us. But I know better.

So, for now, the bowl is going in the refrigerator overnight.

I want it to get nice and cold. Because tomorrow, I'm finally going to bake a pie. From scratch. For Elena.

I do believe I have everything I need: Ty's jay-blue pie plate, a long wooden spoon from Pennsylvania Dutch country, and plenty of rolling pins to choose from. More important, I have sound advice and encouraging words from bakers like Elva, Edgar, Laura, and even young Darrell.

I've carved out the whole morning for nothing but this, because, I've learned, you really have to stop your life to make a pie. That is what makes it the ultimate gift. It is a gift of yourself. A gift of time.

A marriage pie is what I'll make: huckleberry and peach, like the one we loved at the Spruce Park Café in Montana. The California peaches have arrived in my local supermarket. I'm hoping they'll take Elena back to her sunny Santa Monica days. I had to order the purple huckleberries special. Elena could use a whiff of fresh mountain air. Besides, I'm told Montana hucks can pull you through some pretty rough patches.

I will wake up very early, before the cardinals even, to give myself plenty of time for mistakes. And, if the first batch of dough doesn't take, I will "press on," as Calvin Coolidge advised, and try another.

(His ode to persistence, copied from the wall of the Mill Pond Bakery in Munith, Michigan, hangs from my fridge.)

Naturally, Ty has offered to help with the crust. Though I see many joint pies in our future, it's important I tackle this one solo. I've driven more than 20,000 miles chasing tradition. Time to start my very own.

"Il faut mettre la main à la pate," my mother would always say whenever we danced around a challenge. This French expression literally means: "It's time to put your hands in the dough."

Time to surrender to pie.

Dear Pascale,

I would be so grateful if you could include my great-grandmother, Nan, in your book. I am 19 years old and just recently lost my nan in June. She was 88.

My Nan was an amazing woman. My fondest memories revolve around eating her homemade apple pie. I wish that you had had a chance to taste this work of art because words cannot describe it.

Nan never entered contests, never won any awards. She was told time and again to open a bakery. But Nan didn't want to sell her baked goods, because she made them out of love.

She made her crust from scratch and used only the finest apples in the bunch. The crust was always moist and flaky, the perfect color of gold, and the apples never too sweet. She always had a piece ready for me when she took it out of the oven.

I don't know how I am going to survive the upcoming holidays without her and her pies.

I think that anyone can make a good pie with practice, but it takes love to make it perfect. The smell alone of one of her pies baking filled me with such a warm feeling. What I wouldn't give . . .

I thought it would be a nice way for me to thank Nan for everything she baked into her pies by having you include her in your story. I would give you her recipe if she had one, but the thing is, she never used one.

And every pie came out better than the last.

Thank you for your time,

Sincerely,

MORGAN COLE-HATCHARD
Stony Point, New York